CONTENTS

v

vi   CONTENTS

THE
AUTOBIOGRAPHY
OF
A SEAMAN

BY
ADMIRAL LORD COCHRANE
Admiral of the Red, Rear-Admiral of the Fleet

INTRODUCTION BY RICHARD WOODMAN

WITH ELEVEN ILLUSTRATIONS

THE LYONS PRESS

ILLUSTRATIONS

vii

INTRODUCTION

1.

The Autobiography of a Seaman is the simple title for the story of a very complex man. The Tenth Earl of Dundonald, better known to history as Captain Lord Cochrane, the courtesy title he bore in his younger years, was one of the finest British naval commanders in an age that produced many outstanding sea officers. He was also one of the most unorthodox in an age rich in remarkable characters. It is in some ways unfortunate that the era was dominated by Lord Nelson; Nelson's death at Trafalgar, followed by his apotheosis, tends to radiate so bright and exemplary a light, that it has blinded history to the virtues of other officers of his day, and to their achievements in the post-Trafalgar period.

From 1792 to 1814, with a short break between 1801 and 1803, Great Britain was locked in war with France and her allies. Nelson's victory over the Combined Fleets of France and Spain at Trafalgar on October 21, 1805, often mistakenly heralded as an action of total annihilation, was not so much an end of the naval campaign between the two principal protagonists, but an act of empowerment for the British. Up to Trafalgar, the British had been hard-pressed to assert their superiority over their multiple enemies; afterward they had only to maintain it. Not that this was an easy task; it required the complex and enormous exertions of a fleet larger than anything seen before. It was necessary to confine the battle squadrons of the Napoleonic empire, for which major ships were constantly under construction, but it was also imperative to protect the immensely important mercantile trade upon which Britain sustained the war effort of herself and her allies. This fact was well appreciated by the young United States Navy when war broke out between America and Great Britain in 1812.

Nor did Trafalgar prevent the invasion of southern England, for Napoleon had broken up his camp along the coasts of northern France a few weeks earlier and, six weeks later, on December 2, the Grand Army destroyed the forces of Austria and France at Austerlitz, humiliating Prussia at Jena the following autumn. When the British Prime Minister, William Pitt, heard of Austerlitz and the collapse of the Coalition he had worked to build, he presciently commented that the map of Europe might be rolled up, for it would not be wanted for ten years. Pitt knew this was the crux of the war; ruined by disappointment, drink, and overwork, he died in January 1806. British sea power confronted French land power and the decade that followed Trafalgar, although bare of the fleet actions of the earlier period, was a war of attrition, the outcome of which was uncertain.

In addition to hostilities, both sides sought to ruin the other's economy, partly by blockade, but also by a complex system of licensed trade that attempted to divest the enemy of his gold reserves. Despite this form of managed sanctions, it was ultimately sea power that triumphed, not only persuading the Russian, Prussian, and Austrian monarchs to abandon the alliances forced upon them by a victorious Napoleon, but by actively supporting the Spanish insurrection against the rule of Napoleon's otherwise amiable brother Joseph. The struggle of the Spanish guerrillas was supported by a highly professional Anglo-Portuguese army under the Duke of Wellington, and this force was supplied entirely by sea. It was also supported by British cruisers that raided French posts and communications, augmenting the effect of the guerrilla attacks and Wellington's maneuvers by making the French position increasingly untenable. The most notable cruiser commander during the early stage of the Peninsular War was Captain Lord Cochrane.

Although Thomas Cochrane had gone to sea and established his reputation in the period before the Peace of Amiens of 1801, it was in the frigates *Pallas* and *Imperieuse* that he distinguished himself, harrying the coasts of the Napoleonic empire and ever maintaining that by the energetic pursuit of such a policy, a few cruisers could have accomplished all that the heavy blockading squadrons achieved—at a fraction of the cost. History has largely justified Cochrane's high opinion of his own actions. The outreach obtainable by even a modest deployment of sea power is now a tenet of power politics, and in exile Napoleon acknowledged this, afterward ruefully commenting that "wherever there was water to float a ship, there you would find an English man-of-war."

Here is evidence of Cochrane's fierce original thinking and his belief in the absolute justice of logic. Here, too, is his outspokenness: Logical thought prompted him to criticize what he conceived to be the ill-considered, fruitless, or wasteful conduct of his superiors with a relentless energy that is evident in these pages of autobiography written long after the event, when he was an old man.

It is oversimple to attribute this quality to Cochrane's noble birth, though it would be true to claim that his hereditary position undoubtedly swept aside any misgivings a man of humbler birth might have entertained at expressing his opinions! But it is equally true to say that his title automatically attracted a degree of prejudice and hostility from a naval service largely officered by steady, professional, middle- class men. In assessing Cochrane, it is therefore important to set the man within the context of his turbulent times. In fact, as he points out in his autobiography, what was considered outrageously radical in his youth, and now seems no more than common rights of citizenship to us, came to be enshrined within British constitutional law in his own lifetime. However, Cochrane's truculent singleminded pursuit of what he conceived to be just and sensible ends sprang as much from a genetic originality of mind as from an exaggerated sense of fair play, and this ran contrary to the notion of aristocracy itself. One of his midshipmen, the undeniably middle-class Frederic Marryat, was later to enshrine an ironic view of Cochrane's notions in his novel *Mister Midshipman Easy*, just as he recalled many of Cochrane's exploits in his masterwork, *Peter Simple*.

Cochrane's father, the Ninth Earl, was an eccentric inventor and innovator who, by his interests, reduced the comparatively modest family fortune to virtually nothing. Cochrane's birthright thus chiefly consisted of an inherited eccentricity: The application of logic formed his view of life and humanity. When, as he describes in his autobiography, he went into politics, he chose as his platform the then highly radical ideas of reform: reform in parliament, reform in government and in public offices, and, in particular, reform in the Royal Navy. To some extent this was self-serving, for Cochrane undoubtedly sought to reestablish his family fortune, but he wished to achieve this only by giving to serving naval officers what was theoretically theirs by right, and, in doing so, abolishing the many abuses practiced by the bureaucrats who administered the naval service. His exposure of the prize court at Malta is a comic opera that infuriated the place-seekers and jobbers in the British Establishment. This, combined with the enemies he had made among his superiors, presaged his downfall; and in 1814 it became possible to implicate Cochrane in a stock-exchange fraud, which resulted in his total humiliation. To this tragicomedy, Cochrane conspired by his own naïveté.

2.

Thomas Cochrane was born in Scotland in 1775 and in due course entered the navy as a midshipman at the comparatively "old" age of seventeen. By the time he was a lieutenant, Cochrane had quarreled seriously with a senior officer and been reprimanded after a court-martial. In his account of this, Cochrane remains obdurately insistent that he was not insubordinate, merely reasonable, and that Lieutenant Beaver was in the wrong, revealing that Cochrane's own lack of tact was unbowed by age or the lessons of realpolitik!

By 1800, Lord Keith, a fellow Scot and the British Commander in Chief in the Mediterranean, had promoted Cochrane to the command of a small brig-sloop, HMS *Speedy*. In his subsequent cruises, Cochrane proved himself a scourge, capturing prizes and attacking the enemy wherever he could be found. His capture of the Spanish xebec-frigate *El Gamo*, in May of 1801, established his reputation— but his insistence that his badly wounded first lieutenant should be promoted was rejected by Lord St. Vincent, then the First Lord of the Admiralty, the scourge of outspoken officers and a punctilious, unbending man. The Peace of Amiens followed and when the war resumed, it found Cochrane kicking his heels in the ungainly *Arab* on convoy duty. By the spring of 1804 William Pitt was Prime Minister and when the Scotsman Henry Dundas, the First Viscount Melville, became First Lord of the Admiralty, he was told by the Duke of Hamilton, another Scot, that the most promising Scots seaman was languishing in an old tub called the *Arab*.

Cochrane was soon posted into HMS *Pallas* and cruised successfully off the Azores, founding his fortune, despite the rapacity of the parasites, particularly Admiral Young, the port admiral at Plymouth, who shamelessly helped himself to a share of Cochrane's prize money on a bureaucratic technicality. In *Pallas*, Cochrane established a reputation among British seamen that ensured he never afterward had to resort to the press-gang to man any ship he commanded. This reputation was enhanced throughout his period as a seagoing commander by his extreme care for his men. He never needlessly exposed them to danger, always planning his attacks with complete thoroughness, and leading them safely from the front. He was not, however, insensible to the obligations of officers. During the later cruise of the *Imperieuse*, Midshipman Marryat was ashore with him, reconnoitering a French position at Rosas in northeast Spain. Cochrane, over six feet in height and armed with spyglass and notebook, complained when a French musket ball whined past them and Marryat ducked. The shorter Marryat was instructed to "stand steady and to do your duty as a bulwark!"

The *Pallas*'s second cruise in 1806 was directed at attacks on the Biscay coast of western France. By audacity and a ruse, Cochrane deprived the French navy of three corvettes in a single day, an exploit that led Napoleon to call Cochrane "the sea-wolf." Between the two cruises, Cochrane had made his first bid to enter Parliament. As he was only by courtesy Lord Cochrane, not holding the peerage itself, he was eligible to stand for election to the House of Commons.

William Cobbett, the leading radical enemy of parliamentary corruption, advertised for an honest man to stand with him to fight for the two seats of Honiton, a town in the southwest of England and the most corrupt, or "rotten," borough in England. Against them was a ministerial candidate named Bradshaw who paid five pounds per vote. Cochrane arrived at the hustings in some style, but spoke rather disappointingly about naval abuses and appealed to the constituents' patriotism. His audience wanted him to demonstrate the free-spending attitude they had come to regard as characteristic of British seamen. They did not see why they could not sell their votes in the same way they sold their wheat and livestock; and when Bradshaw and Cobbett started abusing each other, a fight broke out. Since Cochrane had brought his boat's crew, and they were accustomed to dealing with heavy odds, it was a fairly lively affair. Cochrane was not elected but afterward he sent the town crier round asking anyone who had voted for him to call on his agent, where the few brave souls who had supported him each received the sum of ten guineas.

On the death of Pitt in January 1806, there was another election. *Pallas* had arrived back from her second cruise on the Biscay coast, so Cochrane returned to Honiton. He was by now a household name and no one dared to raise the matter of cash bribes, though great expectation ran through the limited number of voters. Cochrane won a seat, and when he was asked about payment he retorted he would pay "not one farthing." The angry voters protested that ten guineas had been given before, to which Cochrane responded that this had been a gift to honest men who would not take bribes, and to give money now would be a violation of his own principles. Cochrane had made the Honitonians look foolish, and they revenged themselves by accepting an invitation to dinner, bringing all their relatives and eating and drinking themselves into a stupor. After prolonged litigation, Cochrane was compelled to pay £1,200, but he was no longer a poor man.

Once into the House of Commons, Cochrane managed to get two of his officers their long overdue promotion, but in doing so he made more enemies, particularly the cold and influential John Wilson Croker, who had previously masqueraded as a friend while pumping the naïve and open Cochrane for information. Cochrane also alienated the up-and-coming Palmerston. None of this augured well for the future. The government fell over the issue of Catholic emancipation, and Cochrane went back to sea in *Imperieuse*, a fine thirty-eight-gun frigate. He was ordered to sea before the ship had properly completed fitting out by his old enemy at Plymouth, Admiral Sir William Young. Iron fittings carelessly fitted near the compass induced a deviation of thirty degrees; so, by the time the *Imperieuse* reached the coast of France, she was miles off her course and actually struck a rock off Ushant before she bounced clear, losing her false keel in the process. Despite this inauspicious start, Cochrane again proved his mettle.

When the *Imperieuse*'s successful cruise ended in May 1807 with the frigate coming home to dock and refit, Cochrane decided to stand for the relatively democratic and politically advanced constituency of Westminster. He canvassed as an independent dedicated to naval reform, and was opposed by a ministerial candidate named Elliot and another radical, the immensely rich Sir Francis Burdett.

To the London sophisticates, Cochrane was made out to be, at best, well intentioned and, at worst, a fool. Nevertheless, when asked why he had chosen to stand, Cochrane replied that "a man representing a rotten borough (Honiton) cannot feel himself of equal consequence in the House with one representing such a city as Westminster." Cochrane appeared a cool and dignified figure in his uniform. His watchword was "reform" and he began to denounce Lord St. Vincent, then back at sea in command of the Channel Fleet.

Cochrane and Burdett were elected but Cochrane was not up to the chicanery of the House of Commons. It could scarcely be expected that he would be, and his straightforward, honest, reforming zeal was defeated by procedural tactics, indifference, and the opposition of cunning men determined to protect their self-interests. It was an enmity infinitely more implacable than Cochrane had encountered in war, and it was to be the prelude to his own disgrace. However, he did win admiration for his courage and, as was not uncommon for military and naval officers also serving as Members of Parliament, his electors agreed to give him leave of absence to return to sea.

After further adventures on the *Imperieuse*, he was called home in 1809 to the Admiralty to lead the attack of fireships on a French squadron that had escaped from Brest and was sheltering at the Basque Road. The circumstances of this attack—and the special explosion vessels by which Cochrane and Marryat blasted their way through the protective boom guarding the French anchorage—are recounted in the autobiography. But it was a duty Cochrane did not want, partly because officers senior to him in the supporting fleet would regard him as serving his own interests in seeking glory, but partly because he feared irresolution on the part of the Commander in

Chief of the Channel Fleet, now Lord Gambier. "Dismal Jimmy" Gambier was a religious tractarian much given to sanctimonious pronouncements and the urging of his commanders to exhort their seamen to Christian rather than martial endeavor. Gambier was not a man to seek a battle of annihilation and had refused to approve a plan using fireships, which he regarded as inhumane, so Cochrane was right in his concern. Nevertheless, Cochrane drafted a plan for the First Lord, now Lord Mulgrave, but declined to execute it himself until Mulgrave positively insisted. In the attack, Cochrane did his best and, in the circumstances, did well. Although the French fleet was not destroyed, sufficient damage was done to wreck it and to render most of the ships unserviceable for many months.

But Gambier's failure to support his attack rankled with Cochrane and, despite a complimentary report and the reward of investiture into the Order of the Bath for his own services, Cochrane used his parliamentary position to oppose the customary vote of thanks to Gambier and the fleet. Gambier called for a court-martial on his own conduct; and although Cochrane was effectively Gambier's accuser, he was allowed to give evidence only to a court composed entirely of senior officers sympathetic to Gambier. These officers were, to a man, hostile to the young, presumptuous, and insubordinate Captain Lord Cochrane. Gambier was asked to resubmit his reports, and effectively changed his evidence, denying Cochrane credit for any part in the affair. Under the pressure of cross-examination, Cochrane performed badly and the verdict exonerating Gambier was inevitable. Cochrane was humiliated.

Cochrane was now in disgrace at the Admiralty, so he set off for Malta to expose the injustices in the prize system of which he had so frequently complained in the House of Commons. The outcome is best told in his own words, but the incident, although heard with enthusiasm by his followers, only served to further arouse the hatred of the Establishment. Moreover, Cochrane continued to work for reform in the Royal Navy, zealously attacking the practice of paying a pittance to wounded and disabled officers, deploring the enormous pensions paid to Admiralty civil servants. As these included members of some of the most powerful families in Britain, he thereby continued to attract the enmity of powerful factions, including the influential family of the Duke of Wellington. In short, he set himself up for destruction. It was now that fate interposed and brought Cochrane to his knees; and in this his own family conspired, for Cochrane had an indisputably disreputable uncle, Andrew Cochrane-Johnstone, who was an M.P. for a rotten borough and used his parliamentary privilege to escape his creditors.

3.

It was now 1814, and Napoleon was desperately fighting the Allied forces approaching Paris. While Wellington's army had crossed the Pyrenees and was in southwestern France, the Russians, Prussians, and Austrians had invaded France from the east. Napoleon's series of defensive battles against these ultimately overwhelming forces was a tour de force, and it seemed that matters still hung in the balance on Monday, February 21, when in the early hours a British army officer named Du Bourg arrived at Dover. Claiming to be on the staff of Lord Cathcart, the British ambassador to Russia who was then in the field with Tsar Alexander II's staff, Du Bourg brought the momentous news that Russian Cossacks had captured Napoleon and dismembered him. The Russians were in Paris and the war was over. Du Bourg left this news in Dover to be passed on to Admiral Foley, and then rushed off to London. Foley had to wait until daylight to telegraph the Admiralty, but at dawn Dover was fogbound, so Foley sent a messenger after Du Bourg—by the time he reached London the news was out. Du Bourg had disappeared, but the London Stock Exchange was suddenly buzzing with optimism.

There had been much speculation in stock known as Omnium, which was highly volatile and made up of government stock. Speculation, or buying on margin, in Omnium was common and when business had closed on the Friday, Omnium had been low. That Monday it rose rapidly until it became rumored that no one had received confirmation of the news from Paris. The rise stopped, until a gaily decorated post chaise thundered over London Bridge and into the city. From the chaise French officers threw out pamphlets supporting the Bourbons. The price of Omnium resumed its rise. The next day it was realized that it was all a hoax. Those who had sold when the stock reached its highest point had made a 20 percent profit in three hours, others made 70 percent, but most speculators had their fingers burnt. The only shred of truth was that on January 29, Napoleon had had a brush with some Cossacks, but had escaped from them.

At the time, Cochrane had at last been offered another ship, the eighty-gun *Tonnant*, but that morning he was having breakfast with his uncle, Andrew Cochrane-Johnstone. The extent to which Cochrane was implicated in the hoax remains uncertain. There is no proof as to his absolute innocence, but neither is there any to prove his absolute connivance and his implication seems circumstantial. It is true that he had invested his prize money in Omnium, but with instructions to his broker to sell when the price rose a mere 1 percent. This is a speculation, but not an illegal one, and he would therefore have made about £2000 on £36,000 invested. By this time Cochrane was a wealthy man, and it is highly unlikely that he would have compromised all the principles upon which he had made his name for so disreputable a purpose, while the standing instruction to his broker is a modest, businesslike arrangement.

Andrew Cochrane-Johnstone and his partner, a former pay clerk in the naval dockyard named Butt, were the architects of the fraud and they had done their planning well. While Cochrane went off to attend to the development of one of his inventions, a special convoy lantern, Butt and his uncle went to the Stock Exchange. Cochrane then received a message that a distressed army officer required help. The man was a debtor and known to Cochrane, who had met him at a social function. He wanted to serve with Cochrane aboard *Tonnant* but explained that he could not be seen in public in uniform, as he was only allowed out of the debtor's prison on strict conditions. No doubt embarrassed, Cochrane gave the man a change of clothing. This proved to be a fatal act, though at the time probably seemed no more than a characteristic act of impetuous kindness. In due course, it was to be seen as irrefutable evidence of complicity, for it is certain that this man was De Bourg, and by assisting him Cochrane was implicated in the hoax, because at the same time, acting on instruction, Cochrane's broker was selling his stock at a profit. In the subsequent investigation, one broker swore that Cochrane himself had visited the Stock Exchange, and though this statement was later withdrawn, the wretched Cochrane, having overwhelming alibis to the contrary, was enmeshed. The officer he had helped later himself admitted he had been Du Bourg. Cochrane found himself on trial in the Old Bailey.

Believing himself innocent, Cochrane left his defense in the hands of his legal advisors. He did not even put in an appearance, and this further act of apparent arrogance tipped the partial scales of justice against him. Cochrane had been the dupe of his uncle, Butt, and the other conspirators, who had, of course, masqueraded as French officers. He was now systematically destroyed by the Establishment. Appearing for the Stock Exchange as part of the prosecution was an Admiralty solicitor, Germain Lavrie, who had been involved in Gambier's defense. Moreover, the prosecution was led by Cochrane's own former counsel, Richard Gurney, and held before the anti-radical, highly reactionary judge, Lord Ellenborough, in King's Bench. As if this was not enough, the jury was chosen from city merchants and the defense lawyers decided to conduct a joint defense, so Cochrane's implication was more or less admitted from the start. One of Cochrane's witnesses had been sent to sea while other evidence was flawed or compromised, but the outcome was assured: Cochrane was doomed. Despite an impassioned speech in the Commons that the Hansard reporters filled with asterisks, and a statement by one of the minor conspirators that Cochrane had nothing to do with the matter, Cochrane was fined and sentenced to a year's imprisonment. He was also sentenced to an hour in the pillory, but this was remitted for fear of a riot in Cochrane's favor. Expulsion from the House of Commons and the Royal Navy followed. In the King's Bench Prison, Cochrane learned that the Prince Regent had stripped him of his honors and denounced him; his banner as a Knight of the Bath had been taken down from the King Henry VII chapel in Westminster Abbey and, at midnight, ceremonially kicked down the abbey steps. An unknown man stood as proxy while a pair of spurs were, with equal ceremony, hacked off his heels and Lord Cochrane's degradation was formally announced. Now in exile on the island of Elba, the quondam Emperor Napoleon deplored the treatment meted out to the sea wolf.

Cochrane's autobiography ends at this point, but is not the whole story. One thing he mentions only briefly is the story of his marriage to Kitty Barnes, whom he saw walking Hyde Park as a teenager and instantly decided to marry. The tall, red-haired Cochrane was said to be engaging in appearance, and he succeeded in his suit. Kitty bore him five children and accepted the vicissitudes of a life with her extraordinary husband with apparently uncomplaining equanimity.

4.

In 1817, the disgraced Cochrane accepted the invitation of the emissary of Bernardo O'Higgins, leader of the revolutionaries then fighting for Chilean independence against Spain, to command their ships of war. Cochrane embarked on the kind of warfare in which he was an expert. His capture of the fourteen forts defending Valdivia is an unparalleled feat of arms, while his capture of the Spanish frigate *Esmeralda* off Callao effectively destroyed Spanish power and led to the establishment of Chile and Peru as sovereign states. Cochrane went on to serve as admiral of the Brazilians as they detached themselves from Portugal in 1823, but quarreled with the new government over his pay. By 1827 he had returned to Europe to command the rebellious Greek fleet against the Ottoman Turks. Cochrane's account of these adventures was called *Narrative of Services in Chile, Peru and Brazil*, and were written with the editorial help of a man named Earp, two years before *The Autobiography of a Seaman*.

In 1831 Cochrane returned to Britain to became the Tenth Earl of Dundonald on the death of his father. As a result of successive petitions, he was finally granted a free pardon for his alleged part in the Stock Exchange fraud and in 1832 he was reinstated in the Royal Navy as a rear admiral. This was the year of the great Reform Bill that swept aside the rotten and pocket boroughs and set Britain on the course toward universal suffrage. Later, by order of Albert, Queen Victoria's husband and the Prince Regent, Cochrane's banner and spurs were rehung in Westminster Abbey. From 1848 until 1851 Cochrane commanded the British North America and West Indies

Squadron, but was disappointed when in 1854, at the ripe age of eighty, the Admiralty refused him command of an active battle fleet at the outbreak of the Crimean War against Russia.

He died, aged eighty-five, the year that this autobiography was published, loaded with honors, ennobled in his native land and in Brazil. A photograph of him, taken that year, shows him in his uniform as a full Admiral of the Fleet, the British equivalent of Fleet Admiral. The tough old man appears, even at that late date, to possess a shrewd eye; he was more a man who modern opinion would say had a strong sense of self than he was the supreme egotist his enemies claimed.

In his retirement Cochrane had pursued his career as an inventor, and having introduced a steam warship into the nascent Greek Navy, he proposed and saw steam engines power Britain's fleet of wooden walls. Gas lighting was among many other useful innovations on which he worked, but his concept of war dominated his thinking. He had much in common with Patton's dictum of overwhelming an enemy, thereby ensuring the minimum casualties to one's own side. Having developed theories on the use of sophisticated smoke screens, Cochrane also sought to obviate war by the ultimate deterrent weapon, designed to be so terrible that no enemy would dare to attack. When he proposed his idea to the Admiralty, the authorities were so appalled that they had the papers secured under lock and key. They were not to see the light of day until 1914. What Cochrane had proposed was poison gas.

Although a maverick in his own day, Cochrane was both a supremely professional sea officer and a warrior who would not have felt out of place in the wars of the twentieth century. Despite this, the following pages reveal a man with a strong belief in righteousness and fairness, driven by a courageous refusal to submit to self-interest or an easy life. He had, too, a wry sense of humor, as witness his attitude to arriving aboard ship as both a midshipman and a lord; he had a flair for ingenious extemporization, as when he made water bags out of sails; and he possessed a deep respect for other people, whether it be trying to gain recognition for Lord Keith's prevention of a junction between the French and Spanish fleets in 1799, an appreciation of Jack Larmour, his tarpaulin lieutenant in the *Thetis*, or his long and ultimately successful struggle for promotion for two of his own junior officers,

Lieutenants Haswell and Parker. His originality of mind was not content with mere inventions, such as the convoy lamp, but sought to avoid the ruinous expense of war, particularly the Peninsular War, by the practical application of his theories in harrying the enemy coast. "It is wonderful," he writes, "what an amount of terrorism a small frigate is able to inspire on an enemy's coast!" But the autobiography reveals his flaws with disarmingly honest candor. His account of his conversations with Lord Mulgrave, particularly after the affair at the Basque Road reveal his headstrong and persistent intransigence. This is Cochrane at his most obdurate and it is not surprising that Mulgrave and his ilk turned against such a thorn in their flesh.

The original document contains numerous letters to back up Cochrane's assertions—many of these have been excised from this edition to keep the narrative flowing—but he makes no claims that logical evidence does not support. And while he speaks in the first person, he avoids generating hostility to his egoism. Rather, one is carried along by his modern, raging inveighing against the corruption of his times.

Had Cochrane been a conformist, he would have risen faster in the world, but he could not have retired with more honor. He remains a hero in Chile, where every town of any consequence has a street named after him and the largest ship in their navy retains his name. He was, in fact, a man of strong principle whose example remains an inspiration for those acquainted with him through the story of his life. Nevertheless, one admires the extent of Kitty's love for him; he must have been an exceedingly difficult man to live with.

—RICHARD WOODMAN
June 1999

THE AUTOBIOGRAPHY OF A SEAMAN

The Autobiography of a Seaman

CHAPTER I

MY BOYHOOD, AND ENTRANCE INTO THE NAVY

My birth is recorded as having taken place on the 14th of December, 1775, at Annsfield in Lanarkshire. My father was Archibald, ninth Earl of Dundonald; my mother, Anna Gilchrist, daughter of Captain Gilchrist, a distinguished officer of the Royal Navy.

My father was descended from John, the younger son of the first earl. On default of issue in the elder branch of the family the title devolved on my grandfather, Thomas, who married the daughter of Archibald Stuart, Esq., of Torrence, in Lanarkshire, and had issue one daughter and twelve sons, the most distinguished amongst whom, in a public capacity, was Admiral the Honourable Sir Alexander, father of the present Admiral Sir Thomas Cochrane.

Some of my father's earlier years were spent in the navy, in which he became acting lieutenant. A cruise on the coast of Guinea gave him a distaste for the naval profession, which, in after years, postponed my entrance therein far beyond the usual period. On his return home he quitted the navy for a commission in the army, which was, after a time, also relinquished.

Of our once extensive ancestral domains I never inherited a foot. In the course of a century, and before the title descended to our branch, nearly the whole of the family estates had been alienated by losses incurred in support of one generation of the Stuarts, rebellion against another, and mortgages, or other

A   I

equally destructive process,—the consequence of both. A remnant may latterly have fallen into other hands from my father's negligence in not looking after it, and his unentailed estates were absorbed by expensive scientific pursuits presently to be noticed. So that my outset in life was that of heir to a peerage, without other expectations than those arising from my own exertions.

My father's day was that of Cavendish, Black, Priestley, Watt, and others, now become historical as the forerunners of modern practical science. Imbued with like spirit, and in intimate communication with these distinguished men, he emulated their example with no mean success, as the philosophical records of that period testify. But whilst they prudently confined their attention to their laboratories, my father's sanguine expectations of retrieving the family estates by his discoveries led him to embark in a multitude of manufacturing projects. The motive was excellent; but his pecuniary means being incommensurate with the magnitude of his transactions, its object was frustrated, and our remaining patrimony melted like the flux in his crucibles; his scientific knowledge, as often happens, being unaccompanied by the self-knowledge which would have taught him that he was not, either by habit or inclination, a " man of business." Many who were so knew how to profit by his inventions without the trouble of discovery, whilst their originator was occupied in developing new practical facts to be turned to their advantage and his consequent loss.

An enumeration of some of my father's manufacturing transactions, extensively and simultaneously carried on, will leave no doubt as to their failure in a pecuniary sense. First, the preparation of soda from common salt, as a substitute for *barilla*, —till then the only alkali available for soap and glass making. Secondly, a manufactory for improvement in the production of *alumina*, as a mordant for silk and calico printers. Thirdly, an establishment for preparing British gum as a substitute for *gum Senegal*, these products being in use amongst calico-printers to the present day; the latter especially being at that distant period of great utility, as the foreign gum was scarce and expensive. A fourth manufactory had for its object the preparation of *sal ammoniac*. At a fifth was carried on the manufacture of *white lead*, by a process then new to productive science. A sixth establishment, on a ruinous scale as compared with his resources, was for a new process of extracting tar and other products from pit-coal; the former as an effective agent in protecting timber from decay, whilst the refuse coke was in request amongst ironfounders, whose previous operations for its manufacture were wasteful and unsatisfactory.

After this enumeration, it is unnecessary to dilate on its ruinous results. It is simply the old adage of " too many irons in the fire." One by one his inventions fell into other hands, some by fair sale, but most of them by piracy, when it became known that he had nothing left wherewith to maintain his rights. In short, with seven children to provide for, he found himself a ruined man.

In the present state of manufacturing science, by which the above objects are accomplished through improved means, the mention of such matters may, at first sight, appear unnecessary. Yet, seventy years ago they bore the same relation to the manufacturing processes of our time as at that period did the crude attempts at the steam engine to its modern perfection. In this point of view—which is the true one—reference to my father's patents, though now superseded by improvements, will fairly entitle him to no mean place amongst other inventors of his day, who deservedly rank as benefactors to their country.

One of my father's scientific achievements must not be passed over. Cavendish had some time previously ascertained the existence of hydrogen. Priestley had become acquainted with its inflammable character ; but the Earl of Dundonald may fairly lay claim to the practical application of its illuminating power in a carburetted form.

In prosecution of his coal-tar patent, my father went to reside at the family estate of Culross Abbey, the better to superintend the works on his own collieries, as well as others on the adjoining estates of Valleyfield and Kincardine. In addition to these works, an experimental tar-kiln was erected near the Abbey, and here coal-gas became accidentally employed in illumination. Having noticed the inflammable nature of a vapour arising during the distillation of tar, the Earl, by way of experiment, fitted a gun-barrel to the eduction pipe leading from the condenser. On applying fire to the muzzle, a vivid light blazed forth across the waters of the Frith, becoming, as was afterwards ascertained, distinctly visible on the opposite shore.

Strangely enough, though quick in appreciating a new fact, Lord Dundonald lightly passed over the only practical product which might have realised his expectations of retrieving the dilapidated fortunes of our house ; considering tar and coke to constitute the legitimate objects of his experiments, and regarding the illuminating property of gas merely as a curious natural phenomenon. Like Columbus, he had the egg before him, but, unlike Columbus, he did not hit upon the right method of setting it on end.

The incident just narrated took place about the year 1782, and the circumstances attending it are the more vividly impressed on my memory from an event which occurred during a subsequent journey with my father to London. On our way we paid a visit to James Watt, then residing at Handsworth, near Birmingham, and amongst other scientific subjects discussed during our stay were the various products of coal, including the gas-light phenomenon of the Culross Abbey tar-kiln. This gave rise to some interesting conversation, which, however, ended without further result.

Many years afterwards, Mr Murdoch, then one of Watt's assistants at Soho, applied coal-gas to the illumination of that establishment, though even with this practical demonstration its adoption for purposes of general public utility did not keep pace with the importance of the fact thus successfully developed, until, by the persevering endeavours of Mr Winsor, its advantages overcame prejudice.

It is no detraction from Mr Murdoch's merit of having been

the first to turn coal-gas to useful account, to infer that Watt might, at some period during the interval, have narrated to him the incident just mentioned, and that the fact accidentally developed by my father had thus become the subject of long and careful experiment; for this must have been the case before the complete achievement shone forth in perfection. Mr Murdoch, so far as I am aware, never laid claim to a discovery of the illuminating property of coal-gas, but to its useful application only, to which his right is indisputable. As it is not generally known to whom an earlier practical appreciation of gas-light was in reality due, I have placed these facts on record.

One notice more of my father's investigations may be permissible. To Sir Humphrey Davy is usually ascribed the honour of first pointing out the relation between Agriculture and Chemistry. Reference to a work published in 1795, entitled " A Treatise showing the intimate connection between Agriculture and Chemistry," by the Earl of Dundonald, will decide the priority. Davy's work may in a theoretical point of view surpass that of my father, inasmuch as the analytical chemical science of a more modern date is more minute than that of the last century ; but in point of patient investigation from countless practical experiments, my father's work is more than equal to that of his distinguished successor in the same field, and is, indeed, held in no small estimation at the present time.

The reader will readily pardon me for thus devoting a few pages by way of a tribute to a parent, whose memory still exists amongst my most cherished recollections ; even though his discoveries, now of national utility, ruined him, and deprived his posterity of their remaining paternal inheritance.

During boyhood we had the misfortune to lose our mother, and as our domestic fortunes were even then at a low ebb, great difficulty was experienced in providing us with the means of education—four of us being then at an age to profit by more ample opportunities. In this emergency, temporary assistance was volunteered by Mr Rolland, the minister of Culross, who thus evinced his gratitude for favours received in the more

auspicious days of the family. Highly as was the offer appreciated, family pride prevented our reaping from it the advantage
contemplated by a learned and truly excellent man.

Perceiving our education imperilled, the devotedness of my
maternal grandmother, Mrs Gilchrist, prompted her to apply
her small income to the exigencies of her grandchildren. By
the aid thus opportunely afforded, a tutor was provided, of
whom my most vivid recollection is a stinging box on the ear,
in reply to a query as to the difference between an interjection
and a conjunction; this solution of the difficulty effectually
repressing further philological inquiry on my part.

We were, after a time, temporarily provided with a French
tutor, a Monsieur Durand, who, being a Papist, was regarded
with no complacent eye by our not very tolerant Presbyterian
neighbours. I recollect this gentleman getting into a scrape,
which, but for my father's countenance, might have ended in a
Kirk Session.

As a matter of course, Monsieur Durand did not attend
church. On one side of the churchyard was the Culross Abbey
cherry-garden, full of fine fruit, of which he was very fond, as
were also the magpies, which swarmed in the district. One
Sunday, whilst the people were at church, the magpies, aware no
doubt of their advantage, made a vigorous onslaught on the
cherries—provoking the Frenchman, who was on the watch
to open fire on the intruders from a fowling-piece. The effect of
this reached farther than the magpies. To fire a gun on the
Sabbath was an abomination which could only have emanated
from a disciple of the Scarlet Lady, and neither before nor after
did I witness such a hubbub in the parish. Whatever pains and
penalties were to be found in Scottish church law were eagerly
demanded for Monsieur Durand's benefit, and it was only by
my father's influence that he was permitted to escape the
threatened martyrdom. Annoyed at the ill-feeling thus created,
he relinquished his engagement before we had acquired the rudiments of the French language.

Even this inadequate tuition was abruptly ended by my

father taking me with him to London. His object in visiting the metropolis was to induce the Government to make use of coaltar for protecting the bottoms of inferior ships of war—for in those days copper-sheathing was unknown. The best substitute —by no means a general one—was to drive large-headed iron nails over the whole ship's bottom, which had thus the appearance of being "hobnailed." Even this indifferent covering was accorded to superior vessels only, the smaller class being entirely left to the ravages of the worm. It was for the protection of these small vessels that my father hoped to get his application adopted, and there is no doubt of the benefit which would have resulted had the experiment been permitted.

But this was an innovation, and the Board of Admiralty being then, as too often since, opposed to everything inconsistent with ancient routine, refused to entertain his proposal. It was only by means of political influence that he at length induced the Navy Board to permit him, at his own expense, to cover with his composition one side of the buoy at the Nore. The result was satisfactory, but he was not allowed to repeat the process. As compared with the exposure at that time of ships' bottoms to rapid destruction, without any effort to protect them, my father's plan was even a greater improvement than is the modern substitution of copper-sheathing for the "hobnail" surface which it tardily superseded.

Failing to induce the Government to protect their ships of war, he applied to the mercantile interest, but with no better success. I remember going with my father to Limehouse, in the hope of inducing a large shipbuilder there to patronise his composition; but the shipbuilder had even a greater horror of innovation than the Admiralty authorities. His reply was remarkable. "My lord," said he, "we live by repairing ships as well as by building them, and the worm is our best friend. Rather than use your preparation, I would cover ships' bottoms with honey to attract worms! "

Foiled in London, my father set on foot agencies at the outports, in the hope of inducing provincial shipbuilders to adopt his preservative. Prejudice, however, was not confined to the metropolis, and the objection of the Limehouse man was everywhere encountered. Neither they, nor any artisans in wood, would patronise a plan to render their work durable.

Unsuccessful everywhere, my father turned his attention to myself. My destination was originally the army, whether accordant with my taste or not—for he was not one of those who considered it necessary to consult the inclinations of his children in the choice of a profession ; but rather how he could best bring family influence to bear upon their future interests. Unfortunately for his passive obedience theory, my *penchant* was for the sea ; any hint, however, to this effect was peremptorily silenced by parental authority, against which it was useless to contend.

My uncle, the Hon. Captain, afterwards Admiral, Sir Alexander Cochrane, had the sagacity to perceive that as inclination became more rooted with my growth, passive obedience on this point might one day come to an end. Still further, he was kind enough to provide against such contingency, should it arise. Unknown to my father, he had entered my name on the books of various vessels under his command ; so that, nominally, I had formed part of the complement of the *Vesuvius*, *Carolina*, *La Sophie*, and *Hind*; the object—common in those days—being, to give me a few years' standing in the service, should it become my profession in reality.

Having, however, a relative in the army, who possessed influence at the Horse Guards, a military commission was also procured for me ; so that I had simultaneously the honour of being an officer in his Majesty's 104th Regiment, and a nominal seaman on board my uncle's ship.

By way of initiation into the mysteries of the military profession, I was placed under the tuition of an old sergeant, whose first lessons well accorded with his instructions, not to pay attention to my foibles. My hair, cherished with boyish pride, was formally cut, and plastered back with a vile composition of candle-grease and flour, to which was added the torture incident to the cultivation of an incipient *queue*. My neck, from childhood open to the lowland breeze, was encased in an inflexible leathern collar or stock, selected according to my preceptor's notions of military propriety; these almost verging on strangulation. A blue semi-military tunic, with red collar and cuffs, in imitation of the Windsor uniform, was provided, and to complete the *tout ensemble*, my father, who was a determined Whig partisan, insisted on my wearing yellow waistcoat and breeches; yellow being the Whig colour, of which I was admonished never to be ashamed. A more certain mode of calling into action the dormant obstinacy of a sensitive, high-spirited lad, could not have been devised than that of converting him into a caricature, hateful to himself, and ridiculous to others.

As may be imagined, my costume was calculated to attract attention, the more so from being accompanied by a stature beyond my years. Passing one day near the Duke of Northumberland's palace at Charing Cross, I was beset by a troop of ragged boys, evidently bent on amusing themselves at the expense of my personal appearance, and, in their peculiar slang, indulging in comments thereon far more critical than complimentary.

Stung to the quick, I made my escape from them, and rushing home, begged my father to let me go to sea with my uncle, in order to save me from the degradation of floured head, pigtail, and yellow breeches. This burst of despair aroused the indignation of the parent and the Whig, and the reply was a sound cuffing. Remonstrance was useless; but my dislike to everything military became confirmed; and the events of that day certainly cost his Majesty's 104th Regiment an officer, notwithstanding that my military training proceeded with redoubled severity.

At this juncture, my father's circumstances became somewhat improved by a second marriage, so that my brother Basil and myself were sent to Mr Chauvet's academy in Kensington Square, in order to perfect our military education—Basil, like myself, being destined for the army. At this excellent school we only remained six months; for with slightly increased resources my father resumed his ruinous manufacturing pursuits, so that we were compelled by the " *res angusta domi* " to return to Scotland.

Four years and a half were now wasted without further attempt to secure for us any regular training. We had, however, during the short advantage enjoyed at Kensington, studied diligently, and were thus enabled to make some progress by self-tuition, our tutor's acquirements extending only to teaching the rudiments to the younger branches of the family. Knowing that my future career depended on my own efforts, and more than ever determined not to take up my military commission, I worked assiduously at the meagre elements of knowledge within my reach, in the hope that by unremitting industry my father might be convinced that opposition to his views was no idle whim, but the result of conviction that I should not excel in an obnoxious profession.

Pleased with my progress, and finding my resolution in favour of the naval service unalterable, he at length consented that my commission should be cancelled, and that the renewed offer of my uncle to receive me on board his frigate should be accepted.

The difficulty was to equip me for sea, but it was obviated by the Earl of Hopetoun considerately advancing 100*l*. for the purpose. With this sum the requisite outfit was procured, and a few days placed me in a position to seek my fortune, with my father's gold watch as a keepsake—the only patrimony I ever inherited.

The Dowager Countess of Dundonald, then meditating a journey to London, offered to take me with her. On our arrival in the metropolis, after what was at that time the formidable achievement of a tour through Wales, her ladyship went to reside with her brother, General James Stuart, in Grosvenor Street; but, anxious to become initiated in the mysteries of my profession, I preferred going on board the *Hind* at Sheerness; joining that ship on the 27th of June, 1793, at the mature age, for a midshipman, of seventeen years and a half.

CHAPTER II

CRUISE OF THE HIND

My kind uncle, the Hon. John Cochrane, accompanied me on board the *Hind* for the purpose of introducing me to my future superior officer, Lieutenant Larmour, or, as he was more familiarly known in the service, Jack Larmour—a specimen of the old British seaman, little calculated to inspire exalted ideas of the gentility of the naval profession, though presenting at a glance a personification of its efficiency. Jack was, in fact, one of a not very numerous class, whom, for their superior seaman-ship, the Admiralty was glad to promote from the forecastle to the quarter-deck, in order that they might mould into ship-shape the questionable materials supplied by parliamentary influence—even then paramount in the navy to a degree which might otherwise have led to disaster. Lucky was the com-mander who could secure such an officer for his quarter-deck.

On my introduction, Jack was dressed in the garb of a seaman, with marlinspike slung round his neck, and a lump of grease in his hand, and was busily employed in setting up the rigging. His reception of me was anything but gracious. Indeed, a tall fellow, over six feet high, the nephew of his captain, and a lord to boot, were not very promising recommendations for a mid-shipman. It is not impossible that he might have learned from my uncle something about a military commission of several years' standing; and this, coupled with my age and stature, might easily have impressed him with the idea that he had caught a scapegrace with whom the family did not know what to do, and that he was hence to be saddled with a " hard bargain."

After a little constrained civility on the part of the first lieutenant, who was evidently not very well pleased with the interruption to his avocation, he ordered me to " get my traps below." Scarcely was the order complied with, and myself introduced to the midshipman's berth, than I overheard Jack grumbling at the magnitude of my equipments. "This Lord Cochrane's chest? Does Lord Cochrane think he is going to bring a cabin aboard? The service is going to the devil! Get it up on the main-deck."

The order being promptly obeyed, amidst a running fire of similar objurgations, the key of the chest was sent for, and shortly afterwards the sound of sawing became audible. It was now high time to follow my property, which, to my astonishment, had been turned out on the deck—Jack superintending the process of sawing off one end of the chest just beyond the keyhole, and accompanying the operation by sundry uncomplimentary observations on midshipmen in general, and on myself in particular.

The metamorphose being completed to the lieutenant's satisfaction, though not at all to mine, for my neat chest had become an unshapely piece of lumber, he pointed out the "lubberliness of shore-going people in not making keyholes where they could be most easily got at," viz. at the end of a chest instead of the middle! The observation was, perhaps, made to test my temper, but, if so, it failed in its object. I thanked him for his kindness in imparting so useful a lessson, and left him evidently puzzled as to whether I was a cool hand or a simple one.

Poor Jack! his limited acquaintance with the world—which, in his estimation, was bounded by the taffrail and the bowsprit—rendered him an indifferent judge of character, or he might have seen in me nothing but an ardent desire diligently to apply myself to my chosen profession—with no more pride in my heart than money in my pocket. A short time, however, developed this. Finding me anxious to learn my duty, Jack warmly took me by the hand, and as his only ideas of relaxation were to throw off the lieutenant and resume the functions of the able seaman, my improvement speedily rewarded my kind though rough teacher, by converting into a useful adjunct one whom he had, perhaps not unjustifiably, regarded as a nuisance. We soon became fast friends, and throughout life few more kindly recollections are impressed on my memory than those of my first naval instructor, honest Jack Larmour.

Another good friend in need was Lieutenant Murray, a son of Lord Dunmore, who observing that my kit had been selected rather with a regard to economy than fitness, kindly lent me a sum of money to remedy the deficiency.

The period at which I joined the service was that during which events consequent on the first French revolution reached a crisis, inaugurating the series of wars which for twenty years afterwards devastated Europe. Whatever might have been the faults of the British Government in those days, that of being unprepared for the movements of revolutionary neighbours was not amongst them, for the energy of the Government kept pace with the patriotism of the nation. That fearful system of naval jobbery, which unhappily characterised the subsequent progress of the war, crowding the seas with worthless vessels, purchased into the service in exchange for borough influence—had not as yet begun to thwart the unity of purpose and action by which the whole realm was at first roused into action.

With few of those costly appliances in the dockyards which at the present day absorb vast sums voted by the nation for the support of the navy, to the exclusion of its real strength—*trained men*—the naval ports presented a scene of activity in every way commensurate with the occasion by which it had been called into existence. Their streets abounded with seamen eager to share in anticipated prize-money—for whatever may be the ideas of modern statesmen on this subject, prize-money formed then, as it will ever form, the principal motive of seamen to encounter the perils of war.

To return to our cruise. The destination of the *Hind* was the coast of Norway, to the *fiords* of which country the Government had reason to suspect that French privateers might resort, as lurking-places whence to annoy our North Sea and Baltic commerce. To ascertain this was our primary object. The second was to look out for an enemy's convoy, shortly expected from the West Indies by the northern route round the Orkneys.

We had not, however, the luck to fall in with either convoy or privateers, though for the latter every inlet was diligently searched. The voyage was, therefore, without incident, further than the gratifying experience of Norse hospitality and simplicity; qualities which, it is to be feared, may have vanished before the influence of modern rapidity of communication, without being replaced by others equally satisfactory.

To us youngsters, this Norwegian trip was a perpetual holiday, for my uncle, though a strict disciplinarian, omitted no opportunity of gratifying those under his command, so that we spent nearly as much time on shore as on board ; whilst the few hours occupied in running along the coast from one inlet to another supplied us with a moving panorama, scarcely less to our taste than were the hospitalities on shore.

Our great amusement was sleighing at racing speed, to the musical jingling of bells, without a sound from the catlike fall of the horse's feet on the snow. Other variations in the routine of pleasure were shooting and fishing, though these soon became secondary objects, as the abundance of fish and game rendered their capture uninteresting.

But the principal charm was the primitive aspect of a people apparently sprung from the same stock as ourselves, and presenting much the same appearance as our ancestors may be supposed to have done a few centuries before, without any symptoms of that feudal attachment which then prevailed in Britain. I have never seen a people more contented and happy, not because their wants were few, for even luxuries were abundant, and in common use.

Much, however, cannot be said for Norwegian gallantry at that period. On one occasion my uncle took me to a formal dinner at the house of a magnate named Da Capa. The table literally groaned beneath the feast ; but a great drawback to our enjoyment of the good things set before us, was that, during a five hours' succession of dishes, the lady of the house stood at the head of the table, and performed the laborious duty of carver throughout the tedious repast. Her flushed countenance after the intervals between the various removes, moreover, warranted the suspicion that the very excellent cookery was the result of her supervision. It is to be hoped that the march of civilisation has altered this custom for the better.

It is possible that these remarks may be considered somewhat profound for a midshipman of three months' standing ; but it must be remembered that, from previous hard necessity, no less than maturity, they are those of a reflective midshipman. At any rate, the remarks were duly jotted down, and to this day their reperusal calls forth somewhat of the freshness of boyhood to a mind worn down, not so much with age as with unmerited injuries, which have embittered a long life, and rendered even the failings of age premature.

From boyish impressions to a midshipman's grievances is but a step. At the first moment of my setting foot on board the *Hind* it had been my determination never to commit an act worthy of punishment ; but it was equally the determination of Jack Larmour to punish me for my resolution the first time he caught me tripping. This was certain, for Jack was open and above board, and declared that " he never heard of such a thing as a faultless midshipman ! " For a long time he watched in vain, but nothing occurred more than to warrant his swearing twice as much at me as at any other of my messmates, Jack never troubling himself to swear at a waister. To use his own words, it " was expending wind for nothing.

One day, when his back was turned, I had stolen off deck for a few minutes, but only to hear on my return the ominous words, " Mast-head, youngster ! " There was no alternative but to obey. Certainly not cheerfully—for the day was bitterly cold, with the thermometer below zero. Once caught, I knew my punishment would be severe, as indeed it was, for my sojourn at the mast-head was protracted almost to the limit of human endurance, my tormentor being evidently engaged in calculating this to a nicety. He never mast-headed me again.

By way of return for the hospitality of the Norwegian people, the frigate was freely thrown open to their inspection. On one of their frequent visits, an incident occurred not unworthy of record.

On board most ships there is a pet animal of some kind. Ours was a parrot, which was Jack Larmour's aversion, from the exactness with which the bird had learned to imitate the calls of the boatswain's whistle. Sometimes the parrot would pipe an order so correctly as to throw the ship into momentary confusion, and the first lieutenant into a volley of imprecations, consigning Poll to a warmer latitude than his native tropical forests. Indeed, it was only by my uncle's countenance that the bird was tolerated.

One day a party of ladies paid us a visit aboard, and several had been hoisted on deck by the usual means of a " whip " on the mainyard. The chair had descended for another " whip," but scarcely had its fair freight been lifted out of the boat alongside, than the unlucky parrot piped " Let go ! " The order being instantly obeyed, the unfortunate lady, instead of being comfortably seated on deck, as had been those who preceded her, was soused overhead in the sea ! Luckily for Poll, Jack Larmour was on shore at the time, or this unseasonable assumption of the boatswain's functions might have ended tragically.

On the return of the *Hind* from Norway, my uncle was appointed to the *Thetis*, a more powerful frigate ; for though the *Hind* carried 28 guns, they were only 9-pounders ; an armament truly ridiculous as compared with that of frigates of the present day. It may almost be said, that the use of such an armament consisted in rendering it necessary to resort to the cutlass and boarding-pike—weapons to be relied on. Had such been the object of the Board of Admiralty as regarded the smaller class of frigates, it could not have been better carried out. The lighter class of vessels were even worse provided for. Seven years later a sloop was placed under my command, armed with 4-pounders only. One day, by way of burlesque on such an equipment, I walked the quarter-deck with a whole broadside of shot in my coat pockets.

The *Thetis* was ordered to equip at Sheerness, and knowing that her first lieutenant, instead of indulging himself ashore, would pursue his customary relaxation of working hard aboard, I begged permission to remain and profit by his example. This was graciously conceded, on condition that, like himself, I would put off the officer and assume the garb of a seaman. Nothing could be more to my taste ; so, with knife in belt and marlinspike in hand, the captain of the forecastle undertook my improvement in the arts of knotting and splicing ; Larmour himself taking charge of gammoning and rigging the bowsprit, which, as the frigate lay in dock, overhung the common highway. So little attention was then paid to the niceties of dockyard arrangement.

Dockyards in those days were secondary objects. At Sheerness the people lived, like rabbits in a warren, in old hulks, hauled up high and dry ; yet everything was well done, and the supervision perfect. It would be folly to advocate the continuance of such a state of things, yet it may be doubted whether the naval efficiency of the present day keeps pace with the enormous outlay on modern dockyards, almost (as it appears to me) to ignoring the training of men. I would rather see a mistake in the opposite extreme—men before dockyard conveniences ; and am confident that had such been our practice, we should not have recently heard humiliating explanations, that we were without adequate naval protection, and that our national safety depended on the forbearance of a neighbouring state.

Precision in stone and mortar is no more naval efficiency, than are the absurd coast fortifications (to which there is an evident leaning) national safety. The true fortification of England is, always to be in a position to strike the first blow at sea the moment it may become necessary. To wait for it would, under any circumstances, be folly—to be unprepared for it, national suicide.

The service now seems to savour too much of the dockyard,

B

and too little of the seaman. Formerly, both officers and men had to lend a hand in everything, and few were the operations which, unaided by artificers, they could not perfectly accomplish. On two occasions my own personal skill at pump-work has saved ships and crews, when other assistance was not available.

The modern practice is to place ships in commission with everything perfect to the hands of the officers and crew, little being required of them beyond keeping the ship in order whilst at sea. The practice is to a certain extent praiseworthy; but it has the disadvantage of impressing officers with the belief that handicraft skill on their part is unnecessary, though in the absence of practically acquired knowledge it is impossible even to direct any operation efficiently.

CHAPTER III

THE VOYAGE OF THE THETIS

As soon as the *Thetis* had obtained her complement, she was ordered to join the squadron of Admiral Murray, which was being fitted out for North America; whither, soon after the declaration of war against England by the French Convention, the Government had despatched orders to seize the islands of St Pierre and Miguilon, previously captured from the French in 1778, but restored at the termination of the American war.

It was in order to regain these islands, and for the protection of our commerce and fisheries generally, that a stronger force on the Nova Scotia station was deemed essential. The conduct of the American people was doubtful, as, from the assistance rendered by the French in the War of Independence, and still more from the democratic institutions recently established in France, little doubt existed that their leaning would be upon the side of the enemy. The United States Government, however, did all in its power to preserve neutrality by proclamations and addresses, but as its authority was little more than nominal throughout the various States, a disposition on the part of American shipowners to assist the French in providing stores of every kind was manifested very soon after the declaration of war. On our return from Leith to Plymouth to join the admiral, we detained several American vessels laden with corn and other provisions for French ports; one of the objects of Admiral Murray's squadron being to intercept traffic of this nature.

The squadron sailed from Plymouth; and when about midway across the Atlantic an incident occurred worth relating, as bearing upon a conjecture made a few years ago, by the master and passengers of a merchant vessel, regarding some vessels, supposed, though erroneously, to form part of Sir John Franklin's expedition.

One night, finding the temperature of the atmosphere rapidly decreasing, the squadron was proceeding under easy sail, with a vigilant look-out for icebergs. At dawn we were close to a block of these, extending right across our path as far as the eye could reach. The only alternative was to alter our course and pass to leeward of the group, to which, from the unwonted sublimity of the sight, we approached as nearly as seemed consistent with safety. The appearance of icebergs is now so well known that it would be superfluous to describe them. I shall only remark that on passing one field of great extent we were astonished at discovering on its sides three vessels, the one nearest to us being a polacca-rigged ship, elevated at least a hundred feet; the berg having rolled round or been lightened by melting, so that the vessel had the appearance of being on a hill forming the southern portion of the floe. The story of two vessels answering the description of Sir John Franklin's ships having a few years ago been seen on an iceberg was scarcely credited at the time, but may receive corroboration from the above incident.

Nothing can exceed the extraordinary aspect of these floating islands of ice, either as regards variety of form, or the wonderful display of reflected light which they present. But, however they may attract curiosity, ships should always give them a wide berth, the indraught of water on their weather side being very dangerous. A singular effect was experienced as we passed to leeward of the field ; first, the intense cold of the wind passing over it, and occasionally, the heat caused by the reflection of the sun's rays from the ice whenever the ship came within the angle of incidence.

On our arrival at Halifax we found many American vessels which had been detained, laden with corn and provisions. These had been seized by our predecessors on the station, the act by no means tending to increase our popularity on subsequent visits along the United States coast. Another practice which was pursued has always appeared to me a questionable stretch of authority towards a neutral nation, viz. the forcible detention of English seamen whenever found navigating American ships. Of this the Government of the United States justly complained, as inflicting severe losses on their citizens, whose vessels were thus delayed or imperilled for want of hands.

The practice was defended by the British Government, but on what grounds I am not jurist enough to comprehend. Certain it is, that should another Continental war arise, such a course would be impracticable ; for as American ships, whether of war or commerce, are now for the most part manned by British sea-men, driven from the service of their country by an unwise abrogation of that portion of the navigation laws which fostered our own nursery for the navy—the effect of such an order would be to unman American ships ; and it is questionable whether the United States Government would submit to such a regulation, even if we were inclined to put it in execution.

On the 14th of January, 1795, Admiral Murray appointed me acting third lieutenant of the *Thetis*, though not eighteen months had elapsed since my entrance into the service. Thanks to my worthy friend Jack Larmour, and to my own industry, it may be stated, without vanity, that I was not incompetent to fill the station to which the admiral had promoted me. This unlooked-for reward redoubled my zeal, and on the 13th of April following I was made acting lieutenant of the *Africa*, Captain Rodham Home, who applied to the admiral for my services. This additional promotion was followed on the 6th of July by a provisional commission confirming my rank.

The *Africa* was sent to scour the seaboard of the States in search of enemy's vessels, but not falling in with any, we ran on to Florida, with similar ill-success. An accident here occurred to me which left its mark through life. I had contrived a ball of lead studded with barbed prongs, for the purpose of catching porpoises. One day the doctor laid me a wager against hurling the missile to a certain distance, and in the attempt a hook nearly tore off the forefinger of my right hand. A perhaps not very judicious course of reading had at that time led me to imbibe the notion of a current spurious philosophy, that there was no such thing as pain, and few opportunities were lost of parading arguments on the subject. As the doctor was dressing my hand, the pain was so intense that my crotchet was sadly scandalised by an involuntary exclamation of agony. " What ! " said the doctor, " I thought there was no such thing as pain ! " Not liking to have a favourite theory so palpably demolished, the ready reply was that " my exclamation was not one of pain, but mental only, arising from the sight of my own blood ! " He laughed, whilst I writhed on, but the lesson knocked some foolish notions out of my head.

On the 5th of January, 1796, the first lieutenant of the *Thetis* having been promoted, an order was transmitted for me to quit the *Africa*, and rejoin my uncle's ship, which I did in the *Lynx*, Captain Skene. An incident occurred during the passage worth relating.

The *Lynx* one day overhauled an American vessel from France to New York, professedly in ballast. At first, nothing was found to warrant her detention, but a more minute search brought to light from amongst the shingle ballast, a number of casks filled with costly church plate ; this being amongst the means adopted by the French Convention to raise supplies, an intention in this case thwarted by the vigilance of Captain Skene.

The sagacity of Captain Skene was exemplified in another

instance. Observing one day a quantity of stable litter on the surface of the sea, it was obvious that it could only arise from the transport of animals. Tracking the refuse to the southward, we overtook and captured a vessel laden with mules for the use of one of the French possessions.

The period having arrived at which the Admiralty regulations permitted young officers to offer themselves for examination— on rejoining the *Thetis* I was ordered up, and passed for lieutenant accordingly; my time as a midshipman being made up from my nominal rating on board the *Vesuvius*, etc., as narrated in a former chapter.

The mention of this practice will, perhaps, shock the purists of the present day, who may further regard me as a stickler for corruption, for pronouncing its effect to have been beneficial. First, because—from the scarcity of lieutenants—encouragement was often necessary; secondly, because it gave an admiral a power which he does not now possess, viz. that of selecting for commissions those who exerted themselves, and on whom he could rely, in place of having forced upon him young men appointed by parliamentary or other influence; of whom he could know nothing, except that they did not owe their commissions to practical merit.

In my own subsequent career as captain of a man-of-war, there never was the slightest difficulty as regarded men; yet no commander could, in this respect, be more particular; but of many officers furnished to me through parliamentary influence, it can be only said that they were seldom trusted, as I considered it preferable, on pressing occasions, to do their duty myself; and this, as some of them had powerful influence, no doubt made me many enemies amongst their patrons. It is all very well to talk of the inordinate power exercised by commanding officers in former times, but whilst the Admiralty, even in our day, appears to extend a system in which influence has everything and experience nothing to do, the so-called corruption of old, which was never made use of but to promote merit, had its advantages; no instance in which the power then indirectly pertaining to admirals commanding having, to my knowledge, been abused.

During my absence in the *Africa*, I lost the chance of participating in a gallant attack made by the Hon. Captain Cochrane, in the *Thetis*, and Captain Beresford, in the *Hussar*, on five French ships, which they had been watching near the mouth of the Chesapeake. These ships were fallen in with at sea off Cape Henry, and on the approach of the *Thetis* and *Hussar* formed in line to receive them. The *Hussar*, being the smaller vessel, encountered the two leading ships, whilst the *Thetis* opened her broadside on the centre vessel, and the two in the rear. In half-an-hour, the French commodore and the second in the line gave up the combat, and made sail, leaving the others to the mercy of the two English frigates, which in another half-hour compelled them to surrender, one of them, however, contriving to escape. Two, the *Prevoyant*, 36, and the *Raison*, 18, were secured and taken to Halifax, where they were fitted out as cruisers, and afterwards returned with the squadron to England. This action was the only one of any importance which occurred during the dreary five years that we were employed on the North American coast, and is here mentioned because it has been said I was present, which was not the case.

In the year 1797, Admiral Murray was succeeded in the command by Admiral Vandeput, who, on the 21st of June, appointed me lieutenant in his flag-ship, the *Resolution*. On joining this ship a few days afterwards, my reception was anything but encouraging.

Being seated near the admiral at dinner, he inquired what dish was before me. Mentioning its nature, I asked him if he would permit me to help him. The uncourteous reply was— that whenever he wished for anything he was in the habit of asking for it. Not knowing what to make of a rebuff of this nature, it was met by an inquiry if he would allow me the honour of taking wine with him. " I never take wine with any man, my lord," was the unexpected reply, from which it struck me that my lot was cast among Goths, if no worse.

Never were first impressions more ill-founded. Admiral Vandeput had merely a habit of showing his worst features first, or rather of assuming those which were contrary to his nature. A very short time developed his true character,—that of a perfect gentleman, and one of the kindest commanders living. In place of the hornet's nest figured to my imagination, there was not a happier ship afloat, nor one in which officers lived in more perfect harmony.

The only drawback was that of wanting something better to do than cruise among the fogs of Newfoundland and Nova Scotia,—an inglorious pursuit, the more severely felt, from the fact that each succeeding packet brought accounts of brilliant naval victories achieved in European waters. The French, after my uncle's capture of their store-ships, gave up all attempts to get supplies from America by means of their own vessels; and the United States Government concluded a treaty with England, in which both sides disclaimed all wish to pass the bounds observed by neutral nations, so that the squadron was without beneficial employment.

Tired of the monotony of Halifax, Admiral Vandeput determined to winter in the Chesapeake, where he resided ashore. As it was his practice to invite his officers by turns to remain a week with him, our time was agreeably spent, the more so that there were several families in the vicinity which retained their affection for England, her habits, and customs. Even the inn-keeper of the place contrived to muster a tolerable pack of hounds which, if not brought under the perfect discipline of their British progenitors, often led us into more danger than is encountered in an English field, in consequence of our runs frequently taking us amongst thick forests, the overhanging branches of which compelled us to lay ourselves flat on the horses' backs, in order to avoid the fate intended for the objects of the chase.

Another of our amusements was shooting; and one day a circumstance took place of which I did not for a long time hear the last. Being invited to pass a week with the admiral, who was about to give a dinner to his neighbours, it was my wish to add a delicacy to his table ; and having heard that a particular locality abounded with wild hogs, it seemed practicable that a boar's head might grace the feast. On reaching the forest, nearly the first object encountered was a huge wild-looking sow with a farrow of young pigs, and as the transition from boar's head to sucking pig was not great, a shot from my rifle speedily placed one in a preliminary condition for roasting. But porcine maternal affection had not entered into my calculations. The sow charged me with such ferocity that prompt retreat, however undignified, became necessary, for my weapon was now harmless. In short, so vigorous was the onslaught of the enemy, that it became necessary to shelter myself in the fork of a tree, my gun being of necessity left at the bottom. The enraged animal mounted guard, and for at least a couple of hours waited for my descent ; when, finding no symptoms of unconditional surrender, she at length moved slowly off with the remainder of her family. As the coast was now clear, I came down and shouldered the defunct pig, hoping to be in time to add it to the admiral's table, for which, however, it was too late.

Having told the story with great simplicity, I found myself at dinner roasted instead of the pig ; the changes on this theme being rung till it became rather annoying. By way of variation the admiral asked me for a toast, and on my pleading ignorance of such customs insisted on my giving a sentiment ; whereupon I gave " The Misses Tabbs,"—the point consisting in the fact that these ladies were each over six feet high, and in the gossip of the place were understood to be favourites of the admiral. For a moment Admiral Vandeput looked grave, but thinking, no doubt, the retort a fair one, he joined in the laughter against himself ; though from that day he never asked me for a toast.

Those were days when even gentlemen did not consider it a demerit to drink hard. It was then, as it is now, a boast with me never in my life to have been inebriated, and the revenge was that my boast should be at an end. Rapid circulation of the bottle accordingly set in ; but this I managed to evade by resting my head on my left hand, and pouring the wine down the sleeve of my uniform coat. The trick was detected, and the penalty of drinking off a whole bottle was about to be enforced when I darted from the room, pursued by some of the company, who at length got tired of the chase, and I passed the night at a farmhouse.

Having paid so lengthened a visit to the United States at a period almost immediately following their achievement of independence, a few remarks relative to the temper and disposition of the American people at that period may not be uninteresting. Thoroughly English in their habits and customs, but exasperated by the contumely with which they had been treated by former British governments, their civility to us was somewhat constrained, yet so thoroughly English as to convince us that a little more forbearance and common-sense on the part of the home authorities might have averted the final separation of these fine provinces from the mother country. There is every reason to believe that the declaration of the Confederation of the United Colonies in 1775 was sincere ; viz. that on the concession of their just demands, " the colonies are to return to their former connections and friendship with Great Britain ; but on failure thereof this Confederation is to be perpetual."

In vain, however, did the more far-sighted of the English public remonstrate with the Government, and in vain did the City of London by their chief magistrate urge the wrongs and loyalty of the colonists, even to memorialising the king to dismiss from his councils those who were misleading him. A deaf ear was turned to all remonstrance, and a determination to put down by force what could not at first be called rebellion was the only reply vouchsafed ; it was not till all conciliatory means had failed that the first Congress of Philadelphia asserted the cause and necessity of taking up arms in the defence of freedom ; the second Congress of the same place confederating the provinces under the title of the " United States of America."

The failure of those employed in conciliation to induce the

colonists to return to their allegiance—the co-operation of the King of France in aid of the revolt—the discreditable war which followed—and the singular recoil of his own principles on the head of Louis XVI. himself, are matters of history, and need not here be further alluded to.

When the *Thetis* was first on the coast, the American republic was universally recognised, and it must be admitted that our treatment of its citizens was scarcely in accordance with the national privileges to which the young republic had become entitled. There were, no doubt, many individuals amongst the American people who, caring little for the Federal government, considered it more profitable to break than to keep the laws of nations, by aiding and supporting our enemy, and it was against such that the efforts of the squadron had been chiefly directed; but the way in which the object was carried out was scarcely less an infraction of those international laws which we were professedly enforcing.

The practice of taking English seamen out of American vessels, without regard to the safety of navigating them when thus deprived of their hands, has been already mentioned. To this may be added, the detention of vessels against which nothing contrary to international neutrality could be established, whereby their cargoes became damaged; the compelling them, on suspicion only, to proceed to ports other than those to which they were destined, and generally treating them as though they were engaged in contraband trade.

Of these transactions the Americans had a right to complain; but in other respects their complaints were indefensible; such as that of our not permitting them to send corn and provisions to France, a violation of neutrality into which, after declaration of blockade, none but an inexperienced government could have fallen; though there was perhaps something in the collateral grievance that American ships were not permitted to quit English ports without giving security for the discharge of their cargoes in some other British or neutral port.

It would be wearisome to enter into further details respecting

the operations of a squadron so ingloriously employed, or to
notice the subordinate part which a junior lieutenant could take
in its proceedings. Suffice it to say, that after remaining five
years on the North American station, the *Thetis* returned to
England.

CHAPTER IV

SERVICES IN THE MEDITERRANEAN

TOWARDS the close of the autumn of 1798, Lord Keith was
appointed to relieve Lord St Vincent in the command of the
Mediterranean fleet, and kindly offered to take me with him
as a supernumerary. I therefore embarked, by his lordship's
invitation, in the flag-ship.

We arrived at Gibraltar on the 14th of December, and found
Lord St Vincent residing on shore, his flag flying on board the
Souverain sheer-hulk.

His lordship's reception of me was very kind, and on the 24th
of December, at Lord Keith's request, he gave an order for my
appointment to the *Barfleur*, to which ship Lord Keith had
shifted his flag. This appointment, from a certain dissatisfaction at my having received such a commission after being so
short a time at sea, afterwards brought me into trouble.

Lord St Vincent did not, as was expected, immediately
transfer to Lord Keith the command of the Mediterranean fleet,
but remained at Gibraltar, giving orders to his lordship to
blockade the Spanish fleet in Cadiz.

The first part of the year was spent in this employment,
Lord Keith's force varying from eleven to fifteen sail of the line,
but without frigates, though the commander-in-chief had a
considerable number under his orders. The omission was the
more remarkable, as the blockaded Spanish force numbered upwards of twenty ships of the line, with frigates and smaller
vessels in proportion.

The British force, for upwards of four months, was anchored some seven or eight miles from Cadiz, but without rousing the national spirit of the Spaniards, who manifested no disposition to quit their shelter, even though we were compelled from time to time to leave our anchorage for the purpose of procuring water and cattle from the neighbouring coast of Africa. It was during one of these trips in the *Barfleur* that an absurd affair involved me in serious disaster.

Our first lieutenant, Beaver, was an officer who carried etiquette in the wardroom and on deck almost to despotism. He was laudably particular in all matters visible to the eye of the admiral, but permitted an honest penny to be turned elsewhere by a practice as reprehensible as revolting. On our frequent visits to Tetuan, we purchased and killed bullocks *on board the Barfleur*, for the use of the whole squadron. The reason was, that raw hides, being valuable, could be stowed away in her hold in empty beef-casks, as especial perquisites to certain persons connected with the flag-ship ; a natural result being, that, as the fleshy parts of the hides decomposed, putrid liquor oozed out of the casks, and rendered the hold of the vessel so intolerable, that she acquired the name of " The stinking Scotch ship."

As junior lieutenant, much of the unpleasantness of this fell to my share, and as I always had a habit of speaking my mind without much reserve, it followed that those interested in the raw hide speculation were not very friendly disposed towards me.

One day, when at Tetuan, having obtained leave to go ashore and amuse myself with shooting wild-fowl, my dress became so covered with mud, as to induce me not to come off with other officers in the pinnace which took me on shore, preferring to wait for the launch, in which the filthy state of my apparel would be less apparent. The launch being delayed longer than had been anticipated, my leave of absence expired shortly before my arrival on board—not without attracting the attention of Lieutenant Beaver, who was looking over the gangway.

Thinking it disrespectful to report myself on the quarter-deck in so dirty a condition, I hastened to put on clean uniform, an operation scarcely completed when Lieutenant Beaver came into the wardroom, and in a very harsh tone demanded the reason of my not having reported myself. My reply was, that as he saw me come up the side, he must be aware that my dress was not in a fit condition to appear on the quarter-deck, and that it had been necessary to change my clothes before formally reporting myself.

Lieutenant Beaver replied to this explanation in a manner so offensive that it was clear he wanted to surprise me into some act of insubordination. As it would have been impossible to be long cool in opposition to marked invective, I respectfully reminded him that by attacking me in the wardroom he was breaking a rule which he had himself laid down ; viz. that " Matters connected with the service were not there to be spoken of." The remark increased his violence, which, at length, became so marked as to call forth the reply, " Lieutenant Beaver, we will, if you please, talk of this in another place." He then went on deck, and reported to Captain Elphinstone that in reply to his remarks on a violation of duty, he had received a challenge !

On being sent for to answer the charge, an explanation of what had really taken place was given to Captain Elphinstone, who was kindly desirous that the first lieutenant should accept an apology, and let so disagreeable a matter drop. This was declined on my part, on the ground that, in the conversation which had passed, I had not been in the wrong, and had therefore no apology to make. The effect was, that Beaver demanded a court-martial on me, and this, after manifest reluctance on the part of Lord Keith, was ordered accordingly ; the decision of which was an admonition to be " more careful in future "—a clear proof that the court thought great provocation had been given by my accuser, or their opinion would have been more marked.

The Judge-Advocate on this occasion was the admiral's secretary, one of those who had taken offence about the raw hides before mentioned! After the business of the court was concluded, Lord Keith, who was much vexed with the whole affair, said to me privately : " Now, Lord Cochrane, pray avoid for the future all flippancy towards superior officers." His secretary overheard and embodied the remark in the sentence of the court-martial ; so that shortly afterwards his officiousness or malice formed an impediment to my promotion, though the court had actually awarded no censure.

Lord Keith, who had in vain used every endeavour to induce the Spaniards to risk an engagement, began to get tired of so fruitless an operation as that of watching an enemy at anchor under their batteries, and resolved to try if he could not entice or force them to quit their moorings. With this view, the British force, though then consisting of twelve ships only, without a single frigate to watch the enemy meanwhile, proceeded to water, as usual, at Tetuan, so as to be in readiness for any contingencies that might arise. As the events which followed have been incorrectly represented by naval historians, if not in one instance misrepresented, it is necessary, in order to do justice to Lord Keith, to detail them at some length.

Immediately after our return from Tetuan, the *Childers* arrived with intelligence that five Spanish sail of the line had got out of Ferrol, and she was followed on the same day by the *Success* frigate, which had been chased by a French fleet off Oporto. Lord Keith at once despatched the *Childers* to Gibraltar, to inform Lord St Vincent, as it was undertsood in the squadron, that he intended, if the French fleet came to Cadiz, to engage them, notwithstanding the disparity of numbers. Lord Keith's force, by the arrival of three additional ships of the line and one frigate, now amounted to sixteen sail ; viz. one 112-gun ship, four 98's, one 90, two 80's, seven 74's, and one frigate, and these were immediately got under weigh and formed in order of battle, standing off and on in front of the harbour.

About 8 A.M. on the 6th of May the French fleet was signalled in the offing, and was made out to consist of thirty-three

sail, which, with the twenty-two sail of Spaniards in Cadiz,
made fifty-five, besides frigates, to be encountered by the comparatively small British force. The French fleet was on the
larboard tack, and our ships immediately formed on the same
tack to receive them. To our surprise they soon afterwards
wore and stood away to the south-west; though from our
position between them and the Spaniards they had a fair chance
of victory had the combined fleets acted in concert. According
to Lord Keith's pithily expressed opinion, we lay between " the
devil and the deep sea."

Yet there was nothing rash. Lord Keith calculated that the
Spaniards would not move unless the French succeeded in
breaking through the British line, and this he had no doubt of
preventing. Besides which, the wind, though not dead on
shore, as has been said, was unfavourable for the Spaniards
coming out with the necessary rapidity. The great point to be
gained was to prevent the junction of the enemies' fleets, as was
doubtless intended; the attempt was, however, completely
frustrated by the bold interposition of Lord Keith, who, strange
to say, never received for this signal service the acknowledgment of merit which was his due.

It has been inferred by naval historians that a gale of wind,
which was blowing on the first appearance of the French fleet,
was the cause of their standing away. A better reason was
their disinclination to encounter damage, which they knew
would defeat their ultimate object of forming a junction with
the Spanish fleet elsewhere.

At daylight on the 7th we were still standing off and on before
Cadiz, expecting the enemy to return; when shortly afterwards
four of their ships were seen to windward of the British force,
which immediately gave chase; but the enemy outstripping us,
we returned to the coast, to guard every point by which they
might get into Cadiz. Seeing no symptoms of the main body
of the French fleet, Lord Keith concluded that the four ships
just noticed had been left as a decoy to draw his attention from
their real object of running for Toulon, now that they had been

ADMIRAL VISCOUNT KEITH, K.B.
[Born 1746. Died 1823]

foiled in their expectation of carrying with them the Spanish fleet. We accordingly made all sail for Gibraltar.

From the intelligence forwarded by the *Childers*, there was reason to suppose that Lord St Vincent would have prepared for instant pursuit. To our surprise, the signal was made to anchor and obtain water and provision. Three entire days were consumed in this operation; with what effect as regarded the other ships I do not know, but so far as the *Barfleur* was concerned, and as far as I know of the other ships, the delay was unnecessary. The fleet was greatly disappointed at being thus detained, as the enemy would thereby reach Toulon without molestation, and for any good which could be effected we might as well remain where we lay.

This impatience was, after a lapse of three days, ended by Lord St Vincent hoisting his flag on board the *Ville de Paris*; when, reinforced by the *Edgar*, 74, the fleet shaped its course up the Mediterranean.

After we had proceeded as far as the Bay of Rosas, Lord St Vincent, having communicated with Lord Keith, parted company in the *Ville de Paris* for Minorca, leaving Lord Keith to pursue the enemy with the remaining ships. We now made straight for Toulon, where we learned from some fishing boats that the enemy's fleet had embarked spars, cordage, anchors, and other heavy articles for the equipment of their ships of war built or building at Spezzia—and had sailed to the eastward.

After burning some merchant vessels working into Toulon we again started in chase. It was now of even greater importance to overtake the French fleet, in order to frustrate a double mischief; first, their escape; and secondly, their getting to Spezzia with the materials for so important an addition to their force. With this object the British ships crowded all sail in the direction the enemy had taken, and at length came in sight of their look-out frigates between Corsica and Genoa.

Just as we were upon the point of seeing the fleet also, a fast-sailing transport arrived from Lord St Vincent, with orders to

c

return to Port Mahon; intelligence of the sailing of the French fleet having reached that port, which, Lord St Vincent feared, might become the object of attack. Lord Keith, however, knowing exactly the position of the enemy, within reach of whom we now virtually were, persevered in the pursuit.

Shortly afterwards another fast-sailing transport hove in sight, firing guns for Lord Keith to bring-to, which having done, he received peremptory orders to repair immediately to Minorca; Lord St Vincent still imagining that as the enemy had left Toulon they might catch him in Port Mahon; the fact of their having gone to Spezzia, though known to us, being unknown to him. Compliance with this unseasonable order was therefore compulsory, and Lord Keith made the signal for all captains, when, as reported by those officers, his lordship explained that the bearing up was no act of his, and the captains having returned on board their respective ships, reluctantly changed the course for Minorca, leaving the French fleet to proceed unmolested to Spezzia.

On Lord Keith receiving this order, I never saw a man more irritated. When annoyed, his lordship had a habit of talking aloud to himself. On this occasion, as officer of the watch, I happened to be in close proximity, and thereby became an involuntary listener to some very strong expressions, imputing jealousy on the part of Lord St Vincent as constituting the motive for recalling him. The actual words of Lord Keith not being meant for the ear of anyone, I do not think proper to record them. The above facts are stated as coming within my own personal knowledge, and are here introduced in consequence of blame being cast on Lord Keith to this day by naval historians, who could only derive their authority from *data* which are certainly untrue—even if official. Had the command been surrendered to Lord Keith on his arrival in the Mediterranean, or had his lordship been permitted promptly to pursue the enemy, they could not have escaped.

The French fleet, after we were compelled to relinquish the chase (when in sight of their look-out frigates), were reported to have landed 1000 men at Savona, and convoyed a supply of wheat to Genoa, as well as having landed their naval stores at Spezzia, not one of which services could have been effected had it not been for the unfortunate delay at Gibraltar and the before-mentioned recall of the pursuing fleet.

Immediately after our departure from Gibraltar, the Spanish fleet quitted Cadiz for the Mediterranean, and as no force remained to watch the Straits, they were enabled to pass with impunity ; the whole, after suffering great damage by a gale of wind, succeeded in reaching Carthagena.

On our arrival at Minorca, Lord St Vincent resumed the command, and proceeded for some distance towards Toulon. On the 2nd of June, his lordship again quitted the fleet for Mahon, in the *Ville de Paris*. On the 14th Lord Keith shifted his flag from the *Barfleur* to the *Queen Charlotte*, a much finer ship, to which I had the honour to accompany him.

We once more proceeded in quest of the French fleet, and on the 19th the advance ships captured three frigates and two brigs of war on their way from Egypt to Toulon, but learned nothing of the fleet we were in search of. On the 23rd of June, Lord St Vincent at length resigned the Mediterranean command and sailed for England, so that Lord Keith had no alternative but to return to Port Mahon to make the necessary arrangements.

Scarcely had we come to an anchor when we received intelligence that the French fleet had passed to the westward to join the Spanish fleet at Carthagena !

Without even losing time to fill up with water, every exertion was made for immediate pursuit, and on the 10th we started for Carthagena, but finding the enemy gone, again made sail, and on the 26th reached Tetuan, where we completed our water. On the 29th Lord Keith communicated with Gibraltar, but as nothing was heard of the combined fleets, it was evident they had gone through the Straits in the dark ; we therefore followed and examined Cadiz, where they were not. Pursuing our course without effect along the Spanish and

Portuguese coasts—on the 8th of August we fell in with a Danish brig off Cape Finisterre, and received from her information that she had two days before passed through the combined French and Spanish fleets. We then directed our course for Brest, hoping to be in time to intercept them, but found that on the day before our arrival they had effected their object, and were then safely moored within the harbour. We now shaped our course for Torbay, and there found the Channel fleet under Sir Alan Gardner—the united force being nearly fifty ships of the line.

On our arrival at Torbay, Lord Keith sent me with despatches on board the commander-in-chief's ship, where, after executing my commission, it was imperiously demanded by her captain whether I was aware that my coming on board was an infringement of quarantine regulations ? Nettled at the overbearing manner of an uncalled-for reprimand to an inferior officer, my reply was that, having been directed by Lord Keith to deliver his despatches, his lordship's orders had been executed accordingly ; at the same time, however, assuring my interrogator that we had no sickness in the fleet, nor had we been in any contagious localities. From the captain's manner, it was almost evident that, for being thus plain spoken, he intended to put me under arrest, and I was not sorry to get back to the *Queen Charlotte* ; even a show of resistance to an excess of authority being in those days fatal to many an officer's prospects.

I shall not enter into detail as to what occurred in the Channel ; suffice it to say that despite the imposing force lying at Torbay, the combined French and Spanish fleets found no difficulty in getting out of Brest, and that on the 6th of December Lord Keith returned in pursuit to Gibraltar, where he resumed the Mediterranean command, administered by Lord Nelson during his absence.

It is beyond the province of this work to notice the effectual measures taken by Lord Nelson in the Mediterranean during our absence, as they are matters in which I bore no part. But whilst Nelson and Lord Keith had been doing their best there, little appeared to be done at home to check the enemy's operations.

From Gibraltar we proceeded to Sicily, where we found Lord Nelson surrounded by the *élite* of Neapolitan society, amongst whom he was justly regarded as a deliverer. It was never my good fortune to serve under his lordship, either at that or any subsequent period. During our stay at Palermo, I had, however, opportunities of personal conversation with him, and from one of his frequent injunctions, " Never mind manœuvres, always go at them," I subsequently had reason to consider myself indebted for successful attacks under apparently difficult circumstances.

The impression left on my mind during these opportunities of association with Nelson was that of his being an embodiment of dashing courage, which would not take much trouble to circumvent an enemy, but being confronted with one would regard victory so much a matter of course as hardly to deem the chance of defeat worth consideration.

This was in fact the case ; for though the enemy's ships were for the most part superior to ours in build, the discipline and seamanship of their crews was in that day so inferior as to leave little room for doubt of victory on our part. It was probably with the object of improving his crews that Admiral Bruix had risked a run from the Mediterranean to Brest and back, as just now detailed. Had not Lord Keith been delayed at Gibraltar, and afterwards recalled to Minorca, the disparity of numbers on our side would not have been of any great consequence.

Trafalgar itself is an illustration of Nelson's peculiar dash. It has been remarked that Trafalgar was a rash action, and that had Nelson lost it and lived he would have been brought to a court-martial for the way in which that action was conducted. But such cavillers forget that, from previous experience, he had calculated both the nature and amount of resistance to be expected ; such calculation forming as essential a part of his plan of attack as even his own means for making it. The result justified his expectations of victory, which were not only well founded but certain.

The fact is, that many commanders in those days committed the error of overrating the French navy, just as, in the present day, we are nationally falling into the still more dangerous extreme of underrating it. Steam has, indeed, gone far towards equalising seamanship; and the strenuous exertions of the French department of Marine have perhaps rendered discipline in their navy as good as in ours. They moreover keep their trained men, whilst we thoughtlessly turn ours adrift whenever ships are paid off—to be replaced by raw hands in case of emergency!

To return from this digression. After quitting Palermo, and when passing the Straits of Messina, Lord Keith placed me as prize-master in command of the *Genereux*, 74—shortly before captured by Lord Nelson's squadron—with orders to carry her to Port Mahon. A crew was hastily made up of sick and invalided men drafted from the ships of the fleet, and with these we proceeded on our voyage, but only to find ourselves in imminent danger from a gale of wind. The rigging not having been properly set up, the masts swayed with every roll of the ship to such a degree that it became dangerous to go aloft; the shrouds alternately straining almost to breaking, or hanging in festoons, as the masts jerked from side to side with the roll of the vessel. It was only by going aloft myself together with my brother Archibald, whom Lord Keith had permitted to accompany me, that the men could be induced to furl the mainsail. Fortunately the weather moderated, or the safety of the ship might have been compromised; but by dint of hard work, as far as the ill-health of the crew would allow, we managed, before reaching Mahon, to put the *Genereux* into tolerable order.

It has been stated that Lord Keith permitted my brother to accompany me in the *Genereux*. By this unexpected incident both he and myself were, in all probability, saved from a fate which soon afterwards befell most of our gallant shipmates.

On our quitting the *Queen Charlotte*, Lord Keith steered for Leghorn, where he landed, and ordered Captain Todd to reconnoitre the island of Cabrera, then in possession of the French. Whilst on his way, some hay, hastily embarked and placed under the half-deck, became ignited, and the flame communicating with the mainsail set the ship on fire aloft and below. All exertions to save her proved in vain, and though some of the officers and crew escaped, more than three-fourths miserably perished, including Captain Todd, his first lieutenant, Bainbridge, three other lieutenants, the captain of marines, surgeon, more than twenty master's mates and petty officers, and upwards of 600 marines and seamen.

On our return from England to Gibraltar I had been associated with poor Bainbridge in an affair which—except as a tribute to his memory—would not have been worth mentioning. On the evening of the 21st of September, 1799, we observed from the *Queen Charlotte*, lying in Gibraltar Bay, the 10-gun cutter *Lady Nelson*, chased by some gun-vessels and privateers, all of which simultaneously commenced an attack upon her. Lord Keith instantly ordered out boats, Bainbridge taking command of the barge, whilst another of the boats was put under my orders. Lord Keith's intention was, by this prompt aid, to induce the *Lady Nelson* to make a running fight of it, so as to get within range of the garrison guns ; but before the boats could come up she had been captured ; Lieutenant Bainbridge, though with sixteen men only, dashed at her, boarded, and retook her, killing several and taking prisoners seven French officers and twenty-seven men ; but not without himself receiving a severe sabre cut on the head and several other wounds.

The boat under my command was the cutter with thirteen men. Seeing two privateers which had chiefly been engaged in the attack on the *Lady Nelson* running for Algesiras, we made at the nearest, and came up with her at dark. On laying the cutter alongside, I jumped on board, but the boat's crew did not follow, this being the only time I ever saw British seamen betray symptoms of hesitation. Regaining the cutter, I upbraided them with the shamefulness of their conduct, for the privateer's crew had run below, the helmsman alone being at his post. Their excuse was that there were indications of the privateer's men having there fortified themselves. No reasoning could prevail on them to board. If this boat's crew perished in the *Queen Charlotte*, their fate is not nationally to be regretted.

On the destruction of the *Queen Charlotte* Lord Keith hoisted his flag in the *Audacious*. His lordship was so well satisfied with my conduct of the *Genereux* as to write home to the Admiralty recommending my promotion, at the same time appointing me to the command of the *Speedy*, then lying at Port Mahon.

The vessel originally intended for me by Lord Keith was the *Bonne Citoyenne*, a fine corvette of eighteen guns; but the brother of his lordship's secretary happening at the time to arrive from Gibraltar, where he had been superseded in the command of the sheer-hulk, that functionary managed to place his brother in one of the finest sloops then in the service, leaving to me the least efficient craft on the station.

CHAPTER V

CRUISE OF THE SPEEDY

THE *Speedy* was little more than a burlesque on a vessel of war, even sixty years ago.* She was about the size of an average coasting brig, her burden being 158 tons. She was crowded, rather than manned, with a crew of eighty-four men and six officers, myself included. Her armament consisted of fourteen 4-*pounders*! a species of gun little larger than a blunderbuss, and formerly known in the service under the name of "minion," an appellation which it certainly merited.

Being dissatisfied with her armament, I applied for and obtained

* About 1800.

a couple of 12-pounders, intending them as bow and stern chasers, but was compelled to return them to the ordnance wharf, there not being room on deck to work them ; besides which, the timbers of the little craft were found on trial to be too weak to withstand the concussion of anything heavier than the guns with which she was previously armed.

With her rig I was more fortunate. Having carried away her mainyard, it became necessary to apply for another to the senior officer, who, examining the list of spare spars, ordered the *foretop-gallant-yard* of the *Genereux* to be hauled out *as a mainyard for the " Speedy "* !

The spar was accordingly sent on board and rigged, but even this appearing too large for the vessel, an order was issued to cut off the yard-arms and thus reduce it to its proper dimensions. This order was neutralised by getting down and planing the yard-arms as though they had been cut, an evasion which, with some alteration in the rigging, passed undetected on its being again swayed up ; and thus a greater spread of canvas was secured. The fact of the foretop-gallant-yard of a second-rate ship being considered too large for the mainyard of my " man-of-war " will give a tolerable idea of her insignificance.

Despite her unformidable character, and the personal dis-comfort to which all on board were subjected, I was very proud of my little vessel, caring nothing for her want of accommodation, though in this respect her cabin merits passing notice. It had not so much as room for a chair, the floor being entirely occupied by a small table surrounded with lockers, answering the double purpose of storechests and seats. The difficulty was to get seated, the ceiling being only five feet high, so that the object could only be accomplished by rolling on the locker, a movement sometimes attended with unpleasant failure. The most singular discomfort, however, was that my only practicable mode of shaving consisted in removing the skylight and putting my head through to make a toilet-table of the quarter-deck.

In the following enumeration of the various cruises in which the *Speedy* was engaged, the boarding and searching innumerable neutral vessels will be passed over, and the narrative will be strictly confined—as in most cases throughout this work —to log extracts, where captures were made, or other occurrences took place worthy of record.

" *May* 10.—Sailed from Cagliari, from which port we had been ordered to convoy fourteen sail of merchantmen to Leghorn. At 9 A.M. observed a strange sail take possession of a Danish brig under our escort. At 11.30 A.M. rescued the brig and captured the assailant. This prize—my first piece of luck—was the *Intrepide*, French privateer of six guns and forty-eight men.

" *May* 14.—Saw five armed boats pulling towards us from Monte Cristo. Out sweeps to protect convoy. At 4 P.M. the boats boarded and took possession of the two sternmost ships. A light breeze springing up, made all sail towards the captured vessels, ordering the remainder of the convoy to make the best of their way to Longona. The breeze freshening we came up with and recaptured the vessels with the prize crews on board, but during the operation the armed boats escaped.

" *May* 21.—At anchor in Leghorn Roads. Convoy all safe. 25.—Off Genoa. Joined Lord Keith's squadron of five sail of the line, four frigates and a brig.

" 26, 27, 28.—Ordered by his lordship to cruise in the offing, to intercept supplies destined for the French army under Massena, then in possession of Genoa.

" 29.—At Genoa some of the gun-boats bombarded the town for two hours.

" 30.—All the gun-boats bombarded the town. A partial bombardment had been going on for an hour a day, during the past fortnight, Lord Keith humanely refraining from continued bombardment, out of consideration for the inhabitants, who were in a state of absolute famine."

This was one of the *crises* of the war. The French, about a month previous, had defeated the Austrians with great slaughter in an attempt, on the part of the latter, to retake Genoa ; but the Austrians, being in possession of Savona, were nevertheless able to intercept provisions on the land side, whilst the vigilance of Lord Keith rendered it impossible to obtain supplies by sea.

It having come to Lord Keith's knowledge that the French in Genoa had consumed their last horses and dogs, whilst the Genoese themselves were perishing by famine, and on the eve of revolt against the usurping force—in order to save the carnage which would ensue, his lordship caused it to be intimated to Massena that a defence so heroic would command honourable terms of capitulation. Massena was said to have replied that if the word "capitulation" were mentioned his army should perish with the city ; but, as he could no longer defend himself, he had no objection to "treat." Lord Keith, therefore, proposed a treaty, viz., that the army might return to France, but that Massena himself must remain a prisoner in his hands. To this the French general demurred ; but Lord Keith insisting—with the complimentary observation to Massena that "he was worth 20,000 men"—the latter reluctantly gave in, and on the 4th of June, 1800, a definite treaty to the above effect was agreed upon, and ratified on the 5th, when the Austrians took possession of the city, and Lord Keith of the harbour, the squadron anchoring within the mole.

This affair being ended, his lordship ordered the *Speedy* to cruise off the Spanish coast, and on the 14th of June we parted company with the squadron.

"*June* 16.—Captured a tartan off Elba. Sent her to Leghorn, in the charge of an officer and four men.

"22.—Off Bastia. Chased a French privateer with a prize in tow. The Frenchman abandoned the prize, a Sardinian vessel laden with oil and wool, and we took possession. Made all sail in chase of the privateer ; but on our commencing to fire she ran under the fort of Caprea, where we did not think proper to pursue her. Took prize in tow and on the following day left her at Leghorn, where we found Lord Nelson, and several ships at anchor.

" 25.—Quitted Leghorn, and on the 26th were again off
Bastia, in chase of a ship which ran for that place, and anchored
under a fort three miles to the southward. Made at and brought
her away. Proved to be the Spanish letter of marque *Assuncion*,
of ten guns and thirty-three men, bound from Tunis to Barcelona.
On taking possession, five gun-boats left Bastia in chase of us ;
took the prize in tow, and kept up a running fight with the gun-
boats till after midnight, when they left us.

" 29.—Cast off the prize in chase of a French privateer off
Sardinia. On commencing our fire she set all sail and ran off.
Returned and took the prize in tow ; and the 4th of July anchored
with her in Port Mahon.

" *July* 9.—Off Cape Sebastian. Gave chase to two Spanish
ships standing along shore. They anchored under the protection
of the forts. Saw another vessel lying just within range of the
forts ;—out boats and cut her out, the forts firing on the boats
without inflicting damage.

" *July* 19.—Off Caprea. Several French privateers in sight.
Chased, and on the following morning captured one, the
Constitution, of one gun and nineteen men. Whilst we were
securing the privateer, a prize which she had taken made sail
in the direction of Gorgona and escaped.

" 27.—Off Planosa, in chase of a privateer. On the following
morning saw three others lying in a small creek. On making
preparations to cut them out, a military force made its appearance,
and commenced a heavy fire of musketry, to which it would have
answered no purpose to reply. Fired several broadsides at one
of the privateers, and sunk her.

" 31.—Off Porto Ferraio in chase of a French privateer, with
a prize in tow. The Frenchman abandoned his prize, of which
we took possession, and whilst so doing the privateer got away.

" *August* 3.—Anchored with our prizes in Leghorn Roads,
where we found Lord Keith in the *Minotaur*."

Lord Keith received me very kindly, and directed the *Speedy*
to run down the Spanish coast, pointing out the importance of

harassing the enemy there as much as possible, but cautioning me against engaging anything beyond our capacity. During our stay at Leghorn, his lordship frequently invited me ashore to participate in the gaieties of the place.

Having filled up with provisions and water, we sailed on the 16th of August, and on the 21st captured a French privateer bound from Corsica to Toulon. Shortly afterwards we fell in with H.M.S. *Mutine* and *Salamine*, which, to suit their convenience, gave into our charge a number of French prisoners, with whom and our prize we consequently returned to Leghorn.

On the 14th of September we again put to sea, the interval being occupied by a thorough overhaul of the sloop. On the 22nd, when off Caprea, fell in with a Neapolitan vessel having a French prize crew on board. Recaptured the vessel, and took the crew prisoners.

On the 5th of October, the *Speedy* anchored in Port Mahon, where information was received that the Spaniards had several armed vessels on the look-out for us, should we again appear on their coast. I therefore applied to the authorities to exchange our 4-pounders for 6-pounders, but the latter being too large for the *Speedy's* ports, we were again compelled to forego the change as impracticable.

" *October* 12.—Sailed from Port Mahon, cruising for some time off Cape Sebastian, Villa Nova, Oropesa, and Barcelona ; occasionally visiting the enemy's coast for water, of which the *Speedy* carried only ten tons. Nothing material occurred till November 18th, when we narrowly escaped being swamped in a gale of wind, the sea breaking over our quarter, and clearing our deck, spars, etc., otherwise inflicting such damage as to compel our return to Port Mahon, where we were detained till the 12th of December.

" *December* 15.—Off Majorca. Several strange vessels being in sight, singled out the largest and made sail in chase ; shortly after which a French bombard bore up, hoisting the national colours. We now cleared for action, altering our course to meet her, when she bore up between Dragon Island and the Main.

Commenced firing at the bombard, which returned our fire ; but shortly afterwards getting closer in shore she drove on the rocks. Three other vessels being in the passage, we left her, and captured one of them, the *La Liza*, of ten guns and thirty-three men, bound from Alicant to Marseilles. Took nineteen of our prisoners on board the *Speedy*. As it was evident that the bombard would become a wreck, we paid no further attention to her, but made all sail after the others.

"*December* 18.—Suspecting the passage between Dragon Island and the Main to be a lurking-place for privateers, we ran in again, but found nothing. Seeing a number of troops lining the beach, we opened fire and dispersed them, afterwards engaging a tower, which fired upon us. The prisoners we had taken proving an incumbrance, we put them on shore.

"*December* 19.—Stood off and on the harbour of Palamos, where we saw several vessels at anchor. Hoisted Danish colours and made the signal for a pilot. Our real character being evidently known, none came off, and we did not think it prudent to venture in."

It has been said that the *Speedy* had become the marked object of the Spanish naval authorities. Not that there was much danger of being caught, for they confined their search to the coast only, and that in the daytime, when we were usually away in the offing ; it being our practice to keep out of sight during the day, and run in before dawn on the next morning.

On the 21st, however, when off Plane Island, we were very near " catching a Tartar." Seeing a large ship in shore, having all the appearance of a well-laden merchantman, we forthwith gave chase. On nearing her she raised her ports, which had been closed to deceive us, the act discovering a heavy broadside, a clear demonstration that we had fallen into the jaws of a formidable Spanish frigate, now crowded with men, who had before remained concealed below.

That the frigate was in search of us there could be no doubt, from the deception practised. To have encountered her with

our insignificant armament would have been exceedingly imprudent, whilst escape was out of the question, for she would have
outsailed us, and could have run us down by her mere weight.
There was, therefore, nothing left, but to try the effect of a *ruse*,
prepared beforehand for such an emergency. After receiving
at Mahon information that unusual measures were about to be
taken by the Spaniards for our capture, I had the *Speedy* painted
in imitation of the Danish brig *Clomer* ; the appearance of this
vessel being well known on the Spanish coast. We also shipped a
Danish quartermaster, taking the further precaution of providing
him with the uniform of an officer of that nation.

On discovering the real character of our neighbour, the
Speedy hoisted Danish colours, and spoke her. At first this
failed to satisfy the Spaniard, who sent a boat to board us. It
was now time to bring the Danish quartermaster into play in
his officer's uniform ; and to add force to his explanations, we
ran the quarantine flag up to the fore, calculating on the Spanish
horror of the plague, then prevalent along the Barbary
coast.

On the boat coming within hail,—for the yellow flag effectually
repressed the enemy's desire to board us—our mock officer
informed the Spaniards that we were two days from Algiers,
where at the time the plague was violently raging. This was
enough. The boat returned to the frigate, which, wishing us a
good voyage, filled, and made sail, whilst we did the same.

I have noted this circumstance more minutely than it merits,
because it has been misrepresented. By some of my officers
blame was cast on me for not attacking the frigate after she had
been put off her guard by our false colours, as her hands—being
then employed at their ordinary avocations in the rigging and
elsewhere—presented a prominent mark for our shot. There
is no doubt but that we might have poured in a murderous fire
before the crew could have recovered from their confusion, and
perhaps have taken her, but feeling averse to so cruel a destruction
of human life, I chose to refrain from an attack, which might
not, even with that advantage in our favour, have been successful.

It has been stated by some naval writers that this frigate was the *Gamo*, which we subsequently captured. To the best of my knowledge this is an error.

"*December* 24.—Off Carthagena. At daylight fell in with a convoy in charge of two Spanish privateers, which came up and fired at us ; but being to windward we ran for the convoy, and singling out two, captured the nearest, laden with wine. The other ran in shore under the fort of Port Genoese, where we left her.

" 25.—Stood for Cape St Martin, in hope of intercepting the privateers. At 8 A.M. saw a privateer and one of the convoy under Cape Lanar. Made sail in chase. They parted company ; when, on our singling out the nearest privateer, she took refuge under a battery, on which we left off pursuit.

" 30.—Off Cape Oropesa. Seeing some vessels in shore, out boats in chase. At noon they returned pursued by two Spanish gunboats, which kept up a smart fire on them. Made sail to intercept the gun-boats, on which they ran in under the batteries.

"*January* 10, 1801.—Anchored in Port Mahon, and having refitted, sailed again on the 12th.

" 16.—Off Barcelona. Just before daylight chased two vessels standing towards that port. Seeing themselves pursued, they made for the battery at the entrance. Bore up and set steering sails in chase. The wind falling calm, one of the chase drifted in shore, and took the ground under Castel De Ferro. On commencing our fire, the crew abandoned her, and we sent boats with anchors and hawsers to warp her off, in which they succeeded. She proved to be the Genoese ship *Ns. Senora de Gratia*, of ten guns.

" 22.—Before daylight, stood in again for Barcelona. Saw several sail close in with the land. Out boats and boarded one, which turned out a Dane. Cruising off the port till 3 A.M., we saw two strange vessels coming from the westward. Made sail to cut them off. At 6 P.M. one of them hoisted Spanish colours and the other French. At 9 P.M. came up with them, when after an engagement of half an hour both struck. The Spaniard was the

12-PR. CARRONADE

(From a drawing by E. W. Cooke, R.A.)

Ecce Homo, of eight guns and nineteen men, the Frenchman, *L'Amitie*, of one gun and thirty-one men. Took all the prisoners on board the *Speedy*.

" 23.—Still off Barcelona. Having sent most of our crew to man the prizes, the number of prisoners on board the *Speedy* became dangerous ; we therefore put twenty-five of the Frenchmen into one of their own launches, and told them to make the best of their way to Barcelona. As the prizes were a good deal cut up about the rigging, repaired their damages and made sail for Port Mahon, where we arrived on the 24th, with our convoy in company.

" 28th.—Quitted Port Mahon for Malta, not being able to procure at Minorca various things of which we stood in need ; and on the 1st of February, came to an anchor at Valetta, where we obtained anchors and sweeps."

An absurd affair took place during our short stay at Malta, which would not have been worthy of notice, had it not been made the subject of comment.

The officers of a French royalist regiment, then at Malta, patronised a fancy ball, for which I amongst others purchased a ticket. The dress chosen was that of a sailor—in fact, my costume was a tolerable imitation of that of my worthy friend, Jack Larmour, in one of his relaxing moods, and personated in my estimation as honourable a character as were Greek, Turkish, or other kinds of Oriental disguises in vogue at such reunions. My costume was, however, too much to the life to please French royalist taste, not even the marlinspike and the lump of grease in the hat being omitted.

On entering the ball-room, further passage was immediately barred, with an intimation that my presence could not be permitted in such a dress. Good-humouredly expostulating that, as the choice of costume was left to the wearer, my own taste —which was decidedly nautical—had selected that of a British seaman, a character which, though by no means imaginary, was quite as picturesque as were the habiliments of an Arcadian

D

shepherd ; further insisting that as no rule had been infringed, I must be permitted to exercise my discretion. Expostulation being of no avail, a brusque answer was returned that such a dress was not admissible, whereupon I as brusquely replied that having purchased my ticket, and chosen my own costume in accordance with the regulations, no one had any right to prevent me from sustaining the character assumed.

Upon this a French officer, who appeared to act as master of the ceremonies, came up, and without waiting for further explanation, rudely seized me by the collar with the intention of putting me out ; in return for which insult he received a substantial mark of British indignation, and at the same time an uncomplimentary remark in his own language. In an instant all was uproar ; a French picket was called, which in a short time overpowered and carried me off to the guard-house of the regiment.

I was, however, promptly freed from detention on announcing my name, but the officer who had collared me demanded an apology for the portion of the *fracas* concerning him personally. This being of course refused, a challenge was the consequence ; and on the following morning we met behind the ramparts and exchanged shots, my ball passing through the poor fellow's thigh, and dropping him. My escape, too, was a narrow one— his ball perforating my coat, waistcoat, and shirt, and bruising my side. Seeing my adversary fall, I stepped up to him— imagining his wound to be serious—and expressed a hope that he had not been hit in a vital part. His reply—uttered with all the politeness of his nation—was, that " he was not materially hurt." I, however, was not at ease, for it was impossible not to regret this, to him, serious *dénouement* of a trumpery affair, though arising from his own intemperate conduct. It was a lesson to me in future never to do anything in frolic which might give even unintentional offence.

On the 3rd of February we sailed under orders for Tripoli, to make arrangements for fresh provisions for the fleet. This being effected, the *Speedy* returned to Malta, and on the 20th again left port in charge of a convoy for Tunis.

24th.—At the entrance of Tunis Bay we gave chase to a strange sail, which wore and stood in towards the town, anchoring at about the distance of three miles. Suspecting some reason for this movement, I despatched an officer to examine her, when the suspicion was confirmed by his ascertaining her to be *La Belle Caroline*, French brig of four guns, bound for Alexandria with field-pieces, ammunition, and wine for the use of the French army in Egypt.

Our position was one of delicacy, the vessel being in a neutral port, where, if we remained to watch her, she might prolong our stay for an indefinite period or escape in the night; whilst, from the warlike nature of the cargo, it was an object of national importance to effect her capture. The latter appearing the most beneficial course under all circumstances, we neared her so as to prevent escape, and soon after midnight boarded her, and having weighed her anchor, brought her close to the *Speedy*, before she had an opportunity of holding any communication with the shore.

The following day was employed in examining her stores, a portion of her ammunition being transferred to our magazine, to replace some damaged by leakage. Her crew, now on board the *Speedy* as prisoners, becoming clamorous at what they considered an illegal seizure, and being, moreover, in our way, an expedient was adopted to get rid of them, by purposely leaving their own launch within reach during the following night, with a caution to the watch not to prevent their desertion should they attempt it. The hint was taken, for before daylight on the 27th they seized the boat, and pulled out of the bay without molestation, not venturing to go to Tunis lest they should be retaken. We thus got rid of the prisoners, and at the same time of what might have turned out their reasonable complaint to the Tunisian authorities, for that we had exceeded the bounds of neutrality there could be no doubt.

On the 28th we weighed anchor, and proceeded to sea with our prize. After cruising for some days off Cape Bon, we made sail for Cagliari, where we arrived on the 8th of March, and put to sea on the 11th with the prize in tow.   On the 16th, anchored in Port Mahon.

On the 18th we again put to sea, and towards evening observed a large frigate in chase of us.   As she did not answer the private signal, it was evident that the stranger was one of our Spanish friends on the look-out.   To cope with a vessel of her size and armament would have been folly, so we made all sail away from her, but she gave instant chase, and evidently gained upon us.   To add to our embarrassment, the *Speedy* sprung her maintop-gallant-yard, and lost ground whilst fishing it.

At daylight the following morning the strange frigate was still in chase, though by crowding all sail during the night we had gained a little upon her ; but during the day she again recovered her advantage, the more so, as the breeze freshening, we were compelled to take in our royals, whilst she was still carrying on with everything set.   After dark, we lowered a tub overboard with a light in it, and altering our course thus fortunately evaded her.   On the 1st of April we returned to Port Mahon, and again put to sea on the 6th.

"*April* 11.—Observing a vessel near the shoal of Tortosa, gave chase.   On the following morning her crew deserted her, and we took possession.   In the evening anchored under the land.

"13.—Saw three vessels at anchor in a bay to the westward of Oropesa.   Made sail up to them and anchored on the flank of a ten-gun fort.   Whilst the firing was going on, the boats were sent in to board and bring out the vessels, which immediately weighed and got under the fort.   At 5.30 P.M. the boats returned with one of them ; the other two being hauled close in shore, we did not make any further attempt to capture them.   As the prize, the *Ave Maria*, of four guns, was in ballast, we took the sails and spars out of her, and set her on fire.

"On the following morning at daybreak, several vessels appeared to the eastward.   Made all sail to intercept them, but before we could come up, they succeeded in anchoring under a fort.   On standing towards them, they turned out to be Spanish gun-boats, which commenced firing at us. At 10 A.M. anchored within musket-shot, so as to keep an angle of the tower on our beam, thus neutralising its effect. Commenced firing broadsides alternately at the tower and the gun-boats, with visible advantage. Shortly before noon made preparation to cut out the gun-boats, but a fresh breeze setting in dead on shore, rendered it impossible to get at them without placing ourselves in peril. We thereupon worked out of the bay.

" 15.—Two strange sail in sight. Gave chase, and in a couple of hours came up with and captured them. Made sail after a convoy in the offing, but the wind falling light at dusk, lost sight of them.

" On the 26th we anchored in Mahon, remaining a week to refit and procure fresh hands, many having been sent away in prizes. On the 2nd of May put to sea with a reduced crew, some of whom had to be taken out of H.M.'s prison."

We again ran along the Spanish coast, and on the 4th of May were off Barcelona, where the *Speedy* captured a vessel which reported herself as Ragusan, though in reality a Spanish four-gun tartan. Soon after detaining her we heard firing in the W. N.-W., and steering for that quarter fell in with a Spanish privateer, which we also captured, the *San Carlos*, of seven guns. On this a swarm of gun-boats came out of Barcelona, seven of them giving chase to us and the prizes, with which we made off shore, the gun-boats returning to Barcelona.

On the following morning the prizes were sent to Port Mahon, and keeping out of sight for the rest of the day, the *Speedy* returned at midnight off Barcelona, where we found the gun-boats on the watch ; but on our approach they ran in shore, firing at us occasionally. Suspecting that the object was to decoy us within reach of some larger vessel, we singled out one of them and made at her, the others, however, supporting her so well that some of our rigging being shot away, we made off shore to repair, the gun-boats following. Having thus got them to some distance, and repaired damages, we set all sail, and again ran in shore, in the hope of getting between them and the land, so as to cut off some of their number. Perceiving our intention, they all made for the port as before, keeping up a smart fight, in which our foretop-gallant-yard was so much injured, that we had to shift it, and were thus left astern. The remainder of the day was employed in repairing damages, and the gun-boats not venturing out again, at 9 P.M. we again made off shore.

Convinced that something more than ordinary had actuated the gun-boats to decoy us—just before daylight on the 6th we again ran in for Barcelona, when the trap manifested itself in the form of a large ship, running under the land, and bearing E. S.-E. On hauling towards her, she changed her course in chase of us, and was shortly made out to be a Spanish xebec frigate.

As some of my officers had expressed dissatisfaction at not having been permitted to attack the frigate fallen in with on the 21st of December, after her suspicions had been lulled by our device of hoisting Danish colours, etc., I told them they should now have a fair fight, notwithstanding that, by manning the two prizes sent to Mahon, our numbers had been reduced to fifty-four, officers and boys included. Orders were then given to pipe all hands, and prepare for action.

Accordingly we made towards the frigate, which was now coming down under steering sails. At 9.30 A.M., she fired a gun and hoisted Spanish colours, which the *Speedy* acknowledged by hoisting American colours, our object being, as we were now exposed to her full broadside, to puzzle her, till we got on the other tack, when we ran up the English ensign, and immediately afterwards encountered her broadside without damage.

Shortly afterwards she gave us another broadside, also without effect. My orders were not to fire a gun till we were close to her; when, running under her lee, we locked our yards amongst her rigging, and in this position returned our broadside, such as it was.

To have fired our popgun 4-pounders at a distance would have been to throw away the ammunition; but the guns being doubly, and, as I afterwards learned, trebly, shotted, and being elevated, they told admirably upon her main-deck ; the first discharge, as was subsequently ascertained, killing the Spanish captain and the boatswain.

My reason for locking our small craft in the enemy's rigging was the one upon which I mainly relied for victory, viz. that from the height of the frigate out of the water, the whole of her shot must necessarily go over our heads, whilst our guns, being elevated, would blow up her main-deck.

The Spaniards speedily found out the disadvantage under which they were fighting, and gave the order to board the *Speedy* ; but as this order was as distinctly heard by us as by them, we avoided it at the moment of execution by sheering off sufficiently to prevent the movement, giving them a volley of musketry and a broadside before they could recover themselves.

Twice was this manœuvre repeated, and twice thus averted. The Spaniards finding that they were only punishing themselves, gave up further attempts to board, and stood to their guns, which were cutting up our rigging from stem to stern, but doing little further damage ; for after the lapse of an hour the loss to the *Speedy* was only two men killed and four wounded.

This kind of combat, however, could not last. Our rigging being cut up and the *Speedy's* sails riddled with shot, I told the men that they must either take the frigate or be themselves taken, in which case the Spaniards would give no quarter—whilst a few minutes energetically employed on their part would decide the matter in their own favour.

The doctor, Mr Guthrie, who, I am happy to say, is still living to peruse this record of his gallantry, volunteered to take the helm ; leaving him therefore for the time both commander and crew of the *Speedy*, the order was given to board, and in a few seconds every man was on the enemy's deck—a feat rendered the more easy as the doctor placed the *Speedy* close alongside with admirable skill.

For a moment the Spaniards seemed taken by surprise, as though unwilling to believe that so small a crew would have the audacity to board them ; but soon recovering themselves, they made a rush to the waist of the frigate, where the fight was for some minutes gallantly carried on. Observing the enemy's colours still flying, I directed one of our men immediately to haul them down, when the Spanish crew, without pausing to consider by whose orders the colours had been struck, and naturally believing it the act of their own officers, gave in, and we were in possession of the *Gamo* frigate, of thirty-two heavy guns and 319 men, who an hour and a half before had looked upon us as a certain if not an easy prey.

Our loss in boarding was Lieutenant Parker, severely wounded in several places, one seaman killed and three wounded, which with those previously killed and wounded gave a total of three seamen killed, and one officer and seventeen men wounded.

The *Gamo's* loss was Captain de Torres—the boatswain—and thirteen seamen killed, together with forty-one wounded; her casualties thus exceeding the whole number of officers and crew on board the *Speedy*.

Some time after the surrender of the *Gamo*, and when we were in quiet possession, the officer who had succeeded the deceased Captain Don Francisco de Torres, not in command, but in rank, applied to me for a certificate that he had done his duty during the action; whereupon he received from me a certificate that he had "conducted himself like a true Spaniard," with which document he appeared highly gratified, and I had afterwards the satisfaction of learning that it procured him further promotion in the Spanish service.

Shortly before boarding, an incident occurred which, by those who have never been placed in similar circumstances, may be thought too absurd for notice. Knowing that the final struggle would be a desperate one, and calculating on the superstitious wonder which forms an element in the Spanish character, a portion of our crew were ordered to blacken their faces, and what with this and the excitement of combat, more ferocious-looking objects could scarcely be imagined. The fellows thus disguised were directed to board by the head, and the effect produced was precisely that calculated on. The greater portion of the

Spaniard's crew was prepared to repel boarders in that direction, but stood for a few moments as it were transfixed to the deck by the apparition of so many diabolical-looking figures emerging from the white smoke of the bow guns ; whilst our other men, who boarded by the waist, rushed on them from behind, before they could recover from their surprise at the unexpected phenomenon.

In difficult or doubtful attacks by sea,—and the odds of 50 men to 320 comes within this description,—no device can be too minute, even if apparently absurd, provided it have the effect of diverting the enemy's attention whilst you are concentrating your own. In this, and other successes against odds, I have no hesitation in saying that success in no slight degree depended on out-of-the-way devices, which the enemy not suspecting, were in some measure thrown off their guard.

It became a puzzle what to do with 263 unhurt prisoners now we had taken them, the *Speedy* having only forty-two men left. Promptness was however necessary ; so driving the prisoners into the hold, with guns pointing down the hatchway, and leaving thirty of our men on board the prize—which was placed under the command of my brother, the Hon. Archibald Cochrane, then a midshipman—we shaped our course to Port Mahon—not Gibraltar, as has been recorded—and arrived there in safety ; the Barcelona gun-boats, though spectators of the action, not venturing to rescue the frigate. Had they made the attempt, we should have had some difficulty in evading them and securing the prize, the prisoners manifesting every disposition to rescue themselves, and only being deterred by their own main-deck guns loaded with canister, and pointing down the hatchways, whilst our men stood over them with lighted matches.

The subjoined is Lord Keith's letter in reply to my official announcement of our success.

" ' FOUDROYANT,' off ARAB'S TOWER,
" *9th June*, 1801.

" MY LORD,—I have received your lordship's letter of the 13th ult., enclosing a copy of your letter to Capt. Dixon, detailing your engagement with and capture of the Spanish xebec of 32 guns; and cannot fail to be extremely gratified with the communication of an event so honourable to the naval service, and so highly creditable to your lordship's professional reputation, and to the intrepidity and discipline of the *Speedy's* officers and men, to all of whom I request your lordship will make my perfect satisfaction and approbation known.

" I have the honour to be, my lord, your lordship's most obedient servant,   (Signed)   KEITH.

" The Right Hon. LORD COCHRANE,
      " *Speedy*."

As a matter of course, my report of the capture of the *Gamo* was, in the first instance, made to the commandant at Port Mahon, the commander-in-chief being in Egypt. It should have been forwarded by him to the Secretary of the Admiralty, but was delayed for upwards of a month, thus affording a pretence for not promoting me to post rank, according to the recognised rules of the service.

From information on the affair being thus delayed, it was generally believed at home, that the *Gamo* had been taken by surprise, instead of after a close engagement, deliberately decided on, and announced to the officers and crew of the *Speedy* at five o'clock in the morning, the hands being turned up for the purpose. The consequence of the delay was a postponement of my post commission for upwards of three months, viz. from the 6th of May to the 8th of August; and what was of more consequence, a misunderstanding with Lord St Vincent, which bore most unfavourably upon all my future prospects. Upon this subject much will have to be said in a subsequent chapter.

The subjoined is a copy of my official report to the senior officer commanding at Port Mahon; and also of his remarkably concise comment thereon, when tardily transmitting the same to the Secretary of the Admiralty.

Copy of a letter from Capt. M. Dixon, *of H.M.S. " Genereux," to*
E. Nepean, Esq., *Secretary of the Admiralty, dated Port
Mahon, 9th June,* 1800.

" Sir,—I have the pleasure to transmit a copy of Lord
Cochrane's letter relative to the very spirited and brilliant action
with a Spanish xebec frigate.

" I have the honour, etc.   Manley Dixon.

" E. Nepean, Esq."

      " H.M. Sloop ' Speedy,' off Barcelona,
          " 6th May, 1800.

" Sir,—I have the pleasure to inform you, that the sloop I
have the honour to command, after a mutual chase and warm
action, has captured a Spanish xebec frigate of 32 guns, 22 long
12-pounders, 8 nines, and 2 heavy carronades, viz. the *Gamo*,
commanded by Don Francisco de Torres, manned by 319 officers,
seamen, and marines.

" The great disparity of force rendered it necessary to
adopt some measure that might prove decisive. I resolved to
board, and with Lieut. Parker, the Hon. A. Cochrane, the
boatswain and crew, did so, when, by the impetuosity of the
attack, we forced them to strike. I have to lament, in boarding,
the loss of one man only ; the severe wounds received by Lieut.
Parker, both from musketry and the sword, one wound received
by the boatswain, and one seaman.

" I must be permitted to say that there could not be greater
regularity, nor more cool determined conduct shown by men,
than by the crew of the *Speedy*. Lieut. Parker, whom I beg
leave to recommend to their lordships' notice, as well as the Hon.
Mr Cochrane, deserve all the approbation that can be bestowed.
The exertions and good conduct of the boatswain, carpenter, and
petty officers, I acknowledge with pleasure, as well as the skill
and attention of Mr Guthrie, the surgeon.

" I have the honour to be, etc.   Cochrane.

" M. Dixon, Esq."

" Speedy's force at commencement of action

" Fifty-four officers, men, and boys, 14 4-pounders. Three killed and 8 wounded.

" Gamo's force at commencement of action

" Two hundred and seventy-four officers, seamen, and supernumeraries. Forty-five marines. Guns, 32. Don Francisco de Torres, the boatswain, and 13 men killed, 41 wounded."

CHAPTER VI

CRUISE OF THE SPEEDY CONTINUED

OUR success hitherto had procured us some prize-money, notwithstanding the peculations of the Mediterranean Admiralty Courts, by which the greater portion of our captures was absorbed.

Despite this drawback, which generally disinclined officers and crews from making extraordinary exertions, my own share of the twelve months' zealous endeavours in our little sloop was considerable, and even the crew were in receipt of larger sums than those constituting the ordinary pay of officers ; a result chiefly owing to our nocturnal mode of warfare, together with our refraining from meddling with vessels ascertained to be loading in the Spanish ports, and then lying in wait for them as they proceeded on their voyage.

One effect of our success was no slight amount of ill concealed jealousy on the part of officers senior to myself, though there were some amongst these who, being in command of small squadrons instead of single vessels, might, had they adopted the same means, have effected far more than the *Speedy*, with an armament so insignificant, was calculated to accomplish.

After remaining some days at Port Mahon to refit, we prepared to return to our cruising ground, where, from private information, we knew that other prizes were at hand. In place of being permitted so to do, the *Speedy* received an order to proceed to Algiers, for the purpose of representing to the Dey the illegality of his cruisers having taken a British vessel in retaliation for an Algerine captured whilst violating the law of blockade.

The mission was a singular one to be entrusted to the captain of one of the smallest and worst armed vessels in the British service. Remonstrance, to be effectual with a piratical government, ought to have been committed to an officer armed with sufficient force at least to induce respect. There was, however, no alternative but to obey, and a short time saw us at anchor off the mole of the predatory potentate.

The request for an interview with his highness occasioned no little dissatisfaction amongst his ministers, if those who were quite as much his masters as his subordinates could be so termed. After some consultation, the interview was, however, granted, and a day was appointed to deliver my message.

The invariable Moslem preliminary of taking coffee having been gone through, I was ushered through a series of galleries lined with men, each bearing on his shoulder a formidable-looking axe, and eyeing me with an insolent scowl, evidently meant to convey the satisfaction with which they would apply its edge to my vertebræ, should the caprice of their chief so will.

On reaching the presence of the Dey—a dignified-looking and gorgeously-attired person, seated cross-legged on an elevated couch in one corner of the gallery and surrounded by armed people of most unprepossessing appearance—I was marched up between two janizaries, and ordered to make three salaams to his highness.

This formality being complied with, he rudely demanded, through the medium of an interpreter, " What brought me there ? " The reply was that " I was the commander of an English vessel of war in the roads, and had been deputed, on behalf of my Government, respectfully to remonstrate with his highness concerning a vessel which his cruisers had taken contrary to the laws of nations." On this being interpreted, the ferocious scowls of the bystanders were exchanged for expressions of injured innocence, but the Dey got in a great passion, and told the interpreter to inform me that " remonstrance came with an ill grace from us, the British vessels being the greatest pirates in the world, and mine one of the worst amongst them," which complimentary statement was acknowledged by me with a formal bow.

" If I did right," continued the Dey, through his interpreter,— " I should put you and your crew in prison, till " (naming a captured Algerine vessel) " she was restored ; and but for my great respect for the English Government, and my impression that her seizure was unauthorised, you should go there. However, you may go, with a demand from me that the vessel unjustly taken from us shall be immediately restored."

This decision appeared to be anything but satisfactory to the oligarchy of which his court was composed, as savouring of a clemency to which they were little inclined. From the boisterous conversation which ensued, they were evidently desirous of prolonging my stay to an indefinite period, or perhaps of terminating it summarily through the instrumentality of the axe men who lined the galleries, as a few years afterwards they terminated the existence of the Dey himself.

To confess the truth, there was some room for self-congratulation on quitting the presence of such barbarians, to whom I was not fairly accredited for such a mission. However, the remonstrance confided to me being duly delivered, we returned to Minorca, to report progress, though not without being chased by an Algerine cruiser on our way. As the *Speedy* outsailed her, and as there was no beneficial object to be gained by interfering with her, we stood on without further notice.

On arriving at our former cruising ground, we encountered a Spanish privateer of six guns, which was captured. This vessel was fitted out at my own private expense, and my brother appointed to command her, as a tender to the *Speedy* ; several enemy's vessels having previously escaped for want of such aid.

In a few days after this, we fell in with the *Kangaroo*, Captain Pulling, who, being senior to me, was therefore my commanding officer. Running down the coast in company, we attacked the fort of Almanara, and after silencing it, brought off a Spanish privateer of seven guns.

On the 8th of June, the *Speedy* ran into Oropesa, where, on the 13th and 14th of April, we had the previous action with the fort and gun-boats. Perceiving several vessels at anchor under the fort, it was deemed advisable to make off shore, with the intention of running in again at midnight, and cutting some of them out.

We had not proceeded far, before we again fell in with the *Kangaroo*, when informing Captain Pulling of what we had seen, he declined the night attack, preferring to postpone operations till the following day. Accordingly, at noon on the 9th, we went in, and made out a twenty-gun xebec * and three gun-boats, with ten sail of merchantmen under their convoy. It was determined to attack them as they lay ; the *Kangaroo* anchoring well up to and engaging the fort, whilst the *Speedy* and her tender under my brother's orders encountered the xebec and the gun-boats—the *Speedy* anchoring in a line between those vessels and the *Kangaroo*.

For some hours an incessant cannonade was kept up on both sides, the *Kangaroo's* fire flanking the fort, whilst the slackened fire of the Spanish vessels showed that our shot had told. At this juncture, a twelve-gun felucca and two more gun-boats having arrived from Valentia to their assistance, the Spaniards took heart, and the action became nearly as brisk as before.

The felucca and the newly arrived gun-boats were, however, for a time beat off, and after an hour's additional firing, the xebec, two gun-boats, and some of the convoy were sunk ; the remaining gun-boats shortly afterwards sharing the same fate.

The action had now continued for upwards of nine hours ; during which the *Speedy* had expended nearly all her ammunition, viz. 1400 shot, and the *Kangaroo* was much in the same predica-

* A three-masted vessel used by the corsairs at Algiers.

ment. As the felucca and gun-boats had again come up, it was necessary to effect something decisive. Captain Pulling, therefore, slipping his cable, shifted close to the fort, which was soon afterwards abandoned, and the *Speedy* closed with the felucca and her consorts, which forthwith fled. Had they remained, we had not half-a-dozen rounds left to continue the action.

Both vessels now hoisted out boats, and made for the merchantmen. Three of these had been sunk, and four others driven on shore; we, however, brought away the three still afloat. By this time a number of Spanish troops lined the beach for the protection of the vessels ashore, and as we had scarcely a shot left, it was impracticable to reply to the musketry, within range of which the boats must necessarily have been placed had the attempt been made. We therefore relinquished the endeavour to get off the stranded vessels.

It may be useful here to remark that on board the *Kangaroo* were some guns fitted on the non-recoil principle, and that during the action these broke from their breechings; one, if not more, endangering the vessel by bounding down the hatchways into the hold.

The subjoined letter of thanks for this affair was forwarded to Captain Pulling by Lord Keith, who was then at Alexandria watching the movements of the French in Egypt.

" ' FOUDROYANT,' BAY OF ABOUKIR,
" 10th *July*, 1801.

" SIR,—I have received your letter of the 10th of June, detailing the attack made by the *Kangaroo* and *Speedy* upon the fort of Oropesa and the enemy's armed vessels at anchor under its protection, on 9th of that month; as well as upon the tower of Almanara on a former day : and while I offer my congratulations upon the successful issue of your enterprise, I cannot withhold my approbation of the persevering and determined conduct manifested by you and by Captain Lord Cochrane, as well as by the officers and companies of both the sloops on these occasions, and I request that my satisfaction may be communicated by you to his lordship, and that you and he will make the same known to the officers and companies of the *Kangaroo* and the *Speedy*.

"I am, etc. etc.   KEITH.

"CAPT. PULLING, *Kangaroo*."

On our return to Port Mahon with the prizes, the *Gamo* had not been purchased by the Government ; but, to my regret, this useful cruiser had been sold for a trifle to the Algerines, whilst I was condemned to continue in the pigmy and now battered craft by which she had been taken. To have obtained command of the *Gamo*, even as a means of deception on the enemy's coast, I would scarcely have changed place with an admiral.

But a more cruel thing still was in store for me. The commandant lived in the house of a Spanish merchant who had a contract for carrying the mails to Gibraltar. The vessel employed for this purpose was a notoriously bad sailer, and when the *Speedy* was ready for sea, instead of being permitted to return to our cruising ground, she was ordered to convoy this tub of a packet to Gibraltar, with further instructions to take the letter-bag on board the *Speedy*, protect the packet, put the mail on board her as soon as we arrived off the Rock, and return without holding any communication with the shore ! the evident object of the last injunction being that the service which had been thrust upon us should not become known !

The expectation of the packet-master, doubtless, was that we should put to sea out of privateer reach. In place of this, we ran along the Spanish coast, our superior sailing enabling us, without delay, to scrutinise every creek as we passed. Nothing, however, occurred till we were close in with a bay, or rather indentation of the shore near Alicant, where seeing some vessels at anchor, we made towards them, on which they weighed and deliberately ran ashore. To have stopped to get them off would have been in excess of our instructions. To set fire to them was not, and as one was laden with oil, and the night following

E

very dark, the result was a blaze which illumined the sky for many miles round.

Unluckily for us, three French line-of-battle ships, which afterwards turned out to be the *Indomitable*, the *Dessaix*, and the *Formidable*, were in the vicinity, and being attracted by the light of the burning vessels, ran in shore to see what was the matter.

At daybreak, on the morning of July 3rd, these large ships were observed in the distance, calling up to our imaginations visions of Spanish galleons from South America, and accordingly the *Speedy* prepared for chase. It was not till day dawned that we found out our mistake, the vessels between us and the offing being clearly line-of-battle ships, forbidding all reasonable hope of escape.

It was about four o'clock in the morning when we made out the French ships, which immediately on discovering us gave chase. Being to windward, we endeavoured to escape by making all sail, and, as the wind fell light, by using our sweeps. This proving unavailing, we threw the guns overboard, and put the brig before the wind ; but notwithstanding every effort, the enemy gained fast upon us, and, in order to prevent our slipping past, separated on different tacks, so as to keep us constantly within reach of one or the other ; the *Dessaix*, being nearest, firing broadsides at us as she passed when tacking, at other times firing from her bow chasers, and cutting up our rigging.

For upwards of three hours we were thus within gunshot of the *Dessaix*, when finding it impossible to escape by the wind, I ordered all the stores to be thrown overboard, in the hope of being able, when thus further lightened, to run the gauntlet between the ships, which continued to gain upon us.

Watching an opportunity, when the nearest line-of-battle ship was before our beam, we bore up, set the studding sails, and attempted to run between them, the French honouring us with a broadside for this unexpected movement. The *Dessaix*, however, immediately tacked in pursuit, and in less than an hour got within musket-shot. At this short distance, she let fly at us a complete broadside of round and grape, the object evidently being to sink us at a blow, in retaliation for thus attempting to slip past, though almost without hope of escape.

Fortunately for us, in yawing to bring her broadside to bear, the rapidity with which she answered her helm carried her a little too far, and her round shot plunged in the water under our bows, or the discharge must have sunk us ; the scattered grape, however, took effect in the rigging, cutting up a great part of it, riddling the sails, and doing material damage to the masts and yards, though not a man was hurt.   To have delayed for another broadside would have been to expose all on board to certain destruction, and as further effort to escape was impotent, the *Speedy's* colours were hauled down.

On going aboard the *Dessaix*, and presenting my sword to the captain, Christie Pallière, he politely declined taking it, with the complimentary remark that " he would not accept the sword of an officer who had for so many hours struggled against impossibility," at the same time paying me the further compliment of requesting that " I would continue to wear my sword, though a prisoner "—a request with which I complied ; Captain Pallière at the same time good-naturedly expressing his satisfaction at having terminated our exploits in the cruising line, they having, in fact, special instructions to look out for us.   After this reception it is scarcely necessary to add that I was treated with great kindness by my captors.

Thus ended the thirteen months' cruise of the *Speedy*, during which we had taken and retaken upwards of 50 vessels, 122 guns, and 534 prisoners.

After the capture of the *Speedy*, the French line-of-battle ships stood along the coast, and proceeded with her, and the unlucky packet which had been the primary cause of the disaster, to Algesiras.   During this passage I had ample opportunity of observing the superior manner in which the sails of the *Dessaix* were cut, and the consequent flat surface exposed to the wind ; this contrasting strongly with the bag reefs, bellying sails, and breadbag canvas of English ships of war at that period.

As there was no force at Gibraltar adequate to an attack of the French squadron, the authorities lost no time in transmitting intelligence of their arrival to Sir James Saumarez, then blockading the Spanish squadron in Cadiz. The French meanwhile proceeded to water and refit, evidently with the intention of passing the Straits with the first fair wind.

Quitting Cadiz, Sir James Saumarez immediately sailed for Algesiras with his squadron, consisting of the *Cæsar*, *Venerable*, *Audacious*, *Hannibal*, *Superb*, *Pompée*, *Spencer*, *Calpe*, and *Thames*, these reaching the bay on the 6th of July.

At the time of their first appearance I was conversing with Captain Pallière in his cabin, when a lieutenant reported a British flag over Cabritta point, and soon afterwards the topgallant masts and pendants of a British squadron became visible. We at once adjourned to the poop, when the surprise of the French, at the sight of a more numerous squadron, became not unreasonably apparent ; Captain Pallière asked me " if I thought an attack would be made, or whether the British force would anchor off Gibraltar ? " My reply was " that an attack would certainly be made, and that before night both British and French ships would be at Gibraltar," at the same time adding that when there, it would give me great pleasure to make him and his officers a return for the kindness I had experienced on board the *Dessaix*!

The French admiral, however, determined that his ships should not be carried across the bay if he could help it. Before the British squadron had rounded the point, the French put out boats, with kedges and stream anchors, for the purpose of warping in shore, so as to prevent the approaching squadron from cutting them out ; but the order was so hurriedly executed, that all three ships were hauled aground, with their sterns presented to the approaching British force ; a position which could not have been taken by choice, for nothing could apparently be more easy than to destroy the French ships, which, lying aground stern on, could only use their stern chasers.

To employ their consequently useless hands to some purpose,

the French landed a considerable portion of their crews to man the Spanish batteries on the island, as the ships' guns could not be brought to bear. Two of the British ships anchored, and opened upon the French ships aground, but being exposed to the fire of some of the newly manned forts higher up the bay, the heavy guns of which were admirably handled by the French seamen, both the British vessels slipped their cables, and together with the remainder of the squadron, which did not anchor at all, backed their main-top-sails for the purpose of maintaining their position. The wind, however, blowing from the westward, with a rapid current sweeping round the bay, thwarted this intention, and the British squadron quickly drifted past the enemy, firing as they went.

Perhaps I ought previously to have mentioned an incident demonstrative of the *sang-froid* of my captor. After having satisfied himself that an action with a superior force was inevitable, Captain Pallière remarked, " that it should not spoil our breakfast," in which he had invited me to join him. Before the meal was ended, a round shot crashed through the stern of the *Dessaix*, driving before it a shower of broken glass, the *débris* of a wine bin under the sofa.

We forthwith jumped up from table, and went on the quarter-deck, but a raking shot from Sir James Saumarez's ship sweeping a file of marines from the poop, not far from me, I considered further exposure on my part unnecessary, and went below to a position whence I could nevertheless, at times, see what was going on.

The *Hannibal*, having with the others forged past the enemy, gallantly filled and tacked with a view to get between the French ships and the shore, being evidently unaware of their having been hauled aground. The consequence was that she ran upon a shoal, and remained fast, nearly bow on to the broadsides of the French line-of-battle ships, which with the shore batteries and several gun-boats opened upon her a concentrated fire. This, from her position, she was unable to return. The result was that her guns were speedily dismounted, her rigging shot away, and a third of her crew killed or wounded ; Captain Ferris, who commanded her, having now no alternative but to strike his colours—though not before he had displayed an amount of endurance which excited the admiration of the enemy.

A circumstance now occurred which is entitled to rank amongst the curiosities of war. On the French taking possession of the *Hannibal*, they had neglected to provide themselves with their national ensign, and either from necessity or bravado rehoisted the English flag upside down. This being a well-known signal of distress, was so understood by the authorities at Gibraltar, who, manning all government and other boats with dockyard artificers and seamen, sent them, as it was mistakenly considered, to the assistance of the *Hannibal*.

On the approach of the launches I was summoned on deck by the captain of the *Dessaix*, who seemed doubtful what measures to adopt as regarded the boats now approaching to board the *Hannibal*, and asked my opinion as to whether they would attempt to retake the ship. As there could be no doubt in my mind about the nature of their mission or its result, it was evident that if they were allowed to board, nothing could prevent the seizure of the whole. My advice, therefore, to Captain Pallière was to warn them off by a shot—hoping they would thereby be driven back and saved from capture. Captain Pallière seemed at first inclined to take the advice, but on reflection—either doubting its sincerity, or seeing the real state of the case—he decided to capture the whole by permitting them to board unmolested. Thus boat by boat was captured until all the artificers necessary for the repair of the British squadron, and nearly all the sailors at that time in Gibraltar, were taken prisoners !

In this action the French and Spaniards suffered severely both as regarded ships and men, their masts and hulls being much knocked about, whilst several Spanish gun-boats were sunk. The wonder to me was that the British squadron did not anchor, for the French ships being aground, stern on, could have offered little resistance, and must have been destroyed. It is true that the batteries on shore were admirably served, and thus constituted a formidable obstacle ; but had not the squadron drifted past the French ships, the latter might have been interposed between the batteries and the British force, when the fire of the former would have been neutralised, and the enemy's ships aground destroyed with comparatively little loss. It is not, however, my purpose or province to criticise the action, but simply to give the details, as personally witnessed from that extraordinary place, for a British officer, the deck of a French ship !

Neither the imprisonment of the captured crews, nor my own, was of long duration. The day after the action, Sir J. Saumarez sent Captain Brenton into Algesiras Bay with a flag of truce, to endeavour to effect an exchange of the gallant Captain Ferris, his officers, and crew. At that time there was no regulated system of exchange between the belligerent powers, but Captain Brenton succeeded in procuring the release of the crew of the *Hannibal* and the entrapped artificers, together with the officers and men of the *Speedy*. Admiral Linois would not at first give me up, but, on further consideration, allowed me to go with the other officers to Gibraltar on *parole*. My complete release was eventually effected for the second captain of the *St Antonio*, taken shortly afterwards.

The French ships having lost no time in communicating with the Spanish admiral at Cadiz, he promptly appeared off Algesiras with the reinforcement of six ships of the line, several frigates, and gun-boats. The enemy having by this time warped off their grounded ships, as well as the *Hannibal*, and having by the 12th got them in sea-going order, the whole sailed from Algesiras, followed by the British squadron, which, by great exertions, had been got in readiness for pursuit.

Of the action which subsequently took place I have no personal knowledge, other than that of a scene witnessed by myself from the garden of the commissioner's house, in which I was staying.

The enemy were overtaken at dusk, soon after leaving the bay, and when it had become dark, Captain Keats, in the *Superb*, gallantly dashed in between the two sternmost ships, firing right and left, and passed on. Of course I do not assert myself to have been personally cognisant of the way in which the attack was made, the firing only being visible from the Rock, but that this is the correct version of the affair rests upon indisputable authority. The movement was so rapidly executed, that the *Superb* shot ahead before the smoke cleared away, and the Spanish ships, the *Real Carlos*, 112, and the *San Hermenegildo*, 112, mistaking each other for the aggressor, began a mutual attack, resulting in the *Real Carlos* losing her foretop-mast, the sails of which—falling over her own guns—caught fire. While in this condition the *Hermenegildo*—still engaging the *Real Carlos* as an enemy—in the confusion fell on board her and caught fire also. Both ships burned till they blew up, and nearly all on board perished ; a few survivors only escaping on board the *Superb* as Captain Keats was taking possession of a *third* Spanish line-of-battle ship, the *San Antonio*—for whose second captain, as has been said, I was exchanged.

The remainder of the combined squadron got safely back to Cadiz after an encounter between the *Formidable* and *Venerable*. I am aware that the preceding account of the action with the French ships at Algesiras differs in some respects from that compiled by naval historians from the despatches ; but this circumstance will not prevent me from giving my own version of a conflict in which it was my misfortune to be a reluctant spectator. The *Real Carlos*, one of the ships blown up, bore the flag of the Spanish admiral, Moreno, who with Admiral Linois was said to be at the time on board a Spanish frigate.

CHAPTER VII

ADMIRALTY RELUCTANCE TO PROMOTE ME

IT has been already stated that not only was the action with the *Gamo* for some time unnoticed in the customary manner, but the post rank to which the rule of the service entitled me from

the result of the action, was withheld. My friends, being naturally surprised at the retention of what was no favour on the part
of Lord St Vincent, but my unquestionable right, respectfully
pointed out to his lordship the nature of the services rendered.
The subjoined letter addressed to Lord St Vincent by my kind
uncle, Sir Alexander Cochrane, in reference to the *Speedy's* escape
from a Spanish frigate (see page 46), was written previous to that
relating to the capture of the *Gamo*, but is worthy of record on
grounds generally connected with the naval service.

"My Lord,—Yesterday we received accounts of your lordship's being placed at the head of the Admiralty, on which occasion
I beg to offer my congratulations. I never subscribed to the
opinion that a naval officer ought not to be First Lord of the
Admiralty, and from your lordship's thorough knowledge of the
service, we may now hope for that support on many occasions
which we could not look for from those who—not having borne
the brunt of the day, or being bred to the navy—could be but
bad judges either of officers' characters, or the motives which on
many occasions actuate them.

"Doubtless your lordship has already received numerous
weighty applications for the promotion of young men in the service,
nor would I presume to add to their number but from the obliging
expressions your lordship once made me in favour of Lord
Cochrane, had you remained longer on this station. I have the
less reserve on this occasion, as I think his lordship has a claim
to be made post, from the presence of mind by which he lately
saved H.M.'s sloop *Speedy*, which he at present commands. This
I beg leave to recount.

"He had taken several prizes off Carthagena, when, one
morning, he found himself close under the guns of a Spanish
frigate.

"His only chance of escape was, either to board the frigate, in
the hope of finding her unprepared, or to pass off the *Speedy* as a
Danish sloop of war.

"With one of these objects he stood towards her under Danish colours, but on a near approach, found her too formidable to be carried by the few hands he had on board. On being hailed to know what brig it was, he gave, through the medium of a Danish quartermaster, the name of a Danish brig lately arrived on the station. On being ordered to come on board the frigate with his commission, he informed the Spaniards that his orders from the court of Denmark were not to send a boat on board any foreign man-of-war, but that if they had any doubts of his not being a Danish sloop of war, they were at liberty to board him.

" On this a boat left the frigate, but just as they were almost alongside the *Speedy*, they were informed that she was in quarantine, being only a few days from Algiers, where the plague at that time existed. On this the Spanish officers in the boat refused to touch a rope, and returned to the frigate, when her captain told Lord Cochrane that he knew his brig and wished him a pleasant voyage.*

" I have ever been of opinion that rewards for bold services cannot be too great, and I must confess, that where one of his Majesty's ships is saved by presence of mind similar to what I have related, great praise is due to her commander.

" Your lordship will, I hope, excuse me for trespassing a little longer in favour of my nephew, who is now twenty-five years old, a time of life that promotion can only be of use. His father has expended his whole fortune in discoveries which will be of great use to the public—but the real sufferer is Lord Cochrane. The liberality of your lordship's mind will see this in its true light, and also plead my excuse for the liberty I have taken.

" Hoping that your lordship's health is reinstated, etc. etc., I am, your lordship's, etc. etc.,   ALEXANDER COCHRANE.

" The Right Hon. LORD ST VINCENT."

I was not aware till recently that Sir Alexander had kindly made this application on my behalf. At the time the preceding

* As the reader is aware, we had previously painted the *Speedy* in imitation of the Danish brig.

letter was written he did not know of the capture of the *Gamo* ;
the *Ajax*, which he commanded, being then before Alexandria.
On learning our success, he again wrote to Lord St Vincent as
follows :—

"' AJAX,' off ALEXANDRIA,
"*June* 10*th*, 1801.

" MY LORD,—I some time ago wrote your lordship in favour
of my nephew Lord Cochrane, recommending his being made
post.

"I hope your lordship received my letter, and that you viewed
Lord Cochrane's conduct in the light I did. But if my persua-
sions were not then judged of sufficient weight, I may now with
much confidence come forward and claim for my nephew the
palm of victory in both ways, by an act hardly equalled in this
war of naval miracles, considering the great inequality of force
between the *Speedy*, with fifty-four men, and a xebec frigate of
thirty-two guns and 319 men.

" Well knowing that nothing gives your lordship more
pleasure than having an opportunity of rewarding merit, let the
rank of the person be what it may, I am confident your lordship
will, on the present occasion, do every justice to Lord Cochrane,
though should his promotion have arisen from his former exploits
it would be more grateful to my feelings, more especially as his subsequent conduct will do honour to your lordship's appointment.

"I believe I told your lordship, in my former letter, that Lord
Cochrane has the world before him. He has three younger
brothers to take care of, one of whom boarded at his side * when
the Spaniard was carried. Unfortunately he has not served his
time ; if he had I dare say your lordship would think him worthy
of promotion for his conduct on that occasion.

" It will give me much pleasure to hear that your lordship's
health is quite re-established, and that you may long live to
enjoy it, is the sincere wish of

" Your lordship's most obedient and humble servant,
" A. COCHRANE.

* Archibald.

"*P.S.*—I wish I could give your lordship any pleasing intelligence from this quarter; but ever since the death of Sir R. Abercromby, procrastination has been the order of the day. Never was a gallant army so lost as the present. God grant some man of sense may come out to command them, and save the remnant from destruction. Delay in this climate is worse than death; five men fall a sacrifice to disease for one in the field, and yet I don't think it unhealthy; our troops suffer from being encamped on burning sands."

Even this request from a distinguished officer—preferred unknown to me—failed to obtain what was no favour, but my right according to the invariable rule of the service. There was even then clearly some sinister influence at work, of the real cause for which I am to this day ignorant, and can only surmise that it might have arisen from my, no doubt, freely-expressed opinions on being appointed to convoy the wretched packet which led to my capture; or perhaps from the still more indiscreet plainness with which I had spoken of the manner in which the French fleet had been unfortunately permitted to escape Lord Keith.

Brenton, in his Life of Lord St Vincent, thus alludes to the delay in my promotion: "Lord St Vincent *was so much pressed* on the subject of Lord Cochrane's promotion for taking the *Gamo*, that it became almost a point of etiquette with the earl *not to make him a captain*! An illustrious person is reported to have said, 'My lord, we must make Lord Cochrane "post"'; to which Lord St Vincent replied, 'The First Lord of the Admiralty knows *no must*.'"

There is no doubt that Captain Brenton received this account from Lord St Vincent himself, and as the object of his book was to shield his lordship in questionable matters, we may receive this version as it was given to his biographer.

The only direct application that I was at the time aware of having been made was a letter from my father to Lord St Vincent, *after* the post rank had been reluctantly conceded by placing m *at the bottom of the list,* below others previously my juniors in the service ! My father's letter and Lord St Vincent's reply are subjoined.

"No. 14, MORTIMER-STREET,
"*Sept.* 23, 1801.

" MY LORD,—I beg leave, in behalf of my son, Lord Cochrane, who is now in Scotland, to bring under your lordship's view, for your consideration, some facts and circumstances which may not hitherto *officially* have come to your lordship's knowledge, from the perusal of which I flatter myself it will appear to your lordship that there are few instances of as much being performed by one individual in the like space of time, and with a force so inferior.

" When I first heard of Lord Cochrane's engagement with the *Gamo,* I reckoned it as a matter not admitting of a doubt that your lordship would reward him by immediately appointing him to a post ship, and I was the more confirmed in this belief from the circumstance that the *Gamo was not taken by surprise,* but at noonday, after an action of an hour and ten minutes ; during all of which time the *Gamo's* yards were locked with the *Speedy's* rigging. The determination of the two vessels to engage was mutual ; Lord Cochrane turned up his ship's company at five in the morning, and informed them of his intention to engage the Spanish frigate.

" The anxiety I must naturally feel for whatever concerns the honour and rank of my son, led me, on Wednesday last, to inquire at the Admiralty how his name stood on the post captains' list. And I must be allowed to state the surprise and disappointment I felt on finding several masters and commanders on the Mediterranean station—his juniors long before, and for several months after, the taking of the *Gamo*—now placed before him on that list.

" I beg leave to call your lordship's attention to what Lord Cochrane's feelings must be, and what the situation he will be placed in on service from this supersession ; and whether his being thus postponed in rank will not have a tendency to detract from the merit of one of the most gallant actions during this or any other war ?   And whether it may not induce the public at large, or the navy in particular, to believe that your lordships have had cause to disapprove of some part of Lord Cochrane's conduct ?

" If all the circumstances of the engagement had come to your lordship's knowledge in due time, I am persuaded you would have shown an additional mark of your approbation of Lord Cochrane by making him post from the date of the capture of the *Gamo*, or, at least, that you would not have put over him a number of masters and commanders on the Mediterranean station, who, perhaps equally capable as he of distinguishing themselves, have not been equally fortunate in similar oppor-tunities.   I am likewise convinced, my lord, that those individual officers, who have thus been preferred to him, would not think it any matter of injustice that Lord Cochrane should retain, as post captain, the same seniority he held over them, both before and after his engagement, as master and commander.

" Allow me therefore to request that your lordship will be pleased to give Lord Cochrane that rank in the navy which it is presumed he would have held if the circumstantial accounts of his engagements had reached your lordship at an earlier date, or that he had not been so unfortunate as to have been taken by three French line-of-battle ships.   I cannot suppose any censure is intended to attach to his conduct on that point : for, in the narrative of his capture, your lordship will see that during a chase of several hours upon a wind, he received the broadside and bow chasers of a seventy-four gun ship, and did not strike until, at the distance of a musket shot, he received a full broadside of round and grape from the *Dessaix*.

" I do not, however, my lord, rest my son's claim for seniority in promotion solely upon the capture of the *Gamo*.   Although these particulars, from their being stated in Lord Cochrane's letters to Captain Dixon of the *Genereux*, are known to your lordship, yet I cannot help here repeating them, as *from their not being published in the Gazette* a very erroneous opinion generally prevails that the *Gamo was taken* by surprise, and not after so long and close an engagement as was really the case.

" But perhaps, my lord, I may in the whole of this letter have been impelled, by the ardour and anxiety of my own feelings, to urge that which your lordship's good intentions may have wholly anticipated towards Lord Cochrane. If so, my lord, I have only to entreat your excuse for a zeal on my part for the honour and character of my son, for which I hope parental sensations will plead a forcible apology.

"I have the honour, etc. etc.   DUNDONALD.

" The Right Hon. LORD ST VINCENT."

To this letter Lord St Vincent next day replied as follows :—

" ADMIRALTY,
" *Sept.* 24, 1801.

" MY LORD,—I can have no difficulty in acknowledging that the capture of the *Gamo* reflects the highest degree of credit on Lord Cochrane and the officers and crew of the *Speedy*.

" The first account of that brilliant action reached the Admiralty *very early in the month of August* (it was fought on the 6th of May), previously to which intelligence had been received of the capture of the *Speedy*, by which Lord Cochrane was made prisoner.

" Until his exchange could be effected, and the necessary inquiry into the cause and circumstances of the loss of that sloop had taken place, it was impossible for the Board, consistently with its usual forms, to mark its approbation of his lordship's conduct. Lord Cochrane was promoted to the rank of post captain on the 8th of August, the day on which the sentence of acquittal for the loss of the *Speedy was received*—which was all that could under existing circumstances be done.

" Having entered into this explanation with your lordship, it remains for me only to add that, however disposed the Board might be to pay attention to the merits of his lordship, it could not, consistent with its public duty, give him rank from the time of the capture of the *Gamo*—a measure quite unprecedented—without doing an act of injustice to other deserving officers.

"I have the honour, etc. etc.   ST VINCENT.

"The EARL OF DUNDONALD."

Before quitting the Mediterranean, a letter was addressed by me to Lord St Vincent, requesting him to promote my gallant First Lieutenant Parker, who, as stated in my despatch, was severely wounded in boarding the *Gamo*. No answer being returned to this application, up to the period of my arrival in England, another letter was forwarded to his lordship, which met with the same reception, and afterwards a third, which produced from Lord St Vincent the reply that my application could not be entertained, for that "it was unusual to promote two officers for such a service,—besides which, the small number of men killed on board the *Speedy* did not warrant the application."

It was impossible not to feel nettled at a reply so unexpected : that because few men had been killed on board the *Speedy*, her first lieutenant was considered unworthy of promotion, though terribly cut up. To argue with a First Lord is no doubt an imprudent thing for a naval officer to attempt, and my remonstrance in this instance had such an effect as to get my name placed on the black list of the Admiralty, never again to be erased.

In my letter to Lord St Vincent, the following incautious observations were made, viz. that "his reasons for not promoting Lieutenant Parker, because there were only three men killed on board the *Speedy*, were in opposition *to his lordship's own promotion to an earldom*, as well as that of his flag-captain to knighthood, and his other officers to increased rank and honours : for that in the battle from which his lordship derived his title there was only *one man* killed on board his own flag-ship, so that there were more casualties in my sloop than in his line-of-battle ship."

From the receipt of that letter Lord St Vincent became my bitter enemy, and not he only, but his successors thought it in-

ADMIRAL THE EARL OF ST VINCENT, K.B.
[Born 1735. Died 1823]

cumbent on them to perpetuate his lordship's displeasure. My reply was no doubt keenly felt at the time, when it was a common remark in the navy that the battle of St Vincent was gained by the inshore squadron, under Nelson, the commander-in-chief being merely a spectator, at a distance which involved only the loss of one man in his own ship.

Notwithstanding this refusal of the First Lord to promote my lieutenant, my determination was to persevere with the Board collectively, and accordingly I addressed an official letter to the Secretary of the Admiralty, Mr Nepean, embodying Lord St Vincent's reply, and concluding, that "if their lordships judge by the small number killed, I have only to say that it was fortunate the enemy did not point their guns better "; indeed, had I not taken care to place the *Speedy* in a position where the Spanish guns went over her, many would have swelled the list whom it was my happiness to have saved.

This letter was dated May 12th, 1802, and, receiving no reply, the annexed official letter was addressed to their lordships on the same subject :—

" 14, OLD CAVENDISH-STREET,
" *May* 17, 1802.

" MY LORDS,—The anxiety I feel for the promotion of a meritorious officer, Lieutenant Parker, late of the *Speedy*, whose name I have not seen in the recent list of commanders, even though a very extensive promotion has taken place, induces me to address your lordships.

" Lieutenant Parker served as sole lieutenant of the *Speedy* at the capture of the *Gamo*, of 32 guns and 319 men, carried by boarding, after an action of upwards of an hour ; during the greatest part of which time the yards and rigging of the vessels were locked together. In boarding and carrying the Spanish vessel he was severely wounded by a sword, run through his thigh, and a musket ball lodged in his chest.

" I have always understood it to be an invariable rule with the Board of Admiralty, to promote officers of unimpeachable

F

character who have distinguished themselves in action, or who have been first lieutenants of his Majesty's ships of war at the capture of vessels of superior force—especially of a force so very superior as that of the *Gamo* to the *Speedy* ; the latter, as your lordships know, mounting 14 4-pounders, having on board only 54 men, whilst the force of the *Gamo* was 32 guns, with a comple-ment of men six times greater than that of the *Speedy*.

" When these circumstances are brought to your lordships' recollection, I am fully convinced that you will see proper to reward Lieutenant Parker by appointing him to the rank of commander in his Majesty's service, which will tend to cherish and promote that spirit of exertion among the lieutenants, subordinate officers, and crew, without whose zealous co-operation the endeavours of the captain alone would prove of small avail.

" I have the honour to be, etc. etc.

(Signed)   " COCHRANE.

" To the Right Hon. the LORDS COMMISSIONERS
" OF THE ADMIRALTY."

On the 26th of May the following reply was received from the Secretary :—

" ADMIRALTY OFFICE,
" 26th May, 1802.

" MY LORD,—I have received and read to my Lords Com-missioners of the Admiralty your lordship's letter to me of the 17th inst., and the representation which accompanied it, and am commanded by their lordships to acquaint you that your application to me is perfectly regular, *but that it is not so for officers to correspond with the Board.*

" I am, etc. etc.   E. NEPEAN.

" Captain LORD COCHRANE."

Determined not to be foiled in what I conceived to be the right of Lieutenant Parker, I replied to the Secretary as follows :—

"OLD CAVENDISH-STREET,
"*May 27th,* 1802.

"SIR,—I have been favoured with your letter acknowledging that you had received and read to the Lords Commissioners of the Admiralty my letter of the 17th inst., and that you are commanded by their lordships to acquaint me that my application to you was perfectly regular, but that it is not so for officers to correspond with the Board.

"I have, therefore, to request that you will inform the Lords Commissioners of the Admiralty, that, although I have received your letter, still I wait in expectation to be favoured with an answer to the representation which, through you, I had the honour to transmit to their lordships.

"I am, etc. etc.   COCHRANE.

"E. NEPEAN, Esq., Sec. to the Admiralty."

The reply to this necessarily cut short all further correspondence :—

"ADMIRALTY OFFICE,
"*29th May,* 1802.

"MY LORD—I have received and read to my Lords Commissioners of the Admiralty your letter of the 27th inst., and have nothing in command from their lordships to communicate to you.

"I am, etc. etc.   EVAN NEPEAN.

"Captain LORD COCHRANE."

In spite of this rebuff, I nevertheless continued to persevere, but it was not till some years afterwards that the promotion of Lieutenant Parker was obtained, with a result to that able and gallant officer which proved his ruin, and eventually caused his death.

The circumstances under which this took place were positively diabolical. Despairing of promotion, Lieutenant Parker had retired to a little farm near Kinsale, by the cultivation of which, in addition to his half-pay, he was realising an existence for his family. From my determined perseverance on his behalf, he was at length made commander, and ordered to join the *Rainbow* sloop, represented to be stationed in the West Indies. Selling off everything, even to his household furniture, he proceeded to Barbadoes, and reported himself to Sir Alexander Cochrane ; but, as the vessel could not be found, Sir Alexander furnished him with a passage to look for her at the Bermudas, where he supposed she might be fitting for sea. Not finding her there, Lieutenant Parker returned to Barbadoes, when *it became evident that no such vessel was on the North American station.*

On ascertaining this, poor Parker returned to England a ruined man. Lord Melville, who had succeeded as First Lord, expressed his surprise and regret that such a circumstance should have occurred, and promised the unhappy man that he should not only be amply compensated for the loss and expense attending his outfit and fruitless voyage to the West Indies, but that he should have another command on the first opportunity. This generous intention was however counteracted, for *he never received either the one or the other.*

Lieutenant Parker's loss, consequent to the sale of his property, the expense attendant on settling his family, together with his outfit and voyage, amounted to upwards of 1000*l.* His prospects ruined, his domestic arrangements destroyed, and his pride wounded, his spirit and constitution gradually gave way, and at length overwhelmed with sorrow he sank into a premature grave, leaving a wife and four daughters to deplore the loss of their only protector.

CHAPTER VIII

NAVAL ADMINISTRATION SIXTY YEARS AGO

It will be evident on a perusal of the previous chapter, that there was no fixed principle for the promotion of officers who had distinguished themselves, but that however desirous the Board might be to reward their services, it was in the power of persons holding inferior offices to thwart the intentions of the Board itself.

Were such a principle admitted, nothing could be more detrimental to the service. Let every officer know the regulated reward for a national service, with the certainty that he cannot be deprived of it, and rely upon it, that whenever opportunity presents itself, the service will be performed. There is nothing mercenary, or even selfish about this ; but, on the contrary, an ambition which should be carefully fostered.

In my own case, I can conscientiously avow my leading motive to have been that of exerting myself to the utmost in the hope of thereby attaining promotion in my profession, to which promotion the capture of an enemy's frigate, as well as of a large number of privateers and other vessels, had entitled me, according to a judicious rule for the encouragement of efforts useful to the nation—to a place on the list, from which I conceived myself unjustly excluded by the promotion of a younger man, a junior commander too, for no greater apparent reason than that of his father being a personal and political friend of the First Lord of the Admiralty.

Such was the offence taken by the authorities at my persistence in my own right, and in that of the officers under my command, that an application to the Board for another ship met with refusal ; and as it was clear that Lord St Vincent's administration did not again intend to employ me, the time on my hands was devoted to an investigation of those abuses which were paralysing the navy ; not that this was entered upon from any spirit of retaliation on the Admiralty, but as preparatory to the more ambitious aim of getting into Parliament, and exposing them.

One of the most crying evils of our then naval administration had fallen heavily upon me, though so young in command—viz. the Admiralty Courts ; but for the peculations consequent on which, the cruise of the *Speedy* ought to have sent home myself, officers, and crew, with competence. As it was, we got all the fighting, whilst the Admiralty Court and its hungry parasites monopolised the greater portion of our hard-won prize money. In many cases they took the whole ! and in one case brought me in debt, though the prize was worth several thousand pounds !

Hitherto no naval officer had ventured to expose, in Parliament or out of it, this or indeed any other gross abuse of the naval service ; and having nothing better to do, want of employment appeared to offer a fitting opportunity for constituting myself the Quixote of the profession ; sparing no pains to qualify for the task, though well aware of its arduous, if not hopeless nature—as directed against a mass of corruption, such as—it is to be hoped—may never again strike at the noblest arm of our national safety a blow worse than any enemy can inflict.

After what has been stated with regard to my unpleasant relations with Lord St Vincent and his Board of Admiralty, it will perhaps be better not to enter on the subject of then existing naval abuses, lest I might be suspected of exaggerating their extent.

Suffice it to say, that I used all diligence to store both my memory and note-book with facts, to be used when I might be able to expose them with effect.

No opportunity, however, immediately occurring, I betook myself to the College of Edinburgh, then distinguished by possessing some of the most eminent professors in the kingdom. In the early part of this volume the desultory and imperfect education which fell to my lot has been noticed. It had, nevertheless, sufficed to convince me of the truth of the axiom that " knowledge is power," and also to decide that in my case power if proportioned to knowledge could be of no very high order. It was therefore my determination to increase both to the best of my ability.

It was, perhaps, an unusual spectacle for a post-captain fresh from the quarter-deck to enter himself as a student among boys. For my self-imposed position I cared nothing, and was only anxious to employ myself to the best advantage. With what success may be judged from the fact of my never being but once absent from lectures, and that to attend the funeral of a near relative.

Whilst at Edinburgh I made few acquaintances, preferring secluded lodgings and study without interruption to the gaiety of my contemporaries. Besides which, if my object of getting into Parliament were to be accomplished, it was necessary to be economical, since all that the Admiralty Court had been pleased to leave me of my prize-money would not more than suffice to satisfy the yearnings of a small borough, for which the only hope of election was by outbribing my antagonists.

Amongst my contemporaries at the Edinburgh College was Lord Palmerston, who resided with the most eminent of the then Scotch professors, Dugald Stewart, and attended the classes at the same time with myself.

I might also mention others, of whose society in after life I should have been proud, had not the shameful treatment which it was afterwards my lot to experience from a corrupt faction, driven me from society at a time when it ought to have afforded me a welcome relaxation from hard and unintermitting exertions in the service of my country.

CHAPTER IX

EMPLOYMENT IN THE ARAB

On the renewal of war with France in 1803, application was made by me to the Admiralty for a ship, first taking the precaution to visit the various dockyards to see what vessels were ready, or in preparation. My object was to obtain a suitable vessel, which should enable me to operate inshore and harass the French coast in the Atlantic, as the *Speedy* had done the Spanish coast in the Mediterranean. My success there formed sufficient warrant for such an application, as, previous to the Peace of Amiens, the enemy's coasting trade from Bayonne to Boulogne had been carried on almost with impunity.

My application was made to Lord St Vincent, who informed me that at present there was no vessel available. Having ascertained beforehand what vessels were in preparation for sea, I began to enumerate several, all of which his lordship assured me were promised to others. On mentioning the names of some in a less forward state, an objection was raised by his lordship that they were too large. This was met by a fresh list, but these his lordship said were not in progress. In short, it became clear that the British navy contained no ship of war for me.

I frankly told his lordship as much, remarking that as " the Board was evidently of opinion that my services were not required, it would be better for me to go back to the College of Edinburgh and pursue my studies, with a view of occupying myself in some other employment." His lordship eyed me keenly, to see whether I really meant what I said, and observing no signs of flinching,—for beyond doubt my countenance showed signs of disgust at such unmerited treatment,—he said, " Well, you shall have a ship. Go down to Plymouth, and there await the orders of the Admiralty."

Thanking his lordship, I left him, and repairing to Plymouth, found myself appointed to the *Arab*. There was some difficulty in finding her, for my sanguine imagination had depicted a rakish craft, ready to run over to the French coast, and return with a goodly batch of well-laden coasters. In place of this, a dockyard attendant showed me the bare ribs of a collier, which had been purchased into the service. I would not have cared for this, but a single glance at the naked timbers showed me that, to use a seaman's phrase, " she would sail like a haystack." It was not my wish however to complain, but rather to make the best of the wretched craft provided for me ; and therefore there was nothing to be done but to wait patiently whilst she was completed,—for the most part with old timber from broken-up vessels.

As soon as the *Arab* was ready for sea, instead of being permitted to make a foray on the French coast—for which, however, she was ill-adapted—orders were given to take a cruise round the Land's End, into St George's Channel, and return to Plymouth.

This experimental service being accomplished, without results of any kind, although we sighted several suspicious vessels, which from our bad sailing qualities we could not examine ; on our return, the *Arab* was ordered to join the force then lying in the Downs, quietly watching the movements of the enemy on the opposite coast.

Though Napoleon had not a marine capable of competing with ours, he had, during the last war, become aware that any number of French gun-boats could sail along their own coasts under the protection of the numerous batteries, and hence he conceived the project of uniting these with others at Boulogne, so as to form collectively a flotilla capable of effecting an invasion of England, whose attention was to be divided by an attempt on Ireland, for which purpose an army and fleet were assembled at Brest.

The means by which this invasion of the Kentish or Sussex coast was to be effected is worth adverting to. The various towns of France were invited to construct flat-bottomed boats, to be distinguished by the names of the towns and departments which furnished them. They were divided into three classes, and transported to the nearest port-town, thence coastwise to Boulogne, there to be filled with troops, and convoyed to the English shores by ships of war. It has been the custom to deride this armament, but had it not been for Nelson's subsequent victory at Trafalgar, I see no cause to doubt that sooner or later it might have been successful. In our day of steam-ships the way to prevent the success of a similar project is by the maintenance of a navy more efficiently manned than modern governments appear to think necessary for national safety.

I do not mean efficiency as to the *number* of vessels of war— for in my early day the number was very great, but their efficiency, from causes already mentioned, very trifling. I mean, rather, that every care should be taken to keep a sufficient number in a high state of discipline ; but above all, that the stimulus of reward for merit should be so applied, as that parliamentary influence should not interfere with officers, nor a paltry hankering after saving with the crews.

The *Arab* was sent to watch the enemy in Boulogne. To those acquainted with the collier build, even as they appear in the Thames to this day, it is scarcely necessary to say that she would not work to windward. With a fair wind it was not difficult to get off Boulogne, but to get back with the same wind was—in such a craft—all but impossible. Our only way of effecting this was, by watching the tide, to drift off as well as we could. A gale of wind anywhere from N.E. to N.W. would infallibly have driven us on shore on the French coast.

Under such circumstances, the idea of effectively watching the port, as understood by me,—viz. to look out for troop-boats inshore,—was out of the question, our whole attention being necessarily directed to the vessel's safety. Considering this compromised, I wrote to the admiral commanding, that the *Arab* was of no use for the service required, as she would not work to windward, and that her employment in such a service could only result in our loss by shipwreck on the French coast.

My letter was no doubt forwarded to the Admiralty, for shortly afterwards an order arrived for the *Arab* to convoy the Green-land ships from Shetland, and then to cruise in the North Sea, to *protect the fisheries.* The order was, in fact, to cruise to the N.E. of the Orkneys, *where no vessel fished, and where consequently there were no fisheries to protect!!!* Not so much as a single whaler was seen from the mast-head during the whole of that lonely cruise, though it was as light by night as by day.

The Board had fairly caught me, but a more cruel order could not have been devised by official malevolence. It was literally naval exile in a tub, regardless of expense to the nation. To me it was literally a period of despair, from the useless inactivity into which I was forced, without object or purpose, beyond that of visiting me with the weight of official displeasure.

I will not trouble the reader with any reminiscences of this degrading command, or rather dreary punishment, for such it was no doubt intended to be, as depriving me of the opportunity of exerting or distinguishing myself; and this for no better reason, than my having most truly, though perhaps inconsiderately, urged, in justification of the promotion of the gallant lieutenant of the *Speedy*, that all Lord St Vincent's chief officers had been promoted for an action in which fewer men fell in a three-decker than in my brig.

Of this protracted cruise it is sufficient to state that my appointment to the *Arab* was dated October 5th, 1803, and that she returned to England on the 1st of December, 1804, a period which formed a blank in my life.

On my arrival, Lord St Vincent, fortunately for me, had quitted, or rather had been compelled to retire from the Admiralty. The late Duke of Hamilton, the premier peer of Scotland, and my excellent friend, was so indignant at my ignominious expulsion from active service, where alone it would be beneficial to the country, that, unsolicited by anyone, he strongly impressed upon Lord Melville, the successor of Lord St Vincent, the necessity of relieving me from that penal hulk, the *Arab*, and repairing the injustice which had been inflicted on me, by employing me on more important service. Lord Melville admitted the injustice, and promptly responded to the appeal, by transferring me from the wretched craft in which I had been for fifteen months in exile—to the *Pallas*, a new fir-built frigate of 32 guns.

CHAPTER X

CRUISE OF THE PALLAS

On my appointment to the *Pallas*, Lord Melville considerately gave me permission to cruise for a month off the Azores under Admiralty orders. The favour—the object of which was to give me an opportunity of trying my luck against the enemy, independent of superior command—was no doubt granted in consideration of the lengthened, not to say malevolent, punishment to which I had been condemned in the *Arab*.

My orders were to join my ship at Plymouth, with a promise that my instructions should be forwarded. In place of this, and in disregard of Lord Melville's intention, the Admiralty orders were embargoed by the Port Admiral, Sir W. Young, who had taken upon himself to recopy them, and thus to convert them into orders *issued under his authority*. The effect was, to enable him to lay claim to the admiral's share of any prize-money that we might make, even though captured out of his jurisdiction, which extended no farther than the Sound.

The mention of this circumstance requires brief comment, in order to account for the result which followed. Perhaps the most lucid explanation that can be given will be an extract from a letter of Lord St Vincent to the Admiralty when in command of the Channel fleet. " I do not know," says Lord St Vincent, " what I shall do if you feel a difficulty to give orders to despatch such ships as you may judge necessary to place under my command. I have a notion that he (Admiral Young) *wishes to have the power of issuing orders for their sailing, in order to entitle him to share prize-money ! !* " From this extract from Lord St Vincent, it is evident that if Admiral Young, according to the system then prevailing, had the power—as on his lordship's authority unquestionably appears—of paralysing the operations of a whole fleet, on the question of sharing prize-money, remonstrance on my part against the violation of Admiralty promises, made by Lord Melville himself, would have been disregarded. Nothing was therefore left but to submit.

The first object was to equip the *Pallas* with all speed ; and for this we were obliged to resort to impressment, so much had my do-nothing cruise in the *Arab* operated against me in the minds of the seamen. Having, however, succeeded in impressing some good men, to whom the matter was explained, they turned to with great alacrity to impress others ; so that in a short time we had an excellent crew. This was the only time I ever found it necessary to impress men.

As the cruise off the Western Islands—when arrived there—was restricted to a month, it was matter of consideration how to turn such orders to the best account, without infringing on the letter of my instructions. We therefore crossed the

Bay of Biscay, and having run to the westward of Cape Finisterre, *worked up* towards the Azores, so as to fall in with any vessels which might be bound from the Spanish West Indies to Cadiz.

Scarcely had we altered our course, when, on the 6th of February, we fell in with and captured a large ship, the *Carolina*, bound from the Havannah to Cadiz, and laden with a valuable cargo. After taking out the crew, we despatched her to Plymouth.

Having learned from the prisoners that the captured ship was part of a convoy bound from the Havannah to Spain, we proceeded on our course, and on the 13th captured a second vessel, which was still more valuable, containing, in addition to the usual cargo, some diamonds, and ingots of gold and silver. This vessel was sent to Plymouth as before.

On the 15th, we fell in with another, *La Fortuna*, which proved the richest of all, as, besides her cargo, she had on board a large quantity of dollars, which we shifted into the *Pallas*, and sent the ship to England.

On the 16th, we captured a fine Spanish letter of marque, with more dollars on board ; but as a heavy sea then running prevented us from taking them on board the *Pallas*, these were therefore despatched with her to Plymouth.

Whilst securing the latter vessel, we observed at sunset an English privateer take possession of a large ship. On seeing us —evidently knowing that we were an English man-of-war, and therefore entitled to share in her capture—the privateer crowded all sail and made off with her prize in company. Unluckily for this calculation, the prize was subsequently taken by a French squadron, when it turned out that the captured vessel—the *Preciosa*—was the richest of the whole Spanish convoy, having, in addition to her cargo, no less than a million dollars on board. Singularly enough, the privateer belonged to my agent, Mr Teed, from whom I afterwards learned the value of the vessel which his captain's mistaken greed had sacrificed.

The sensation created on the arrival of the prizes at Plymouth was immense, as the following curious extracts from a local paper will show :—

" *February* 24.—Came in the *Carolina* from Havannah, with sugar and logwood. Captured off the coast of Spain by the *Pallas*, Captain Lord Cochrane. The *Pallas* was in pursuit of another with a very valuable cargo when the *Carolina* left. His lordship sent word to Plymouth, that if ever it was in his power, he would fulfil his public advertisement (stuck up here) for entering seamen, of filling their pockets with Spanish ' pewter ' and ' cobs,' nicknames given by seamen to ingots and dollars."

" *March* 7.—Came in a rich Spanish prize, with jewels, gold, silver, ingots, and a valuable cargo, taken by the *Pallas*, Captain Lord Cochrane. Another Spanish ship, the *Fortuna*, from Vera Cruz, had been taken by the *Pallas*, laden with mahogany and logwood. She had 432,000 dollars on board, but has not yet arrived."

' *March* 23.—Came in a most beautiful Spanish letter of marque of fourteen guns, said to be a very rich and valuable prize to the *Pallas*, Captain Lord Cochrane."

A still greater sensation was excited by the arrival of the *Pallas* herself, with three large golden candlesticks, each about five feet high, placed upon the mast-heads. The history of these is not a little curious. They had been presented by the good people of Mexico, together with other valuable plate, to some celebrated church in Spain, the name of whose patron saint I forget, and had been shipped on board one of the most seaworthy vessels.

Their ultimate destination was, however, less propitious. It was my wish to possess them, and with this view an arrangement had been made with the officers and crew of the *Pallas*. On presenting the candlesticks at the Custom-house, the authorities refused to permit them to pass without paying the full duty, which amounted to a heavier sum than I was willing to disburse. Consequently, although of exquisite workmanship, they were broken in pieces, and thus suffered to pass as old gold.

The following incident relating to the capture of one of the vessels had escaped my recollection, till pointed out in the *Naval Chronicle* for 1805. It is substantially correct.

" Lord Cochrane, in his late cruise off the coasts of Spain and Portugal, fell in with, and took, *La Fortuna*, a Spanish ship bound to Corunna, and richly laden with gold and silver to the amount of 450,000 dollars (132,000*l.*), and about the same sum in valuable goods and merchandise. When the Spanish captain and his supercargo came on board the *Pallas*, they appeared much dejected, as their private property on board amounted to the value of 30,000 dollars each. The captain said he had lost, in the war of 1779, a similar fortune, having then been taken by a British cruiser, so that now, as then, he had to begin the world again. Lord Cochrane, feeling for the dejected condition of the Spaniards, consulted his officers as to their willingness to give them back 5000 dollars each in specie. This being immediately agreed to, his lordship ordered the boatswain to pipe all hands, and addressing the men to the like purpose, the gallant fellows sung out, ' Aye, aye, my lord, with all our hearts,' and gave the unfortunate Spaniards three cheers."

Another curious circumstance must not be passed over. In one of the captured vessels was a number of bales, marked " *invendebles*." Making sure of some rich prize, we opened the bales, which to our chagrin consisted of pope's bulls, dispensations for eating meat on Fridays, and indulgences for peccadilloes of all kinds, with the price affixed. They had evidently formed a venture from Spain to the Mexican sin market, but the supply exceeding the demand, had been reconsigned to the manufacturers. We consigned them to the waves.

On our way home we were very near losing our suddenly acquired wealth and the frigate too. Whilst between the Azores and Portugal, one of those hazes common in semi-tropical climates, had for some time prevailed on the surface of the sea, the mast-heads of the ship being above the haze, with a clear sky. One day the look-out reported three large ships steering for us, and on going aloft I made them out to be line-of-battle ships in chase of the *Pallas*. As they did not show any colours, it was impossible to ascertain their national character, but, from the equality of the fore and maintopgallant masts, there was little doubt they were French.

The course of the frigate was immediately altered, and the weather changing, it began to blow hard, with a heavy sea.

The *Pallas* was crank to such a degree, that the lee main-deck guns, though housed, were under water, and even the lee quarter-deck carronades were at times immerged.

As the strange ships were coming up with us hand over hand, the necessity of carrying more sail became indispenasble, notwithstanding the immersion of the hull.

To do this with safety was the question. However, I ordered all the hawsers in the ship to be got up to the mast-heads and hove taut. The masts being thus secured, every possible stitch of sail was set, the frigate plunging forecastle under, as was also the case with our pursuers, which could not fire a gun—though as the haze cleared away we saw them repeatedly flashing the priming. After some time the line-of-battle ships came up with us, one keeping on our lee-beam, another to windward, each within half a mile, whilst the third was a little more distant.

Seeing it impossible to escape by superior sailing, it appeared practicable to try a manœuvre, which might be successful if the masts would stand. Having, as stated, secured these by every available rope in the frigate, the order was given to prepare to clew up and haul down every sail at the same instant. The manœuvre being executed with great precision,—and the helm being put hard a-weather, so as to wear the ship as speedily as possible,—the *Pallas*, thus suddenly brought up, shook from stem to stern, in crossing the trough of the sea. As our pursuers were unprepared for this manœuvre, still less to counteract it, they shot past at full speed, and ran on several miles before they could shorten sail, or trim on the opposite tack. Indeed, under the heavy gale that was now blowing, even this was no easy matter, without endangering their own masts.

There was no time for consideration on our part, so having rapidly sheeted home, we spread all sail on the opposite tack. The hawsers being still fast to the masts, we went away from our pursuers at the rate of thirteen knots and upwards; so that a considerable distance was soon interposed between us and them; and this was greatly increased ere they were in a condition to follow. Before they had fairly renewed the chase night was rapidly setting in, and when quite dark, we lowered a ballasted cask overboard with a lantern, to induce them to believe that we had altered our course, though we held on in the same direction during the whole night. The trick was successful, for, as had been calculated, the next morning, to our great satisfaction, we saw nothing of them, and were all much relieved on finding our dollars and his Majesty's ship once more in safety. The expedient was a desperate one, but so was the condition which induced us to resort to it.

Of the proceeds of the above-mentioned captures—all made within ten days—Sir William Young, on the strength of having recopied my orders from the Admiralty, *claimed and received* half my share of the captures. No wonder that Lord St Vincent said of him, that he wished to " *have the power of giving orders, and so share prize-money.*"

Being then young and ardent, my portion appeared inexhaustible. What could I want with more ? The sum claimed and received by Admiral Young was not worth notice.

On our return to Plymouth the country was on the eve of a general election, and the time appeared a fitting one to carry out my long-cherished scheme of getting into Parliament. The nearest borough in which there was a chance was Honiton, and accordingly I applied to the port admiral for leave of absence to contest that " independent " constituency. The prize-money procured it without scruple.

G

My opponent was a Mr Bradshaw, who had the advantage of a previous canvass. From the amount of prize-money which was known to have fallen to my share, that gentleman's popularity was for a moment in danger, it being anticipated that I should spend my money sailor fashion, so that it became unmistakably manifest that the seat in Parliament would be at my service, if my opponent were outbid! To use the words of " an independent elector " during my canvass : " You need not ask me, my lord, who I votes for, I always votes for Mister Most."

To the intense disgust of the majority of the electors, I refused to bribe at all, announcing my determination to " stand on patriotic principles," which, in the electioneering *parlance* of those days, meant " no bribery." To my astonishment, however, a considerable number of the respectable inhabitants voted in my favour, and my agent assured me that a judicious application of no very considerable sum, would beat my opponent out of the market. This, however, being resolutely refused, the majority voted in favour of his five-pound notes, and saved my friends of the Admiralty Court and other naval departments from an exhibition of misplaced zeal, which, as subsequently proved, could only have ended in my parliamentary discomfiture.

To be beaten, even at an election, is one thing ; to turn a beating to account is another. Having had decisive proof as to the nature of Honiton politics, I made up my mind that the next time there was a vacancy in the borough, the seat should be mine without bribery. Accordingly, immediately after my defeat, I sent the bellman round the town, having first primed him with an appropriate speech, intimating that " all who had voted for me might repair to my agent, J. Townsend, Esq., and *receive ten pounds ten !* "

The novelty of a defeated candidate paying double the current price expended by the successful one—or, indeed, paying anything—made a great sensation. Even my agent assured me that he could have secured my return for less money, for that the popular voice being in my favour, a trifling judicious expenditure would have turned the scale.

I told Mr Townsend that such payment would have been bribery, which would not accord with my character as a reformer of abuses—a declaration which seemed highly to amuse him. Notwithstanding the explanation that the ten guineas were paid as a reward for having withstood the influence of bribery, the impression produced on the electoral mind by such unlooked-for liberality was simply this—that if I gave ten guineas for being beaten, my opponent had not paid half enough for being elected ; a conclusion which, by a similar process of reasoning, was magnified into the conviction that each of his voters had been cheated out of five pounds ten.

The result was what had been foreseen. My opponent, though successful, was regarded with anything but a favourable eye ; I, though defeated, had suddenly become most popular. The effect at the next election must be reserved for its place in a future chapter.

It was this election that first induced me to become a parliamentary Reformer, or, as anyone holding popular opinions was called in those days, a " Radical," i.e. a member of a political class holding views not half so extreme as those which form the parliamentary capital of Reformers in the present day, and even less democratic than were the measures brought in during the last session of Parliament by a Tory Government, whose predecessors consigned to gaol all who, fifty years ago (1800), ventured to express opinions conferring political rights on the people.

It is strange that, after having suffered more for my political faith than any man now living, I should have survived to see former Radical yearnings become modern Tory doctrines. Stranger still, they should now form stepping-stones to place and power, instead of to the bar of a criminal court, where even the counsel defending those who were prosecuted for holding them became marked men.

Still it is something worth living for—even with the remembrance of my own bitter sufferings, for no greater offence than the advocacy of popular rights, and the abolition of naval abuses.

CHAPTER XI

SERVICES IN THE PALLAS CONTINUED

ON the 28th of May, 1805, the *Pallas* again sailed from Portsmouth in charge of a convoy for Quebec. On this voyage little occurred worthy of note, beyond the fact that when we made the American coast we were, from a cause presently to be mentioned, no less than thirteen degrees and a half out in our *dead reckoning*! The reader must not imagine that we were 800 miles out of our course, for that was corrected whenever observations of the sun or stars could be obtained; but as these might at any time be rendered uncertain from the fogs prevalent on the banks, the most vigilant care was necessary to prevent the ship and convoy from being wrecked.

In my former voyage in the *Thetis* we had the advantage of a very clever man on board—a Mr Garrard—who not being able to subsist on his salary as assistant astronomer and calculator at Greenwich, was glad to accept the birth of schoolmaster on board my uncle's frigate. From the instructions of this gentleman, I had formerly profited considerably, and was not a little pleased when he applied to me for a similar birth on board the *Pallas*. With so skilful an observer, there could be no mistake about the error just mentioned ; which arose from this circumstance, that for the sake of economy, the Navy Board or the dockyard authorities had surrounded the binnacle of the *Pallas* with iron instead of copper bolts ; so that the compass was not to be depended upon. Fortunately the atmosphere was tolerably clear, so that no danger was incurred.

As, however, I had no inclination to risk either the ship or my own reputation amongst the fogs of Canada for the sake of false economy, the course of the *Pallas* and her convoy was directed to Halifax, there to free the compass from the attraction of iron. On demanding copper bolts from the dockyard officers, they were refused, on the ground that permission must be first obtained from the authorities in London! To this I replied, that if such were the case, the *Pallas* should wait with the convoy at Halifax whilst they communicated with the Admiralty in England! for that on no account should she enter the Gulf of St Lawrence till our compass was right. The absurdity of detaining a convoy for six months on account of a hundredweight of copper bolts was too much even for dockyard routine, and the demand was with some difficulty conceded.

It would be wearisome to detail the uninteresting routine of attending the convoy to Quebec, or of my taking charge of another for the homeward voyage ; further than to state, that from the defect of having no proper lights for the guidance of the convoy by night, the whole lost sight of us before reaching the Lizard ; where we arrived with only one vessel, and that in tow.

The carelessness of merchant captains when following a convoy can only be estimated by those who have to deal with them. Not only was this manifested by day, but at night their stern cabins glittered with lights, equally intense with the convoy light, which therefore was not distinguishable. The separation of the convoy on the following day was thus rather a matter of course than of surprise.

This want of proper distinguishing lights, and the consequent dispersion of convoys, were thus frequent causes of the capture of our merchantmen, and to remedy this I constructed a lamp powerful enough to serve as a guide in following the protecting frigate by night. The Admiralty, however, neglected its application, or even to inspect my plan.

Some few years afterwards, the clamour of shipowners compelled the Board to direct its attention to the subject, and, passing over my communications, they offered a reward of fifty pounds to the inventor of the most suitable lamp for the purpose. On this I directed my agent, Mr Brooks, to offer my lamp *in his own name*, feeling convinced that my connection with it would, if known, insure its rejection. He did so, and after repeated trials against others at Sheerness, Spithead, and St Helen's, the fifty-pound prize was adjudged to Mr Brooks *for my lamp*!! The fact afterwards becoming known, *not a lamp was ever ordered*, and the merchantmen were left to the mercy of privateers as before. I do not relate this anecdote as telling against the *directing* powers of the Admiralty, but with the *administrative* powers, it was then and afterwards clearly a fixed rule that no invention of mine should be carried into effect.

On our way home, we one day made an experiment which even now I believe might occasionally be turned to account; viz. the construction of gigantic kites to give additional impetus to ships. With this view a studdingsailboom was lashed across a spare flying jibboom to form the framework, and over this a large spread of canvas was sewn in the usual boys' fashion. My spars were, however, of unequal dimensions throughout, and this and our launching the kite caused it to roll greatly. Possibly, too, I might not have been sufficiently experienced in the mysteries of " wings and tail," for though the kite pulled with a will, it made such occasional lurches as gave reason to fear for the too sudden expenditure of his Majesty's stores. The power of such machines, properly constructed, would be very great ; and in the case of a constant wind, might be useful. The experiment, however, showed that kites of smaller dimensions would have answered better.

On our return to England in December, the *Pallas* was ordered to join the squadron of Admiral Thornborough, appointed to operate on the French and Spanish coasts. Instructions were, however, given to cruise for a few days off Boulogne before finally proceeding to Plymouth.

We sailed from the Downs on the 23rd of January, 1806, and on the 31st seeing a French merchant vessel at anchor near the mouth of the river Somme, the boats were sent inshore to cut her out. On nearing her, a battery opened fire on them, when we wore and engaged the battery, whilst the boats brought off the vessel, with which we anchored in Dover roads on the following morning.

On the 8th of February, the *Pallas* sailed from Dover, and stood over towards the French coast, where we captured a fast-sailing lugger, having on board a number of letters addressed to various persons in London. Shortly after this we were ordered to join the admiral.

On the 22nd the *Pallas* sailed with Vice-Admiral Thornborough's squadron from Plymouth, and remained in company till the 24th of March, when seeing some vessels off Isle Dieu, the boats went in chase, and returned with seven French fishing-smacks ; to the surprise of whose crews we bought their fish, and let them go.

From information communicated by the fishing-boats the *Pallas* ran off shore, and in the night following, returned and captured a vessel freighted with wine, which was taken on board the frigate. The next night the boats again went in, and brought off another vessel similarly laden. On the following morning we made sail with our two prizes, but observing a brig at anchor off Sable d'Olonne, ran in again after dark, and sent the boats to cut her out. A fire being opened on the boats from the town, we discharged several broadsides, on which the townspeople desisted, and the brig was brought off. Whilst engaged in this operation, another brig was seen to run ashore for safety. On the morning of the 28th, the boats were again despatched to get her off, when, the people mustering along shore to attack them, we fired several shotted guns to warn them from interfering, and the brig was safely brought out.

This propensity of French crews thus to run their vessels ashore—on being chased by boats—was principally caused by a galley which had been constructed at my own expense by the Deal boatbuilders, and shipped on board the *Pallas*. She rowed double-banked, and required eighteen hands at the oars, and this together with her beautiful build rendered her perhaps the fastest boat afloat. Escape from such a craft being hopeless, she became so notorious, that the enemy's coasters ran their vessels ashore, and jumping into their boats, thus saved themselves from being made prisoners.

On the 29th, we manned the largest prize, the *Pomone*, and sent her to England in charge of the others. On the same day we fell in with the admiral, and supplied the squadron with prize wine, of which a large quantity had been taken, most of the vessels captured being laden with wine of fine quality, on its way to Havre for the Parisian market.

On quitting the squadron, we proceeded to the southward in chase of a convoy, one of which we captured, and on the 5th of April ran for the Garonne, having received intelligence that some French corvettes were lurking in the river and its vicinity, one of which vessels was reported to be lying some miles up the river as a guardship. Keeping out of sight for the remainder of the day, I determined on making an attempt to cut her out on the following night.

After dark the *Pallas* came to an anchor off the Cordovan lighthouse, and the boats, manned with the whole crew of the frigate, except about forty men, pulled for the corvette, under the command of their gallant First Lieutenant Haswell, who found her at 3 A.M. on the morning of the 6th, anchored near two batteries. As the weather was thick when the attack was made, the boats came upon the enemy unawares, and after a short but gallant resistance, the corvette was carried, proving to be the *Tapageuse* of 14 guns.

No sooner was this effected, than two others, whose presence was unexpected, came to her rescue. Lieutenant Haswell, however, promptly manned the guns of the captured vessel, and beat off his assailants, the tide rendering it imprudent for the prize or the boats to follow in pursuit.

Whilst this was going on, the *Pallas* remained at single anchor waiting for the boats, and soon after daylight three strange sail appeared to windward, making for the river. As the private signal was unanswered, there could be no doubt but that they were enemies, to oppose whom we had only forty hands on board, the remainder of the crew, as previously stated, being in the prize brig.

There was no time to be lost, and as it was of the first importance to make a show of strength, though we possessed none, I immediately set the few hands we had to fasten the furled sails with rope yarns; the object being to cut the yarns all at once, let fall the sails, and thus impress the enemy with an idea that from such celerity in making sail we had a numerous and highly disciplined crew.

The manœuvre succeeded to a marvel. No sooner was our cloud of canvas thus suddenly let fall than the approaching vessels hauled the wind, and ran off along shore, with the *Pallas* in chase, our handful of men straining every nerve to sheet home, though it is surprising that the French officer did not observe the necessary slowness of the operation.

By superior sailing we were soon well up with one of them, and commenced firing our bow guns—the only guns, in fact, we were able to man. Scarcely had we fired half-a-dozen shots, when the French captain deliberately ran his ship ashore as the only way of saving himself and crew. The corvette was dismasted by the shock and immediately abandoned by the crew, who got ashore in their boats; though had they pulled on board the *Pallas* instead, we were literally incapable of resistance.

After the crew had abandoned the wreck, we ran nearly close, and fired several broadsides into her hull, to prevent her floating again with the tide. Whilst thus engaged, the other corvettes, which had previously run out of sight, again made their appearance to the S.S.-W. under a press of sail, evidently coming up fast to the assistance of their consort.

As it was necessary once more to take the initiative, we quitted the wreck, ran up our colours, and gave chase, firing our bow guns at the nearest, which soon afterwards followed the example of the first, and ran ashore too,—with the same result of being dismasted—the crew escaping as in the case of the other.

Of the remaining corvette we for a time took no notice, and made sail towards the mouth of the Garonne to pick up our crew, which had necessarily been left on board the vessel cap-

tured on the river. As the *Pallas* neared the Cordovan lighthouse, we observed the third corvette making for the river.
Finding herself intercepted she also ran on shore, and was
abandoned in like manner.

The chase of these corvettes forms one of my most singular
recollections, all three being deliberately abandoned and wrecked
in presence of a British frigate with only forty men on board!
Had any one of the three known our real condition, or had we
not put a bold face on the matter, we might have been taken.
The mere semblance of strength saved us, and the panic thereby
inspired destroyed the enemy.

Having joined our prize—the *Tapageuse*—the prisoners were
shifted on board the *Pallas*, which made sail in quest of the
squadron, rejoining it on the 10th, when, by order of Admiral
Thornborough, the prisoners were distributed among different
ships.

The subjoined despatches will afford further explanation of
the events just narrated.

" 'PALLAS,' off CHASSERON,
" *8th April*, 1806.

" SIR,—Having received information—which proved correct—
of the situation of the corvettes in the river of Bordeaux, a little
after dark on the evening of the 5th, the *Pallas* was anchored
close to the shoal of Cordovan, and it gives me satisfaction to
state that about 3 o'clock on the following morning the French
national corvette, *La Tapageuse*, of 14 long 12-pounders and 95
men, who had the guard, was boarded, carried, and cut out,
about twenty miles above the shoal, and within two heavy
batteries, in spite of all resistance, by the first lieutenant of the
Pallas, Mr Haswell, the master, Mr Sutherland, Messrs Perkyns,
Crawford, and Thompson, together with the quartermasters
and such of the seamen and crew as were fortunate enough to
find places in the boats.

" The tide of flood ran strong at daylight. *La Tapageuse*
made sail. A general alarm was given. A sloop-of-war followed,

and an action continued—often within hail—till by the same
bravery by which the *Tapageuse* was carried, the sloop-of-war,
which before had been saved by the rapidity of the current alone,
was compelled to sheer off, having suffered as much in the hull
as the *Tapageuse* in the rigging.

" The conduct of the officers and men will be justly appreciated. With confidence I shall now beg leave to recommend them to the notice of the Lords Commissioners of the
Admiralty.

" It is necessary to add, that the same morning, when at anchor
waiting for the boats (which, by-the-by, did not return till this
morning), three ships were observed bearing down towards the
Pallas, making many signals, and were soon perceived to be
enemies. In a few minutes the anchor of the *Pallas* was weighed,
and with the remainder of the officers and crew we chased,
drove on shore, and wrecked one national 24-gun ship, one of
22 guns, and the *Malicieuse*, a beautiful corvette of 18 guns.
Their masts went by the board, and they were involved in a
sheet of spray.

" All in this ship showed great zeal for his Majesty's service.
The warrant officers and Mr Tattnall, midshipman, supplied
the place of commissioned officers. The absence of Lieutenant
Mapleton is much to be regretted. He would have gloried in
the expedition with the boats. The assistance rendered by Mr
Drummond of the Royal Marines was such as might have been
expected. Subjoined is the list of wounded, together with that
of vessels captured and destroyed since the 26th ult.

" I am, etc. etc.   COCHRANE.

" To VICE-ADMIRAL THORNBOROUGH."

' " PRINCE OF WALES,' off ROCHEFORT,
"9th April, 1806.

" MY LORD,—I have the honour to transmit to your lordship
a copy of a letter I have this day received from Captain Lord
Cochrane of H.M.S. *Pallas*, under my orders. It will not be

necessary for me, my lord, to comment on the intrepidity and good conduct displayed by Lord Cochrane, his officers and men, in the execution of a very hazardous enterprise in the Garonne, a river the most difficult, perhaps, in its navigation, of any on the coast. The complete success that attended the enterprise, as well as the destruction of the vessels of war mentioned in the said letter on the coast of Arcasson, speaks their merits more fully than is in my power to do.   To which may be fairly added, that nothing can show more clearly the high state of discipline of the crew of the *Pallas* than the humanity shown by them in the conflict.

" I have the honour, etc. etc.   EDWARD THORNBOROUGH.

" The Right Hon. the EARL ST VINCENT."

" ' HIBERNIA,' off USHANT,
" *April* 14*th*, 1806.

" SIR,—I yesterday received from Admiral Thornborough a letter with its enclosure from Captain Lord Cochrane, of which copies are herewith transmitted for the information of my Lord Commissioner of the Admiralty.

" The gallant and successful exertions of the *Pallas* therein detailed, reflect very high honour on her captain, officers and crew, and call for my warmest approbation.
" I am, etc. etc.   ST VINCENT.

" W. MARSDEN, Esq."

The cold, reluctant praise bestowed by this letter was no doubt intended by Lord St Vincent as a wet blanket on the whole affair, and contrasts strongly with the warm-hearted sailor-like frankness of Admiral Thornborough.   It had its full effect ; not a word of approbation did I receive from the Admiralty.   The *Tapageuse* was not bought into the navy, though a similar vessel, subsequently captured by another officer at the same place, was purchased. My first lieutenant, Haswell, was not promoted. In short, if we had done something worthy of disapprobation, it could scarcely have been more marked. On this subject further comment will presently become necessary.

To return to our cruise. On the 14th of April we again quitted the squadron, and made for the corvettes run on shore on the 7th. The French had erected a battery for the protection of one of them which was still sound in the hull ; but we silenced the battery and set fire to the corvette. After this the *Pallas* proceeded towards the wreck of the northernmost vessel stranded, but as strong breezes came on, and she was evidently breaking up in the surf, we deemed it prudent to work off shore, and in so doing captured another vessel, which turned out to be a French packet.

On the 20th the *Pallas* ran down abreast of the remaining corvette, and out boats for the purpose of burning her ; but these being exposed to the fire of another battery, which had been thrown up to protect the wreck, and the *Pallas* not being able, on account of the shoaliness of the water, to get near enough to fire with effect, we desisted from the attempt, and again made sail.

On the 23rd we came to an anchor off the Malmaison passage, and on the following day reconnoitred the French squadron inside Isle Rhe. Whilst thus engaged, the British squadron appeared to windward, and shortly afterwards came to an anchor.

On the 24th we worked up to windward to join the admiral, and on the following day stood into Basque Roads to reconnoitre the enemy's squadron. On approaching within gunshot, a frigate and three brigs got under weigh, and we made sail to meet them, endeavouring to bring them to action by firing several broadsides at them. On this they tacked after returning the fire, and stood in under their batteries. Having completed our reconnoissance, we beat out again and rejoined the admiral, to whom I made the annexed report.

"H.M.S. 'PALLAS,' off ISLE D'AIX,
"*April 25th*, 1806.

"SIR,—Having stood within gunshot of the French squadron this morning, I find it to consist of the following vessels.

"One of three decks, 16 ports below; one of 80 guns, 15 ports; three of 74, 14 ports; two heavy frigates, of 40 guns; three light frigates, 13 ports on main-deck, and three brigs of from 14 to 16 guns.

"The *Calcutta* * is not among them. Neither are there any corvettes, unless a very clumsy 20-gun ship can be called one. The ships of the line have all their topmasts struck and top-gallant yards across. They are all very deep, more so than vessels are in general for common voyages.

"They may be easily burned, or they may be taken by sending heie eight or ten thousand men, as if intended for the Mediterranean. If people at home would hold their tongues about it, † possession might thus be gained of the Isle d'Oleron, upon which all the enemy's vessels may be driven by sending fire vessels to the eastward of Isle d'Aix.

"A frigate and the three brigs were ordered to get under weigh. These stood towards the *Pallas* and exchanged a few broadsides. After waiting from ten o'clock till past two, close to Isle d'Aix, we were obliged to come out no better than we went in. They could not be persuaded to stand from under their batteries.

"I have the honour, etc. etc.   COCHRANE.

"EDW. THORNBOROUGH, Esq.,
"Vice-Admiral of the *Blue*."

Having found by experience that the French had organised a system of signal-houses, by means of which they were able to

---

* An Indiaman, recently captured by the French off St Helena.

† It is a curious fact, that there being no such thing as confidence or secrecy in official quarters in England, the French were as well advised as to our movements as were our own commanders, and were consequently prepared at all points.

indicate the exact position of an enemy, so as to warn their coasters from impending danger, I resolved on destroying one of their principal stations on Isle Rhe, at the town of St Martin. The result will be gathered from the subjoined despatch to Admiral Thornborough.

" ' PALLAS,' ST MARTIN'S ROAD, ISLE RHE,
" *May 10th*, 1806.

" SIR,—The French trade having been kept in port of late, in a great measure by their knowledge of the exact position of his Majesty's cruisers, constantly announced at the signal-posts ; it appeared to me to be some object, as there was nothing better to do, to endeavour to stop this practice.

" Accordingly, the two posts at Point Delaroche were demolished, next that of Caliola. Then two in L'Anse de Repos, one of which Lieutenant Haswell and Mr Hillier, the gunner, took in a neat style from upwards of 100 militia. The marines and boats' crews behaved exceedingly well. All the flags have been brought off, and the houses built by government burnt to the ground.

" Yesterday, too, the zeal of Lieutenant Norton of the *Frisk* cutter, and Lieutenant Gregory of the *Contest* gun-brig, induced them to volunteer to flank the battery on Point d'Equillon, whilst we should attack in the rear by land ; but it was carried at once, and one of fifty men who were stationed to three 36-pounders was made prisoner—the rest escaped. The battery is laid in ruins—guns spiked—carriages burnt—barrack and magazine blown up, and all the shells thrown into the sea. The convoy got into a river beyond our reach. Lieutenant Mapleton, Mr Sutherland, master, and Mr Hillier were with me, and as they do on all occasions so they did at this time whatever was in their power for his Majesty's service. The petty officers, seamen, and marines failed not to justify the opinion that there was before reason to form ; yet it would be inexcusable were not the names of the quartermasters Barden and Casey particularly mentioned, as men highly deserving any favour that can be shown in the line to which they aspire.

"I have the honour, etc. etc.   COCHRANE.

"EDW. THORNBOROUGH, Esq.,
"Vice-Admiral of the *Blue*."

Early in the morning on the 14th May, the *Pallas* again stood in close to the Isle of Aix, to renew her reconnoissance of the French squadron under Admiral Allemand, then anchored at the entrance of the Antioche passage, and also in the hope of once more getting within range of the vessels which we had failed to bring to an action on the 25th ultimo. In order to prevent their again taking shelter under the batteries on Isle d'Aix, we cleared for action and ran within range of the latter; the frigate shortly afterwards getting under weigh to meet us.

Scarcely had she done so, than the three brigs also got under weigh to support her, making a formidable addition to the force to be encountered, the frigate alone showing a broadside superior to ours. We however remained under our topsails by the wind to await them, and when the brigs came within point-blank shot, a broadside from the *Pallas* dismantled one of them. We then veered and engaged the frigate and the other brig—the batteries on Isle d'Aix meanwhile firing at us.

After an hour's fighting, we observed that considerable damage had been done by the fire of the *Pallas* to the frigate and another of the brigs, the maintopsail-yard of the latter being cut through, and the aftersails of the frigate shot away, though the action was not continuous, owing to the frequent necessity on our part of tacking to avoid shoals.

About one o'clock we managed to gain the wind of the frigate, and running between her and the batteries gave her two or three smart broadsides, on which her fire slackened, and she showed signs of meditating a retreat. Perceiving this, I directed Mr Sutherland, the master, to lay us aboard, which at 1.40 P.M. was gallantly but rather too eagerly effected.

Just at this moment, unobserved by us, the French frigate grounded on a shoal, so that on coming in contact, the spars and rigging of both vessels were dismantled. The concussion drove our guns back into the ports, in which position the broadside was again discharged, and the shot tore through her sides with crushing effect, her men taking refuge below, so that the only return to this broadside was three pistol-shots fired at random. The French captain was the only man who gallantly remained on deck.

To clear away our own wreck was one object ; to board the frigate the next ; but two more frigates were observed to quit the enemy's squadron, and crowd all sail to her assistance. This, in our crippled condition, was too much ; there was, therefore, nothing for it but to quit the grounded ship and save ourselves. Accordingly we bore up, and made what sail was possible, cutting away and repairing the wreck as best we could, the two frigates following in chase.

Fortunately the sloop *Kingfisher*, commanded by the gallant Captain, now Admiral, Seymour, seeing our disabled condition, promptly ran down and took us in tow ; on which the enemy desisted from the pursuit, turning their attention to their disabled consort. The subjoined report to Admiral Thornborough details a few other particulars of the action, though at that time we neither knew the names nor the strength of our opponents.

" His Majesty's Ship ' Pallas,' 14*th May*,
" Off the Island of Oleron, *May* 15*th*, 1806.

" Sir,—This morning when close to Isle d'Aix, reconnoitring the French squadron, it gave me great joy to find our late opponent, the black frigate, and her companions the three brigs getting under sail ; we formed high expectations that the long wished-for opportunity was at last arrived.

" The *Pallas* remained under topsails by the wind to await them ; at half-past eleven a smart point-blank firing commenced on both sides, which was severely felt by the enemy. The maintopsailyard of one of the brigs was cut through, and the

H

frigate lost her aftersails. The batteries on l'Isle d'Aix opened on the *Pallas*, and a cannonade continued, interrupted on our part only by the necessity we were under to make various tacks to avoid the shoals, till one o'clock, when our endeavour to gain the wind of the enemy and get between him and the batteries proved successful ; an effectual distance was now chosen, a few broadsides were poured in, the enemy's fire slackened. I ordered ours to cease, and directed Mr Sutherland, the master, to run the frigate on board, with intention effectually to prevent her retreat.

" The enemy's side thrust our guns back into the ports, the whole were then discharged, the effect and crash were dreadful ; their decks were deserted ; three pistol-shots were the unequal return.

" With confidence I say that the frigate was lost to France had not the unequal collision tore away our foretopmast, jibboom, fore and maintopsailyards, spritsailyards, bumpkin, cathead, chain plates, forerigging, foresail, and bower anchor, with which last I intended to hook on, but all proved insufficient. She was yet lost to France had not the French admiral, seeing his frigate's foreyard gone, her rigging ruined, and the danger she was in, sent two others to her assistance.

" The *Pallas* being a wreck, we came out with what sail could be set, and his Majesty's sloop the *Kingfisher* afterwards took us in tow.

" The officers and ship's company behaved as usual ; to the names of Lieutenants Haswell and Mapleton, whom I have mentioned on other occasions, I have to add that of Lieutenant Robins, who had just joined.

" I have the honour to be, etc. etc.   COCHRANE."

" *Killed.*—David Thomson, marine.
" *Wounded.*—Mr Andrews, midshipman, very badly ; John Coger, and three other seamen, slightly.

" EDW. THORNBOROUGH, Esq.,
" Vice-Admiral of the *Blue*."

On the 17th, being still ignorant of the name of the frigate we had engaged, we landed some French prisoners under a flag of truce, and thus learned that she was the 40-gun frigate *La Minerve*. The brigs were ascertained to be the *Lynx*, *Sylphe*, and *Palinure*, each carrying 16 guns.

On the 18th, the *Pallas* was ordered to Plymouth in charge of a convoy of transports, and arrived on the 27th without any other occurrence worthy of notice.

A device practised by us when, at various times, running close in to the French shore, must not be omitted. A number of printed proclamations, addressed to the French people, had been put on board, with instructions to embrace every opportunity of getting them distributed. The opportunities for this were, of course, few, being chiefly confined to the crews of boats or small fishing craft, who would scarcely have ventured on their distribution, had the proclamation been entrusted to them.

The device resorted to was the construction of small kites, to which a number of proclamations were attached. To the string which held the kite, a match was appended in such a way, that when the kite was flown over the land, the retaining string became burnt through, and dispersed the proclamations, which, to the great annoyance of the French government, thus became widely distributed over the country.

CHAPTER XII

MY ENTRANCE INTO PARLIAMENT

On the termination of the cruise, the *Pallas* was thoroughly refitted, the interval thus occupied affording me time for relaxation, but nothing occurred worthy of record till, in the July following, the electors of Honiton chose me as their representative in Parliament.

The story of this election is worth relating. My former discomfiture at Honiton, and the ten guineas a head paid to those who had voted for me on the previous occasion, will be fresh in the recollection of the reader. A general election being at hand, no time was lost in proceeding to Honiton, where considerable sensation was created by my entrance into the town in a *vis-à-vis* and six, followed by several carriages and four filled with officers and seamen of the *Pallas*, who volunteered to accompany me on the occasion.

Our reception by the townspeople was enthusiastic, the more so, perhaps, from the general belief that my capture of the Spanish galleons—as they were termed—had endowed me with untold wealth ; whilst an equally fabulous amount was believed to have resulted from our recent cruise, during which my supporters would have been not a little surprised to learn that neither myself, officers, nor crew, had gained anything but a quantity of wine, which nobody would buy ; whilst for the destruction of three French corvettes we never received a shilling !

Aware of my previous objection to bribery, not a word was asked by my partisans as to the price expected in exchange for their suffrages. It was enough that my former friends had received ten guineas each after my defeat, and it was judged best to leave the cost of success to my discretion.

My return was triumphant, and this effected, it was then plainly asked, what *ex post facto* consideration was to be expected by those who had supported me in so delicate a manner.

" Not one farthing ! " was the reply.

" But, my lord, you gave ten guineas a head to the minority at the last election, and the majority have been calculating on something handsome on the present occasion."

" No doubt. The former gift was for their disinterested conduct in not taking the bribe of five pounds from the agents of my opponent. For me now to pay them would be a violation of my own previously expressed principles."

Finding nothing could be got from me in the way of money payment for their support, it was put to my generosity whether I would not, at least, give my constituents a public supper.

"By all means," was my reply; "and it will give me great satisfaction to know that so rational a display of patriotism has superseded a system of bribery, which reflects even less credit on the donor than the recipients."

Alas! for the vanity of good intentions. The permission thus given was converted into a public treat; not only for my partisans, but for my opponents, their wives, children, and friends; in short, for the whole town! The result showed itself in a bill *for some twelve hundred pounds*! which I refused to pay, but was eventually compelled to liquidate, in a way which will form a very curious episode hereafter.

One of my first steps, subsequent to the election, was to apply to the Admiralty for the promotion of my first lieutenant, Haswell, who had so gallantly cut out the *Tapageuse* from the Bordeaux river; and also for that of poor Parker, whose case has been notified in connection with the *Speedy*, though it was not till after my becoming a member of the House of Commons that he was promoted after the fashion previously narrated.

It is unnecessary to recapitulate the services of these gallant officers, further than to state briefly, that on the 6th of April, 1806, Lieutenant Haswell, with the boats of the *Pallas* alone, acting under my orders, cut out the French guardship, *La Tapageuse*, from the river Garonne, and brought off his prize, in the face of heavy batteries, and despite the endeavours of two vessels of war—each of equal force to the captured corvette. For this service Lieutenant Haswell remained unpromoted.

On the 15th of July, in the same year, the boats of Sir Samuel Hood's squadron, under the orders of Lieutenant Sibley, performed the somewhat similar, though certainly not superior exploit, of cutting out *Le Cæsar*, of 16 guns and 86 men, from the same anchorage. Within three weeks after the performance of this service, Lieutenant Sibley was *promoted to the rank of commander*, and so palpable an instance of favouritism determined me to urge afresh the neglected claims of both Parker and Haswell.

My renewed application being met with evasion in the case

of both officers, I plainly intimated to the Admiralty authorities that it would be my duty to bring before the House of Commons a partiality so detrimental to the interests of the navy. The threat produced what justice refused to concede, and these deserving officers were both made commanders on the 15th of August, 1806 ; Parker, for a service performed upwards of five years before, and Haswell for one four months previously. Notwithstanding this lapse of time, Haswell's promotion was dated *eleven days after* that of Lieutenant Sibley ; though the former officer had effected with the boats of a small frigate, and against *three* ships of war, as much as Lieutenant Sibley had accomplished against *only one*, though with the boats of a whole squadron ! viz. the boats of the *Centaur, Conqueror, Revenge, Achilles, Prince of Wales, Polyphemus, Monarch, Iris*, and *Indefatigable*. Lieutenant Sibley's exploit with this overwhelming force had a medal awarded, and appears in the Navy List to this day ; Lieutenant Haswell's capture of the *Tapageuse* under my directions was unnoticed in any way.

Another curious circumstance connected with the *Pallas* may be here mentioned. As the reader is aware, that ship—on her last cruise—had taken a number of chasse-marées, some of which were laden with the finest vintages of the south of France. Independently of the wine gratuitously supplied by the *Pallas* to the squadron of Admiral Thornborough, a large quantity of the finest had been reserved to be sold for the benefit of the captors ; so much, in fact, that in an easily glutted market, like that of Plymouth, it was not saleable for anything beyond the duty.

An offer was made to the Victualling Board to accept, for our claret, the price of the villainous small beer then served out to ships' companies, so that Jack might have a treat without additional expense to the nation. The offer was unwisely refused, despite the benefit to the health of the men.

As customs officers were placed on board the prize vessels containing the wine, considerable expense was incurred. We therefore found it imperative that something should be done with it, and as the Victualling Board refused to take it, there was no alternative but to knock out the bungs of the casks, and empty the wine overboard.

My agent had, however, orders to pay duty on two pipes, and to forward them, on my account, to my uncle the Honourable Basil Cochrane, who had kindly offered to stow them in his cellars in Portman Square. Knowing the quality of the wine, the agent took upon himself to forward seven pipes instead of two, and on these duty was paid. As it was impossible to consume such a quantity, the whole was bottled, in order to await opportunity for its disposal.

On this wine hangs a curious story. My residence in town was in Old Palace Yard, and one of my constant visitors was the late Mr Croker, of the Admiralty, then on the look-out for political employment. This gentleman had an invitation to my table as often as he might think proper, and of this—from a similarity of taste and habit, as I was willing to believe—he so far availed himself as to become my daily guest; receiving a cordial reception, from friendship towards a person of ardent mind, who had to struggle as I had done to gain a position.

Croker was one day dining with me, when some of the *Pallas* wine was placed on the table. Expressing his admiration of my " superb claret," for such it really was, notwithstanding that the Victualling Board had rejected wine of a similar quality for the use of seamen, though offered at the price of small beer, he asked me to let him have some of it. The reply was, that he should have as much as he pleased, at the cost of duty and bottling, taking the wine as I had done from the French, for nothing : jocosely remarking, that the claret would be all the better for coming from a friend instead of an enemy, he stated his intention to avail himself of my offer.

Shortly after this incident, Croker, who had previously been in Parliament, was appointed Secretary to the Admiralty, and from that day forward he never presented himself at my apartments ; nor did I, by any chance, meet him till some time afterwards we encountered each other, by accident, near Whitehall.

Recognising me in a way meant to convey the idea, that as he was now my master, our relations were slightly altered, I asked him why he had not sent for his wine. His reply was, " Why, really I have no use for it, my friends having supplied me more liberally than I have occasion for ! " Well knowing the meaning of this, I made him a reply expressive of my appreciation of his conduct towards me personally, as well as of the wine sources from which he had been so liberally supplied. This, of course, was conclusive as to any future acquaintance, and we parted without one additional word.

This incident converted into a foe one who had been regarded by me in the spirit of sincere and disinterested friendship. He was, moreover, in a position to make his enmity felt, and when I was hunted down by that infamous trial which blasted at a blow my hopes and reputation, the weight of official vengeance was all the more keenly felt, as being the return of former hospitality.

On the 23rd of August, 1806, I was appointed to the command of the *Imperieuse* frigate, which was commissioned on the 2nd of September following, the crew of the *Pallas* being turned over to her.

We left Plymouth on the 17th of November, but in a very unfit condition for sea.

The alacrity of the port authorities to obtain praise for despatching vessels to sea before they were in fit condition was reprehensible. It was a point in those days for port admirals to hurry off ships, regardless of consequences, immediately after orders for their sailing were received ; this " *despatch*," as it was incorrectly termed, securing the commendation of the Admiralty, whom no officer dared to inform of the danger to which both ships and crews were thereby exposed.

The case of the *Imperieuse* was very near proving the fallacy of the system. She was ordered to put to sea, the moment the rudder—which was being hung—would steer the ship. The order was of necessity obeyed. We were therefore compelled to leave port with a lighter full of provisions on one side, a second with ordnance stores on the other, and a third filled with gun-powder towing astern. We had not even opportunity to secure the guns; the quarter-deck carronades were not shipped on their slides; and all was in the utmost confusion.

The result of this precipitation was—for it had no object—that as soon as the land was out of sight, we were obliged to heave-to, in mid-channel, to unstow the after hold, get down the ballast, and clear the decks. Worse still—the rigging had not been effectually set up, so that had a gale of wind come on, the safety of the frigate might have been compromised; or had we been attacked by an enemy—even a gun-boat—we could not have fired a shot in return, as, from the powder coming on board last, we had not a cartridge filled.

The weather becoming thick on the following day, no obser-vation could be taken. The consequence was, that from the current and unknown drift of the frigate whilst hove-to, to set up the new rigging, secure the masts, and stow the hold, we drifted towards Ushant, and in the night struck heavily three or four times on a shelf, but fortunately forged over into a deep pool, in which, as it was blowing hard, we had to let go three anchors to hold the ship till the following morning.

As soon as it became daylight, it was found that the *Imperieuse* was inside of Ushant, instead of outside, to the manifest peril of the frigate. As it was, we sounded our way out with difficulty, and happily without material injury.

I afterwards demanded a court-martial on my conduct in this affair, but it was not granted; because it was known that the blame would have fallen on others, not on me. This unwise and arbitrary conduct, in hastily and prematurely forcing vessels to sea, was mistaken by the public as a manifestation of official zeal in carrying on the service!

It would be easy to mention numerous instances of the like nature, but this being my own case, I can vouch for its authen-ticity.

On the 29th we joined the blockading squadron in Basque Roads, and were ordered by the admiral to cruise off shore in the vicinity, but without effect, till the 19th of December, when we captured two vessels off Sable d'Olonne, and on the 31st a third at the entrance of the Garonne.

On the 4th of January we gave chase to several vessels which ran in the direction of Arcassan. On the following day the boats were sent in chase of a galliot and another vessel in shore, but the cutter being swamped in the surf, both escaped into the creek or basin, and ran ashore. We then anchored about three miles from the entrance.

On the 6th we again hoisted out boats and sent them with the stream anchors to warp off the vessels, in which operation they were successfully obstructed by a battery on an island at the entrance of the creek. As the water was too shoal for the frigate to approach with safety, the boats were manned, and before daylight on the 7th we carried the battery by assault, spiking or otherwise destroying the guns, which consisted of four 36-pounders, two field-pieces, and a 13-inch mortar. This done, we collected their carriages, and what wood we could find, with which we set fire to the fort. Several gun-boats being at anchor in the rear of the island, we burned them, as well as the vessels previously chased, not thinking it prudent to remain and get them off, as a general alarm had been excited along the coast.

Having destroyed this battery, we again sailed for the Garonne, and on the 9th anchored off Cordovan, in the hope of intercepting any vessels entering or quitting the river; but notwithstanding we remained here till the 19th, none showed themselves, nor was any attempt made by the enemy to dislodge us from our position. Our anchorage was, however, exposed, and heavy gales coming on, we were compelled to make sail on the 19th.

Shortly after this the *Imperieuse* was ordered home, arriving at Plymouth on the 11th of February, without further incident. Indeed the cruise would not be worthy of record, except to preserve the order of time in this narrative of my services unbroken.

On the 26th we chased some vessels off Isle Dieu, but they

ran under the protection of a battery with which we exchanged some shots, and then made sail in the direction of Sable d'Olonne. On the 29th joined the squadron, and were ordered to supply the *Atalante* with provisions and water.

CHAPTER XIII

DISSOLUTION OF PARLIAMENT

On the 27th of April, 1807, the short but busy Parliament was dissolved, "his Majesty being anxious to recur to the sense of his people." In other words, it was dissolved for political reasons not within the scope of the present work to enter.

In the following month of May writs were issued for a general election, and as my Honiton constituents, even during the short period I had been ashore, had heartily sickened me of further connection with them, by the incessant cry for places with which they had assailed me, I made up my mind to become a candidate for Westminster, with the object of adding the weight of an important constituency to my own representations on naval or other abuses whenever opportunity might occur. Or, as I told the electors of Westminster, at a meeting convened at the St Alban's Tavern, my motive for soliciting their suffrages was, that "a man representing a rotten borough could not feel himself of equal consequence in the House with one representing such a city as Westminster—that disclaiming all attachment to parties or factions, it was not only my wish to be independent, but to be placed in a position where I could become so with effect, and that as this was impossible with no more efficient backers than my late constituents, my connection with them had ceased, and I had taken the liberty of soliciting the suffrages of the electors for Westminster."

The candidates for Westminster were, the Right Hon. Brinsley Sheridan, Mr Elliot, Mr Paul, and myself. It was not till the poll had commenced, that Sir Francis Burdett—at that time confined to his bed by a dangerous wound received in a duel with Mr Paul—was put in nomination, without his knowledge, the nature of his wound not permitting any person to communicate with him, except his medical attendant.

I was regarded as the opponent of Mr Sheridan, and for want of better argument that gentleman's partisans in the press sought to depreciate me in the estimation of the electors by representations of the most unjust character, a far more reprehensible act than that of pointing out to them the advantage of retaining an eminent and tried man in preference to one of whose political tendencies they could practically know nothing.

In electioneering all devices are considered fair, so in place of resenting or retaliating, they were met by my declaration, that—

" Whatever gentlemen might say of their long political services—to the electors belonged the privilege of judging for themselves, and that in looking for security for the performance of pledges, they should also consider the character of those who gave them. I was not a mere professed reformer, but the zealous friend of reform, earnestly desiring to see it thoroughly carried out as regarded many abuses which had crept into our constitution. Much had been said of profligacy and profusion of public money. But what was to be said of a commander-in-chief of the navy, who would give away those commissions which formed the stimulus, and should be the reward of honourable merit, in exchange for borough interests ? If I had the honour of being returned for Westminster, I should feel confident in rising to arraign such abuses. But in representing a rotten borough, I was under restriction."

This explanation was favourably received, and the result was, that on the 10th of May I was at the head of the poll, whilst my detractors were at the bottom ; Sir Francis Burdett being third,

and Mr Sheridan fourth,—a circumstance which called forth
from the latter gentleman one of those diatribes for which he had
become famous.

At the final close of the poll, Sir Francis Burdett and myself,
being at the head, were declared elected, and I had the honour
of representing a body of constituents whose subsequent support, under the most trying events of my life, forms one of my
most gratifying recollections. I must also record it, to the
honour of my Westminster friends, that during my long connection with them, no elector ever asked me to procure for himself
or relatives a place under Government, whilst the multitude of
applications for place from my late constituents formed, as has
been said, a source of intolerable annoyance.

This election was remarkable as being the first in which public
opinion firmly opposed itself to party faction. It had become
unmistakably manifest that the two great factions into which
politicians were divided had no other object than to share in
the general plunder, and, as a first step to this, to embarrass the
Government of the " *ins* " by the factious opposition of the
" *outs*." Indeed, so obvious had this become, that the appella-
tions of Whig and Tory were laid aside by common consent, and
the more descriptive names of " *outs* " and " *ins* " substituted in
their stead. My election had no doubt been secured by the
emphatic declaration, that I would belong to neither party,
supporting or opposing either as in my judgment might seem
conducive to the national good.

The animosity of these respective parties against each other
was favourable to such a course. Each accused the other of
grasping at offices for the sake of personal or dependent
advantage, and averred that the aim of their opponents was
neither the administration of government—which, as has been
seen, was left to administer itself in its own way—nor the good
of the country, but the possession and distribution of the public
money. So virulent did these mutual recriminations become,
that it cannot be wondered at if people took the disputants
at their word ; the more so as the moment either party was in

power they threw aside the principles which had gained momentary ascendancy, and devoted their sole attention to their former practices, knowing that, as their possession of office might be short, a tenure so uncertain must be made the most of. Statesmanship amongst such people was out of the question. Neither party could even foresee that the very disgust which their scramble for office was exciting in the public mind must one day overthrow both factions.

It was at this very Westminster election that the patriotism of the electors made itself felt throughout the length and breadth of the land, and laid the foundation of that reform which has been obtained by the present generation. To the error which had been committed both factions became speedily alive, and each in turn persecuted the expression of public opinion whenever opportunity offered. The press, as far as possible, was gagged; public writers and speakers heavily fined, and sentenced to lengthened imprisonment; and, where the rank or position of the offender rendered this impracticable, both parties joined in the most uncompromising hostility to him, as afterwards I had but too much reason to know to my cost.

On the 24th of June, the electors of Westminster insisted on carrying Sir Francis Burdett from his house in Piccadilly to a magnificent entertainment at the Crown and Anchor Tavern in the Strand. A triumphal car was provided, which on its passage through immense crowds of spectators was enthusiastically greeted, the illustrious occupant reclining with his wounded leg on a cushion, whilst the other was placed on a figure inscribed with the words " VENALITY AND CORRUPTION," which were thus emblematically trampled under foot.

On the 26th the House was formally opened by the delivery of his Majesty's speech, through the instrumentality of commissioners, viz. Lord Chancellor Eldon, and the Earls of Aylesford and Dartmouth. In the course of the debate on the address, during which much party recrimination took place, I excited great animosity by expressing a hope that, " as each party charged the other with making jobs in order to influence the elections, the conduct of both might in this respect be inquired into, and that hence, some third party would arise, which would stand aloof from selfish interests and sinecure places, for that, as parties were at present constituted, I would not support either unless they were prepared to act on other principles than those by which their present course appeared to be guided."

On the 10th of July, I brought forward a motion on naval abuses.

The motion was negatived without a division. It however produced a *cessation of my legislative functions* ! for immediately afterwards I was ordered to join Lord Collingwood's fleet in the Mediterranean ; it being perhaps anticipated that I should vacate my seat in consequence ; but this the electors of Westminster prevented, by giving me unlimited leave of absence from my parliamentary duties.

CHAPTER XIV

CRUISE OF THE IMPERIEUSE

ON the 12th of September, 1807, the *Imperieuse* sailed from Portsmouth to join Lord Collingwood's fleet in the Mediterranean, having in charge a convoy of thirty-eight sail of merchantmen destined for Gibraltar and Malta. We reached Malta on the 31st of October, and finding that Lord Collingwood was cruising off Palermo, sailed on the 5th of November to join his fleet.

On the 14th, under the land of Corsica, two strange sail were discovered, and it being calm, the boats were manned and gave chase, the larger of the vessels showing English colours. Finding that this *ruse* did not check the progress of the boats, she hove-to, and when they had advanced within musket-shot, hauled in her colours and commenced firing with musketry and long guns ; the boats, however, dashed alongside, and in five minutes, after considerable slaughter, were in possession.

She proved to be a Maltese privateer of 10 guns ; her crew,

however, consisting of Russians, Italians, and Sclavonians, the captain only being a Maltese. In this affair we lost one man killed, and two officers and thirteen men wounded. The loss of the privateer was far more considerable, her treachery being severely punished.

I was much vexed at this affair, for the vessel, though hailing from Malta, was in reality a pirate, and ought to have been treated as such. After despatching her to Malta, I addressed the following letter on the subject to Lord Collingwood :—

"H.M.S. 'IMPERIEUSE,' off CORSICA,
"14th November, 1807.

"MY LORD,—I am sorry to inform your lordship of a circumstance which has already been fatal to two of our best men, and I fear of thirteen others wounded two will not survive. These wounds they received in an engagement with a set of desperate savages collected in a privateer, said to be the King George, of Malta, wherein the only subjects of his Britannic Majesty were three Maltese boys, one Gibraltar man, and a naturalised captain ; the others being renegadoes from all countries, and great part of them belonging to nations at war with Great Britain.

" This vessel, my lord, was close to the Corsican shore. On the near approach of our boats a union-jack was hung over her gunwale. One boat of the three, which had no gun, went within hail, and told them that we were English. The boats then approached, but when close alongside, the colours of the stranger were taken in, and a volley of grape and musketry discharged in the most barbarous and savage manner, their muskets and blunderbusses being pointed from beneath the netting close to the people's breasts.

" The rest of the men and officers then boarded and carried the vessel in the most gallant manner. The bravery shown and exertion used on this occasion were worthy of a better cause.

" I have the honour, etc.   COCHRANE.

" The Right Hon. LORD COLLINGWOOD."

ELECTION CANDIDATES, MAY 1807

The figures on the pole represent (at top) Sir Francis Burdett, Lord Cochrane,
Eliott, Sheridan, Paull

This pirate, for the capture of which, as was subsequently learned, 500*l.* had been offered, was after much trouble condemned as a *droit of Admiralty* ! it being evidently hoped that by this course such influence might be brought to bear as would eventually procure her restoration : for it was currently reported at Malta that certain persons connected with the Admiralty Court had a share in her ! Be this as it may, we never obtained the premium for her capture, but in place thereof were *condemned by the Court of Admiralty to pay five hundred double sequins* ! After this, the Maltese Court always threw every obstacle in the way of condemning our prizes, and, when this was effected, with such costs as to render the term " prize " almost a misnomer ; a subject on which some strange stories will have to be told in another place.

On the 19th we joined Lord Collingwood's fleet off Toulon, consisting of the *Ocean, Malta, Montague, Tiger, Repulse, Canopus,* and *Espoir.* The *Imperieuse* was forthwith ordered to Malta, to land the wounded, after which we were directed by Lord Collingwood to proceed to the Archipelago, his lordship giving me an order to supersede the officer in command of the blockading squadron there.

On the 26th we again fell in with the fleet off Sardinia, and on the 29th anchored in Valetta, our pirate prize having arrived on the preceding evening. On the 6th of December, the *Imperieuse* sailed for the Archipelago, and on the 8th passed between Zante and Cephalonia. On the 11th we joined the blockading squadron in the Adriatic, consisting of the *Unite, Thames, Porcupine,* and *Weasel,* which were then watching some French frigates in Corfu. On the 12th, the *Imperieuse* overhauled three Russian vessels, one of which threw overboard three bundles of letters. By prompt exertion we were lucky enough to rescue these, and found them to contain important intelligence.

On arriving off Corfu, and pending the necessary arrangements for transferring the command of the blockading squadron to myself, I asked leave of the senior officer still in command to take

I

a run to the north end of the island. This being granted, we sailed forthwith, and to our surprise soon afterwards fell in with thirteen merchantmen, as leisurely proceeding along the blockaded coast as though we had belonged to their own nation! Singling out the three nearest to us, we took possession of them, and to our astonishment found that each had a pass from the officer I was ordered to supersede!

Despite this unlooked-for protection, I sent them to Malta for adjudication, and they were, I believe, condemned. The immediate result to myself, however—as Lord Collingwood long afterwards told me—was the *withdrawal of my appointment to the command of the blockading squadron*! The commanding officer, whose passes I had intercepted, promptly took the initiative, and without apprising me, despatched one of his vessels to Lord Collingwood, with a letter stating generally that, "*from my want of discretion I was unfit to be entrusted with a single ship, much less with the command of a squadron*"! Lord Collingwood acted on the representation without making inquiry into its cause, and the consequence was my recall to receive further orders from his lordship, this amounting to my deposition from the only command of a squadron that was ever offered to me.

I was, of course, ignorant of Lord Collingwood's reasons for recalling me, though greatly disappointed at such a result. It was not till some time afterwards, when too late to remedy the injury, that I ventured to ask his lordship the reason of such a proceeding. He frankly told me, when I as frankly informed him of the intercepted passes, and that my senior officer had traduced me to his lordship, by way of first blow in a serious scrape. Lord Collingwood was very indignant, but from the lapse of time, and probably from having neglected to investigate the matter at the time, he thought it better not to reopen it, and thus my traducer continued his pass trade with impunity.

I give the above incident as it occurred. Those to whom such a statement may appear incredible will find, on consulting the pages of Captain Brenton, that it was not an isolated instance.

I shall add, that on my return from the Mediterranean, in 1809, an officer, who shall be nameless, waited on me at Portsmouth, and begged me not to make official or public mention of the preceding circumstance, or it would be his ruin. I made him no promise, but having then the preparation for the Basque Roads attack on my hands, there was no time to attend to the matter, and as the circumstance had not been officially reported by me at the time—as indeed it did not come within my province to report it—I never afterwards troubled myself about it, though this shameless proceeding had deprived me of the only chance I ever had to command more than a single ship !

On the 17th we fell in with a brig bound from Trieste to Lord Collingwood with despatches, announcing that Russia had declared hostilities against England. This intelligence was fortunate, as there were several Russian ships of war in the Gulf, with one of which—a line-of-battle ship—we had fallen in only two days previous.

The professed origin of the declaration of Russia against England was our questionable conduct at Copenhagen. But notwithstanding the assumption by Russia, that she had endeavoured to serve our cause at Tilsit, there is no doubt but that she was secretly leagued with Napoleon against us. I never knew what was in the letters we rescued, as they were sent to Lord Collingwood; but no doubt they contained important intelligence for the French squadron then in the Archipelago, and, coming from a Russian source, there was little question as to the nature of their contents, which appeared to be conclusive in the estimation of the British authorities.

On the 22nd the *Imperieuse* stood into the Gulf of Valona under French colours, and saw some vessels close in under the batteries. As soon as it became dark, we manned the boats and brought out a Turkish vessel under the fire of a battery. On the 30th again joined the squadron, and learned that the Russian fleet, consisting of five sail of the line and three frigates, had left Corfu and gone up the Adriatic. On the 2nd of January, 1808, we joined Lord Collingwood, the fleet then bearing up in the direction of Syracuse. On the 8th gave chase to some vessels off the south point of Cephalonia, sending the boats after them into the bay ; but the enemy being on the alert, and the vessels being run on shore, it became necessary to recall the boats. On the 12th, when off Otranto, we captured a vessel from Corfu to that place laden with clothing and iron.

On the 23rd we again joined Lord Collingwood off Corfu, and were despatched to Malta with sealed orders, arriving there on the 28th. Having filled up our water and provisions, the *Imperieuse* was then ordered to Gibraltar, for which port we sailed on the 31st, my expectations of increased command, thanks to the adroit turn given to my seizure of the intercepted passes, being thus at an end.

The instructions now given me by Lord Collingwood were to harass the Spanish and French coast as opportunity served. These instructions, though forming a poor equivalent for the command of a squadron, were nevertheless complimentary, as acknowledging the good effected by my former cruises in the *Speedy*. Consequently, I determined to make every exertion to merit his lordship's approbation in the present instance.

On the 9th of February we made the high land of Spain to the eastward of Barcelona, and at daylight on the following morning fell in with two vessels bound from Carthagena to Marseilles, both of which were captured and sent to Malta with the prisoners.

On the 11th looked into Barcelona, where a considerable number of vessels lay at anchor, but knowing the fortifications to be too strong to warrant success in an attempt to cut any of them out, the *Imperieuse* again made sail. On the 18th we ran in close to Valencia, and having on the previous day perceived some vessels anchored within a mile of the town, the boats were sent off after dark to capture them, but as they unfortunately proved to be American, our labour was abortive.

On the 15th we arrived off Alicant, and at daylight stood close to the town under American colours. Two boats came out, but finding their mistake when within gun-shot, they immediately made for the shore, and the batteries opened fire upon us. As there was no purpose to be answered in returning this, we passed by Cape Palos, where four gun-boats showing Russian colours were observed at anchor under the protection of one of the numerous batteries with which the Spanish coast was studded.

On the 17th entered a bay about eight miles to the westward of Carthagena to intercept some vessels observed running along shore. After a long chase with the boats, we succeeded in capturing two. As I had made up my mind to get possession of the gun-boats seen two days previously, we stood off out of sight of land in order to lull suspicion, and at sunset on the 19th again steered for the bay in which they were at anchor. At 9 P.M. we distinctly saw them quit their anchorage, on which we cleared for action, remaining undiscovered till they had passed the point which forms one extremity of the bay. They now attempted to return, but too late. Running in amongst them, we opened both our broadsides with effect, and dashing at them with the boats, took one, armed with a 32-pounder, a brass howitzer, and two smaller guns. Another sank with all hands, just as the boats were alongside, and a third sank shortly afterwards. A fourth escaped by running for Carthagena, where we did not think it politic to follow her, lest we might bring upon us the Spanish fleet at anchor there. A brig with a valuable cargo also fell into our hands.

Having received information from the prisoners taken in the gun-boats that a large French ship, laden with lead and other munitions of war, was at anchor in the Bay of Almeria, I determined on cutting her out, and the night being dark, it became necessary to bring to. At daylight on the 21st, we found ourselves within a few miles of the town, and having hoisted American colours, had the satisfaction to perceive that no alarm was excited on shore.

The boats, having been previously got in readiness, were forthwith hoisted out, and the large pinnace, under the command of Lieutenant Caulfield, dashed at the French ship, which, as the pinnace approached, commenced a heavy fire, in the midst of which the ship was gallantly boarded, but with the loss of poor Caulfield, who was shot on entering the vessel. The other pinnace coming up almost at the same moment completed the capture, and the cable being cut, sail was made on the prize.

Some smaller vessels were also secured, but before we could get clear the wind died away ; and the *Imperieuse* and her prizes were becalmed. The batteries of the town and citadel opened upon us a heavy fire, which lasted till 11 A.M., when a light breeze carried us out of gun-shot.

Of these batteries our most formidable opponent was a four-gun tower, situated on an eminence above us ; but by exercising great care in laying our guns, we contrived to keep this battery from doing mischief, except that now and then they managed to hull the prize, which had been placed between the battery and the frigate. By midday, however, we were clear of the batteries, with the prize safe. It was fortunate for us that a breeze sprang up, for had it continued calm, we could not have brought a vessel out in the face of such batteries, not more than half-a-mile distant.

Neither, perhaps, should we ourselves have so easily escaped, on another account,—for about four o'clock in the afternoon a Spanish ship of the line suddenly appeared in the offing, no doubt with the intention of ascertaining the cause of the firing. We, however, kept close to the wind, and got clear off with the French ship, mounting 10 guns, and two brigs laden with cordage. The scene must have been an interesting one to the people of Almeria, great numbers of the inhabitants lining the shore, though at some risk, as from our position many shots from the *Imperieuse* must have passed over them.

On the 23rd the frigate arrived at Gibraltar with the prizes in company, and on the following day we attended the remains of Lieutenant Caulfield to the grave.

On the 2nd of March, we received orders again to proceed up the Mediterranean together with the *Hydra*, with which vessel we sailed in company on the 4th. Heavy weather setting in prevented our return to Almeria, as had been intended ; but on the 12th we stood close in to the entrance of Carthagena, where only the guardship and a sloop of war were at anchor under strong fortifications. As nothing could be done here, we anchored about two miles to the eastward of the port, in the hope of catching vessels running along shore. At daylight the next morning we gave chase to a ship rounding Cape Negretti, but she escaped into a bay in the vicinity, under the protection of a powerful battery and several gun-boats. As we knew nothing of the anchorage we did not attempt to molest them.

On the 13th the *Imperieuse* steered in the direction of Majorca, near which, on the 19th, we captured a vessel bound to Port Mahon. At daylight on the 21st went in close to the entrance of Mahon, where we found the Spanish fleet at anchor, and captured a brig within three miles of the shore, sending her on the following day to Gibraltar, with some prisoners taken out of another brig on the previous evening by the *Hydra*.

On the 23rd fell in with the *Renomme*, to which we reported that the Spanish fleet was in Mahon harbour. After supplying us with water, she parted company for Gibraltar. On the 26th we again made Port Mahon, where six sail of the Spanish fleet appeared to be in readiness for sea. Seeing a sloop to leeward, we made sail in chase, and captured her in the evening ; she was bound from Port Mahon to Sardinia.

On the 28th at daylight, having observed some vessels in Alcudia Bay, we sent in the boats ; these soon afterwards returning with a tartan laden with wine, which we sent to Gibraltar ; soon afterwards we captured another partly laden with wine, which we took out and set her adrift. On the 29th gave chase to two vessels rounding an island ; one succeeded in getting in safe, the other, under Moorish colours, we took, notwithstanding the fire of the forts, and sent her to Malta ; she had several male and female passengers on board, who were highly delighted when, two days afterwards, we put them on shore.

On the 2nd of April the *Imperieuse* was again close to Minorca, when reconnoitring a small bay we observed a strong tower, apparently just built. Landed, and blew it up without molestation from the inhabitants. Though ready for an armament, none had been placed upon it.

On the 5th, at daylight, passed close to Cittadella in chase of a vessel which escaped ; made sail after a brig coming from the direction of Majorca ; at 3 P.M. she ran in shore, and anchored under a small fort, which opened a smart fire upon us, but was soon silenced. The crew then abandoned the brig, which was brought off and sent to Gibraltar.

On the 6th, again reconnoitred Port Mahon, and saw three sail of the line at the entrance of the harbour, ready for sea. On the 8th, captured a French brig, laden with 163 pipes of wine for the use of the Spanish fleet at Port Mahon ; sent her to Gibraltar, and put the prisoners on shore.

On the 11th, off Cittadella, we captured another vessel, sailing under Moorish colours, but laden with Spanish wine ; took out the wine, and as she belonged to the unfortunate Moors who manned her, to their great gratification we gave them back the vessel.

On the 13th it blew so hard, that we were compelled to anchor within range of a pile of barracks placed upon a high cliff—a position certainly not taken by choice. The troops commenced firing, which we returned, and by 4 P.M. had pretty well demolished the barracks. I then despatched an officer in the gig with a barrel of powder to complete the work, but just as they had got up, a large reinforcement of troops came upon them and compelled them to make a retreat, leaving the powder behind them. After this we got under weigh.

On the 18th fell in with the *Leonidas*, which on the previous day had left Lord Collingwood with 16 sail of the line. Parted company in quest of the fleet, but did not fall in with it.

On the 22nd we re-entered Alcudia Bay, and sent the pinnace ashore, when she captured some sheep. On the following day another boat's crew managed to procure some bullocks and pigs, which were very acceptable, but all their efforts to obtain water failed.

A few days previous to this, when close to Majorca, we had been fired upon from the small battery of Jacemal, and having subsequently reconnoitred it more closely, it appeared practicable to destroy it by a night attack. Accordingly, we again ran in, and soon reaching the tower, blew it up, dismounting three guns. A guard-house near the battery was set on fire, after which we returned to the frigate without loss. At daylight on the following morning we had the gratification to perceive that our work had been effectual, the whole being in ruins. As the place stood on an eminence very difficult of access, and commanding two bays, its demolition was desirable.

On the 26th fell in with the *Leonidas*, which had been in quest of, but had not succeeded in falling in with, Lord Collingwood's fleet. From her we learnt that the French fleet was at anchor in Corfu. On ascertaining this, I determined on paying another visit to the Spanish coast, and accordingly parted company with the *Leonidas*.

At daylight on the 27th, observing a brig and a smaller vessel in shore, made sail in chase. The brig got safe into Palamos Bay, where there were several other vessels deeply laden, but well protected by forts and gun-boats. The smaller vessel was boarded by Mr Harrison in the gig, before she had time to get under the forts, but perceiving a large galley full of men in pursuit of him, he was obliged to relinquish the prize, and made for the frigate ; the galley pressed him hard, but on perceiving the *Imperieuse* bringing to for her reception, she gave up the chase, and the gig returned in safety.

We were now in great distress from want of water, and as it could only be obtained from the enemy's coast, we sent a boat on shore to the westward of Blanes, but she returned without success, having been fired upon from a fortification on an eminence in the vicinity. As a supply of this essential fluid had become essentially necessary, even if it had to be fought for, we made every preparation for a second attempt on a sandy beach, between Blanes and Calella, where a large river was found, on which the frigate was brought to an anchor about a quarter of a mile from the place, and, thanks to our bold front, we obtained an abundant supply without molestation ; though, as we came off, a considerable body of troops showed themselves, and a fire of musketry was opened upon us, but the frigate promptly replying with round shot, our assailants retreated into the woods as hastily as they had emerged from them, and we again made sail.

On the 5th of May, observing a vessel under Moorish colours to leeward, we made all sail in chase, and by ten o'clock she was in our possession, proving to be a xebec from Marseilles to Tripoli, laden with lead. Her crew were Genoese, and having given us information that on the preceding evening they were in company with a large French ship also laden with lead, and other munitions of war, destined for the use of the French fleet, we despatched the prize to Gibraltar, and made sail for the mainland, in order to intercept the Frenchman.

On nearing the coast, we observed several vessels running along shore, and singling out the one which most nearly answered the description given us by the Genoese, she struck after a few shots ; the information thus proving correct. She was bound from Almeria to Marseilles, laden with lead and barilla. Despatched her after the other to Gibraltar.

At daylight on the 6th, gave chase to three ships, running under the land. On observing us they parted company, one going round a shoal near Oliva, and another running into a small harbour. The third, a fine vessel, we chased into Valencia, but she escaped, as we did not venture after her. Retracing our course, we saw on the following morning one of the others anchored close in shore, and sent the boats to bring her off. On nearing her she opened a smart fire, which being steadily returned by our men, her crew abandoned her, and we took possession without loss. As soon as she was boarded it was found that she had just touched the ground, but the boats promptly taking her in tow, succeeded in getting her afloat, and brought her safely off despite the fire of two towers close to the town of Cullera, in the neighbourhood of Valencia. A considerable number of people assembled to witness the attack from the neighbouring hills.

On the 8th, perceived a vessel rounding Cape St Antonio. On seeing us, she made sail, as we also did in chase. At sunset lost sight of her, and despatching our prize to Gibraltar, altered our course so as to cut her off from Marseilles, whither we suspected she was bound. At daylight we again caught sight of her, and by ten o'clock had gained upon her considerably, when to our disappointment she sent a boat on board, proving to be a Gibraltar privateer instead of a Spaniard.

At daylight the following morning we ran close to Tarragona, and captured a large xebec under Moorish colours. At twelve o'clock observed a fine vessel coming round the shoals of Fangalo, and knowing that she could not have witnessed the capture of the xebec we immediately furled all sail in order to escape observation. An alarm was, however, promptly raised along the coast, and this causing her to alter her course, we immediately started in pursuit. At sunset it fell calm, the ship being then distant about twelve miles. At 3 A.M. she was discovered close in shore, when we hoisted out boats and pulled smartly for her, but on arriving almost within gun-shot, she caught a breeze and went away from us, endeavouring to get into a creek ; but the boats being in a position to cut her off, and making every effort to head her, she bore up, and at 7 A.M. anchored under a two-gun battery, which kept up a constant fire on the boats.

The *Imperieuse* now rapidly approaching, gave the tower a gun and recalled the boats, in order to send other crews, those engaged in the chase being necessarily much fatigued. About 3 P.M. we were joined by the Gibraltar privateer, which bore up to engage the tower, keeping up a smart fire, as did also the ship. The *Imperieuse* now came to an anchor, and opened her broadside on the tower, which was soon silenced. The boats were once more manned, as were also those of the privateer, and the prize towed out, proving to be a large Spanish ship—the same as we had chased into Valencia—bound from Alicant to Marseilles. We learned from her the unpleasant news of one of our lieutenants, Mr Harrison, having been captured by some gun-boats, and taken into Denia ; this intelligence being subsequently confirmed by a fishing-boat boarded off Denia on the 17th.

On the 20th passed close to Cape Palos, the forts on which fired several shots at us, but without damage. At 9 o'clock on the 21st, observed twelve vessels coming round the Cape, four of which were evidently gun-boats. We at once made all sail in chase, and as we tacked, the gun-boats opened a smart fire upon us, continuing this till we again tacked and stood towards them, when they made off, with the exception of one which stood towards the Cape ; the other three running aground on the beach. As we were now very close to the gun-boats, the *Imperieuse*, whilst in stays, also took the ground, but luckily got off again, and opened a fire of musketry upon them, which, in about twenty minutes, obliged two crews to quit the vessels, the third keeping her colours flying till her captain was mortally wounded.

It now came on to blow hard, and as there was no probability of saving the prizes, we set fire to the two gun-boats and a large vessel laden with barilla, the crews having all escaped on shore. The other gun-boat, which had gallantly kept her colours flying to the last, we got off, bringing her wounded captain and two other officers on board the frigate. About 6 P.M. both gun-boats blew up with a great explosion.

Our own situation was at this time critical, as we were in only four fathom water, and it was blowing a gale of wind. By nine o'clock the wind fortunately came off the land, which enabled us to run out a couple of miles and anchor for the night. We learned from the officers, that the convoy was bound from Carthagena to Barcelona, and that each gun-boat had a long gun in the bow, and two aft, with a complement of 50 men.

Two other vessels having run on shore on the morning of the 22nd, we again despatched the boats to bring them off if possible, as well as to recover our anchor and cable, which had been slipped when getting the *Imperieuse* afloat. They succeeded in bringing off one of the vessels, which was laden with barilla, but the other vessel, being immovable, was set fire to. This done we put to sea with our prizes in tow.

In the course of the night the Spanish captain died, his wounds having been from the first hopeless. Every attention possible was paid to the poor fellow, from admiration of his gallantry, but anything beyond this was out of our power. On the following morning we committed his remains to the deep, with the honours of war.

We now made sail for Gibraltar with our prizes, one of which was with difficulty kept afloat. On the 25th passed Malaga, and on the 31st arrived at Gibraltar with all the prizes except one, which had been placed in charge of the Hon. Mr Napier (afterwards Lord Napier), then a midshipman.

On the 1st of June, the *Trident* arrived from England with convoy, and the intelligence of a revolution in Spain, which, being shortly afterwards confirmed by proclamation, a friendly communication was opened between the garrison and the Spaniards, and on the 8th Lord Collingwood arrived at Gibraltar in the *Ocean*, to be in readiness to act as circumstances might require.

A few words on our altered relations with Spain, though coming rather within the province of the historian than the biographer, may here be necessary, in order to account for so sudden a change in my own personal operations.

On the 6th of June, 1808, Napoleon issued a decree, notifying that, as it had been represented to him by the Spanish authorities that the well-being of Spain required a speedy stop to be put to the provisional government, he had proclaimed his brother Joseph, King of Spain and the Indies !

To this extraordinary proclamation the Supreme Junta, *on the same day*, replied by another, accusing Napoleon of violating the most sacred compacts, forcing the Spanish monarch to abdication, occupying the country with troops, everywhere committing the most horrible excesses, exhibiting the most enormous ingratitude for services rendered by the Spanish nation to France, and generally treating the Spanish people with perfidy and treachery, such as was never before committed by any nation or monarch against the most barbarous people.

On these and other accounts the Junta declared war against France by land and sea, at the same time proclaiming durable and lasting peace with England, and commanding that no further molestation be offered to English ships or property, whilst, by the same proclamation, an embargo was laid on all French ships and property.

Another proclamation, more immediately concerning the ensuing chapters, is an order of the Junta, forming the Spaniards generally into an organised national militia for the defence of the country. The French, pretending to consider this militia in the light of non-combatants, having no right to engage in war, committed amongst them the most barbarous atrocities, in retaliation for which many of the succeeding operations of the *Imperieuse* were undertaken, in pursuance of orders from Lord Collingwood to assist the Spaniards by every means in my power.

CHAPTER XV

CRUISE OF THE IMPERIEUSE CONTINUED

SHORTLY after Lord Collingwood's arrival at Gibraltar, his lordship ran down to Cadiz, to watch events, and wait instructions from the Government. On the 18th of June the *Imperieuse* sailed from Gibraltar to join Lord Collingwood's fleet before Cadiz, and on the 21st was ordered by his lordship to cruise in the Mediterranean, and render every possible assistance to the Spaniards against the French. On the 22nd we returned to Gibraltar for our prize tender, which had been fitted as a gunboat, and manned with twenty men, under the command of a lieutenant.

At daylight on the 23rd we passed close to Almeria, with English and Spanish colours flying at the main, and on the evening of the 25th came to an anchor in the outer road of Carthagena. On the following morning a number of Spanish officers came off to bid us welcome, and at noon we paid a visit to the governor, by whom, as well as by the populace, we were received with every mark of friendship, notwithstanding our recent hostile visits in the vicinity. Indeed, our whole passage along the coast was one continued expression of good feeling.

On the 2nd of July the *Imperieuse* arrived off Majorca. The inhabitants were at first shy, apparently fearing some deception, but as we were bearers of the good news that the English and Spaniards were now friends, confidence was soon restored, and presents of all kinds were sent off to the ship, payment being resolutely refused. We had also the satisfaction of here recovering our lost midshipman, Harrison, and the late Lord Napier, who, whilst in charge of prizes, had been taken and carried into Port Mahon.

On the 5th the *Imperieuse* passed close to Barcelona, and hoisting English and Spanish colours at the main, fired a salute of 21 guns! The French, who were in possession of the place, to our great amusement resented the affront by firing at us from all their batteries, but their shot fell short. We could distinctly see the inhabitants crowding the house-tops and public places of the city by thousands, and the French cavalry and infantry meanwhile patrolling the streets. Knowing that the French held their own with difficulty, especially in the adjacent towns, we again hove-to and displayed English colours over French, and then Spanish over French, firing an additional salute, which increased the cannonade from the batteries, but to no purpose.

We then bore up along the coast, and when clear of the enemy's lines, a number of boats came off complaining bitterly of the French troops, who were burning their towns on the least resistance, or even pretended resistance, and were permitted by their officers to plunder and kill the inhabitants with impunity. Perhaps it would be more in accordance with military justice to say, that with the ideas of equality and fraternity then prevalent amongst the soldiers, their officers had no control over them.

On the 6th, the *Imperieuse* came to an anchor between the towns of Blanes and Mataro, in nearly the same position as that taken up on the last cruise. Great numbers of people came off, and the frigate was speedily filled with visitors of both sexes, bringing with them all kinds of presents ; being most politely oblivious of all the mischief ₁we had been effecting in their vicinity for months past. On the 7th, after paying a visit to Blanes, we got under weigh, the Spaniards having sent us word that the French had entered the town of Mataro, at the same time requesting our co-operation against them.

On the 8th we were becalmed close to several villages, one of which had been nearly destroyed by the French on pretence of some trifling resistance. A deputation from the inhabitants of one village came off, and informed us that their church had been plundered of everything, and that forty-five houses had been burned to the ground. A wretched policy truly, and one which did the French great harm by the animosity thus created amongst the people, who were treated as rebels, rather than in the light of honourable adversaries.

The *Imperieuse* could effect nothing against the French in Mataro, from its unassailable position, but having received intelligence that a considerable force under General Duhesme was advancing towards Barcelona, it occurred to me that their progress might be checked. Landing accordingly with a party of seamen, we blew down the overhanging rocks and destroyed the bridges so effectually as to prevent the passage either of cavalry or artillery, at the same time pointing out to the Spaniards how they might impede the enemy's movements else-where along the coast by cutting up the roads,—an operation on which they entered with great alacrity, after being shown how to set about their work.

The nature of these operations will be readily comprehended by the statement that a considerable portion of the main road ran along the face of the precipitous rocks nearest the sea. By blowing up the roads themselves in some places, and the over-hanging rocks in others, so as to bury the road beneath the *débris*, it was rendered impassable for cavalry or artillery, whilst removal of the obstructions within reasonable time was out of the question—indeed, so long as the frigate remained in the vicinity, impossible, as any operation of the kind would have been within reach of our guns.

Having effected all the damage possible, and there being no beneficial end to be answered by longer stay in the vicinity of Mataro, we again made sail, and on the 17th the *Imperieuse* arrived at Port Mahon, where we found a squadron embarking Spanish troops for Catalonia, the crews of the six ships of the line in harbour taking their places in manning the batteries. On the 19th the troops sailed under convoy of some English frigates, as did others destined for Tortosa.

Having filled up with provisions and water, we quitted Port Mahon for another cruise on the Spanish coast, and on the 22nd were close to San Felin, when the whole of the convoy entered the harbour to the great delight of the inhabitants, who reported that, despite the obstacles created, the French had, in the absence of the *Imperieuse*, forced the pass from Mataro, and marched for Gerona, to which place the Spanish troops, just disembarked, were next day despatched, together with 1200 militia, raised from amongst the peasantry in the neighbourhood. Heavy firing was heard shortly afterwards in the interior, and at night it was ascertained that the French had made an attack on Hostalrich and were beaten back. This place was about nine miles from San Felin.

On the 24th we again anchored about four miles from Mataro, and there learned the mode in which the French had surmounted the obstacles interposed by the Spaniards in cutting up the roads, viz. by compelling the inhabitants to fill up the gaps with everything movable, even to their agricultural implements, furniture, and clothes. After this, the French, by way of deterring the Spaniards from again interfering with the highways, sacked and burned all the dwelling-houses in the neighbourhood.

K

Taking a party of marines on shore, we again blew up additional portions of the road to the eastward, and as the gaps made on our last visit had been chiefly filled up with wood, and other inflammable articles just mentioned, we set fire to them, and thus not only renewed the obstacles, but created fresh ones, in the assurance that as everything movable was now destroyed, the obstruction must become permanent. Whilst this was going on the seamen and marines of the *Imperieuse* destroyed a battery completed by the French, and threw over the cliff the four brass 24-pounders. These were next day recovered.

On the 26th we dropped down to the town of Canette, and embarked some more brass guns which the enemy had placed in position on the top of a high cliff. These guns were got on board by means of hawsers carried from the frigate to the cliff, one end being made fast to the masthead. By the application of the capstan and tackles, the guns were thus hopped on board. After these had been secured, I again took a party of seamen and marines on shore, and broke down or blew up the road in six different places. On paying a visit to the town, there was scarcely a house which the French had not sacked, carrying off everything that was valuable, and wantonly destroying the remainder. The inhabitants were in a miserable condition.

The two next days were employed in blowing down rocks, and otherwise destroying roads in every direction which the French were likely to take, the people aiding heart and soul, anxiously listening to every suggestion for retarding the enemy's movements, and evincing the greatest alacrity to put them in practice. In short, I had taken on myself the duties of an engineer officer, though occupation of this kind was, perhaps, out of my sphere as commander of a frigate ; and there is no doubt that I might have better consulted my personal interests by looking after prizes at sea, for, except from Lord Collingwood, not so much as an acknowledgment of my persevering exertions was vouchsafed. I was, however, indignant at seeing the wanton devastation committed by a military power, pretending to high notions of civilisation, and on that account spared no pains to instruct the persecuted inhabitants how to turn the tables on their spoilers ; making—as throughout life I have ever done—common cause with the oppressed.

Having effected all the mischief possible, we weighed for Mongat, ten miles from Barcelona, and anchored off the place at sunset. I had previously received intelligence that General Duhesme was approaching Barcelona with a strong force to relieve the French garrison in possession, and my object was to destroy the fort at Mongat before Duhesme's force came up. For this, however, we were too late, the advanced guard having occupied the fort before our arrival. The people, however, came off with an assurance that, if we would attack the French, 800 Spaniards were ready to assist us. As the destruction of the fort was my principal object, I at once assented, and we commenced blowing up the road between Barcelona and Mongat, so that the communication on that side was effectively cut off, whilst the guns of General Duhesme's force were rendered immovable on the other ; these he afterwards abandoned.

On the 30th it fell calm, and having weighed anchor we drifted down as far as Mataro, but too distant from the shore to attempt anything. Having received intelligence of the continued advance of General Duhesme, we again returned, and anchored within five miles of Mongat, the inhabitants coming off to beg for assistance, as the French in the fort were keeping up a constant fire on their party in the woods, though without venturing to dislodge them.

It is, perhaps, here necessary to explain that General Duhesme had on the 26th of July been compelled, by a well-executed movement on the part of the Count de Caldagues, to raise the siege of Gerona, in which he had been employed for upwards of a fortnight, his force being driven to Sarria, where they were protected by their cavalry. During the night they separated into two divisions, one retreating towards Figueras, and the other in the direction of Barcelona.

It was to the latter division that my attention was directed. To reach Barcelona with heavy guns, the enemy must of necessity proceed by way of Mongat, the castle or fort of which place commanded a pass on their way. By breaking up the roads, the passage of the guns was impeded, as has been described ; but, as the French had possession of the castle, it was essential that they should be dislodged as speedily as possible. The Spanish militia, being eager to second our efforts, I determined to make the attack forthwith.

At 8 A.M. on the 31st the *Imperieuse* got under weigh, and stood towards the castle, whilst I landed in the gig, and mounted the hills overhanging the position, for the purpose of reconnoitring ; finding an attack practicable, I returned on board, and we cleared for action.

The Spaniards, seeing the *Imperieuse* stand in, and being eager for the onset, gallantly dashed up a hill where the French had established an outpost, and either killed or took the whole prisoners ; upon which the garrison in the fort opened a heavy fire to dislodge the victorious Spaniards, but without effect. By this time I had got the *Imperieuse* well in, and had given the castle a couple of well-directed broadsides when the enemy hung out flags of truce.

On this I landed with a party of marines, but the exasperated Spaniards, elated by their recent victory, paid no attention to the flags of truce, and were advancing up the hill to storm the place, the French still firing to keep them in check. I was immediately conducted to the castle, where the French troops were drawn up on each side of the gate. On entering, the commandant requested me not to allow the peasantry to follow, as they would only surrender to me, and not to the Spaniards, of whose vengeance they were evidently afraid.

After giving the commandant a lecture on the barbarities that had been committed on the coast, and pointing out the folly of such a course, inasmuch as, had his troops fallen into the hands of the Spanish peasantry, not a man would have escaped with life, I acceded to the request to surrender to us alone, and promised the escort of our marines to the frigate.

The commandant then gave me his sword, and his troops forthwith laid down their arms. We had, however, even after this surrender, some trouble in keeping out the irritated Spaniards, who were actuated rather by the excitement of vengeance than by the rules of war ; and it was not without a few blows, and forcing some of the assailants over the parapet, that we succeeded in keeping them off.

The Spaniards were with some difficulty made to understand that, however exasperated they might be at the conduct of the French, the latter were British prisoners, and not a hair of their heads should be hurt. When we were somewhat assured of their safety, the prisoners were marched down to the boats ; and glad enough they were to get there, for the Spaniards accompanied them with volleys of abuse, declaring that they might thank the English for their lives, which, had the Spanish party succeeded in storming the fort, should have been sacrificed.

What became of the men forming the captured outpost I never knew, and was not anxious to inquire. Having placed the troops on board, we took off four brass field-pieces with their appendages, and threw the iron guns over the parapet ; after which the Spaniards were allowed to ransack the fort. At 6 p.m. we laid a train to the French ammunition, and soon after the whole blew up. Spanish colours were then hoisted on the ruins, amidst the hearty cheers of thousands with arms in their hands, who had by this time flocked to the spot, though when we landed not a single inhabitant was to be seen. Soon after we gained possession, men, women, and children came from their hiding-places in abundance, expressing grateful satisfaction at the capture of the enemy.

It would have been well if the leaders of the French army in other parts of Spain could have seen the exasperation produced by the barbarous propensities of these detachments of troops, who appeared to be under no moral discipline. Except, perhaps, in actual fight, their officers had no control over them, so that their path was marked by excesses of every kind. This is a fatal mistake in armies, as the French afterwards found elsewhere—it degrades war into extermination. Our prisoners did not even deny that the Spaniards would only have exercised a just retaliation by immolating them, but contented themselves by saying that they would never have given in to the Spaniards whilst a man remained alive.

After we had blown up the castle, the *Cambrian* arrived, and to her, by permission of her captain, we transferred half our prisoners. On the following morning we sailed from Mongat, having first presented the chief commanding the Spaniards with two of the field-pieces taken the day before, together with a sufficient supply of powder and ammunition.

General Duhesme reached Barcelona by making a *détour* into the interior, after an absence of about a month, during which the destruction of the roads had been going on. He was highly exasperated with the unfortunate inhabitants, though for no better reason than that all his plans had been thwarted, and, pointing the guns of the citadel on the town, he threatened it with destruction, unless his force was supplied with 12,000 rations daily, with wine and brandy in proportion ; following up this injustice by seizing the most respectable inhabitants for the purpose of extorting ransoms for their liberation.

Great credit is due to the Catalans for the spirit thus manifested at a time when all the more important strongholds of Catalonia were in the hands of the enemy. I say Catalonia, as being concerned with that province only, though there was reason to know that the like patriotism was manifested in the western provinces, though, from the preponderance of the enemy, with less effect.

Even when Duhesme had reached Barcelona, he had great difficulty in maintaining himself, as the activity of the patriots in cutting off his supplies by land was worthy of their cause, and the *Imperieuse* and other English vessels of war took care that he got no supplies by sea.

On the 31st of July I addressed the subjoined despatch to Lord Collingwood :—

"H.M.S. 'IMPERIEUSE,' off MONGAT, CATALONIA,
"31st July, 1808.

"MY LORD,—The castle of Mongat, an important post, completely commanding a pass on the road from Gerona to Barcelona, which the French are now besieging, and the only post between these towns occupied by the enemy, surrendered this morning to his Majesty's ship under my command.

"The Spanish militia behaved admirably in carrying an outpost on a neighbouring hill. Lieutenant Hoare of the marines took possession of the castle, which, by means of powder, is now levelled with the ground, and the pending rocks are blown down into the road, which in many other places is also rendered impassable to artillery, without a very heavy loss of men, if the French resolve to repair them.

"I enclose to your lordship a list of the prisoners, and of the material part of the military stores, all of which that could be useful to the Spaniards have been delivered to them.

"I have the honour, etc.   COCHRANE.

"The Right Hon. LORD COLLINGWOOD."

Having effected everything possible at Mongat, we made sail on the 4th of August, and anchored off San Felin, where— whilst the ship was employed in filling up water—I rode five miles into the country to inspect a battery which the Spaniards had erected to prevent the French from marching on the town. It was situated on an eminence, commanding the road to Gerona and Mataro, and was completely surrounded by high trees, so as not to be visible from the road. If properly defended, it would have presented a formidable obstacle, but as it was, the French infantry would have taken it in a few minutes. I gave the Spaniards instructions how to strengthen the position, but as they told me they could in a short time collect 3000 armed peasantry, I bid them rather rely on these by maintaining a guerilla warfare, which, if conducted with their usual judgment and activity, would harass the enemy more than the battery.

The Catalans made capital guerilla troops, possessing considerable skill in the use of their weapons, though previously untrained. A character for turbulence was often attributed to them ; but, in a country groaning under priestcraft and bad government, the sturdy spirit of independence, which prompted them to set the example of heroic defence of their country, might be, either mistakenly or purposely—the latter the more probable—set down for discontent and sedition. At anyrate, the descendants of men who, in a former age, formed the outposts of the Christian world against Mahomedanism, in no way disgraced their ancestors, and became in the end the terror of their enemies. One quality they pre-eminently possess, viz. patience and endurance under privation ; and this added to their hardy habits and adventurous disposition, contributed to form an enemy not to be despised—the less so that they were in every way disposed to repay the barbarities of the French with interest.

At 8 A.M. on the 6th, the *Imperieuse* got under sail from San Felin, and passing close to Palamos, arrived in the afternoon at Rosas, where we found the *Montague* and *Hind*, to the latter of which we transferred the prisoners. The *Hind* was bound for Port Mahon with the Governor of Figueras and his family, who had to be escorted to the ship by the marines of the *Montague* in order to protect him from popular vengeance, so exasperated were the Spaniards on account of the governor's cowardice or treachery in allowing the French to enter the fortress he had commanded, though from its position and strength he could easily have held out.

The fortress of Figueras was about twelve miles from Rosas, and was a place of amazing strength, having been constructed for the defence of one of the principal passes on the borders of Spain, and being well garrisoned and provisioned, it ought certainly to have withstood a considerable force. The Rosas people had a right to be indignant at its pusillanimous surrender, for not only did this expose their town, but it formed a marked contrast to one of their own exploits, when, being attacked by a large French force, they drove them back with the loss of 300 men.

On the 7th we filled up with water at a wretched place on the opposite side of the Bay of Rosas, and on the 8th sailed for San Felin, where we arrived on the 9th.   On the 10th we were again off Barcelona, when a flag of truce was sent by the French to ask what had become of the troops we had taken at Mongat. On the 11th we bore up for San Felin and were joined by our gun-boat, after which we proceeded to see what was being done on the French coast, and bore up for Marseilles.

My object in proceeding in this direction was, that as the French troops kept out of our reach, there was no beneficial object to be gained by remaining on the Spanish coast ; and it occurred to me, that by giving the French, in the neighbourhood of Marseilles, a taste of the evils they were inflicting on their Spanish neighbours, it would be possible to create an amount of alarm, which would have the effect of diverting troops intended for Catalonia, by the necessity of remaining to guard their own seaboard.   It is wonderful what an amount of terrorism a small frigate is able to inspire on an enemy's coast.   Actions between line-of-battle ships are, no doubt, very imposing ; but for real effect I would prefer a score or two of small vessels, well handled, to any fleet of line-of-battle ships.

On the 15th we stood into the Bay of Marseilles, nad anchored off the mouth of the Rhone, which was distant about eight miles.   Sent the gun-boat in chase of a small vessel, but the crew ran her on shore, and escaped.   The gun-boat burned her, and joined us again on the following morning, when we anchored abreast of a telegraph employed in signalising our appearance on the coast.   Here was a hint, the beneficial nature of which could not be doubted, and at once I decided on destroying the enemy's communications along shore.   As a commencement, this telegraph was demolished without opposition.

On the 16th sent the gun-boat in chase of two vessels close to Cette. They escaped, but she brought back a boat with four men, who gave such information as induced me to send her on a cruise.

On the 17th, there being nothing in sight, we made preparations for destroying the signal-station on the island of Boni, which commands the entrance to the Rhone. Landing ninety men in the boats, we were just in time to see the troops in charge of the station abandon it; and having possessed ourselves of the signals, we blew up the place and returned to the ship.

We then got under weigh, and by 4 o'clock were close to Montpellier, firing on a fort as we passed. Perceiving another signal-station in the vicinity, we again out boats, and proceeded to destroy it, but found this not so easy a matter as on the last occasion, for we had two rivers to ford, each mid-leg in mud, and had moreover to encounter a fire of musketry, but at a distance which did no harm, so that with some difficulty we accomplished our object. This station was called Frontignan, the one last blown up being named La Pinede. At 8 P.M. we returned to the *Imperieuse*, with no other damage than being thoroughly encased in mud.

In the night we ran out about ten miles, having no confidence in the anchorage, and at daylight on the 19th again went in shore, carefully feeling our way by the lead, which showed us that the soundings were highly dangerous. We, nevertheless, came to an anchor off a place called Dumet, when we again out boats and destroyed another signal-tower, together with four houses connected with it. At 2 P.M. we got under sail and bore up, joining the gun-boat to leeward. Supplying her with a new yard and bowsprit, her former spars being carried away, we sent her in shore.

On the 21st it fell so calm that the *Imperieuse* had to be brought to an anchor in Gulf Dumet. At 3 A.M. the boats were manned to destroy a building which we had been informed was a custom-house. This having been set fire to, they returned on board, and were shortly afterwards despatched to destroy another signal-station ; but as troops were now perceived on the look-out, it was not worth while to risk the men, and the boats were recalled. We then got under sail, passing once more close to Montpellier and Cette, where we again joined the gun-boat, and stood into the Bay of Perpignan—forming the west portion of Marseilles Bay—where we destroyed another signal-station called Canet.

At 3 A.M., on the 24th, the morning being still dark, we manned three boats to destroy another signal-station called St Maguire, about three miles distant, and at about half-past four, when within ten yards of the beach, were saluted by two heavy guns with grape, which, passing over the boats, luckily did no damage. Fearing an ambuscade, we pulled out of reach of musketry, but calculating that the French would not venture far in the dark—my favourite time for attacks of any kind— instead of returning to the ship, we made straight for the signal-station, and blew it up amidst a dropping fire of musketry, which, as we could not be distinguished, failed in its direction, and consequently did no harm. Having completed our work, we next marched along the beach in line towards a battery, observed on the previous evening, skirmishing as we proceeded, our boats meanwhile covering us with their 9-pounders ; the French also keeping up a constant fire with their guns, but in a wrong direction.

On storming the battery, with the usual British cheer, the enemy rushed out in an opposite direction, firing as they went, but without effect. We then took possession of two brass 24-pounders, but whilst making preparations to get them off were alarmed by recall guns from the frigate, from the mast-head of which, as day was now beginning to break, a force of cavalry had been seen making for us over the crest of a hill.

We had already had one narrow escape, for on taking possession of the battery it was found that the magazine was prepared for blowing us up, but fortunately, in the hurry of its late occupants to escape, the match had not caught fire. There was, however, now no time to be lost, so placing a barrel of powder under each gun and setting fire to the matches, both were blown up, as was also the battery itself by lighting the match attached to the magazine.

This somewhat staggered the cavalry in pursuit, but they soon recovered, and some smart skirmishing took place on our retreat to the boats, which all the time maintained a well-directed fire on the enemy, keeping them in check, so that we got clear off with the loss of one seaman only—a gallant fellow named Hogan—who was blown up and terribly shattered, in consequence of a cartouch box buckled round his waist having exploded while setting fire to the trains. We otherwise arrived safe on board about 7 A.M., somewhat fatigued by the night's adventure.

We now got under sail, passing close to Perpignan, and were fired upon from Point Vendré, where a French brig of war lay at anchor under the fortification, and therefore was too well protected to be safely interfered with.

In this cruise against the French signal-stations, the precaution of obtaining their signal-books before destroying the semaphores was adopted ; and in order to make the enemy believe that the books also were destroyed, all the papers found were scattered about in a half-burnt condition. The trick was successful, and the French authorities, considering that the signal-books had been destroyed also, did not deem it necessary to alter their signals, which were forwarded by me to Lord Collingwood, who was thus informed by the French semaphores, when re-established, of all the movements of their own ships, as well as of the British ships from the promontory of Italy northward !

CHAPTER XVI

CRUISE OF THE IMPERIEUSE CONTINUED

ON the 2nd of September the *Imperieuse* rejoined the fleet off Toulon, and received orders from Lord Collingwood to renew operations on the enemy's coasts. As the French, though by our previous operations, and by the spirit thereby inspired amongst the inhabitants, were disinclined to advance into Catalonia, they were nevertheless in considerable force in the neighbourhood of Figueras and Rosas, we therefore leisurely sailed in the direction of the latter port.

Keeping well in with the French coast, some gun-boats were observed at 8 A.M. on the following morning close in with the town of Ciotat, between Toulon and Marseilles. One of these being somewhat detached, we hoisted out all boats in chase, but on the remaining gun-boats and a battery on shore opening a heavy fire on them, they were recalled, and we cleared for action. At 10 A.M. six sail of French line-of-battle ships were observed to quit Toulon, but as they were far to leeward, there was nothing to apprehend from their interference; indeed after manœuvring for a short time, they returned to port, no doubt satisfied that the firing which had taken place was of little importance.

At 11 A.M. we anchored under an island, within range of our main-deck guns, but in such a position as to shelter us from the fire of the battery, which, finding that their guns could not be brought to bear, commenced a constant discharge of shells; but as no accurate aim could be taken, these inflicted no damage, though occasionally dropping near us. Taking no notice of these, we out boats, and sending them to a point out of sight of the battery, commenced throwing rockets into the town, which was twice set on fire; but as the houses were for the most part built of stone, the conflagration was confined to the spot where it had broken out. Our reason for molesting the town was that the inhabitants everywhere showed themselves in arms to oppose us.

Finding the place impervious to rockets, and the ship being too far out for a successful cannonade, we got under weigh, and took up a position within range of the fort, on which we continued firing till 8 P.M., almost every shot falling in the place. As it now came on to blow hard from the N.W., we were obliged to anchor.

During the night the enemy had got up a large gun close to the lighthouse, and by 10 o'clock on the following morning, a squadron consisting of four line-of-battle ships and three frigates left Toulon and commenced beating up towards us. We therefore did not again open fire, being unwilling to excite the squadron to pursue us.

However, at 3 P.M., as a large settee was running into the mole of Ciotat, we discharged two shots at her, which went over and fell in the town. Upon this the mortar battery, seeing their squadron approaching, again opened fire, but, as before, without effect. We took no notice of this, but seeing the enemy manning the gun at the lighthouse, we beat to quarters, and prepared everything in case they should fire upon us, which was done at 4 P.M.

We again opened a heavy fire upon the town, every shot telling upon the houses, from which the inhabitants fled, no person being anywhere visible. At the expiration of an hour the lighthouse people left off firing, and the gun was pointed eastward to show that they did not intend to renew the conflict, upon which we ceased also, my object being not to batter the town, but to get possession of some of the numerous vessels anchored within the mole.

This purpose was, however, defeated by the perseverance of the Toulon squadron, the headmost ship of which — a fine frigate—was now within six miles of us, and coming up fast, supported by the others. We therefore thought best to get under weigh, and did so under fire of batteries and mortars, none of which touched us. As soon as the enemy's fleet saw us under sail, they bore up and again ran into Toulon.

On the 6th, at midday, we anchored in the Bay of Marseilles, within half-a-mile from the shore, just out of range of the strongly fortified islands in the bay. Our appearance created the greatest alarm on the coast, from which people were hurrying with their movables beyond the reach of shot. We had, however, no intention to molest them.

The *Imperieuse* was now becalmed till midday on the 7th,

when a breeze springing up, we again got under sail, and exchanged signals with the *Spartan*, which shortly afterwards joined company. Having discovered three vessels lying in a small cove, we out boats, and brought out two of them, setting fire to the other. As the enemy had numerous troops ashore, they opened a brisk fire on the boats, and would probably have defeated our intention, had not the ships kept up a fire upon them whenever they approached. Thus aided, the boats lost only one man, with another wounded.

On the 8th the *Spartan* and *Imperieuse* stood towards the Gulf of Foz, where, seeing a number of troops placed for the defence of a signal telegraph, both ships manned boats, and in addition to the seamen, the marines of the *Imperieuse* were sent with a 9-pounder field-piece—one of our prizes from Duhesme's army. On effecting a landing, the enemy's troops retired to the interior, when, firing two volleys after them, the telegraph named Tignes was taken and blown up, the signals being secured as before.

On the 9th we passed close to Port Vendré, *Spartan* in company, and anchored about a mile from the shore ; but an alarm having been raised, and the troops on shore having got our range, we were, at 3 A.M. on the 10th, compelled to shift our position.

Before daylight the boats of both ships were manned, and pulled on shore, a battery firing at us, but as the shot went over, no mischief was done. Our seamen and marines having landed to the right of the battery, the enemy's troops fled, and we took possession, spiking the guns, destroying their carriages, and blowing up the barracks. These operations were scarcely completed, when a considerable body of troops made their appearance in the distance, and by the time we returned on board, a number of cavalry and artillery had assembled on the site of their demolished battery.

We now passed close to a small fishing town, where other guns were observed in position, both on the right and on the left, these being manned by regular troops and backed by hundreds of armed peasantry, who showed a bolder front than had the garrison of the battery recently destroyed. By way of feint, to draw off the attention of the cavalry, both *Spartan* and *Imperieuse* manned their small boats and the rocket boats with the ships' boys, dressed in marines' scarlet jackets, despatching these at some distance towards the right, as though an attack were there intended. The device was successful, and a body of cavalry, as we anticipated, promptly set off to receive them.

Meanwhile the ships stood towards the town, under a smart fire from the batteries, the shot from which several times took effect. When close in, the *Imperieuse* opened her broadside, and the *Spartan* following, an incessant fire was kept up for an hour, at the expiration of which the marines of both ships were landed. As soon as the boats touched the shore, the enemy fled from the battery, the guns of which were immediately spiked.

The cavalry, which had gone off to repel the sham attack to the right, having found out the trick which had been played upon them, were now seen galloping back to save the battery, which had just been rendered useless, and from which our marines were now re-embarking. So intent were they on rescuing their guns, that they did not appear to have noticed the altered position of the ships, which, as soon as the horsemen approached within musket-shot, opened upon them with grape so effectually, that all who were not knocked out of their saddles rode off as fast as they could, and the marines leisurely returned to their respective ships.

As the French troops had now taken shelter in the town, and the people were everywhere armed, I returned to the *Imperieuse* for the large boats, in each of which a gun was mounted, with the object of clearing the beach and silencing the other battery. By 6 o'clock this was accomplished, not only the battery, but many of the houses and vessels being destroyed. As our boats neared the town, a numerous body of troops again began a brisk fire with musketry ; and by the time one of the largest

ADMIRAL LORD COLLINGWOOD
[Born 1750.   Died 1810]

vessels, which yet remained undemolished, could be blown up, the fire became so warm that it was advisable to cease from further operations, and we returned to the frigate.

In this affair a considerable number of people must have been killed ashore during the five hours and a half continued firing, the cavalry and infantry engaged amounting to several hundreds, whilst the armed inhabitants mustered in equal, if not superior numbers. Neither *Spartan* nor *Imperieuse* had any killed, and only a few wounded, though, from their proximity to the shore, the rigging of both ships was a good deal cut up, and several shots passed through their hulls. Besides the seamen, we had only fifty marines engaged, thirty from the *Imperieuse*, and twenty from the *Spartan*.

On the 11th at 8 P.M. we anchored off the town of Cette, just out of gun-shot, the batteries on shore however maintaining a brisk fire, which was consequently thrown away.

At midnight two boats were despatched from the *Imperieuse* and one from the *Spartan*, to throw rockets into the town, the batteries continuing their fire in all directions till daylight, but doing no damage.

At 4 A.M. on the 12th we got under weigh, and when within a mile of the shore, between Cette and Montpellier, sent the boats to burn two large pontoons, close to the signal-station, which the *Imperieuse* had attempted to destroy on the 18th ultimo. One of the pontoons was burned, and the other blown up without opposition, together with the signal-station and other public buildings which we had not been able to destroy on the former occasion. A number of troops showed themselves, but were contented with firing at a harmless distance. As nothing more remained to be done, we again made sail.

On the morning of the 13th a convoy was discovered in shore. As soon as they saw us, the vessels composing it altered their course, and by 12 o'clock had taken refuge in a deep bay in the vicinity, it being, do doubt, calculated that we should not venture to pass over an extensive shoal, which almost closed up the entrance of the bay. By careful sounding we, however,

L

managed to effect a passage, and three of the smaller vessels perceiving that we should attain our object, passed over the opposite end of the shoal and got away.

About midday it blew a hurricane, and both ships were rapidly driving towards shore, but by letting go another anchor they were brought up. In about a couple of hours, the wind abated, when we weighed and anchored close to the remaining vessels, taking possession of the whole that remained, viz. a ship, two brigs, a bombard, a xebec, and a settee, but all aground. We, however, succeeded in getting off the ship, one brig, the bombard, and settee. The remainder were burned. During these operations a body of French troops lined the beach ; we did not, however, attempt to molest them, as it was still blowing so hard that the prizes were with difficulty got off.

On the 16th we despatched some of the prizes to Gibraltar, and the remainder to Rosas. The *Spartan* now parted company with us to rejoin the Toulon fleet, and the *Imperieuse* held on her course for Rosas with the prize brig in tow, she having been so much damaged by beating on the shoals before she was captured as to require the greatest exertion to keep her afloat.

On the 18th we came to an anchor off Rosas, and on the 23rd, having patched up our prize, she was sent to Gibraltar in charge of Lieutenant Mapleton.

On the 24th the *Imperieuse* again sailed for the French coast, and passing Cette, stood into the Gulf of Foz.

In these cruises our greatest difficulty was to procure fresh water, which was only to be obtained on the enemy's coast, so that the men had frequently to be placed on short allowance. As we were now destitute of this necessary, I determined to run for the entrance of the Rhone, and fill up with water by a novel expedient. Our foretopmast studding-sails were sewn up and converted into huge bags nearly water-tight, these—as the water at the river's mouth was brackish—were sent in the boats higher up the stream where it was pure. The bags being there filled were towed alongside the ship, and the water pumped as quickly as possible into the hold by means of the fire-engine, the operation being repeated till we had obtained a sufficient supply. Having thus replenished our water, we made an attempt to obtain fresh meat also at the enemy's expense. Whilst engaged in watering, a number of cattle had been observed grazing on the banks of the river, and a party was taken on shore to secure some. But this time circumstances were against us. The low-lands on the banks of the river having been flooded, we found on landing a complete morass ; the men nevertheless gave chase to the cattle, but they were so wild, that after a run of three miles, often up to the middle in water, nothing was caught but the herdsman, a poor wretch, who no doubt believing, according to current report in France, that the English killed all their prisoners, began to prepare for death in the most exemplary manner, scarcely crediting the evidence of his senses on being liberated.

In this excursion we had perceived a new telegraph station, about three miles from Foz, the building being complete, with the exception of the machine. We set fire to the building, but the destruction not being fully accomplished, the boats were again sent on shore to blow it up, which was done in the presence of about a hundred troops assembled for its protection. A shot from the ship was so well aimed that it fell right amongst the party, killing one man and wounding several. A few more shots completely dispersed them in such haste as to compel them to relinquish their dead comrade.

On inspecting the abandoned body through a glass, it evidently appeared to be that of an officer, and hence it occurred to me that he might have papers about him which would prove useful. In order to secure them, if there were any, the frigate's barge was again despatched on shore, but before the men could land, a horse was brought from the interior, and the body being laid across him, a shot was fired from the ship over the heads of the party in charge of the horse, which becoming restive, the body was again abandoned. The boat's crew having by this time landed, found it to be that of an officer, as I had conjectured, the poor fellow having been nearly cut in two by a round shot.

As no papers of any consequence were found, our men wrapped him in a sheet which the troops had brought with the horse, and again returned on board.

The *Imperieuse* continued her course along the coast, and on the 30th, seeing some small vessels at anchor near Boni, the boats were sent to destroy them. This being effected in the face of a detachment of troops and the armed population of a small fishing town, the latter also shared the same fate. Passing close to Boni, we saw several vessels at anchor, and made preparations to attack them, but it coming on to blow hard from the westward, we held on our course towards Marseilles, off which a large polacca-rigged ship passed astern of the *Imperieuse*, out of gun-shot. The boats were lowered, but the wind increasing, they had to be taken on board again, and the polacca got into Marseilles, which was then distant about eight miles.

On the 1st of October we again passed close to Ciotat, but saw nothing to attract our attention. On the 2nd some French ships were discovered at anchor near the land to the westward of Toulon, and several guns were fired at us from four batteries on the coast, but without damage, as we were not within reach of shot.

Seeing a frigate to leeward, we exchanged numbers, and found her to be our former consort the *Spartan*, which had been engaged in reconnoitring the enemy's port. Shortly afterwards she bore up and made all sail, the French line-of-battle ships quitting port in pursuit. When within about four miles of these we came to the wind, and the *Spartan* signalled that, since the previous evening, five of the enemy's frigates and a store-ship had sailed from Toulon.

As the *Spartan* again signalled for us to pass within hail, I went on board, and from the information communicated, bore up in search of the admiral. Not finding him where we expected to fall in with him, we ran with a fair wind for Minorca, arriving off Port Mahon on the 5th.

As there was only a Spanish ship of the line in harbour, we again proceeded in quest of the flag-ship, and soon after midday fell in with her on her way to Minorca. On communicating to

Lord Collingwood intelligence of the escape of the five frigates from Toulon, his lordship ordered the *Imperieuse* to Gibraltar with despatches. We therefore wore ship and made sail for that port, where we arrived without further incident.

For these operations on the coast of France I never received the slightest acknowledgment from the Admiralty, though, regardless of prize-money, I had completely disorganised the telegraphic communication of the enemy, from the seat of war in Catalonia to one of the principal naval arsenals of France ; and had created an amount of terrorism on the French coast, which, from inculcating the belief that it was intended to be followed up, prevented the French Government from further attempts at throwing a military force on the Mediterranean coast of Spain. This, as has been said, was my object, as the Spaniards were now in alliance with us. For the panic thus created on the French coast, and its consequences, French writers have given me credit, but the British Government none !

By people of narrow views it has been said that such operations formed no business of mine, and that my zeal exceeded my discretion, which I deny. The commander-in-chief, Lord Collingwood—confiding in my discretion—had sent me to do what I could to assist the Spaniards and annoy the French—and I am proud to say that both objects were effected to his lordship's satisfaction, as will appear from his letters. What damage can I do to the enemy ? was my guiding principle, and the excitement of accomplishing the mischief was my only reward,—for I got no other.

To the disgrace of the then corrupt British administration, which withheld not only reward, but praise, because I had connected myself with a radical constituency, and had set up as a reformer of naval abuses, nothing was manifested in return for these services but hatred. I am proud, however, to make known the subjoined testimony of Lord Collingwood, who gave me the credit of paralysing the enemy's operations by the panic which the *Imperieuse* created on the coast of France ; thus neutralising military expeditions intended to act against Catalonia, or, in other words, preventing, by means of a single frigate, the march of an army into the Mediterranean provinces of Spain, where it could at the time have operated with complete effect. Posterity may not believe the effect of these exertions as narrated by myself. To Lord Collingwood they *must* give credit.

"ADMIRALTY OFFICE,
"*Jan. 7th*, 1809.

"*Copy of a Letter from* Vice-Admiral LORD COLLINGWOOD, *Commander-in-Chief of His Majesty's ships and vessels in the Mediterranean, to the* Hon. WELLESLEY POLE, *dated on board the* '*Ocean*,' *off Toulon, the* 19th *of October*, 1808.

" SIR,—I enclose a letter which I have just received from the Right Honourable Lord Cochrane, captain of the *Imperieuse*, stating the services in which he has been employed on the coast of Languedoc. Nothing can exceed the zeal and activity with which his lordship pursues the enemy. The success which attends his enterprises clearly indicates with what skill and ability they are conducted, besides keeping the coast in constant alarm—causing a general suspension of the trade, and harassing a body of troops employed in opposing him. He has probably prevented *these troops which were intended for Figueras from advancing into Spain, by giving them employment in the defence of their own coasts.*

*   *   *   *   *

" I have the honour to be, etc.   COLLINGWOOD."

(Enclosure.)

" ' IMPERIEUSE,' GULF of LYONS,
" 28th *Sept.* 1808.

" MY LORD,—With varying opposition, but with unvaried success, the newly-constructed semaphoric telegraphs—which are of the utmost consequence to the safety of the numerous convoys that pass along the coast of France—at Bourdique, La Pinede, St Maguire, Frontignan, Canet, and Fay, have been blown up and completely demolished, together with their telegraph houses, fourteen barracks of *gens d'armes*, one battery, and the strong tower on the lake of Frontignan.

"Mr Mapleton, first lieutenant, had command of these expeditions. Lieutenant Johnson had charge of the field-pieces, and Lieutenant Hoare of the Royal Marines. To them, and to Mr Gilbert, assistant-surgeon, Mr Burney, gunner, Messrs. Houston Stewart and Stoven, midshipmen, is due whatever credit may arise from such mischief, and for having, with so small a force, drawn about 2000 troops from the important fortress of Figueras in Spain for the defence of their own coasts.

"The conduct of Lieutenants Mapleton, Johnson, and Hoare, deserves my praise, as well as that of the other officers, Royal Marines, and seamen.

"I have the honour to be, my lord, your obedient servant, etc.   COCHRANE.

"Vice-Admiral LORD COLLINGWOOD."

"*Imperieuse.*—None killed, none wounded, one singed in blowing up the battery.

"*French*—One commanding officer of troops killed. How many others unknown."

CHAPTER XVII

CRUISE OF THE IMPERIEUSE CONTINUED

ON the 19th of October we again quitted Gibraltar for the eastward, having learned that the French frigates which had succeeded in getting out of Toulon were at anchor in St Fiorenzo bay, in the island of Corsica. After leaving Gibraltar, we stood over towards the Spanish possessions on the Barbary coast, and finding everything right there, passed on to the Zaffarine Islands, inside of which we anchored for the purpose of painting and refitting the ship, which stood much in need of renovation.

This being accomplished, we again sailed on the 29th, and on the 31st arrived in the harbour of Carthagena, where we found the Russian ambassador to Austria on his way to Trieste. No English man-of-war having been here since our former visit, we were received with great hospitality and attention by the authorities and inhabitants, who unanimously expressed their delight at being at peace with England ; though, as a Spanish fleet lay dismantled in the harbour, it struck me that they might aid England to better purpose by looking after the enemy. Even their convoys had to be protected by English ships, for whilst we lay at Carthagena, the *Myrtle* arrived from Tarragona, with twelve sail of transports which she had convoyed thither with Spanish troops from Lisbon, and again returned for more.

The *Imperieuse* left Carthagena on the 10th of November, and rounding Cape Palos, passed between Majorca and the mainland, where, on the 11th, we captured a settee. On the 12th we anchored off Barcelona, which place was still in possession of the French. The *Cambrian* was at anchor in the roads.

At night we sent the boats of the *Imperieuse* to throw rockets into the fort, and at daylight on the following morning got under weigh, but perceiving two boats full of men in chase of some Spanish settees,* we lowered ours, and pulled for the boats, which on seeing our intention, abandoned their prey, and ran in under the forts for protection.

On our arrival at Barcelona the *Cambrian* went out for a run, leaving the *Imperieuse* to watch the enemy. On her return we again out boats, and proceeded to blow up a fort close to the entrance of Llogrebat river, and succeeded in so far shattering its foundations as to render it useless. On the 14th the *Imperieuse* anchored near the mouth of this river for the purpose of watering, sending at the same time a boat to throw rockets

---

* Single-decked Mediterranean vessels with long prow and lateen sails.

into the barracks, in order to divert the attention of the Barcelona garrison.

Having completed watering on the 15th, we again got under sail, and resumed our position before the town, shortly after which we observed about 2000 of the French army march out and ascend the hills, where they soon became engaged with a large body of Spanish peasantry. The ships followed, keeping as far as practicable in shore ; but still at too great a distance to render any material assistance to the patriots, who were at last forced from their position. As soon as this action was over, the batteries commenced firing shells at us. In place of replying to this, both ships opened a heavy fire on the portion of the town occupied by French troops, amongst whom, as we afterwards learned from the Spaniards, our shot told with great effect.

Irritated by this unexpected movement, the whole of the batteries ashore began to ply us with shot and shell, the latter of which were thrown with excellent precision as regarded their direction, but fell either over or short of us, two only bursting near the *Imperieuse*, but without doing us any harm. The *Cambrian*, lying a little farther out, escaped with similar impunity. With round shot the batteries were in our case more lucky, one of these passing through the barge and galley, and another striking the muzzle of a brass 32-pounder on the forecastle, in such a way as to render it useless, though without injury to the men who were at the time working the guns.

The circumstances under which the destruction of this gun was effected are too curious to be passed over.

By an extraordinary coincidence the enemy's shot entered the muzzle at the moment our men were firing it, so that the two shots met in the bore ! The consequence was, that the gun was blown up nearly in the middle, the exterior being forced into a globular form—to our great annoyance, for this gun was one of our most useful weapons.

On the 17th another action took place between the mountaineers and a French force on the hills, the object of the patriots being to get possession of the heights, where the French had established a battery, but which on every side annoyed the *cordon* of irregular troops employed in intercepting provisions, from which the Spaniards could not dislodge them, though they appeared to make their attacks with so much judgment and vigour as to compel the enemy to remain on the defensive. In the present case the attack was unsuccessful, the patriots being compelled to retire without accomplishing their object.

After this affair was concluded, several Spanish officers came on board the *Imperieuse*, and spoke confidently of being able to drive in the French advanced force as soon as General Reding's force joined. They informed me that the presence of the *Imperieuse* and *Cambrian* had been of great use, by compelling the French to keep a considerable portion of their troops in the town, and to employ others in manning the coast batteries, so that few were available for operations elsewhere ; but beyond this we had no opportunity of assisting the patriots, as the heights to which the enemy clung so tenaciously were beyond the reach of shot or shell from the ships.

On the 19th I received information of the French having invested Rosas, and knowing that Lord Collingwood attached considerable importance to this place, I considered it my duty, in accordance with his lordship's instructions, to proceed in that direction, hoping that the *Imperieuse* might there render substantial service ; we therefore left the *Cambrian* before Barcelona, and made sail for Rosas, where we arrived on the following day. As it fell calm, the ship was compelled to anchor ten miles from the fortress.

On our arrival a heavy cannonade was going on between the ships and a French battery thrown up on the cliff above Fort Trinidad. The *Imperieuse*, as has been said, being out of range, I took the gig and landed in the town, to ascertain how we might best employ ourselves. Having satisfied myself on this point, I sent back the gig with orders for the frigate to make every effort to get within range of the French troops surrounding the town, so as to enfilade them. As the calm continued, she was, however, unable to approach till the following day, I meanwhile remaining in Rosas, to encourage the Spanish troops, whose spirit was beginning to give way.

Previous to our arrival the marines of the *Excellent*, together with some Spanish troops, had occupied the citadel. Many of these having been wounded, the *Excellent* took upwards of forty on board and sailed, leaving the *Fame* to watch the place, and her commander withdrew some thirty marines, who, with sixty or seventy Spaniards, occupied Fort Trinidad. The departure of the *Excellent* in the first place, and the withdrawal of the marines in the second, greatly dispirited the Spaniards, who on the evening of the 21st began to quit the town in boats.

A brief outline of what had occurred previous to my arrival in the *Imperieuse* will here be requisite, in order to comprehend the events which followed. On the 6th of November a body of 6000 French, or rather Italians, coming from Figueras, had taken possession of the town and the heights commanding the roads. The inhabitants forthwith fled ; but the *Excellent* and *Meteor*, then lying in the harbour, speedily drove out the invaders.

On the assault of the town some of the inhabitants had fled to the citadel, which was in a wretched condition, one of its bastions having been blown down during the last war ; and such had been the negligence of the Spanish military authorities, that it had received no better repair than a few planks and loose stones ; whilst the stores were even in a more wretched condition than the works. It was, however, necessary to put it, as far as possible, in a defensible condition, and to this Captain West, of the *Excellent*, energetically applied himself.

To the eastward of the town, on an eminence commanding the harbour, stood Fort Trinidad, of which a description will presently be given. In this fortress Captain West placed five-and-twenty of the *Excellent's* marines, in addition to the Spaniards who manned the fort ; and, at the same time, sent fifty seamen into the citadel to support the garrison.

The Spanish governor, O'Daly, now sent a request to the Junta of Gerona for reinforcements ; but the French, managing to intercept his despatches, caused it to be reported to the Junta that the English had taken forcible possession of the fortress, and deposed the governor ; whereupon, in place of sending reinforcements, the Junta wrote to Captain West, demanding an explanation of conduct so extraordinary, and, till this explanation revealed the trick, it remained undiscovered.

On the 9th the citadel was attacked by General Reille, and a breach effected ; but Captain West, placing the *Meteor* in a position to flank the breach, and sending some boats to enfilade the shore, prevented the assault, and despatching more seamen to the citadel, the next day it was again in a tolerably defensive state, so much so that Captain West had sallied out with the seamen and effected the rescue of a party of Catalonian militia.

The French commander, thus foiled by the gallantry and judgment of Captain West, now deemed it necessary to proceed against Rosas by regular siege, but first made an attempt to storm Fort Trinidad, in which he was repulsed with considerable loss ; but the fort was so much in danger that, in order to prevent surprise, Captain West reinforced it with thirty additional marines, who entered by means of rope ladders.

The French now, despite opposition from the ships, began to erect batteries on the heights for the demolition of Fort Trinidad, and threw up an intrenchment 300 yards from the citadel, for the purpose of breaching that also. A 3-gun battery opened against the town walls, and the joint effect of these being occasionally directed against the ships, compelled them to retire out of range.

Captain West was now superseded by Captain Bennett of the *Fame*, and, as a breach had nearly been effected in the lower bomb-proof of Fort Trinidad, Captain Bennett withdrew the marines. At this juncture I arrived at Rosas in the *Imperieuse*, having, indeed, come there to render what assistance I could to the Spaniards, and, knowing the endurance, as well as indomitable bravery of the Catalan or *Michelet* * character ; feeling, moreover, assured that the Junta of Gerona would supply early assistance,

* A name given at this period to the irregular Catalonian troops.

I determined to replace the marines which Captain Bennett had withdrawn with others from my own frigate. As it was generally known amongst vessels on the Mediterranean station that I was acting under discretionary orders from Lord Collingwood, Captain Bennett, though he had withdrawn his own men, and notwithstanding that he was my senior officer, did not attempt to thwart my resolution, probably because he considered that by so doing he might be interfering with the instructions given me by Lord Collingwood.

On the 22nd, after having given further instructions on board the *Imperieuse* for annoying the enemy during my absence, I again went on shore to the citadel, into which the French were incessantly throwing shells, but without much effect; for although every shell fell within the place, the shelter was excellent, and no great damage was done.

Having ascertained the position of the enemy's intrenchments, I returned on board, and despatched a party from the frigate to fire upon them at the distance of about 600 yards, as well as to harass the batteries in course of construction. The work was so well performed by our men as to embarrass the troops in the batteries, and thus lessen their fire on the citadel, the preservation of which, till further assistance should arrive, was my principal object. A battery of 24-pounders on the top of a cliff, and therefore inaccessible to our fire, kept up, however, an unremitting fire on Fort Trinidad, every shot striking; but the fort being bomb-proof, without injury to the little garrison, which, like that of the citadel, was well sheltered, but had no means of returning the fire except occasionally by musketry.

After pounding away at the fort for several days, the French made up their minds to storm, but on coming within range of musket-shot, they got such a reception from the garrison as to render a hasty retreat imperative. As their discomfiture was visible from the ship, we fired a salute of twenty-one guns by way of sarcastic compliment, but the enemy had not the politeness to return the courtesy.

The *Imperieuse* now got under weigh, and cleared for action, taking up a position to the left of the citadel, and within musket-shot of the French lines, into which we poured such a storm of shot as to drive out the enemy. Satisfied with the success, I went on shore at Rosas, and got 700 Spaniards to embark in the boats, afterwards putting them on board a light vessel, with the intention of landing them at the back of Fort Trinidad, so as to dislodge the troops from the battery on the cliff, and throw the guns over. The movement was, however, detected by the French commander, and a force which had just been engaged at a distance was hastily recalled, and rushed on, driving the Spaniards and some Germans before them. Manning the batteries, the French instantly turned their attention to the *Imperieuse*, against which they directed such a well-aimed shower of shells as rendered it imperative to get under sail and anchor out of range.

The firing between the batteries and the citadel was kept up during the night without intermission, and at daylight the Spaniards we had landed for the attack on the cliff battery appeared in such confusion, that it became necessary to despatch the boats to bring off a party of marines, who had been put on shore with them. Our men reported that the Spaniards had unaccountably refused to follow them to the attack, and, as is usual in such cases, had suffered far more severely than they would have done had they persevered in the attempt to capture the battery. On sending boats to bring off the Spaniards we only got 300 out of the 700, the remainder being either killed or made prisoners.

On the 23rd we again ran in under Fort Trinidad, but this time on the opposite side to the battery on the cliff, where we could effect considerable mischief, without receiving much in return. It now fell dead calm, so that it was lucky we had not taken up our former position, where we might have been terribly annoyed.

The French, without paying much attention to us, now appeared to redouble their efforts against both castle and citadel, whilst their troops mustered strongly on the hills, with the evident intention of an attack on both, the moment a breach became practicable.

Finding this to be the case, the *Fame* withdrew her marines from Fort Trinidad, upon which I went ashore, and after careful inspection of the breach in course of formation, considering it still capable of prolonged defence, begged the commandant to hold out till next day, when he should be reinforced with marines from the *Imperieuse*, promising at the same time to remain myself in the fortress with the men. With some difficulty he was induced to consent to this arrangement, after telling me that it had been his intention to capitulate on the same evening.

Nor was the Spanish governor at all to blame for his intention to surrender the fortress. Captain Bennett had withdrawn his men, thinking, no doubt, that it was untenable, and that therefore nothing was to be gained by their exposure; so that the Spanish governor might fairly plead that further resistance had been deemed unavailing by the English themselves.

Lord Collingwood had, however, entrusted me with discretionary orders to assist the Spaniards, and it appeared to me that the present was an instance where those orders might be carried into effect, for I had no doubt, if assistance arrived promptly, that the French would be compelled to raise the siege of Rosas, as they had done that of Gerona. In which case they would find themselves isolated at Barcelona; and being cut off, as they already were by land, and exposed to bombardment by sea, must surrender. The occupation of Catalonia, in short, turned on two points; 1st, whether the Junta of Gerona supplied an adequate reinforcement; and, 2ndly, whether I could hold Fort Trinidad till it arrived. Neither do I blame Captain Bennett for withdrawing his men. It was simply matter of opinion; his being that neither fort nor citadel would long hold out—mine, formed on actual inspection of the fort, that it was still in a condition to maintain itself, and being so, that its retention was essential for the preservation of the town and citadel. And had there been a little more alacrity on the part of the Gerona Junta in supplying reinforcements, that opinion would have been justified. Captain

Bennett perhaps knew the dilatory habits of the Spaniards better than I did ; but although my senior officer, he was disinterested enough not in any way to interfere with my plans.

Before daylight on the 24th we landed fifty men, ordering all the marines to follow after sunset. Our first object was to effect such repairs as would put the fort in a better state of defence, and this was accomplished without any great difficulty, as the French were confining their attention to one particular spot, where, by a constant succession of quick firing, they hoped to make a practicable breach. This we could not prevent, having no artillery to reply to theirs.

My principal ground for a belief in the practicability of holding the fort arose from the peculiar form and thickness of the walls, to penetrate which was no easy matter, if resolutely defended. Even if eventually successful, it would not be difficult to evacuate the fort by the lower portion, before the enemy could establish themselves in the upper, whilst a well-constructed mine would involve both them and the castle in one common ruin.

The Castle of Trinidad stood on the side of a hill, having by no means a difficult descent to the sea, but this hill was again commanded by a higher and more precipitous cliff, which would have enabled an enemy to drive out the occupants with ease, but for the peculiar construction of the fortress.

Next to the sea was a fort constructed with strong walls some 50 feet high. Behind this, and joined to it, rose another fort to the height of 30 or 40 feet more, and behind this again was a tower rising some 20 or 30 feet still higher, the whole presenting the appearance of a large church with a tower 110 feet high, a nave 90 feet high, and a chancel 50 feet. The tower, having its back to the cliff, as a matter of course sheltered the middle and lower portions of the fortress from a fire of the battery above it. Nothing, in short, for a fortress commanded by adjacent heights could have been better adapted for holding out against offensive operations, or worse adapted for replying to them ; this on our part being out of the question, as the French battery was too much elevated on the cliff for artillery to reach, whilst the tower which prevented their shot from annoying us, would also have prevented our firing at them, even had we possessed artillery.

It was to this tower therefore that the French chiefly directed their attention, as a practicable breach therein, followed by a successful assault, would in their estimation place the fortress at their mercy, so that we must either be driven out or forced to surrender. In consequence of the elevated position of the enemy's battery on the cliff, they could however only breach the central portion of the tower, the lowest part of the breach being nearly sixty feet above its base, so that, when practicable, it could only be reached by long scaling ladders.

A pretty correct idea of our relative positions may be formed if the unnautical reader will imagine our small force to be placed in the nave of Westminster Abbey, with the enemy attacking the great western tower from the summit of a cliff 100 feet higher than the tower, so that the breach in course of formation nearly corresponded to the great west window of the abbey. It will hence be clear that, in the face of a determined opposition, it would be no easy matter to scale the external wall of the tower up to the great west window, and more difficult still to overcome impediments presently to be mentioned, so as to get down into the body of the church. These were the points I had to provide against, for we could neither prevent the French from breaching nor storming.

It so happened, that just at the spot where the breach was in process of formation, there was a lofty bomb-proof interior arch, upwards of fifty feet in height. This arch, reaching from the lower part of the breach to the interior base of the tower, was without much difficulty converted into an obstacle, of which the French little dreamed ; viz. into a chasm, down which they must have plunged headlong had they attempted to penetrate an inch beyond the outer wall, even after they had gained it.

The only operation necessary was to break in the crown of the arch, so that all who on an assault ventured on penetrating farther than the outer wall of the breach, must of necessity be hurled to the bottom. But as the fall of a portion of the enemy

M

might not deter the rest from holding possession of the outer wall till they were provided with the means of overcoming the obstacle, I got together all the timber at hand, and constructed a huge wooden case, exactly resembling the hopper of a mill—the upper part being kept well greased with cooks' slush from the *Imperieuse*, so that to retain a hold upon it was impossible. Down this, with the slightest pressure from behind, the storming party must have fallen to a depth of fifty feet, and all they could have done, if not killed, would have been to remain prisoners at the bottom of the bomb-proof.

The mantrap being thus completed,—and to do the Spaniards justice, they entered with ardour into the work,—the next object was to prepare trains for the explosion of the magazines, in case evacuation of the fort became compulsory. This was done in two places; the first deposit of powder being placed underneath the breach, with the portfire so arranged as to go off in about ten mintues; the other beneath the remaining part of the fortress, with a portfire calculated to burn until we ourselves were safe on board the frigate.

The French were highly exasperated on finding that the castle had been reinforced from the *Imperieuse*, of which ship they had by this time not a few unpleasant reminiscences; they therefore adopted additional measures to put a stop to our co-operation.

In addition to the previously mentioned battery, another was erected on the cliff commanding the fortress; and on the 25th, upwards of 300 shots were directed at the tower, the result being a hole, which speedily widened into a tolerable breach. Our men were now engaged in blocking it up as fast as it was made, and working as they did under cover, no loss was sustained, though every shot brought down large masses of stone within the fortress; the French thus supplying us with materials for repair, though rendering a sharp look-out against splinters necessary.

On this day I received a wound, which caused me intolerable agony. Being anxious, during an ominous pause, to see what the enemy were about, I incautiously looked round an angle of the tower towards the battery overhead, and was struck by a

stone splinter in the face ; the splinter flattening my nose and
then penetrating my mouth. By the skill of our excellent doctor,
Mr Guthrie, my nose was after a time rendered serviceable.

Whilst the enemy were breaching the tower, the boats of the
Imperieuse inflicted on them such severe chastisement, that detachments of infantry were stationed on the hills to drive off the
boats with musketry ; but our people managed to keep out of
harm's way, whilst directing a destructive fire upon the nearer
portion of our opponents.

On the 26th the French renewed their fire ; but as during the
previous night we had filled up the breach with loose rubble,
their progress was by no means rapid, the rubble forming almost
as great an obstacle as did the wall itself. It was, however,
evident that the breach must sooner or later become practicable,
so that we turned our attention to the erection of interior barricades, in case of a sudden attempt to storm.   In addition to these
barricades festoons of top chains were brought from the ship, and
suspended over the hopper and elsewhere ; the chains being moreover armed with large fish-hooks, so securely fastened, that there
was little danger of those who were caught getting away before
they were shot.

The barricades constituted what may be termed a rampart
within the breach, constructed of palisades, barrels, bags of earth,
etc., these supplying the place of walls, whilst the descent from
the crown of the bomb-proof to the bottom constituted a formidable substitute for a ditch.

We got to-day a trifling though welcome reinforcement of sixty
regular Spanish, or rather Irish, troops in the Spanish service,
and sent an equal number of peasants to Rosas ; for though these
men were brave, as are all Catalans, and ready enough, yet their
want of military skill rendered them ill adapted to the work in
hand.   As soon as the Irish comprehended our means of defence,
and the reception prepared for the enemy, their delight at the
prospective mischief was highly characteristic, and could not have
been exceeded had they been preparing for a " scrimmage " in
their native country.

At midnight the French made a general assault on the town of Rosas, and after several hours' hard fighting obtained possession. The *Imperieuse* and *Fame* now approached, and commenced a fire which must have caused great loss to the besiegers, but which failed to dispossess them. Towards morning—when too late—a detachment of 2000 Spanish troops arrived from Gerona! Six hours earlier would have saved the town, the preservation of which was the only object in retaining the fortress.

The practice of the French when breaching the walls of Rosas was beautiful. So skilfully was their artillery conducted, that, to use a schoolboy similitude, every discharge " ruled a straight line " along the lower part of the walls ; this being repeated till the upper portion was without support, as a matter of course, the whole fell in the ditch, forming a breach of easy ascent. This operation constituted an object of great interest to us in the fortress, from which the whole proceedings were clearly visible.

Having secured the town, the French redoubled their efforts against the castle, and had they continued with the same vigour, we must have been driven out. Two of our marines were killed by shot, as was a third by a stone splinter, so that with all my desire to hold out, I began to doubt the propriety of sacrificing men to the preservation of a place which could not be long tenable.

The French being also heartily tired of the loss they were sustaining from the fire of the ships and boats, sent us a flag of truce, with the offer of honourable capitulation. This being declined on our part, the firing recommenced more heavily than before.

On the 28th the fire of the enemy slackened, their troops being engaged in throwing up intrenchments and constructing batteries in the town, a second detachment of Spanish troops being on its way now that the place had fallen. Soon after midday they sent a small party with another flag of truce. As it was, however, evident that their object was this time to spy out the state of our defences, we threw some hand grenades towards them, to show that we would not hold any parley, on which they retired, and the firing was again renewed.

On the 29th the French opened upon the castle from five different batteries on the hills, but without damage to life, as our men were now kept close. The ships and bombs, however, directed upon them a destructive fire with shot and shell, which considerably damped their ardour. To-day all access to the citadel was cut off, the French having succeeded in erecting batteries on both sides the sea gates, so that all communication with the boats was rendered impossible.

The dawn of the 30th might have been our last, but from the interposition of what some persons may call presentiment. Long before daylight I was awoke with an impression that the enemy were in possession of the castle, though the stillness which prevailed showed this to be a delusion. Still I could not re-compose myself to sleep, and after lying for some time tossing about, I left my couch and hastily went on the esplanade of the fortress. All was perfectly still, and I felt half ashamed of having given way to such fancies.

A loaded mortar, however, stood before me, pointed, during the day, in such a direction that the shell should fall on the path over the hill which the French must necessarily take whenever they might make an attempt to storm. Without other object than that of diverting my mind from the unpleasant feeling which had taken possession of it, I fired the mortar. Before the echo had died away, a volley of musketry from the advancing column of the enemy showed that the shell had fallen amongst them just as they were on the point of storming.

Rushing on, their bullets pattered like hail on the walls of the fort. To man these was the work of a moment; for, as may be supposed, our fellows did not wait for another summons, and the first things barely discernible amidst the darkness were the French scaling ladders ready to be placed at the foot of the breach, with an attendant body of troops waiting to ascend, but hesitating, as though the unexpected shell from our mortar rendered them uncertain as to our preparations for defence. To the purposeless discharge of that piece of ordnance we owed our safety, for otherwise they would have been upon us before we even suspected their presence ; and so exasperated were they at our obstinate defence, that very little attention would have been paid to any demand for quarter. The French deserved great credit for a silence in their movements which had not even attracted the attention of the sentries on the tower.

Whilst the enemy were hesitating, we became better prepared, our men being ready at every point which commanded the breach. It was not in the nature of the French to slink off on being detected. In a few minutes on they came up the ladders, to the certainty of getting either into the mantrap, or of being hurled from the walls as fast as they came up, retreat being for a short time impossible, on account of the pressure from behind. There was now just light enough for them to see the chasm before them, and the wall was crowded with hesitating men. About forty had gained the summit of the breach, all of whom were swept off with our fire ; whilst a crowd was waiting below for the chance of sharing the same fate. Giving them no time for deliberation, several shells which had been suspended by ropes half-way down the wall, were ignited, our hand grenades were got to work, and these, together with the musketry, told fearfully on the mass—which wavered for a few moments, and then retreated amidst the loud huzzas of our fellows. The French, however, gallantly carried off their wounded, though they were compelled to leave their dead, who, till the following morning, lay in a heap close to the foot of the tower.

Scarcely had we got rid of our assailants, when a numerous body of troops came down from the hills with muskets firing and drums beating, nothing doubting that their comrades were in possession of the fortress. Our lads, having their hands now free, returned their fire with excellent effect, dropping some at every discharge ; when at length, finding that the assault had failed, and that we were able to offer effectual resistance, the detachment retreated up the hills as fast as they could, amidst the derisive cheering of our men.

The force which formed the storming party, consisted, as we afterwards learned from our prisoners, of one company of grenadiers, two of carabineers, and four of the voltigeurs of the 1st Light Regiment of Italy, in all about 1200 men. They were gallantly led, two of the officers attracting my especial attention. The first was dropped by a shot, which precipitated him from the walls, but whether he was killed or only wounded, I do not know, probably wounded only, as his body was not seen by us amongst the dead. The other was the last man to quit the walls, and before he could do so, I had covered him with my musket. Finding escape impossible, he stood like a hero to receive the bullet, without condescending to lower his sword in token of surrender. I never saw a braver or a prouder man. Lowering my musket, I paid him the compliment of remarking, that so fine a fellow was not born to be shot down like a dog, and that, so far as I was concerned, he was at liberty to make the best of his way down the ladder ; upon which intimation he bowed as politely as though on parade, and retired just as leisurely.

In this affair we had only three men killed—one of the marines and two Spaniards, another Spaniard being shot through the thigh and the Spanish governor of the fortress through the hand ; there were, however, a few minor casualties. The total loss of the enemy, judging from the dead left behind—upwards of fifty— must have been severe. My determination not to quit the fortress was therefore increased, as there was every reason to be satisfied with the efficaey of my hopper trap and fish-hook chains. In short, it was impossible for any one to get over the one or through the other. Not a Frenchman had advanced beyond the outer wall.

After this the enemy did not molest us much, except with musketry, which did no damage, as our men were well under cover. They, however, turned their attention to the citadel, the Spanish garrison replying smartly to their fire. The Spaniards with us in the castle likewise behaved with great gallantry, as did the soldiers of the Irish brigades in the Spanish service, by whom the peasants before mentioned had been supplanted. Had the latter remained, the repulse of our assailants might have been more difficult, though equally certain.

On the 1st of December we passed a tolerably quiet day, the

French being engaged in erecting a new battery, to annoy our boats when coming on shore, with which they appeared to content themselves.

The 2nd passed over in the same quiet way.

On the 3rd the troops in the citadel made a sortie, apparently in the hope of dislodging the French from their intrenchments, and an obstinate engagement ensued, with considerable loss on both sides. By the time this was over, our friends on the hill had nearly completed another new battery, and were trying its effect on us somewhat unpleasantly, every shot knocking down great quantities of stone. A still more unpleasant circumstance was, that a heavy gale of wind had arisen, before which the *Imperieuse* was visibly dragging her anchors, and might be compelled to go to sea, leaving us to defend ourselves till her return.

On the 4th, the French opened all their batteries on the citadel, eleven of their guns being brought to bear upon the old breach elsewhere mentioned as never having been properly repaired. At this point an immense number of shot and shell were directed, and towards night a breach was nearly practicable. This operation against the citadel seeming decisive, the new battery on the hill began upon us in the castle with redoubled vengeance, and every shot told with effect; the object no doubt being to storm both fortresses simultaneously on the following day.

An unfortunate accident occurred in the castle to-day. Five of our men were loading a gun, intended for employment against a body of French troops, who were throwing up an intrenchment below us, with the evident object of cutting us off from retreat or communication with the frigate; by some mischance the gun exploded, blowing off the arms of a marine, who died soon after, and knocking a seaman over the castle wall, a depth of fifty feet. The poor fellow was taken up by the boat's crew, and carried on board in a dreadfully shattered condition.

At daylight on the 5th, the French again opened their batteries on the citadel, and by 8 A.M. the breach was quite practicable.

A large body of troops had assembled for the assault, but the firing suddenly ceased on both sides, and from the number of men lounging about the breach, it was clear that a capitulation was in progress. Under these circumstances it became my duty not to sacrifice our marines and seamen to the mere excitement of fighting a whole army which could now pay us undivided attention. We therefore began to think of taking our departure ; and getting our baggage collected, we made signals to the *Imperieuse* for all boats to be in readiness to take us off if the garrison in the citadel should capitulate. The battery, however, continued firing upon us as usual, and with decisive effect on the tower. Without taking any notice of this, we laid trains ready for blowing up the fort.

Soon after our signals were made, the *Fame* and *Magnificent*— the latter of which had recently come into the anchorage—got under weigh and beat towards the landing-place. Our signals having been also understood by the French, the batteries overhead ceased firing, and a number of troops approached to take possession. At 11 A.M. we made the signal for the boats—the *Imperieuse* attending them close in shore.

We now commenced evacuating the fortress, sending down the troops of the Bourbon regiment first ; the Irish brigade next, and our marines and seamen last. On the boats pulling in, the ships opened fire with shot and shell upon the French. We did not, however, receive any molestation from the latter, whilst our men went down the rope ladders out of the fort, and by one o'clock all were out of the castle except the gunner and myself, we having remained to light the portfires attached to the trains.

After this we got into the boats also unopposed, but the moment they pulled off from the shore the French opened upon us with musketry and round shot, fortunately without injury to any one. A stiff breeze now blowing, enabled the *Imperieuse* to get close in, so that we were soon on board.

The French having become practically acquainted with some of our devices were on their guard, and did not take possession of the castle immediately on our quitting it, and it was lucky for them that they did not, for shortly after we got on board the first explosion took place, blowing up the portion of the fortress which they had been breaching; but the second train failed, owing, no doubt, to the first shock disarranging the portfire. Had not this been the case, scarcely one stone of the castle would have remained on the other.

In the evening I directed the *Imperieuse* to get under weigh and stand towards La Escala, where we landed the Spanish troops. On the following morning the *Fame* parted company for Lord Collingwood's fleet; and leaving the *Magnificent* at anchor with the bombs, we stood towards San Felin, having the mortification of seeing the French flag flying over what remained of the Castle of Trinidad, which we had so pertinaciously endeavoured to defend, and failing in this, should have wholly destroyed but for the accident of the second portfire becoming out of order.

In the defence of this fortress, we lost only three killed and seven wounded; the loss of the Spaniards amounting to two killed and five wounded. Next to the thorough accomplishment of the work in hand my care was for the lives of the men. Indeed, it is matter of congratulation to me that no commander having gone through such service ever had fewer men killed. Lord St Vincent on a former occasion gave this as a reason for not promoting my officers, but even a rebuff so unworthy failed to induce me to depart from my system of taking care of the men, the death of one of whom would have affected me more than the death of a hundred enemies, because it would, in my estimation, have been attributable to my own want of foresight.

The destruction of the French must have been very great. We who were cooped up in the fortress had only one collision with them, but in that they suffered fearfully, whilst we escaped scot free. But the fire of the ships must have told upon them to a great extent.

The subjoined letters from Lord Collingwood to the Secretary of the Admiralty constitute the only commendations I received for the services detailed in the preceding chapters.

Extract of a letter from Vice-Admiral LORD COLLINGWOOD *to the* Hon. W. W. POLE, *dated on board the " Ocean," Dec.* 14, 1808.

" My letter of the 1st instant would inform you of the enemy having laid siege to the castle of Rosas, and of the measures taken by the British ships in that Bay in aid of the Spaniards for its defence. The *Scout* joined the squadron off Toulon on the 7th, and by her I received further accounts from Captain Bennett, of the *Fame*, of the progress the enemy was making against that important fortress.

" Captain Lord Cochrane has maintained himself in the posses- sion of Trinity castle with great ability and heroism. Although the fort is laid open by the breach in its works, he has sustained and repelled several assaults, having formed a sort of rampart within the breach with his ship's hammock cloths, awnings, etc., filled with sand and rubbish. *The zeal and energy with which he has maintained that fortress excites the highest admiration. His resources for every exigency have no end.* The Spanish governor of the castle is wounded and on board the *Meteor*.

" COLLINGWOOD."

This expression of opinion on the part of Lord Collingwood should have procured me some commendation from the naval authorities at home ; the more so as it was spontaneous on his lordship's part, no official despatch from me on the subject having at that time reached him. I was, however, a black sheep at the Admiralty, and, had it been my good fortune to have been instrumental in raising the siege of Rosas, the only care taken by the Tory government at home would, in all probability, have been how to conceal a knowledge of the fact from the public. After the evacuation and destruction of the fortress I addressed to Lord Collingwood the subjoined despatch.

" H.M. SHIP ' IMPERIEUSE,' BAY OF ROSAS, " *5th December*, 1808.

" MY LORD,—The fortress of Rosas being attacked by an army of Italians in the service of France (in pursuance of discretionary orders which your lordship gave me, to assist the Spaniards whenever it could be done with most effect), I hastened here. The citadel on the 22nd instant was already half invested, and the enemy was making his approaches towards the south-west bastion, which your lordship knows was blown down last war by the explosion of a magazine and tumbled into the ditch ; a few thin planks and dry stones had been put up by the Spanish engineers, perhaps to hide the defect ; all things were in the most deplorable state without and within ; even measures for their powder and saws for their fuses were not to be had, and mats and axes supplied their place. The castle of Trinity, situated on an eminence, but commanded by heights, was also invested. Three 24-pounders battered in breach, to which a fourth was afterwards added, and a passage through the wall to the lower boom-proof being nearly effected on the 23rd, the marines of the *Fame* were withdrawn. I went to examine the state of the castle, and, as the senior officer in the bay had not officially altered the orders I received from your lordship, I thought this a good opportunity, by occupying a post on which the acknowledged safety of the citadel depended, to render them an effectual service. The remaining garrison consisted of about eighty Spaniards, who were on the point of surrendering ; accordingly, I threw myself into the fort with fifty seamen and thirty marines of the *Imperieuse*. The arrangements I made need not be detailed to your lordship ; suffice it to say, that about a thousand bags (made of old sails, besides barrels and palisades), supplied the place of walls and ditches, and that the enemy, who assaulted the castle on the 30th with full 1000 picked men, were repulsed with the loss of their commanding officer, storming equipage, and all who had attempted to mount the breach. The Spanish garrison having been changed, gave good assistance. As to the officers, seamen, and marines of the ship, the fatigues they underwent, and the gallant manner in which they behaved, deserve every praise. I must, however, particularly mention Lieutenant Johnson, of the navy, Lieutenant Hoare, of the marines, Mr Burney, the gunner, Mr Lodowick, the carpenter, and Messrs Stewart, Sloven, and Marryat, midshipmen.

" Captain Hall, of the *Lucifer*, at all times and in every way gave his zealous assistance. I feel also indebted to Captain Collens, of the *Meteor*, for his aid.

" The citadel of Rosas capitulated at twelve o'clock this day. Seeing, my lord, farther resistance in the castle of Trinity useless, and impracticable against the whole army, the attention of which had naturally turned to its reduction ; after firing the trains for exploding the magazines, we embarked in the boats of the *Magnificent, Imperieuse,* and *Fame.*

" I have the honour to be, etc. (Signed) COCHRANE.

" The Right Hon. LORD COLLINGWOOD."

LORD COLLINGWOOD'S *Letter to the Admiralty*

" H.M. SHIP ' OCEAN,'
" *Jan.* 7, 1809.

" SIR,—The *Imperieuse* having with other ships been employed in the Bay of Rosas, to assist the Spaniards in defending the fortress, and Captain Lord Cochrane having taken on himself the defence of Trinity Castle, an outwork of that garrison, I have received from him a letter, dated the 5th of December, a copy of which is enclosed, stating the surrender of Rosas by the Spaniards on that day, and of his having embarked the garrison of Trinity Castle on board his ship from the castle destroyed.

" The heroic spirit and ability which have been evinced by Lord Cochrane in defending this castle, although so shattered in its works against the repeated attacks of the enemy, is an admirable instance of his lordship's zeal ; and the distinguished conduct of Lieutenants Johnson and Hoare, of the Royal Marines, and the officers and men employed in this affair under his lordship, will, doubtless, be very gratifying to my Lords Commissioners of the Admiralty.

(Signed, etc.) " COLLINGWOOD.

" To the SECRETARY OF THE ADMIRALTY."

To these despatches I may be pardoned for appending the following extract from the *Gerona Gazette*, as it appeared in the Naval Chronicle of 1809.

LORD COCHRANE

The Spanish *Gerona Gazette*, when inserting a letter from Lord Cochrane, January 1, 1809, subjoins the following liberal testimony to his noble conduct :—

" This gallant Englishman has been entitled to the admiration and gratitude of this country from the first moment of its political resurrection. His generosity in co-operating with our earliest efforts, the encouragement we received from the interest he took with the commanders of the Balearic islands, to induce them to succour us with troops and ammunition, can never be erased from our recollection. The extraordinary services which we owe to his indefatigable activity, particularly this city and the adjacent coast, in protecting us from the attempts of the enemy, are too well known to be repeated here. It is a sufficient eulogium upon his character to mention, that in the defence of the castle of Trinidad, when the Spanish flag, hoisted on the wall, fell into the ditch, under a most dreadful fire from the enemy, his lordship was the only person who, regardless of the shower of balls flying about him, descended into the ditch, returned with the flag, and happily succeeded in placing it where it was."

Without any degree of egotism, I may—considering that no praise beyond Lord Collingwood's was ever awarded to me for my defence of Trinidad—be excused from adducing the following remarks, known to be from the pen of Sir Walter Scott.

" Thus, in consequence of our co-operation, were the French detained a whole month before a neglected and ill-provided fortress, which, without that co-operation, could not have resisted the first attack. The event might have been different had there been a floating army off the coast—the whole of the besieging force might then have been cut off. Of the errors which the English Government committed in the conduct of the Spanish war, the neglect of this obvious and most important means of annoying the enemy, and advantaging our allies, is the most extraordinary. Five thousand men, at the disposal of Lord Cochrane or Sir Sidney Smith, or any of those numerous officers in the British navy who have given undoubted proofs of their genius as well as courage, would have rendered more service to the common cause *than five times that number on shore*, because they could at all times choose their points of attack, and the enemy, never knowing where to expect them, would everywhere be in fear, and everywhere in reach of the shore in danger.

" Lord Cochrane, during the month of September, 1808, with his single ship, the *Imperieuse*, kept the whole coast of Languedoc in alarm,—destroyed the numerous semaphoric telegraphs, which were of the utmost consequence to the numerous coasting convoys of the French, and not only prevented any troops from being sent from that province into Spain, but even excited such dismay that 2000 men were withdrawn from Figueras to oppose him, when they would otherwise have been marching farther into the peninsula. The coasting trade was entirely suspended during this alarm ; yet with such consummate prudence were all Lord Cochrane's enterprises planned and executed, that *not one of his men were either killed or hurt*, except one, who was singed in blowing up a battery."

For none of the services detailed in the last two chapters did I ever receive praise or reward from the Admiralty authorities ! though from the nature of the services they were necessarily accompanied by the deprivation of all chance of prize-money, either to myself, officers, or crew. The check opposed to the advance of the French in Catalonia—as testified by Lord Collingwood— was therefore made at *my expense*, without costing a farthing to the nation beyond the expenditure of ammunition ; a strange contrast to some of the costly expeditions of the period for less results, and one which ought to have secured for me anything but the political animosity with which all my services were regarded.

CHAPTER XVIII

CRUISE OF THE IMPERIEUSE CONTINUED

WHEN in the roads of San Felin, on the 7th of December, a boat came off with a request from the Spanish commandant that I would reconnoitre the enemy's position in the direction of Gerona. I had, at first, considerable doubts whether compliance with a request to act in a military capacity came within the sphere of a naval officer's duty ; but considering that Lord Collingwood's instructions were to aid the Spaniards by any means within my power, I resolved for once to forego my reluctance to leave the frigate, and accordingly accompanied the commandant and his staff in the direction of the enemy, whom we found assembled in such numbers as to render successful opposition out of the question.

Being unable to advise the Spaniards in this locality to adopt any beneficial course, or indeed how to act in any effective way against the enemy, we again sailed in the direction of Barcelona, where a Spanish force of 40,000 men, under General Vives, was closely investing the town so as to cut off supplies from the French garrison. As the consequent scarcity of provisions affected the inhabitants also, all who could afford to hire boats were quitting the place with their families ; the garrison offering no obstacle.

On the 17th, a body of French—or rather Italian troops embodied in the French army—made their appearance for the purpose of relieving the garrison. As they numbered only about 10,000, and the Spaniards fully 40,000, posted on the top of a hill, with every advantage in their favour, the defeat of the Franco-Italians appeared so much a matter of course as to induce me to go on shore to witness the engagement.

To my surprise, Vives allowed his flank to be turned, and the French attacking in front and rear at the same time the Spaniards became panic-struck, and fairly ran away. The rout was complete ; and it was with difficulty that I managed to get on board the frigate.

Shortly after gaining the ship, a boat full of officers was seen to put off from the shore and make for the *Imperieuse*. On coming alongside, it was reported to me that General Vives was amongst their number, on which I returned a message expressive of disbelief : adding that it could not be the general, for that to my certain knowledge he was on shore, driving back the French who were attempting to relieve Barcelona. After some hesitation, General Vives personally avowed himself, and demanded a conveyance for himself, officers, and 1000 men to Tarragona ; which demand being flatly refused, they left for the *Cambrian*, which lay at anchor not far off.

On the 19th we got under weigh, and soon after fell in with a vessel bound for Palamos, and crowded with families escaping from Barcelona, all of whom bitterly complained of the shameful treatment they had experienced at the hands of the French soldiery. On the 21st we came to off St Philou, which had just been plundered of everything.

Nothing material occurred till the 30th, when, beating up towards Caldagues Bay, we received intelligence that several French vessels, bound to Barcelona with provisions for the relief of the French army, were at anchor there. To attack these, as we had reason to believe that there was a considerable body of the enemy at Caldagues, and as the harbour was not more than half-a-mile broad, was a dangerous affair, on account of the necessity of anchoring within point-blank range of musketry. It was, however, of great importance that the provisions should not reach their destination, and, in place of waiting for them to proceed on their voyage, I decided on attacking them as the convoy lay at anchor.

At midday we were close to the entrance of the harbour, and made out the convoy and two vessels of war in charge of them,

N

the whole being protected by a battery and a number of French troops on the hills. Bringing the *Imperieuse* to an anchor we commenced firing on the vessels of war, one of which shortly afterwards sank ; when directing our attack on her consort, she also sank and fell on her broadside, the crew escaping on shore.

The protecting vessels being thus disposed of, we warped closer in shore for the purpose of silencing some guns which whilst engaged in sinking them had repeatedly struck us. In order to divide the enemy's attention, a party of marines was despatched to make a feint of landing near the town, whilst with the other marines and the blue jackets we dashed on shore between the former and the French, who were still firing on us from the battery. The latter, seeing the double attack and afraid of being cut off from their comrades in the town, ran off to the hills, abandoning their guns, which, on landing, we threw over the cliff, with the exception of four brass 18-pounders and one 24-pounder, which were taken on board the *Imperieuse*. We then blew up the magazine.

The coast being now clear, all boats were sent in to bring out eleven vessels laden with provisions, and by dark they were all close alongside, with our marines safely on board. They had, indeed, met with no opposition, the French troops in the town having run away and joined their comrades on the hills, the whole shortly afterwards marching in the direction of Rosas. During this affair the inhabitants remained quiet spectators on the hills— afraid to assist us, lest the French, who were certain to return on our departure, should retaliate after their usual fashion.

On the 21st we made an effort to raise the vessels of war which had sunk in shallow water near the shore, and after some time succeeded in stopping the leak of the one which had fallen over on her broadside, and was full of water, which being pumped out she floated and was towed alongside the frigate.

By this time a number of Spanish boats from the neighbouring coast came in, and without ceremony set to work plundering our prizes ! It was not till after some rough treatment from a party of marines sent for the protection of the captured vessels, that the

Spaniards were made to comprehend that the prizes belonged to us and not to them !

Towards midnight the Spaniards gave us information that the French, with reinforcements from Rosas, were on the point of re-entering the town.   We therefore sent a party of marines on board the brig-of-war, to protect her from recapture.

Early in the morning of the 1st of January, 1809, the enemy opened upon the brig with a smart fire of musketry, which the marines as smartly returned,—the frigate and a gun in the pinnace meanwhile plying the assailants with grape so effectually that they immediately abandoned their position, and marching round a hill, commenced firing from the other side, where, as the movement was anticipated by the frigate, they met with a similar reception immediately on showing themselves.   Finding us fully prepared at all points, they followed the example of their predecessors, and retreated to the hills, offering no further opposition, whilst we were engaged in weighing the other vessel of war, in which we succeeded also.   As soon as the French saw that they could not save either of these vessels, they abandoned the victuallers, and again marched off in the direction of Rosas.

The 2nd was employed in repairing our prizes, and in getting off other brass guns found on shore.   On the 3rd we blew up the barrack and another magazine close to the town, without any further interference on the part of the enemy.   Our operations being now completed, the smallest vessel of war was despatched to Lord Collingwood, off Toulon, with the following account of our success.

" HIS MAJESTY'S SHIP ' IMPERIEUSE,' CALDAGUES,
" 2nd January, 1809.

" MY LORD,—Having received information of two French vessels of war, and a convoy of victuallers for Barcelona being in this port, I have the honour to inform your lordship, that they are all—amounting to thirteen sail—in our possession.

" The French have been driven from the tower of Caldagues

with the loss of nine cannon, which they had mounted or were mounting on the batteries.

"I have the honour, etc.   COCHRANE.

"The Right Hon. LORD COLLINGWOOD."

"*La Gauloise*, cutter, 7 guns and 46 men, commanded by Mr Avanet, Member of the Legion of Honour.

"*La Julie*, lugger, 5 guns, 4 swivels, 44 men, commanded by Mr Chassereau.

"And eleven victuallers."

In consequence of which his lordship was pleased to write to the Admiralty as follows :—

"*Copy of a letter from* Vice-Admiral LORD COLLINGWOOD, *Commander-in-Chief of His Majesty's ships and vessels in the Mediterranean, to the* Hon. W. W. POLE, *dated on board the* '*Ocean*' *at sea, the 6th of May,* 1809.

"SIR,—I inclose—to be laid before their Lordships—a letter I have received from Lord Cochrane, captain of his Majesty's ship *Imperieuse*, who has been for some time past employed on the coast of Catalonia, and where the good services of his lordship in aid of the Spaniards and in annoyance of the enemy could not be exceeded.

"I have, etc.   COLLINGWOOD."

Having put to sea with our prizes, except the smallest, which we gave to the Spaniards,—the *Imperieuse* stood, on the 9th of January, towards Silva, anchoring in that port at 4 P.M. Observing a battery of ten guns mounted ashore, we landed, rolled them into the sea, and afterwards demolished the battery without opposition.

On the 10th, the Spaniards gave us intelligence of a large detachment of French troops being on their march from Rosas. Anticipating much the same kind of opposition as we had ex-

perienced at Caldagues, the marines were directed to take possession of the hill on which the demolished battery had been placed,
and soon afterwards the enemy was seen advancing in three
divisions. Shortly before reaching the hill, they halted and reconnoitred, after which they filed off towards the opposite
mountain, and piled their arms in sight of the ship.

About noon they were reinforced by great numbers, and the
whole advanced down the hill, their skirmishers keeping up a
brisk fire upon our marines. As it was impossible for these to
hold their position against such numbers, and as there was no
particular object in so doing, it became necessary to embark
them, for which purpose the boats had been placed in readiness.
On the first appearance of the reinforcement, the French re-
entered their battery, but only to find the iron guns thrown in the
sea and the brass ones in our possession. Exasperated at this,
they opened upon us so heavy a fire of musketry that we were
glad to get off as fast as we could, with the loss of three men.

Scarcely had we pushed off, when they manned a lower
battery, which we had not had time to destroy—but though they
fired very smartly, we had only two men wounded. It was fortunate we took precautions to re-embark the marines in time—
five minutes later would have lost us half their number, and we
might have been compelled to leave some of the wounded. It
was no less fortunate that, from the entrance being high and
narrow, I had, before anchoring in a passage so exposed, taken
the precaution of laying out a kedge to seaward, with something
like a mile of coir rope attached, to be used in case of emergency.
Hauling on this, we were quickly out of reach of the battery, but
again anchored just within our own range of the enemy, when the
frigate re-opened her fire with shot and shell, keeping up an inter-
mitting cannonade till after nightfall.

We learned in a curious way that the principal portion of the
troops who attacked us were Swiss! About midnight a boat
was reported alongside with a letter from the commandant of
the troops with which we had been engaged. Wondering what
he could want with me, I opened the letter, and found it to contain

a rigmarole account of himself and the extraordinary achievements of his regiment, which belonged to some canton whose
name I forget ; the letter concluding with a request for a few
bottles of rum ! ! I sent him the rum, together with a reply not
very complimentary to his country or present occupation.

On the 11th some of our missing men got on board, and reported that the French had received still larger reinforcements,
with heavy artillery, of which, indeed, we had ample proof, they
having this morning got their guns to bear so accurately, that
almost every shot struck us, so that it became necessary to display
the better part of valour, and be off.   The wind, unluckily for us,
had died away, but a southerly air at length springing up, we put
our prisoners ashore, and stood out of the bay, anchoring on the
following day at Caldagues.

It would be tedious to narrate the remainder of our cruise,
which chiefly consisted in sailing along the Spanish coast, and
firing upon French troops wherever they came within reach, this
being principally in the vicinity of Barcelona.

On one occasion only did we make much havoc amongst them,
viz., on the 22nd.   On the previous day we had been reconnoitring Barcelona, and fell in with the *Cyrene*.   Whilst rounding
a small promontory in company, we observed a foraging expedition of at least 5000 troops, with immense numbers of mules laden
with provisions,—the spoil of the surrounding country,—coming
along a road close to the sea.   Both ships immediately beat to
quarters, and running well within shot and shell range,commenced
a heavy fire, which told admirably on the troops and convoy, as
was evident from the disorder into which they were thrown.
After about two hours persevering—though not continuous fire,—
as from the strong breeze blowing, we were occasionally carried
past the enemy, and lost time in regaining our position ; the
French abandoned their line of march, and filed off into the
interior, the ships harassing their retreat with shells till they were
out of range.   The loss of the enemy on this occasion must
necessarily have been very severe.

On the 30th we joined Admiral Thornborough's squadron of

thirteen sail at Minorca. On the following day we received the unwelcome intelligence of Lieutenant Harrison's having been taken prisoner by the French. I had placed this excellent officer in command of the man-of-war cutter taken with the French convoy at Caldagues, and when off Tarragona he imprudently went on shore with only two hands, to gain information about us. On landing he was immediately surrounded by French troops, a body of whom was embarked in boats to regain possession of his cutter, but by promptly making sail she escaped.

Some time previous to this period I had applied to the Admiralty for permission to return to England. My reasons for the application were various, the ostensible ground being the state of my health, which had in reality suffered severely from the incessant wear and tear of body and mind to which for nearly two years I had been exposed. A more urgent reason was to get back to my place in the House of Commons, in order to expose the robberies of the Admiralty Courts in the Mediterranean, the officials of which were reaping colossal fortunes at the expense of naval officers and seamen, who were wasting their lives and blood for official gain! The barefaced peculations of these courts would be almost incredible, especially as regarded the Maltese Court, were there not some living at the present time who can testify to their enormity. To such an extent was this now carried, that a ship captured without cargo never yielded a penny to the captors, the whole proceeds being swallowed up by the Admiralty Court. With cargo, some trifling surplus might remain, but what between pilfering and official fees, the award was hardly worth the trouble of capture.

The effect of this upon the navy generally was most disastrous, and not upon the navy only, but upon the nation also, which had upwards of 1000 ships in commission without any result at all commensurable with the expenditure. Captains were naturally disinclined to harass themselves and crews for nothing, and avoided making prizes certain to yield nothing but the risk and trouble of capture, and which, in addition, might bring them in debt, as was the result in my own case.

It will now be evident why I preferred harassing the French army in Spain to making prizes for the enrichment of the officials of the Maltese and other Admiralty courts. It was always my aim to serve my country before my own interests, and in this case I judged it better to do so where the service could be most effectual. Prizes, of which the proceeds were monopolised by a body of corrupt officials, neither under the eye nor control of the government, were not worth troubling ourselves about; so I determined on a course of service where there were no prizes to take, but abundance of highly interesting operations to be undertaken. The frigate's officers and crew willingly seconding my views, I now—more on their account than my own—put on record that *none* of the services previously narrated, though lauded by the admirals commanding them, and by historians subsequently, were ever rewarded, either as regarded myself, or any one under my command, even promotion to the officers being shamefully withheld; their fault, or rather misfortune, consisting in having served under my command.

My chief motive, however, for wishing to return to England was, that during our operations against the French on the Spanish coast, I had seen so much of them as to convince me, that if with a single frigate I could paralyse the movements of their armies in the Mediterranean—with three or four ships it would not be difficult so to spread terror on their Atlantic shores, as to render it impossible for them to send an army into Western Spain. My object then was—as from long and unceasing experience I considered myself entitled to the command of more than one ship—to propose to the Government to take possession of the French islands in the Bay of Biscay, and to let me with a small squadron operate against the enemy's seaboard there, as I had previously done with the *Speedy* and *Imperieuse*, from Montpellier to Barcelona.

Had this permission been granted, I do not hesitate to stake my professional reputation that *neither the Peninsular war, nor its enormous cost to the nation, from* 1809 *onwards would ever have been heard of.* It would have been easy—*as it will always be easy in case of future wars*—that is, provided those who have the direction of national affairs have the sagacity to foresee disaster, and, *foreseeing it, to take the initiative*, so to harass the French coast as to find full employment for their troops at home, and thus to render any operations in Western Spain, or even in foreign countries, next to impossible.

By members not aware of this power of harassing an enemy's coast by means of a few frigates, the ministry was greatly blamed for not having sent a military force to Catalonia, instead of despatching the very inadequate force under Sir John Moore to the western shores of the Peninsula. That the latter step was a great mistake, likely only to end in disaster, is now admitted. But what I contend for is, that no military force was at all needed in Spain, had the government seized and held, by a comparatively small military force, the isles on the coast of France, viz., Isles Dieu, Rhe, Oléron, and a few others ; following up or preceding this seizure by a limited number of active frigates harassing the whole western coast of France, which, in consequence, would not have been able to send a single regiment into Spain, and hence, as has been said, we should have had no Peninsular war with its hundreds of millions of national debt. Had the French been thus employed in the defence of their own coasts, the Spaniards on the west coast would have been a match for their enemies, as, with the assistance of a few small British frigates, they were rendered a match for them on the east coast. This was the work I was prepared to recommend to the British Government ; considering, moreover, that from the part the *Imperieuse* had taken in harassing the enemy on the east coast of Spain, I was fairly entitled to ask that any small squadron of frigates, appointed for the purpose of operating on the west coast of France, should be placed under my command.

How my plans for this end, and together with them, my own career as a naval officer, were sacrificed by an occurrence which forms the subject of the next chapters, will there be seen.

The reader will by this time have gathered some idea of what the *Imperieuse* had effected, as testified by the warmly expressed satisfaction of Lord Collingwood ; yet it will scarcely be believed that, in place of approbation, I was reproached for the expenditure of more sails, stores, gunpowder, and shot than had been used by any other captain in the service !

CHAPTER XIX

APPOINTMENT TO COMMAND FIRE-SHIPS IN BASQUE ROADS

ALMOST immediately after the arrival of the *Imperieuse* at Plymouth, I received the subjoined letter from the Hon. Johnstone Hope, Second Lord of the Board of Admiralty :—

" ADMIRALTY,
" *March* 21, 1809.

" MY DEAR LORD,—I congratulate you on your safe arrival after the fatigues you underwent at Trinity. Be assured your exertions there were highly applauded by the Board, and were done most ample justice to by Lord Collingwood in all his despatches.

" There is an undertaking of great moment in agitation against Rochefort, and the Board thinks that your local knowledge and services on the occasion might be of the utmost consequence, and, I believe, it is intended to send you there with all expedition ; I have ventured to say, that if you are in health, you will readily give your aid on this business.

" Before you can answer this I shall be out of office, and on my way to Scotland, as I found I could not continue here and keep my health. But if you will write to Sir R. Brotherton in reply, and state your sentiments on the getting at the enemy at Rochefort, I am sure it will be kindly taken.

" I am, my dear Lord, yours faithfully,
" W. JOHNSTONE HOPE.

" Captain LORD COCHRANE."

On the receipt of this letter hope appeared to dawn. The St Vincent or any other official *animus* against me had evidently been satisfied with the punishments with which I had in one shape or other been visited. I was now to be consulted and employed on matters in which my experience and services were to be fully recognised, and my ambition of being ranked amongst those brave defenders of my country, to whose example I had looked up, was about to be fulfilled! Alas, for the simplicity of my ideas! Nothing could be farther from the intention of those who wanted to consult me!

Scarcely had the letter reached me, when a telegraphic message was transmitted from the Admiralty, requiring my immediate presence at Whitehall. A brief narrative of recent events will show the reason for the summons.

Early in the year Lord Gambier had been appointed to blockade the French fleet at Brest. Towards the end of February they, however, contrived to elude his vigilance, and got out without leaving a trace as to the direction taken. Despatching Admiral Duckworth in pursuit, his lordship returned to Plymouth. Admiral Duckworth meanwhile reached Cadiz, where he ascertained that the Brest fleet had not entered the Mediterranean. He then ran for Madeira, in the hope of obtaining intelligence of them, should they, as was feared in England, have made for the West Indies.

The fact was that the French squadron, consisting of eight sail of the line and two frigates, had gone to L'Orient, and liberated the ships there blockaded. They next made for Isle d'Aix, intending further to reinforce themselves with the ships at that anchorage, and thence proceed to harass our West India colonies. By the vigilance of Admiral Stopford they were, however, discovered and thwarted as to their ultimate purpose, though successful in forming a junction with the Rochefort squadron. On finding Admiral Stopford in their vicinity, though with four ships of the line only, they put into Basque Roads, subsequently withdrawing into Aix Roads, where Admiral Stopford having been reinforced, blockaded them with seven ships of the line. On the

7th of March Lord Gambier arrived in Basque Roads with an additional five sail, several frigates and small vessels, the British squadron being now numerically superior to that of the enemy.

On presenting myself at the Admiralty, the First Lord (Mulgrave) did me the honour to consult me confidentially as to the practicability of destroying or disabling the French squadron as it lay at anchor under the protection of the batteries of Isle d'Aix, where, as his lordship told me, the commander-in-chief did not consider it prudent to attack them. Lord Mulgrave further stated that the Board of Admiralty, fearing that "the French fleet might again slip out, as it had done at Brest, were extremely desirous that it should forthwith be destroyed. With that view they had already consulted various naval officers on the practicability of accomplishing the object by means of fire-ships ; but that their opinions were discouraging."

"Now," added his lordship, "you were some years ago employed on the Rochefort station, and must, to a great extent, be practically acquainted with the difficulties to be surmounted. Besides which, I am told that you then pointed out to Admiral Thornborough some plan of attack, which in your estimation would be successful. Will you be good enough again to detail that or any other plan, which your further experience may suggest ? But first let me tell you what Lord Gambier has written to the Admiralty on the subject."

Lord Mulgrave then read me an extract from Lord Gambier's letter, to the following effect, that " an attack by means of fire-ships was hazardous, if not desperate " ; but that " if the Board of Admiralty wished to order such an attack, it should be done secretly and quickly."

I respectfully reminded his lordship that he was asking me to suggest means for an attack which the admiral commanding considered " hazardous, if not desperate " ; and which other naval officers, no doubt my seniors in the service, had pronounced impracticable. On both these accounts there was reason to fear that if means suggested by me were adopted, the consequence would be an amount of ill-feeling on the part of those officers, which any naval officer in my position should feel reluctant to provoke.

Lord Mulgrave replied that "the present was no time for professional etiquette. The Board was, if possible, bent on striking some decisive blow before the French squadron had an opportunity of slipping out; for if their sailing were not prevented they might get off to the West Indies, and do our commerce an immense amount of mischief. However," added his lordship, "there is Lord Gambier's letter. Give me your opinion on it."

As this letter was afterwards made public, there can be no reason for withholding it.

"'CALEDONIA,' off the NERTUIS D'ANTIOCHE,
"11th March, 1809.

"MY DEAR LORD,—The advanced work between the Isles of Aix and Oleron, which I mentioned in my last letter, I find was injured in its foundation, and is in no state of progress; it is, therefore, no obstacle to our bombarding the enemy's fleet, if you should be disposed to attempt to destroy it.

"A trial was made six years ago, when a Spanish squadron lay at the same anchorage, but without effect. The report of it you will find in the Admiralty. It was made by Sir C. Pole.

"The enemy's ships lie much exposed to the operation of fire-ships, *it is a horrible mode of warfare, and the attempt hazardous if not desperate*; but we should have plenty of volunteers for the service. If you mean to do anything of the kind, it should be with secrecy and quickly, and the ships used should not be less than those built for the purpose—at least a dozen, and some smaller ones.

"Yours, my dear Lord, most faithfully,   GAMBIER.

"The Right Hon. LORD MULGRAVE."

"You see," said Lord Mulgrave, "that Lord Gambier will not take upon himself the responsibility of attack, and the

Admiralty is not disposed to bear the *onus* of failure by means of an attack by fire-ships, however desirous they may be that such attack should be made."

It was now clear to me why I had been sent for to the Admiralty, where not a word of approbation of my previous services was uttered. The Channel fleet had been doing worse than nothing. The nation was dissatisfied, and even the existence of the ministry was at stake. They wanted a victory, and the admiral commanding plainly told them he would not willingly risk a defeat. Other naval officers had been consulted, who had disapproved of the use of fire-ships, and, as a last resource, I had been sent for, in the hope that I would undertake the enterprise. If this were successful, the fleet would get the credit, which would be thus reflected on the ministry ; and if it failed, the consequence would be the loss of my individual reputation, as both ministry and commander-in-chief would lay the blame on me.

I had, however, no fear of failure in the plans at that moment uppermost in my mind, but from the way in which my co-operation was asked, I determined to have nothing to do with the execution of the plans, believing that I should have to deal with some who would rather rejoice at their failure than their success.

My reply to Lord Mulgrave, therefore, was, that, " the opinion of Lord Gambier, and the naval officers consulted by the Admiralty, as to the use of fire-ships, coincided with my own ; for if any such attempt were made upon the enemy's squadron, the result would in all probability be, that the fire-ships would be boarded by the numerous row-boats on guard,—the crews murdered,—and the vessels turned in a harmless direction. But that if, together with the fire-ships, a plan were combined which I would propose for his lordship's consideration, it would not be difficult to sink or scatter the guard-boats, and afterwards destroy the enemy's squadron, despite any amount of opposition that might be offered." I further told Lord Mulgrave that my opinion agreed with the expression of Lord Gambier, that the fortifications on Isle d'Aix were " no obstacle " ; though this opinion on my part was expressed for different reasons to the one assigned by his lordship, my own previous knowledge of the anchorage satisfying me that the channel was of sufficient breadth to enable an attacking force to interpose the enemy's fleet between itself and Isle d'Aix, as well as to keep out of reach of the fortifications on Aix, even though those fortifications might be in a state of efficiency, in place of being "no obstacle," from their dilapidated condition, as Lord Gambier had, no doubt, correctly described them.

I then briefly recapitulated to his lordship the outline of my plan, which, if seconded by the fleet, must certainly result in the total destruction of the French squadron. His lordship appeared very much gratified by the communication, and after praising its novelty and completeness, frankly expressed his entire confidence in the result, requesting me to put the substance of my suggestion in writing, so that he might at once lay it before the Board of Admiralty, which was then sitting.

The request was immediately complied with, and the letter placed in the hands of Lord Mulgrave, who shortly afterwards personally communicated to me his own satisfaction, and the entire concurrence of the Board in my plan. His lordship at the same time asked me "if I would undertake to put it in execution?"

I told him that "for reasons before assigned I would rather not do so, as being a junior officer, it would excite against me a great amount of jealousy. Besides which Lord Gambier might consider it presumptuous on my part to undertake what he had not hesitated to describe as 'hazardous, if not desperate.' It was, moreover, by no means certain that Lord Gambier would be satisfied to put my plans in execution, as it was not impossible that he might deem them still more 'desperate' and 'horrible' than those to which he had already objected. I, however, assured his lordship that the plans were at the service of the Admiralty, and Lord Gambier also, irrespective of any share in their execution to which I might be considered entitled."

"But," objected his lordship, "all the officers who have been consulted deem an attack with fire-ships impracticable, and after such an expression of opinion, it is not likely they would be offended by the conduct of fire-ships being given to another officer who approved of their use."

My answer was, " that the plan submitted to his lordship was not an attack with fire-ships alone, and when its details became known to the service, it would be seen that there was no risk of failure whatever, if made with a fair wind and flowing tide. On the contrary, its success on inspection must be evident to any experienced officer, who would see that as the enemy's squadron could not escape up the Charente, their destruction would not only be certain, but, in fact, easy. The batteries on Isle d'Aix were scarcely worth notice, not so much from their dilapidated condition, though that was rightly estimated in Lord Gambier's letter, as from there being plenty of room to steer clear of them, as well as from the ease with which the enemy's ships might be brought between the fortifications and the ships attacking ; the channel being sufficient for this purpose, as well as for their passage without any exposure to shot likely to be detrimental. As all this would be apparent to the officers of the fleet whenever the plan submitted should be communicated to them, I must emphatically repeat my objection to undertake its execution, not only on this ground, but for the additional reason that my health had been so much shattered by recent exertions as to require repose."

Lord Mulgrave did not deny the reasonableness of my objections, admitting that " although he did not believe Lord Gambier would feel hurt at my undertaking to put my own plan in execution, other officers might not be well pleased that its superintendence should be committed to a junior officer. On this ground he would reconsider the matter, and endeavour to find some one else to put it in execution."

I then took leave of Lord Mulgrave, who, next day, again sent for me, when he said, " My lord, you must go. The Board cannot listen to further refusal or delay. Rejoin your frigate at once. I will make you all right with Lord Gambier. Your own confidence in the result has, I must confess, taken me by surprise, but it has increased my belief that all you anticipate will be ac-

ADMIRAL LORD GAMBIER, G.C.B.
[Born 1756.   Died 1833]

complished. Make yourself easy about the jealous feeling of senior officers ; I will so manage it with Lord Gambier that the *amour propre* of the fleet shall be satisfied."

On this I requested a short time for final consideration, and before its expiration sent a letter to his lordship again declining the command ; but at the same time informing him that it had ever been a maxim with me not to shrink from duty to my country under any circumstances, however disadvantageous to myself, and that if officers my seniors could not be found to put the project in execution, I would then waive further objection.

The immediate result was the following letter from Lord Mulgrave, who, contrary to the tenour of mine, had construed it into an unqualified acceptance of the command.

[Private.]

"ADMIRALTY,
"*March* 25, 1809.

" MY DEAR LORD,—The letter I have just received from your lordship is truly characteristic of the whole tenour of your professional life. If your health will admit of your undertaking the important service referred to, I am fully persuaded that I cannot so well commit it to any others.

" I have the honour to be, with the highest esteem, your lordship's most faithful servant, MULGRAVE.

" The LORD COCHRANE."

" *P.S.*—I think the sooner you go to Plymouth the better. You will there receive an order to join Lord Gambier, to whom a secret letter will be written, directing him to employ your lordship on the service which we have settled against the Rochefort fleet."

I have been thus minute in detailing the circumstances connected with my acceptance of a command so unusual, because it has been said, and for anything that has appeared to the contrary, may still be considered, that I thrust myself into the

o

position, which, as my own foresight had anticipated, became eventually a very serious one for me, as bringing upon my head an amount of enmity, such as even my own misgivings had not considered possible.

Having made the requisite suggestions to Lord Mulgrave relative to the contents and mode of fitting up the explosion vessels, the fire-ships to be employed being of the usual description, I returned on board the *Imperieuse* at Plymouth, there to await further orders from the Admiralty.

Such was the despatch used, that by the 19th of March the Board was in a position to apprise Lord Gambier of the steps taken, by the following letter addressd to his lordship by the Board of Admiralty.

"ADMIRALTY OFFICE,
"*March* 19, 1809.

" MY LORD,—I am commanded by my Lords Commissioners of the Admiralty to acquaint your lordship, that they have ordered twelve transports to be fitted as fire-ships, and to proceed and join you off Rochefort ; and that Mr Congreve (afterwards Sir W. Congreve) is under orders to proceed to your lordship in a coppered transport (the *Cleveland*), containing a large assortment of rockets, and supplied with a detachment of marine artillery, instructed in the use of them, and placed under Mr Congreve's orders.

" That the vessels named in the margin (*Etna, Thunder, Vesuvius, Hound,* and *Fury*), are likewise under orders to fit for sea with all possible expedition, and to join you as soon as they may be ready. That all preparations are making with a view to enable your lordship to make an attack upon the French fleet at their anchorage off Isle d'Aix, if practicable ; and I am further commanded to signify their Lordships' directions to you, to take into your consideration the possibility of making an attack upon the enemy, either conjointly with your line-of-battle ships, frigates, and small craft, fire-ships, bombs, and rockets—or separately by any of the above-named means.

" It is their Lordships' further direction, that you state to me for their information, whether any further augmentation of force of any description is in your opinion necessary to enable you to perform this service with full effect, that it may be prepared and forwarded to you without a moment's delay—their Lordships having come to a determination to leave no means untried to destroy the enemy's squadron.

(Signed) " W. W. POLE.

" The Right Hon. LORD GAMBIER."

Lord Gambier's reply to this intimation, that on the receipt of the above-mentioned appliances he would be expected to attack the French squadron, was, that " *if the Board* deemed an attack practicable, he would obey any orders with which they might honour him, however great might be the loss of men and ships." A plain declaration that he *still declined to take upon himself the responsibility of attack.*

It will be necessary to bear this fact in mind, as after the attack was made, Lord Gambier, in his first despatch to the Admiralty, gave me credit for everything but the success of my plan, and in his second despatch *omitted my name altogether as having had anything to do with either planning or executing it* ! ! ! and in the vote of thanks subsequently given to his lordship in parliament, the officers under my orders were thanked, but no mention whatever was made of me, either as having conducted, or even taken any part in the attack, the whole merit of which was ascribed to Lord Gambier, who was never nearer than nine miles to the scene of action, as will subsequently appear.

Lord Gambier's answer to the previous letter from the Board is, however, so material to the right understanding of the events which followed, that it will be better to subjoin the whole of it.

" ' CALEDONIA,' in BASQUE ROADS,
" *March* 26, 1809.

" SIR,—In obedience to their Lordships' directions to me, contained in your letter of the 19th instant, I beg leave to state that it is advisable that I should be furnished with six gun-brigs in addition to those I may be able to collect of such as are under my command ; at present there are only two at this anchorage. I shall, however, order the *Insolent* and *Contest* to join me from Quiberon Bay ; and I should hope that the *Martial* and *Fervent* will shortly return from Plymouth.

" It is proper I should state for their Lordships' information, the position in which the French fleet is at present anchored under the Isle d'Aix, that their Lordships may be able to form a judgment of the success that may be expected to attend an attack upon the enemy's fleet, in either of the modes directed by their Lordships in your letter above-mentioned.

" The enemy's ships are anchored in two lines, very near each other, in a direction due south from the Isle d'Aix, and the ships in each line not farther apart than their own length ; by which it appears, as I imagined, that the space for their anchorage is so confined by the shoaliness of the water, as not to admit of ships to run in and anchor clear of each other. The most distant ships of their two lines are within point-blank shot of the works on the Isle d'Aix ; such ships, therefore, *as might attack the enemy would be exposed to be raked by red-hot shot, etc., from the island, and should the ships be disabled in their masts, they must remain within range of the enemy's fire until they are destroyed*—there not being sufficient depth of water to allow them to move to the southward out of distance.

" The enemy having taken up their position apparently with the view not only to be protected by *the strong works on the Isle d'Aix*, but also to have the entrance of the Charente open to them, that in case of being attacked by fire-ships and other engines of the kind, they can run up the river beyond the reach of them. The tide and wind that are favourable to convey this kind of annoyance to the enemy, serve equally to carry them up the river.

" With respect to the attempt that may be made to destroy the enemy's ships with shells, etc., I am not competent to give an opinion until it is ascertained whether the booms can be placed within the reach of their mortars from the enemy's ships, without being exposed to the fire of the Isle d'Aix.

" I beg leave to add that, *if their Lordships* are of opinion that an attack on the enemy's ships by those of the fleet under my command is practicable, I am ready to obey any orders they may be pleased to honour me with, *however great the risk may be of the loss of men and ships.*

" I have the honour, etc.   GAMBIER.

" The Hon. W. W. POLE."

I have marked some passages of this singular letter in italics, for the purpose of showing their important bearing on subsequent events. On the 11th Lord Gambier had informed the Board of Admiralty—as to my own personal knowledge was the fact—that " the advanced work on the Isle d'Aix was *no obstacle to bombardment.*" " Now," says his lordship, " *the ships attacking would, from the fire of this fort, be exposed to be raked by red-hot shot, and if disabled in their masts, must be destroyed.*" In the former letter his lordship stated that the fort was " *injured in its foundations*, and in no state of progress." It is now characterised as " *the strong works* " on *the* Isle d'Aix.

That there was really little damage to be feared from these fortifications, either to ships or bombs, was afterwards corroborated by the fact, that when a partial attack only was reluctantly made, neither suffered from their fire, the result proving that these works had from the first been rightly characterised by Lord Gambier as "*forming no obstacle*," though magnified into " strong works."

In my interview with Lord Mulgrave, I had stated to his lordship, that the works on the Isle d'Aix were no impediment, because of the facility with which the enemy's ships could be brought between the attacking British force and the fortifications, so as completely to interpose between the fire of the latter. Lord Gambier does not appear to have taken this view, but he completely proved its soundness by stating that the enemy's ships lay within point-blank shot of their own works, so as to expose them to the fire of their own forts, on Aix, if these fired at all, whilst my previous knowledge of the anchorage made it a matter of certainty to me, that it was not difficult for the British fleet to place the enemy in such a position. Lord Gambier's assertion was one of the main points relied on in the subsequent court-martial, and his lordship's own letter just quoted is in direct contradiction to the evidence upon which he relied for acquittal.

A more singular declaration is made by his lordship, that if the enemy were attacked by " fire-ships and other engines of the kind, they could run up the river beyond their reach." In place of this the result, as will presently be seen, proved that the attempt to do so only ended in all running ashore, with the ex-ception of two, and they ultimately escaped up the river because they were not attacked at all ! But we must not anticipate.

Had Lord Gambier been, as I was, from having previously blockaded Rochefort in the *Pallas*, practically acquainted with the soundings, he must have taken the same views that I had laid before Lord Mulgrave, and in place of writing to the Admiralty all sorts of evil forebodings to " men and ships," he would have seen that the attack, with the means indicated, was certain in effect, and easy of accomplishment.

CHAPTER XX

ARRIVAL AT BASQUE ROADS

WITHOUT waiting to convoy the fire-ships and explosion vessels, the *Imperieuse* sailed forthwith for Basque Roads in order to expedite the necessary arrangements, so that on their arrival no time might be lost in putting the project in execution ; a point on which the Board of Admiralty was most urgent, not more in a belligerent than a political point of view, for as has been stated, the public was dissatisfied that the enemy had been permitted to escape from Brest; whilst our West Indian merchants were in a state of panic lest the French squadron, which had escaped the vigilance of the blockading force before Brest, might again slip out, and inflict irretrievable disaster on their colonial interests, then the most important branch of our maritime commerce.

The *Imperieuse* arrived in Basque Roads on the 3rd of April, when I was received with great urbanity by the commander-in-chief; his lordship without reserve communicating to me the following order from the Admiralty :—

"ADMIRALTY OFFICE,
"25th March, 1809.

"My LORD,—My Lords Commissioners of the Admiralty having thought fit to select Captain Lord Cochrane for the purpose of conducting, under your lordship's direction, the fire-ships to be employed in the projected attack on the enemy's squadron off Isle d'Aix, I have their Lordships' commands to signify their direction to you to employ Lord Cochrane in the above-mentioned service accordingly, whenever the attack shall take place ; and I am to acquaint you that the twelve fire-ships, of which you already had notice, are now in the Downs in readiness, and detained only by contrary winds, and that Mr Congreve is also at that anchorage, with an assortment of rockets, ready to proceed with the fire-ships.

" I am also to acquaint you that the composition for the six transports, sent to your lordship by Admiral Young, and 1000 carcases for 18-pounders, will sail in the course of three or four days from Woolwich, to join you off Rochefort.

" I have, etc. etc.   W. W. POLE.

" Admiral LORD GAMBIER."

Whatever might have been the good feeling manifested by Lord Gambier, it did not, however, extend to the officers of the fleet, whose *amour propre* Lord Mulgrave had either not attempted, or had failed to satisfy. Every captain was my senior, and the moment my plans were made known, all regarded me as an interloper, sent to take the credit from those to whom it was now considered legitimately to belong. " Why could we not have done this as well as Lord Cochrane ? " was the general cry of the fleet, and the question was reasonable ; for the means once devised, there could be no difficulty in effectually carrying them out. Others asked, " Why did not Lord Gambier permit us to do this before ? " the second query taking much of the sting from the first, as regarded myself, by laying the blame on the commander-in-chief.

The ill-humour of the fleet found an exponent in the person of Admiral Harvey, a brave Trafalgar officer, whose abuse of Lord Gambier to his face was such as I had never before witnessed from a subordinate. I should even now hesitate to record it as incredible, were it not officially known by the minutes of the court-martial in which it some time afterwards resulted.

On ascertaining the nature of my mission, and that the conduct of the attack had been committed to me by the Board of Admiralty, Admiral Harvey came on board the flag-ship with a list of officers and men who volunteered, under his direction, to perform the service which had been thrust upon me. On Lord Gambier informing him that the Board had fixed upon me for the purpose, he said, " he did not care ; if he were passed by, and Lord Cochrane or any other junior officer was appointed in preference, he would immediately strike his flag, and resign his commission ! "

Lord Gambier said he " should be sorry to see him resort to such an extremity, but that the Lords of the Admiralty having fixed on Lord Cochrane to conduct the service, he could not deviate from their Lordships' orders."

On this explanation being good-naturedly made by Lord Gambier, Admiral Harvey broke out into invectives of a most extraordinary kind, openly avowing that " he never saw a man so unfit for the command of the fleet as Lord Gambier, who instead of sending boats to sound the channels, which he (Admiral Harvey) considered the best preparation for an attack

on the enemy, he had been employing, or rather amusing himself with mustering the ships' companies, and had not even
taken the pains to ascertain whether the enemy had placed any
mortars in front of their lines ; concluding by saying, that had
Lord Nelson been there, he would not have anchored in Basque
Roads at all, but would have dashed at the enemy at once."

Admiral Harvey then came into Sir Harry Neale's cabin, and
shook hands with me, assuring me that " he should have been
very happy to see me on any other occasion than the present.
He begged me to consider that nothing personal to myself was
intended, for he had a high opinion of me ; but that my having
been ordered to execute such a service, could only be regarded
as an insult to the fleet, and that on this account he would
strike his flag so soon as the service was executed." Admiral
Harvey further assured me that " he had volunteered his
services, which had been refused."

To these remarks I replied : " Admiral Harvey, the service on
which the Admiralty has sent me was none of my seeking. I
went to Whitehall in obedience to a summons from Lord Mulgrave, and at his lordship's request gave the Board a plan of
attack, the execution of which had been thrust upon me, contrary to my inclination, as well knowing the invidious position
in which I should be placed."

" Well," said Admiral Harvey, " this is not the first time I
have been lightly treated, and that my services have not been
attended to in the way they deserved ; because I am no canting
methodist, no hypocrite, no psalm-singer, and do not cheat old
women out of their estates by hypocrisy and canting ! I have
volunteered to perform the service you came on, and should
have been happy to see you on any other occasion, but am very
sorry to have a junior officer placed over my head."

" You must not blame me for that," replied I : " but permit
me to remark that you are using very strong expressions relative
to the commander-in-chief."

" I can assure you, Lord Cochrane," replied Admiral Harvey,
" that I have spoken to Lord Gambier with the same degree of

prudence as I have now done to you in the presence of Captain Sir H. Neale."

" Well, admiral," replied I, " considering that I have been an unwilling listener to what you really did say to his lordship, I can only remark that you have a strange notion of prudence."

We then went on the quarter-deck, where Admiral Harvey again commenced a running commentary on Lord Gambier's conduct, in so loud a tone as to attract the attention of every officer within hearing, his observations being to the effect that "Lord Gambier had received him coldly after the battle of Trafalgar, that he had used him ill, and that his having forwarded the master of the *Tonnant's* letter for a court-martial on him, was a proof of his methodistical, jesuitical conduct, and of his vindictive disposition ; that Lord Gambier's conduct, since he took the command of the fleet, was deserving of reprobation, and that his employing officers in mustering the ships' companies, instead of in gaining information about the soundings, showed himself to be unequal to the command of the fleet." Then turning to Captain Bedford, he said, " You know you are of the same opinion."

Admiral Harvey then left the ship, first asking Captain Bedford " whether he had made his offer of service *on any duty* known to the commander-in-chief ? " To which Captain Bedford replied in the affirmative.

My reason for detailing this extraordinary scene, the whole of which, and much more to the same effect, will be found in the minutes of the court-matrial previously referred to—is to show into what a hornet's nest my plans had involuntarily brought me. It may readily be imagined that I bitterly regretted not having persisted in my refusal to have anything to do with carrying them into execution, for now they were known, all believed—and, being my senior officers, had no doubt a right to believe—that they could execute them better than myself.

So far as regarded the neglect to take soundings of even the approaches to the channel leading to the enemy's fleet, Admiral Harvey was quite right in his statement. Nothing of the kind had been attempted beyond some soundings on that part of the Boyart shoal, *farthest from the French fleet*! Had not my previous knowledge of the anchorage, as ascertained in the *Pallas* a few years before, supplied all the information necessary for my conduct of the plans proposed, this neglect would in all probability have been fatal to their execution. Unlike Admiral Harvey, I am not, however, prepared to blame Lord Gambier for the neglect, as a slight acquaintance with the masters, whose duty it was to have made the examination, showed me that they were quite capable of misleading the commander-in-chief, by substituting their own surmises for realities. Certain it was, that although no soundings whatever of the approaches to the enemy's fleet had been taken, those whose duty it was to have made them, as far as practicable, pretended to know more of the anchorage than I did! and had, no doubt, impressed the commander-in-chief that their reports were founded on actual observations.

How far Admiral Harvey was justified in his intemperate allusions to the "*musters*" and *quasi* religious practices on board the fleet, is a point upon which I do not care to enter, further than to state that these "musters" were found to relate to catechetical examinations of the men, and that I had not been many days in the fleet before the commander-in-chief sent a number of tracts on board the *Imperieuse*, with an injunction for their distribution amongst the crew.

Having by this time ascertained that, rightly or wrongly, the fleet was in a state of great disorganisation on account of the orders given to various officers for the distribution of tracts, and being naturally desirous of learning the kind of instruction thereby imparted, I found some of them of a most silly and injudicious character, and therefore declined to distribute them, but imprudently selected some, and sent them to my friend Cobbett, together with a description of the state of the fleet, in consequence of the tract controversy. It was a false step, though I did not at the time contemplate the virulent animosity which might be excited at home from Cobbett's hard-hitting comments, nor the consequent amount of enmity to myself, which only ceased with my eventual removal from the navy !

The fact was, that the fleet was divided into two factions, as bitter against each other as were the Cavaliers and Roundheads in the days of Charles I. The above-mentioned imprudent step incurred the ill-will of both parties. The tractarian faction, consisting for the most part of officers appointed by Tory influence or favour of the Admiral, and knowing my connection with Burdett and Cobbett, avoided me ; whilst the opposite faction, believing that from the affair of the tracts I should incur the irreconcilable displeasure of Lord Gambier, lost no opportunity of denouncing me as a concocter of novel devices to advance my own interests at the expense of my seniors in the service.

Strange as it may appear, almost the only persons who treated me with consideration were Lord Gambier, his second in command, Admiral Stopford, and his flag-captain, Sir H. Neale.

For this urbanity Lord Gambier had to incur the bitter sarcasm of the fleet—that when the Admiralty wanted to attack the enemy with fire-ships, he had denounced the operation as a " horrible and anti-Christian mode of warfare " ; but that now he saw my plan of explosion vessels, in addition to fire-ships, was likely to be crowned with success, he no longer regarded it in the same light.

It was evident that amidst these contending factions, so fatal in a fleet where all ought to be zeal and unity of action—I should have to depend on myself. Disregarding, therefore, the disunion prevalent, and, indeed, increased four-fold by the further division of opinion with respect to Admiral Harvey's disrespectful expressions to the commander-in-chief, I determined to reconnoitre for myself the position of the French ships, especially as regarded their protection by the batteries on Isle d'Aix, and for this purpose made as minute a *reconnaissance* as was practicable.

Perhaps it ought to have been previously mentioned, that on

the evening of our arrival, I had gone close in to the island, and had embodied the result of my observations in the following letter to Lord Mulgrave, to whom I considered myself more immediately responsible.

"'IMPERIEUSE,' BASQUE ROADS,
"3rd April.

"MY LORD,—Having been very close to the Isle d'Aix, I find that the western sea wall has been pulled down to build a better. At present the fort is quite open, and may be taken as soon as the French fleet is driven on shore or burned, which will be as soon as the fire-ships arrive. The wind continues favourable for the attack. If your lordship can prevail on the ministry to send a military force here, you will do great and lasting good to our country.

"Could ministers see things with their own eyes, how differently would they act! but they cannot be everywhere present, and on their opinion of the judgment of others must depend the success of war—possibly the fate of England and all Europe.

"No diversion which the whole force of Great Britain is capable of making in Portugal or Spain, would so much shake the French government as the capture of the islands on this coast. A few men would take Oleron; but to render the capture effective, send twenty thousand men, who, without risk, would find occupation for a French army of a hundred thousand.

"The batteries on Oleron are all open, except two of no importance. Isle Gros would also be of infinite use to our cruisers in the destruction of the French trade.

"The commerce on this coast—and indeed on all the French coasts—is not inferior to that of England in number of vessels and men employed, though not in size of coasting craft.

"The coasting trade is the great nursery of English seamen, and yet we strangely affect to despise the French coasting trade. Must not the corn of the French northern provinces give food to the south? Are the oil and wine of the south of no consequence to those who grow none for themselves? I do not state these matters to your lordship but as an answer to the opinions generally current in England, and indeed, too much entertained in the naval service also.

" Ships filled with stones would ruin for ever the anchorage of Aix, and some old vessels of the line well loaded would be excellent for the purpose.

" I hope your lordship will excuse the way in which I have jumbled these thoughts together. My intentions are good, and if they can be of any use, I shall feel happy.

" I have the honour to be, my Lord, your most obedient servant,   COCHRANE.

" The Right Hon. LORD MULGRAVE."

In this hurried letter the reader will readily recognise the principles laid down by me in a former chapter, for the most advantageous mode of warfare, viz. by harassing the enemy on his own coast, and by a perpetual threat of a descent thereon at any moment, to prevent his employing his forces elsewhere.

In place of the advice being even taken in good part, I had afterwards reason to know, that the views briefly expressed in this letter were regarded by the government as an act of impertinence. Yet nothing could be more sound. The French islands captured, and occupied by an adequate force, protected by a few ships, would have kept the enemy's coasts in a constant state of alarm, so that it would have been impossible for the enemy to detach armies to the Spanish peninsula ; had this policy been pursued, the Peninsular war, as has been stated in a former chapter, and its millions of National Debt, would never have been heard of. So much does the useful or useless expenditure of war depend on the decision of a cabinet, which can practically know little of the matter.

As it was—the French laughed at the clouds of cruisers intent on watching their coasting trade, which was carried on almost without interruption ; our vessels going in shore in the day time, when the French coasters kept close under their batteries, and going off shore in the night, when they pursued their course unmolested. Provisions and stores were thus moved as wanted from one part of the enemy's coast to another with absolute safety. The great number of prizes which had fallen to the lot of the *Speedy*, *Pallas*, and *Imperieuse* was almost solely owing to our working in shore at night, when the enemy's coasters were on the move. In the day time we are usually out of sight of land, with the men fast asleep in their hammocks.

To return from this digression to the *reconnaissance* of the enemy's works on Isle d'Aix.

The opinion which I had expressed to Lord Mulgrave respecting the trifling importance of these works was strengthened on actual inspection ; indeed any opposition which they could have offered was too insignificant for notice, as was afterwards proved when a partial attack took place.

I could not say as much to Lord Gambier, after the opinion he had expressed in his letter to the Admiralty, for this would have amounted to a flat contradiction of his judgment, even though, as was afterwards known, such opinion had been formed on the reports of others, who gave his lordship their surmises as ascertained facts, an assertion which will be hereafter fully demonstrated.

In place, therefore, of officially reporting the result of my *reconnaissance*, I urged upon his lordship not to wait the arrival of the fire-ships from England, but as the fleet had abundance of materials, rather to fit up, as fire-ships and explosion vessels, some transports which happened to be present.

With this request Lord Gambier promptly complied, manifesting his anxious desire that my project should be put in execution without delay. Several vessels were, therefore, chosen for the purpose ; the fire-ships being prepared by the fleet, whilst I worked hard at the explosion vessels, two, at least, of which I determined to conduct personally ; not because I deemed myself more competent to conduct them than others, but because being novel engines of warfare, other officers could not have given that attention to their effect which long deliberation on my part had led me to anticipate, if directed according to the method on which their efficacy depended; it being certain, even from the novelty of such a mode of attack, that the officers and crews of the line-of-battle ships would be impressed with the idea that every fire-ship was an explosion vessel, and that in place of offering opposition, they would, in all probability, be driven ashore in their attempt to escape from such diabolical engines of warfare, and thus become an easy prey. The creation of this terrorism amongst the enemy's ships was indeed a main feature of the plan, the destruction or intimidation of the guard-boats being secondary, or rather preparatory.

The nature of the explosion vessels will be best understood from the subjoined description of the manner in which one was prepared under my own directions. The floor of the vessel was rendered as firm as possible, by means of logs placed in close contact, into every crevice of which other substances were firmly wedged, so as to afford the greatest amount of resistance to the explosion. On this foundation were placed a large number of spirit and water casks, into which 1500 barrels of powder were emptied. These casks were set on end, and the whole bound round with hempen cables, so as to resemble a gigantic mortar, thus causing the explosion to take an upward course. In addition to the powder casks were placed several hundred shells, and over these again nearly three thousand hand grenades; the whole, by means of wedges and sand, being compressed as nearly as possible into a solid mass.

This was the vessel in which I subsequently led on the attack. A more striking comment on the "red-hot shot," etc., of which Lord Gambier made so much in one of his letters to the Admiralty, could scarcely be found. Of course, had a red-hot shot from the batteries on Aix reached us—and they were not half-a-mile distant—nothing could have prevented our being "hoist with our own petard." I can, however, safely say, that such a catastrophe never entered into my calculations, for the simple reason, that from previous employment on the spot, on several occasions, I well knew there was plenty of room in the channel to keep out of the way of red-hot shot from the Aix batteries, even if, by means of blue lights or other devices, they had discovered us. The explosion vessels were simply naval mines, the effect of which depended quite as much on their novelty as engines of war, as upon their destructiveness. It was calculated that, independently of any mischief they might do, they would cause such an amount of terror, as to induce the enemy to run their ships ashore as the only way to avoid them and save the crews. This expectation was fully answered, but no adequate attack on the part of the British force following up the effect of the explosion vessels, the stranded ships were permitted to heave off, and thus escaped, for the most part, as will be detailed in the succeeding chapter.

CHAPTER XXI

THE ATTACK

On the 10th of April, the *Beagle*, having arrived from England with the fire-ships in company, I pressed Lord Gambier to permit an attack to be made on the same night; but, notwithstanding that the weather was favourable, his lordship saw fit to refuse. My reasons for pressing an immediate attack was, that as the enemy could not remain in ignorance of the character of the newly arrived vessels, they might have less time to make additional preparations for their reception.

Notwithstanding the importance of prompt action in this respect, argument was unavailing. His lordship urged that the fire-ships might be boarded, and the crews murdered, though there was more danger of this from delay than from attacking unawares. There was in reality no danger; but I urged in vain that it was an essential part of my plan personally to embark in an explosion vessel, *preceding* the fire-ships, so that in conducting and firing her all risk would fall on myself and the volunteer crew which would accompany me; it not being prob-

P

able that after the explosion the enemy's guard-boats would board the fire-ships which might follow, as every one would certainly be taken for a mine similarly charged. Under that impression, however gallant the enemy, there was little chance of the fire-ships being boarded.

His lordship replied, that " if I chose to rush on self-destruction that was my own affair, but that it was his duty to take care of the lives of others, and he would not place the crews of the fire-ships in palpable danger."

To this I rejoined, that there could not be any danger, for the use of explosion-vessels being new to naval warfare, it was unlikely that, after witnessing the effect of the first explosion, the enemy's officers and men would board a single fire-ship. I further told his lordship that my brother, the Hon. Basil Cochrane, and Lieut. Bissel were on Board the *Imperieuse* as my guests, and so well satisfied were both of the little danger to be apprehended that they had volunteered to accompany me. Lord Gambier, however, remained firm, and further remonstrance being useless, I had no alternative but to delay, whilst the French, who quickly became aware of the character of the newly arrived vessels, adopted all necessary precautions.

A most favourable opportunity was thus thrown away. The French admiral, however, lost no time in turning the delay to account, by altering the positions of his fleet, so as to expose it to the smallest possible amount of danger.

The enemy's ships of the line struck their topmasts, got their topgallant yards on deck, and unbent sails, so as to expose as little inflammable matter aloft as possible ; the frigates only being left in sailing trim, ready to act as occasion might require ; whilst the boats and launches of the fleet, to the number of seventy-three, were armed and stationed in five divisions for the purpose of boarding and towing off the fire-ships.

The French admiral, Allemand, disposed his force in the following manner :—The ten sail of the line, which before the arrival of the fire-ships had been moored in two lines overlapping each other, were formed afresh in a double line, nearly north

and south ; the outer line comprising five, and the inner six
ships, including the *Calcutta* ; the inner line being so anchored
as to face the openings between the ships of the outer line, the
extremity of which was somewhat more than a mile from the
batteries on the Isle of Aix. About half-a-mile in advance
of the whole lay the four frigates, and immediately in front of
these a boom of extraordinary dimensions.

The French, no doubt, considered their position secure against
fire-ships, having no expectation of other means of attack ; and
so it undoubtedly was, from the protection afforded by the
boom, which, from its peculiar construction, could neither be
destroyed nor burned by fire-ships—as well as further defended
by the guard-boats, which were judged sufficient to divert the
course of such fire-ships as might drift past the boom. Their
fleet was anchored so as to expose the smallest possible front ;
and what added no little to their sense of security was the delay
which had taken place on the part of the British admiral without
attack of any kind. On such grounds, therefore, they not
unreasonably felt confident that, if the fire-ships failed, as
from the judicious preparations made, Admiral Allemand had
every reason to anticipate, no attack on the part of the British
fleet would follow. In this belief, on altering their position,
the French dressed their fleet with flags, and, by way of contempt for their assailants, hung out the English ensign of the
Calcutta—which, as has been said, was a captured English
vessel—under her quarter gallery ! The peculiar nature of the
insult needs not to be explained—to naval men it is the most
atrocious imaginable.

As narratives of the attack on the French fleet in Basque
Roads have been often, though in some of the main points
incorrectly, written from the contradictory, and in many instances
incomprehensible, evidence on the subsequent court-martial, as
compared with the no less contradictory despatches of Lord
Gambier, I shall in the following account strictly confine myself
to what took place under my own personal conduct and observation.

On the 11th of April, it blew hard with a high sea. As all preparations were complete, I did not consider the state of the weather a justifiable impediment to the attack, to which Lord Gambier had now consented ; so that after nightfall, the officers who volunteered to command the fire-ships were assembled on board the *Caledonia,* and supplied with instructions according to the plan previously laid down by myself.

The *Imperieuse* had proceeded to the edge of the Boyart shoal, close to which she anchored with an explosion vessel made fast to her stern, it being my intention, after firing the one of which I was about to take charge, to return to her for the other, to be employed as circumstances might require. At a short distance from the *Imperieuse* were anchored the frigates *Aigle, Unicorn,* and *Pallas,* for the purpose of receiving the crews of the fire-ships on their return, as well as to support the boats of the fleet assembled alongside the *Cæsar* to assist the fire-ships. The boats of the fleet were not, however, for some reason or other, made use of at all.

The enemy had calculated on the impending attack, and as was afterwards ascertained, by way of precaution against fire-ships, sent two divisions of their guard-boats, with orders to lie under the boom till two in the morning ; but wind and tide being against them, they were compelled to put back, without effecting their orders. Both wind and tide, however, though dead against the French boats, were favourable for the boats of the British fleet, had they been employed as arranged ; and they would have been of great use to the less efficient boats of the fire-ships, some of which in returning, were nearly swamped.

For want of such assistance, as will presently be seen, most of the fire-ships were kindled too soon, no doubt to save the men the terrible pull back, against a gale of wind and a high sea.

Having myself embarked on board the largest explosion vessel, accompanied by Lieut. Bissel and a volunteer crew of four men only, we led the way to the attack ; the *Imperieuse* afterwards, in accordance with my instructions, signalising the fire-ships to " proceed on service."

The night was dark, and as the wind was fair, though blowing hard, we soon neared the estimated position of the advanced French ships, for it was too dark to discern them. Judging our distance, therefore, as well as we could, with regard to the time the fuse was calculated to burn, the crew of four men entered the gig, under the direction of Lieut. Bissel, whilst I kindled the portfires ; and then, descending into the boat, urged the men to pull for their lives, which they did with a will, though, as wind and sea were strong against us, without making the progress calculated.

To our consternation, the fuses, which had been constructed to burn fifteen minutes, lasted little more than half that time, when the vessel blew up, filling the air with shells, grenades, and rockets ; whilst the downward and lateral force of the explosion raised a solitary mountain of water, from the breaking of which in all directions our little boat narrowly escaped being swamped. In one respect it was, perhaps, fortunate for us that the fuses did not burn the time calculated, as, from the little way we had made against the strong head wind and tide, the rockets and shells from the exploded vessel went over us. Had we been in the line of their descent, at the moment of explosion, our destruction, from the shower of broken shells and other missiles, would have been inevitable.

The explosion vessel did her work well, the effect constituting one of the grandest artificial spectacles imaginable. For a moment, the sky was red with the lurid glare arising from the simultaneous ignition of 1500 barrels of powder. On this gigantic flash subsiding, the air seemed alive with shells, grenades, rockets, and masses of timber, the wreck of the shattered vessel ; whilst the water was strewn with spars, shaken out of the enormous boom, on which, according to the subsequent testimony of Captain Proteau, whose frigate lay just within the boom, the vessel had brought up, before she exploded. The sea was convulsed as by an earthquake, rising, as has been said, in a huge wave, on whose crest our boat was lifted like a cork, and as suddenly dropped into a vast trough, out of which, as it closed

upon us with a rush of a whirlpool, none expected to emerge.
The skill of the boat's crew, however, overcame the threatened
danger, which passed away as suddenly as it had arisen, and in
a few minutes nothing but a heavy rolling sea had to be encountered, all having again become silence and darkness.

This danger surmounted, we pulled in the direction of the
Imperieuse, whose lights could be distinguished at about three
miles' distance. On our way we had the satisfaction of seeing
two fire-ships pass over the spot where the boom had been
moored. Shortly afterwards we met the *Mediator* steering in
the direction of the enemy, whose ships of the line were now
firing towards the spot where the explosion had taken place,
and consequently on their own advanced frigates ! which, as was
afterwards learned, cut their cables, and shifted their berths to
a position in the rear of the larger ships.

On reaching the *Imperieuse*, I found, to my great mortification, that the second explosion vessel, which, by my orders, had
been made fast to the frigate's stern, had been cut away and
thus set adrift : a fire-ship in flames having come down on her
instead of the enemy ! The *Imperieuse* herself had a narrow
escape of being burned, and was only saved by veering cable ;
the fire-ship which caused the disaster drifting harmlessly away
on the Boyart shoal. This clumsy occurrence completely
frustrated the intention with which I had reserved her, viz. for
further personal operations amongst the enemy's fleet, now
that the first explosion vessel had cleared the way.

Of all the fire-ships, upwards of twenty in number, *four only
reached the enemy's position, and not one did any damage* ! The
way in which they were managed was grievous. The *Imperieuse*,
as has been said, lay three miles from the enemy, so that the
one which was near setting fire to her became useless at the
outset ; whilst several others were kindled a mile and a half
to windward of this, or four miles and a half from the enemy.
Of the remainder, many were at once rendered harmless, from
being brought to on the wrong tack. Six passed a mile to
windward of the French fleet, and one grounded on Oleron. I

could scarcely credit my own vision when I saw the way in which they were handled ; most of them being fired and abandoned before they were abreast of the vessels anchored as guides.

The fear of the fire-ships operated strongly enough ; but, notwithstanding the actual effect attributed to them by naval historians, they did no damage whatever—a matter of little consequence, had the British fleet, or even a portion thereof, subsequently taken advantage of the panic created amongst the enemy.

As the fire-ships began to light up the roads, we could observe the enemy's fleet in great confusion. Without doubt, taking every fire-ship for an explosion vessel, and being deceived as to their distance, not only did the French make no attempt to divert them from their course, but some of their ships cut their cables and were seen drifting away broadside on to the wind and tide—whilst others made sail, as the only alternative to escape from what they evidently considered certain destruction from explosive missiles !

Had the commander-in-chief witnessed this scene, he would never again have deemed such extraordinary precaution on his part requisite to guard against fire-ships being boarded when preceded by explosion vessels. In place of becoming the aggressors, as his lordship had anticipated, the only care of the enemy was how to get out of the way, even at the risk of running their ships ashore. Unfortunately the commander-in-chief was with the fleet, fourteen miles distant.

At daylight on the morning of the 12th not a spar of the boom was anywhere visible, and with the exception of the *Foudroyant* and *Cassard, the whole of the enemy's vessels were helplessly aground.* The former of these ships lying out of the sweep of the tide, and being therefore out of danger from the fire-ships, appeared not to have cut her cable, and the *Cassard,* which had at first done so, again brought up about two cables' length from the *Foudroyant.*

With these exceptions, every vessel of the enemy's fleet was ashore. The flag-ship of Admiral Allemand, *L'Ocean,* three-decker, drawing the most water, lay outermost on the north-west edge of the Palles shoal, nearest the deep water, where she was most exposed to attack; whilst all, by the fall of the tide, were lying on their bilge, with their bottoms completely exposed to shot, and therefore beyond the possibility of resistance.

The account given by the captain of the *Indienne*, French frigate, Captain Proteau, of the position of the grounded ships, will not be called in question. It is as follows :—" The *Indienne* aground on Point Aiguille, near the fort ; the *Pallas* off Barques ; the *Elbe* and *Hortense* on the Fontenelles ; the *Tourville, Patriote,* and *Tonnerre*, as seen from the *Indienne*, in a line on the Palles shoal ; the *Calcutta, Regulus, Jemappes* on the extremity of that shoal ; the *Varsovie* and *Aquilon* aground on Charenton ; and the *Ocean*, three-decker, close to the edge of the Palles."

We did not reach the *Imperieuse* till after midnight. At daylight, observing seven of the nearest enemy's ships ashore, amongst which was the admiral's ship *L'Ocean*, and a group of four others lying near her, in a most favourable position for attack, without the possibility of returning it, at 6 A.M. we signalised the admiral to that effect. As the *Imperieuse* at this time lay just within range of the batteries on Aix, which had commenced to fire upon us, we weighed, and stood in the direction of the fleet, letting go our anchor as soon as the ship was out of range. At 7 A.M. we signalised again, " *All the enemy's ships, except two, are on shore* " ; this signal, as well as the former one, being merely acknowledged by the answering pennant ; but to our surprise, no movement was visible in any part of the fleet indicating an intention to take advantage of the success gained.

Reflecting that, from the distance of the British force from the stranded enemy's ships, viz. from twelve to fourteen miles, the commander-in-chief could not clearly be acquainted with their helpless condition, I directed the signal to be run up, " *The enemy's ships can be destroyed* " ; this also meeting with the same cool acknowledgment of the answering pennant.

Not knowing what to make of such a reply, another signal

was hoisted, "*Half the fleet can destroy the enemy.*" This signal was again acknowledged by the answering pennant, the whole fleet still remaining motionless as before. On this I made several telegraph signals, one of which was probably regarded as impertinent, viz. "*The frigates alone can destroy the enemy,*" though it was true enough, their ships aground being perfectly helpless. To my astonishment the answering pennant was still the only reply vouchsafed!

Eight and nine o'clock passed without any indication of movement on the part of the fleet, though the tide was now fast rising, so that any ships sent to the attack of the stranded vessels would have had the flood-tide to go in and the ebb to return, after having accomplished their destruction ; whilst it was evident that if not attacked, the same flood-tide would enable the French ships aground to float and escape, with which view some were heaving their guns and stores overboard. On ascertaining this, I again signalised, "*The enemy is preparing to heave off*" ; and entertaining no doubt that the commander-in-chief would not permit such a catastrophe, the *Imperieuse* dropped her anchor close to the Boyart shoal, in readiness for any service that might be required.

As much has been said respecting the alleged narrowness of the channel leading to Aix Roads, by way of excuse for the British fleet not having followed up the advantage gained by the panic created on the previous night, from terror of the explosion vessels, I may here mention, that on our coming to an anchor, a fort on Isle d'Oleron commenced firing shells at us. As not one of these reached us, the French gunners adopted the expedient of loading their mortars to the muzzle, this being evident from the fact that they now discharged them by means of portfires, the men gaining a place of security before the mortars exploded. Not a shell, even thus fired, reached our position, a clear proof that had the British fleet come to the attack, it could have been in no danger from Oleron, though even these distant batteries were afterwards brought forward as an obstacle, in default of stronger argument.

At 11 A.M. the British fleet weighed, and stood towards Aix Roads. By this time the *Ocean*, three-decker, and nearest ships aground were busily employed in heaving off, with a view of making sail for the Charente ! ! The advance of our fleet had been too long delayed ; nevertheless, as the bulk of the enemy's ships were still aground, good service might have been rendered. To our amazement, the British fleet, after approaching within seven or eight miles of the grounded ships, *again came to anchor about three and a half miles distant from Aix, i.e.*, just out of range.

There was no mistaking the admiral's intention in again bringing the fleet to an anchor. Notwithstanding that the enemy had been four hours at our mercy, and to a considerable extent was still so, it was now evident that *no attack was intended*, and that every enemy's ship would be permitted to float away unmolested and unassailed ! I frankly admit that this was too much to be endured. The words of Lord Mulgrave rang in my ears, " *The Admiralty is bent on destroying that fleet before it can get out to the West Indies.*"

The motive of Lord Gambier in bringing the ships to an anchor being beyond doubt, I made up my mind, if possible, to force him into action by attacking the enemy with the *Imperieuse*, whatever might be the consequence. It was, however, a step not to be taken without consideration, and for some time I hesitated to carry out this resolution, in the hope that a portion, at least, of the British fleet would again weigh and stand in.

Noon passed. The *Ocean*, three-decker, had now got afloat, and the group of four others on shore near her, seeing the British fleet anchor, proceeded with additional energy to heave off. From her position the three-decker, lying as she did on the edge of the shoal, nearest the deep water, ought to have been the easiest prize of the whole ; for whilst she lay on her bilge, close to the most accessible part of the channel, even a single gunboat might have so riddled her bottom as to have prevented her from floating off with the rising tide !

The surprise of the enemy at seeing the fleet anchor was

probably greater than my own. Before that, they had been making great exertions to lighten and heave off, but no sooner had the fleet brought up, than, seeing the possibility of escape, they strained every nerve to hasten the operation.

In place of the fleet, or even the frigates, a single bomb, which, being armed with a 13-inch mortar, could project her shells to a great distance, without being exposed to danger from shot, was ordered in to shell the ships aground. On my asking her commander, " *what attack was going to be made on the enemy by the fleet ?* " he replied, that " he knew nothing further than that he was ordered to bombard the ships ashore." This was proof enough that no intention of attacking with the fleet, or any part of it, existed.

In despair, lest the ships still aground should also effect their escape, at 1 P.M. I ordered the anchor of the *Imperieuse* to be hove atrip, and thus we drifted stern foremost towards the enemy. I say " *drifted,*" for I did not venture to make sail, lest the movement might be seen from the flag-ship, and a signal of recall should defeat my purpose of making an attack with the *Imperieuse* ; the object of this being to *compel* the commander-in-chief to send vessels to our assistance, in which case I knew their captains would at once attack the ships which had not been allowed to heave off and escape.

Had this means not been resorted to, *not a single enemy's ship would have been destroyed,* for all could have hove off almost without damage, and that, to all appearance, without the slightest attempt at molestation on the part of the British fleet. It was better to risk the frigate, or even my commission, than to suffer such a disgraceful termination to the expectations of the Admiralty, after having driven ashore the enemy's fleet ; and therefore we drifted by the wind and tide slowly past the fortifications on Isle d'Aix, about which the commander-in-chief had expressed so many fears in his last letter to the Board ; but though they fired at us with every gun that could be brought to bear, the distance was too great to inflict damage.

Proceeding thus till 1.30 P.M., and then suddenly making sail after the nearest of the enemy's vessels escaping, at 1.40 P.M. the signal was run up to the peak of the *Imperieuse*, "*Enemy superior to chasing ship, but inferior to the fleet.*" No attention being paid to this signal, at 1.45 P.M. I again signalled, "*In want of assistance*," which was true enough, being in a single frigate, close to several enemy's ships of the line.

As this signal, according to the code then in use, was coupled with the one signifying "*In distress*," the signal officer on board the flag-ship thus interpreted it to the commander-in-chief; a circumstance which will require brief explanation.

In order to divert our attention from the vessels we were pursuing, these having thrown their guns overboard, the *Calcutta*, which was still aground, broadside on, began firing at us. Before proceeding farther, it became, therefore, necessary to attack her, and at 1.50 we shortened sail, and returned the fire. At 2 the *Imperieuse* came to an anchor in five fathoms; and veering to half a cable, kept fast the spring, firing upon the *Calcutta* with our broadside, and at the same time upon the *Aquilon* and *Ville de Varsovie* with our forecastle and bow guns, both these ships being aground stern on, in an opposite direction.

This proceeding—though there could be no doubt of our being "*In want of assistance*," seeing that our single frigate, unaided, was engaging three line-of-battle ships—did not look much like being "*In distress*," as the signal officer of the *Caledonia* had interpreted the signal; the nature of which could not, however, have deceived the commander-in-chief, who must have witnessed the circumstances under which the signal had been made by the *Imperieuse*.

After engaging the *Calcutta* for some time, and simultaneously firing into the sterns of the two grounded line-of-battle ships, we had at length the satisfaction of observing several ships sent to our assistance, viz., *Emerald*, *Unicorn*, *Indefatigable*, *Valiant*, *Revenge*, *Pallas*, and *Aigle*. On seeing this, the captain and crew of the *Calcutta* abandoned their vessel, of which the boats of the *Imperieuse* took possession before the vessels sent to our " assistance " came down.

On the subsequent court-martial, it was declared that the *Calcutta* did not strike to the *Imperieuse*, but to the ships sent to her assistance. This was deliberately untrue ; as proved beyond question by the fact that the French government ordered a court-martial on the captain of the *Calcutta*, Lafon, and condemned him to be shot, clearly *for having abandoned his ship to inferior force.* The French did not shoot any of the other captains for abandoning their ships, and would not have shot Captain Lafon for fighting his vessel as long as he could, and then abandoning her to two line-of-battle ships and five frigates. On the contrary, they would have highly rewarded him, for saving his crew against such odds. There cannot be a stronger proof, if proof in addition to my word be wanted, that Captain Lafon abandoned the *Calcutta* to the *Imperieuse*, and not to the line-of-battle ships which came up afterwards, as was subsequently asserted.

On the arrival of the two line-of-battle ships and the frigates, the *Imperieuse* hailed them to anchor, or they would run aground on the Palles shoal, on the very edge of which the *Imperieuse* had taken up her berth. They anchored immediately and commenced firing on the *Calcutta, Aquilon,* and *Ville de Varsovie.* On this I signalled the *Revenge* and others to desist from firing, as the *Calcutta* had already struck to the *Imperieuse,* and we had at that time a boat's crew on board her.

On this they desisted, and turned their fire wholly on the other two vessels. At 3.30 P.M. the *Imperieuse* ceased firing, the crew being thoroughly exhausted by fatigue ; whilst I was so much so, as to be almost unable to stand. My reason, however, for ordering the *Imperieuse* to cease firing was, that the ships sent to our assistance were more than sufficient to destroy the enemy which remained, and had they been sent in time— not to our " *assistance,*" but for the more legitimate object of attacking the grounded ships—they would have been abundantly sufficient, had they not been recalled, to have destroyed all those that got away.

At 5.30 P.M. the *Aquilon* and *Ville de Varsovie* struck.

Shortly afterwards, the *Calcutta* was set on fire, and in half-an-hour was burning furiously. At 6 P.M. the crew of the *Tonnerre*, which was not attacked, set fire to her, escaping in their boats. At 7 the *Tonnerre* blew up, and at 9 the *Calcutta* also, with an effect, from the large quantity of ammunition on board, almost equalling that of the explosion vessels the night before. The *Calcutta* was the storeship of the French fleet.

It has been said, that my having rushed single-handed amongst the enemy's ships, and then hoisted the signal "*In want of assistance*," was unjustifiable, as forcing the commander-in-chief to attack against his judgment. My answer to this is, that the expectations entertained by the Admiralty of destroying the enemy's fleet would not have been in any way carried out, had not this means been adopted ; because, as has been said, not a ship belonging to the enemy would have sustained even the slightest damage from the measures of the commander-in-chief.

The fire-ships entrusted to my command had failed, not from any fault of mine, but of those who were entrusted with them. It was, then, a question with me, whether I should disappoint the expectations of my country ; be set down as a *charlatan* by the Admiralty, whose hopes had been raised by my plan ; have my future prospects destroyed ; or force on an action which some had induced an easy commander-in-chief to believe impracticable.

Some proof has been given of the jealousy of a portion of the fleet towards me. Another instance of this occurred even after the two line-of-battle ships and the frigates came down. Perceiving that the shot from two sloops, or rather brigs, ordered to protect the *Etna* bomb, did not reach the enemy, from the long range at which she had anchored, I made the signal for them to close. As no signal was at hand to express brigs only to the exclusion of frigates or larger vessels, I endeavoured to explain my meaning that the signal was intended for the brigs, by firing towards them from the main-deck of the *Imperieuse*, the object of this being to *avoid giving offence* to my senior officers in command of the frigates and line-of-battle ships now present. The signal "*to close*" in the same defective code expressing also "*to close the Admiral*," it was construed by my seniors into an insult to them, as arrogating to myself the position of chief-in-command, which was simply absurd ; as, being my seniors, I had no power to order them, nor was I so ignorant of my duty as wantonly to usurp the functions of the commander-in-chief. Yet this at the time gave great offence, though afterwards satisfactorily explained, to Lord Gambier.

I may here mention a singular incident which occurred some time after the *Aquilon* and *Ville de Varsovie* had struck, and after their officers and crews had been removed on board the British ships. The captain of the *Aquilon* having informed me that he had left his personal effects behind, I volunteered to take him on board in my boat and procure them. As we left the *Aquilon* a shot from a heated gun on board one of the vessels to which the French had set fire—the *Tonnerre*, if I recollect rightly—struck the stern sheets of the boat on which he and I were sitting, and lacerated the lower part of the gallant officer's body so severely that he shortly afterwards expired.

Before daybreak on the following morning the officer of the watch called me, and reported that three lights were hoisted in the squadron outside. This proved to be a signal, afterwards reported to have been made by Admiral Stopford, for the recall of the ships that had been sent in on the previous evening ! In obedience to this signal, they, at 4 A.M., got under weigh, having previously kindled the French line-of-battle ships *Aquilon* and *Ville de Varsovie*; an act for which there was not the slighest necessity, as they could easily have been got off. Fatigued, and mentally harassed as I was, I had neither time nor opportunity to protest against this wanton destruction ; besides which, not knowing that the magazines of the burning ships had been drowned, my attention was directed to the preservation of the *Imperieuse*, which was in close proximity.

The two ships *Foudroyant* and *Cassard*, had cut their cables and made sail, when on the previous evening the British fleet stood towards Aix Roads, but afterwards so unaccountably came to an anchor. On seeing this they shortened sail, but ran aground in the middle of the channel leading to the Charente.

It being clear to me that these ships were not in a fighting condition, I determined, notwithstanding the recall of the British vessels, to remain and attack them; considering the signal of recall to be addressed only to the ships sent to our assistance, which, in obedience to that signal, were working out of the inner anchorage without any attempt to destroy other ships which were clearly at their mercy. As they were passing out I hailed the *Indefatigable*, and asked the captain if he would go on one quarter of the three-decker (*l'Ocean*), whilst the *Imperieuse* engaged the other? The reply was that "he would not, and that they *were going out to join the fleet.*"

To his infinite credit, Captain Seymour, of the *Pallas* (the present distinguished admiral, Sir George Seymour), hailed us to know "if he should remain with the *Imperieuse*?" he being evidently as reluctant as myself to give up advantages so manifest. I replied, that if no orders had been given him to the contrary, I should be obliged to him so to do; whereupon the *Pallas* anchored, and four brigs, the *Beagle*, *Growler*, *Conflict*, and *Encounter*, followed her example.

We now commenced clearing the decks for further action, throwing overboard a boat which had been shot to pieces. The carpenters were then set to stop shot holes in the sides and decks, and the seamen to repair the rigging, and shift the foretopmast, which had been shot through. The brave, but unfortunate captain of the *Calcutta* had, in our short action, inflicted on us an amount of damage which the forts on Aix and Oleron had in vain attempted to effect; neither the one nor the other having once touched us.

Whilst the refitting of the frigate was going on, I ordered our only bomb, the *Etna*, protected by the brigs, to fire on the enemy's Vice- and Rear-Admiral's ships, as well as on the *Foudroyant* and *Cassard*, which, having thrown all overboard, were now pressing sail to get up the Charente, thus taking upon myself to commence

LORD MULGRAVE
[Born 1755. Died 1831]

the action anew, *after the auxiliary line-of-battle ships and frigates had retired* !

To my regret a signal of recall was immediately hoisted on board the *Caledonia* ! To this I replied by another, "*The enemy can be destroyed* "; of which no notice was taken. Shortly afterwards a boat brought me the following letter from Lord Gambier :—

" ' CALEDONIA,'
" 13*th of April.*

"MY DEAR LORD,—*You have done your part so admirably that I will not suffer you to tarnish it by attempting impossibilities,* which I think, as well as those captains who have come from you, any further effort to destroy those ships would be. You must, therefore, join as soon as you can, with the bombs, etc., as I wish for some information, which you allude to, before I close my despatches.

" Yours, my dear Lord, most sincerely, GAMBIER.

" Capt. LORD COCHRANE.

"*P.S.*—I have ordered *three brigs and two rocket-vessels to join you,* with which, and the bomb, you may make an attempt on the ship that is aground on the Palles, or towards Ile Madame, but I do not think you will succeed ; and I am anxious that you should come to me, as I wish to send you to England as soon as possible. You must, therefore, come as soon as the tide turns."

I felt deep regret at what must be considered as the evasions of this letter. First, Lord Gambier ordered me to come out of the anchorage and join the fleet ! but evidently not choosing to take upon himself the responsibility of ordering me out, in opposition to my own views, he told me he would send some brigs with which I might attack vessels which his own neglect had permitted to escape up the Charente ! and thirdly, I was ordered to come out as soon as the tide turned !

As the commander-in-chief's letter was thus indecisive, I

Q

chose to construe it as giving me the option of remaining, and returned his lordship the following answer :—

"' IMPERIEUSE,'
" 13*th April.*

"MY LORD,—I have just had the honour to receive your Lordship's letter. We *can* destroy the ships that are on shore, which I hope your Lordship will approve of.
"I have the honour, etc.   COCHRANE.

" The Right Hon. LORD GAMBIER."

At daylight on the 14th the enemy were still in the same condition, but with a number of chasse-marées quietly taking out their stores. Three of them were getting out their guns, evidently in expectation of certain destruction from the small vessels which remained after the line-of-battle ships and heavy frigates were recalled ; and, had we been permitted to attack them *even now*, their destruction would have been inevitable.

In place of this the recall signal was once more hoisted on board the *Caledonia*, to which I replied by the interrogatory signal " *Shall we unmoor ?* " considering that his lordship would understand the signal as a request to be permitted to resume the attack. I did not repeat the signal that the enemy could be destroyed, because, having conveyed to him by letter my opinion on that subject the day before, I thought a repetition of that opinion unnecessary,—the more so, as, from the enemy heaving overboard their guns, its soundness was more than ever confirmed.

In place of being ordered to attack, as from his lordship's previous letter I had every reason to expect, the recall signal was repeated, and shortly afterwards came the following letter :—

"' CALEDONIA,'
"13th (14th) April.

"MY DEAR LORD,—It is necessary I should have some communication with you before I close my despatches to the Admiralty. *I have, therefore, ordered Captain Wolfe to relieve you* in the services you are engaged in. I wish you to join me as soon as possible, that you may convey Sir Harry Neale to England, who will be charged with my despatches, or you may return to carry on the service where you are. I expect two bombs to arrive every moment, they will be useful in it.

"Yours, my dear Lord, most sincerely, GAMBIER.

"Capt. LORD COCHRANE."

Here was a repetition of the same thing. I was ordered away from the attack, to "convey Sir H. Neale to England," or I "might return to carry on the service where I was," viz. after the enemy had got clear off, *and after being formally superseded in the service to which the Board of Admiralty had appointed me, by a senior officer whom I could not again supersede*!!!

There was, however, no evading Lord Gambier's letter this time without positive disobedience to orders, and that was not lightly to be risked, even with the Board's instructions to back me. I therefore returned to the *Caledonia*, and at once told Lord Gambier that the extraordinary hesitation which had been displayed in attacking ships helplessly on shore, could only have arisen from my being employed in the attack, in preference to senior officers. I begged his lordship, by way of preventing the ill-feeling of the fleet from becoming detrimental to the honour of the service, to set me altogether aside, and send in Admiral Stopford, with the frigates or other vessels, as with regard to him there could be no ill-feeling ; further declaring my confidence that from Admiral Stopford's zeal for the service, he would, being backed by his officers, accomplish results more creditable than anything that had yet been done. I apologised for the freedom I used, stating that I took the liberty as a friend, for it would be impossible, as matters stood, to prevent a noise being made in England.

His lordship appeared much displeased ; and making no remark, I repeated, " My Lord, you have before desired me to ' speak candidly to you,' and I have now used that freedom."

Lord Gambier then replied, " *If you throw blame upon what has been done, it will appear like arrogantly claiming all the merit to yourself.*"

I assured his lordship that I had no such intention, for that no merit was due, and told him that I had no wish to carry the despatches, or to go to London with Sir Harry Neale on the occasion, my object being alone that which had been entrusted to me by the Admiralty, viz. to destroy the vessels of the enemy.

His lordship, however, cut the matter short by giving me written orders immediately to convey Sir Harry Neale to England with despatches. In obedience to this order we quitted Basque Roads for Plymouth on the following morning.

CHAPTER XXII

ARRIVAL IN ENGLAND

On the 26th of April, his Majesty was pleased to confer on me the Knighthood of the Order of the Bath.

Soon after Lord Gambier's arrival in England, Lord Mulgrave informed me that a vote of thanks to the commander-in-chief would be proposed in the House of Commons. Whereupon I told Lord Mulgrave that it was my duty to apprise him that in my capacity as one of the members for Westminster, I would oppose the motion, on the ground that the commander-in-chief had not only done nothing to merit a vote of thanks, but had neglected to destroy the French fleet in Aix Roads, when it was clearly in his power to do so.

Lord Mulgrave entreated me not to persist in this determination, as such a course would not only prove injurious to the government, but highly detrimental to myself, by raising up against me a host of enemies. The public, said his lordship, was satisfied with what had been done, and gave me full credit for my share therein, so that as I should be included in the vote of thanks, the recognition of Lord Gambier's services could do me no harm.

I told his lordship that, speaking as a member of the House of Commons, I did not recognise Lord Gambier's services at all, for that none had been rendered ; and as for any thanks to myself, I would rather be without them, feeling conscious that I had not been enabled satisfactorily to carry out the earnest wishes of the Admiralty by the destruction of the enemy's fleet, as impressed on me by his lordship before accepting the command with which I had been entrusted. I nevertheless begged his lordship to consider that in my professional capacity as a naval officer, I neither did offer nor had offered, any opinion whatever on Lord Gambier's conduct, but that my position as member of Parliament for Westminster forbade my acquiescence in a public misrepresentation.

Lord Mulgrave replied, that I was even now accusing Lord Gambier in my professional capacity ; the public would not draw the distinction between my professional and parliamentary conduct. I expressed my regret for the public want of discrimination, but told his lordship that this would not alter my determination.

Soon after this conversation Lord Mulgrave sent for me, and again entreated me, for my own sake, to reconsider my resolution, saying that he had reported our former conversation to the government, which was highly dissatisfied therewith. His lordship further assured me that he was anxious about the matter on my account, as the course intimated would certainly bring me under high displeasure. To this I replied, that the displeasure of the government would not for a moment influence my parliamentary conduct, for which I held myself answerable to my constituents.

His lordship then said, " If you are on service, you cannot be in your place in parliament. Now, my lord, I will make you a proposal. I will put under your orders three frigates, with *carte blanche* to do whatever you please on the enemy's coasts in the Mediterranean. I will further get you permission to go to Sicily, and embark on board your squadron my own regiment, which is stationed there. You know how to make use of such advantages."

I thanked Lord Mulgrave for the offer, at the same time expressing my gratitude for his anxiety to preserve me from the evils of acting contrary to the wishes of the government; but told his lordship that, were I to accept this offer, the country would regard my acquiescence as a bribe to hold my peace, whilst I could not regard it in any other light. Self-respect must, therefore, be my excuse for declining the proposal.

The anxiety of the then government was, no doubt, to convert what had been effected in Aix Roads into political capital, as a victory which merited the thanks of parliament. My tacit acquiescence in the object of government would have subjected me, and rightly, to a total loss of political confidence in the estimation of those with whom I acted. No man with the slightest pretensions to personal honesty or political consistency could, therefore, have decided otherwise than I did, even with the kind warning of Lord Mulgrave, that evil consequences to myself would follow—a prediction subsequently verified to the letter.

The upshot of the matter was, that on Lord Mulgrave communicating my determination to Lord Gambier, the latter demanded a court-martial.

As soon as my fixed resolution of opposing the vote of thanks became known to the government, the Board of Admiralty directed Lord Gambier to make a *fresh report* of the action in Basque Roads! requiring his lordship to call upon various officers for further reports as to the part they took therein!

Accordingly, on the 10th of May, Lord Gambier forwarded *a new despatch* to the Admiralty, *in which my services were altogether passed over* ! ! ! notwithstanding that, in Lord Gambier's previous report, he had written as follows :—" I cannot speak in sufficient terms of admiration and applause of the vigorous and gallant attack made by Lord Cochrane upon the French line-of-battle ships which were on shore ; as well as of his judicious manner of approaching them, and placing his ship in a position most advantageous to annoy the enemy and preserve his own ship, which could not be exceeded by any feat of valour hitherto achieved by the British navy."

Still more singularly, in the second despatch, Lord Gambier inadvertently confirms the fact that *no attack on the French fleet would have been made at all,* had it not been for my having commenced an attack with the *Imperieuse* alone, which movement, as has been said, was executed literally *by stealth,* under the fear that the signal of recall would be hoisted by the commander-in-chief !

It having, for reasons described in a former chapter, become imperative on Lord Gambier to send us assistance, he, nevertheless, construed this into an *intention* on his part to attack the enemy. "*Observing the 'Imperieuse' to advance, and the time of flood nearly done running, the Indefatigable, etc., etc.,* were ordered to the attack !" It is not very probable that, had Lord Gambier intended an attack, he would have let the flood-tide go by, without taking advantage of it in a channel which was afterwards declared unsafe for want of water !

This passage alone of Lord Gambier's second despatch ought to have decided the result of any court-martial. The Board of Admiralty would not, however, see anything inculpatory of their former colleague ; but, on the 29th of May, ordered me, through their secretary, to become the accuser of the commander-in-chief : " I am commanded by their Lordships to signify their directions that you state fully to me, for their information, the grounds on which your lordship objects to the vote of thanks being moved to Lord Gambier, to the end that their Lordships' objections may be of a nature to justify the suspension of the intended motion in Parliament, or to call for any further information."   (Signed)   " W. W. Pole."

This command was manifestly intended to entrap me into the position of Lord Gambier's prosecutor, and was, moreover, an improper interference with my parliamentary capacity, in which alone I had declared my intention to oppose an uncalled-for vote of thanks to the commander-in-chief. I therefore wrote to the Secretary of the Admiralty the subjoined reply.

"Portman Square,
"30th May, 1809.

"Sir,—I have to request that you will submit to their Lordships that I shall, at all times, entertain a due sense of the honour they will confer by any directions they may be pleased to give me ; that in pursuing the object of these directions, my exertions will invariably go hand in hand with my duty ; and that, to satisfy their Lordships' minds in the present instance, I beg leave to state that the log and signal log-books of the fleet in Basque Roads contain all particulars, and furnish premises whence accurate conclusions may be drawn ; that, as these books are authentic public documents, and as I cannot myself refer to them, anything I could offer to their Lordships on the subject would be altogether superfluous, and would appear presumptuous interruptions to their Lordships' judgment, which will, doubtless, always found itself upon those grounds only that cannot be disputed.

"I have, etc. etc.   Cochrane.

"The Hon. W. W. Pole,
"Secretary to the Admiralty."

This reply, though plain, was respectful ; but, as I had afterwards good reason to know, was deemed very offensive ; the result being that, *after two months' delay* to enable Lord Gambier to get up his defence, a court-martial was assembled on the 26th of July, on board the *Gladiator*, at Portsmouth, the court being composed of the following members :—

President—Sir Roger Curtis, Port-Admiral.

ADMIRALS—Young, Stanhope, Campbell, Douglas, Duckworth, and Sutton.

CAPTAINS—Irwin, Dickson, Hall, and Dunn.

It may perhaps be asked in what way a court-martial on Lord Gambier can so far concern me as to occupy a prominent place in this autobiography ? The reply is, that, notwithstanding my repudiation, I was regarded at the court-martial as his accuser, though not permitted to be present so as to cross-examine witnesses ; the whole proceeding being conducted in my absence, rather as a prosecution against me than Lord Gambier ; and that the result was injurious to myself, as Lord Mulgrave had predicted, involving the punishment of not being employed with my frigate at Flushing, there to put in execution plans for the certain destruction of the French fleet in the Scheldt ; so that, in order to punish me, the enemy's fleet was suffered to remain in security, when it might easily have been destroyed.

CHAPTER XXIII

LORD GAMBIER'S DESPATCH

THE despatch brought to England by Sir Harry Neale set out with the perversion, that the fire-ships, " arranged according to my plan," were " led on in the most undaunted and determined manner by Captain Wooldridge in the ' *Mediator*,' *preceded by some vessels filled with powder and shells, as proposed by Lord Cochrane, with a view to explosion* " !

The omission of the fact that before Captain Wooldridge " led the fire-ships " I had myself preceded them in the explosion vessel, and that, even before the *Mediator* proceeded on service in obedience to the signals made by my order from the *Imperieuse*, the explosion vessel under my personal command was half-way towards the French fleet ; the suppression of my name as having anything at all to do with the attack by means of the explosion vessels, notwithstanding that by going first I ran all the risk of being boarded by the French guard-boats, and myself and crew murdered, as would have been the case had we been captured, showed that the object of the commander-in-chief was to suppress all mention of me, my plans, or their execution, as entitled to any credit for the mischief done to the enemy.

The despatch leads the reader to infer that the success subsequently obtained arose from the "undaunted and determined manner in which Captain Wooldridge led the fire-ships," from "Admiral Stopford's zealous co-operation with the boats," though not one of these ever stirred from alongside the *Cæsar*, anchored full four miles from the scene of action, and from the plans of the commander-in-chief himself.

That this suppression of all mention of the success of my plans in driving the whole enemy's fleet ashore with the exception of two ships of the line, was deliberately intended by the commander-in-chief, is placed beyond question by the contemptuous manner in which he speaks of the means which really effected the mischief,—" *some vessels filled with powder and shells, with a view to explosion.*" That these means, conducted by myself, not Captain Wooldridge, *did* drive the French ships ashore, has been admitted by every French and English historian since that period ; and that this was done by my personal presence and instrumentality is a historical fact which nothing can shake or pervert. The only person ignoring the fact was the commander-in-chief of the British force, who not only gives me no credit for what had been done, but does not even mention my name, as having, by the above means, contributed to the result !

Throughout the whole despatch, there is not a word to indicate that the terror caused by the explosion vessels had anything to do with the success gained. On the contrary, the success is attributed to causes purely imaginary. Great credit is given to me "for the vigorous and gallant attack on the French line-of-battle ships ashore," and for " my judicious manner of approaching them, and placing my ship in a position most advantageous to annoy the enemy, and *preserve my own ship* ! which," continued his lordship, " could not be exceeded by any feat of valour hitherto achieved by the British navy ! "

The plain fact is, and it will by this time be evident to others besides nautical men, that the just quoted piece of claptrap was considered in the light of a sop to my supposed vanity, sufficient to insure my holding my peace on the subject of the fleet not having even contemplated an attack till forced into it by my signal being mistaken for being " in distress."

Instead of being praised for what my plans really effected, I was praised for what was neither done nor intended to be done. Instead of adopting " a judicious manner of approaching the enemy, so as *to preserve my ship*," I drifted the *Imperieuse* in like a log with the tide, and stern foremost, for fear of being recalled, and then went at the enemy with a determination, not to preserve, but *to lose* my ship, if the commander-in-chief did not relieve her before she was riddled with shot ; this being my only hope of forcing on an attack of any kind. My motive was, no doubt, fathomed from seeing me attack three line-of-battle ships simultaneously. Not a moment was to be lost, and for the first time, since the French ran their ships ashore in terror, two British line-of-battle ships, and some frigates, approached the spot where the enemy's vessels had been lying aground *ever since the previous midnight*, helpless, and, as every French authority admits, hopeless of escape, had the slightest effort been made to prevent it.

In place, then, of attacking these with a single frigate, in such a way as to " *preserve my ship*," I here avow that I rushed at the enemy in the bitterness of despair, determined that if a portion of the fleet was not sent in, the *Imperieuse* should never again float out ; for rather than incur the stigma which would have awaited me in England, from no fault of mine, but because it was not expedient that plans which had been partially successful should be fully accomplished, she should have been destroyed.

This despatch, inexplicable as it was felt to be, naturally suggested to the public mind in England, that, despite its assumption of a great victory, the result of the victory was by no means commensurate with the tone of exultation assumed. The French fleet was *not* destroyed ; and it was equally manifest, that if but little had been effected, it was owing to the time which had been suffered to elapse between my first signals and the tardy aid reluctantly yielded in support of them. By that kind of intuitive perception characteristic of the British press, it was agreed that there had been mismanagement somewhere, but *where* was not to be gathered from the commander-in-chief's despatch, in which everything "by favour of the Almighty," as the despatch most reprehensibly set forth, had succeeded.

CHAPTER XXIV

CONDUCT OF THE COURT-MARTIAL

THE most damnatory point connected with the court-martial is —that on finding me inflexible with regard to the vote of thanks to Lord Gambier, the Board of Admiralty ordered his lordship, AFTER HIS RETURN TO ENGLAND, to *write a second despatch containing fresh details of the action*! thus superseding the first despatch written by himself as commander-in-chief at the time of the action ! !

With this extraordinary demand Lord Gambier appears to have gladly complied on the 10th of May, 1809 ; so that there are two despatches, the first highly praising me for what I neither did nor intended to do—the second IGNORING MY SERVICES ALTO-GETHER ! ! In fact, only mentioning me by name, as *lying* "*about three miles from the enemy.*" One step more in the second despatch, viz. that I was not in Aix Roads at all ! would only have been in keeping with the assertion just quoted. Were not these contradictory documents now adduced, the denial of such an act by suppressing all mention of it in the despatches would be incredible. Nevertheless, I fearlessly assert, that to my personal conduct of the explosion vessel was solely attributable the panic produced in the enemy's fleet, and that such conduct was one of the most desperate acts on record.

There is nothing like this in the records of the British or any other naval service, and the reasons for a precedent so unusual must themselves have been extraordinary. It is clear to me, that from the order of the Board of Admiralty to the commander-in-chief to make a second report of the action in Aix Roads the court-martial took its cue. This may be a harsh conclusion, and perhaps would be so were it not corroborated by circumstances, not the least significant of which was, that the commander-in-chief's official report had been long before *published in the Gazette* ! No naval reason to invalidate this official report was alleged, or could have existed.

During my examination before the court I alluded to the fact of having " reported to the commander-in-chief the ruinous state of the Isle of Aix, it having the *inner fortifications completely blown up and destroyed.* This I not only ascertained from the deck of the *Imperieuse* with perfect precision as to the side towards us, but also as to the opposite side, from personal observations made from the main-topgallant mast-head. There were thirteen guns mounted."

This evidence, if admitted, and its truth was fully proved by the testimony of other officers, completely confirmed Lord Gambier's previous statement to the Admiralty, that " *the fortifications were no obstacle.*" But now it was expedient that these fortifications should constitute the bugbear which, as was asserted, would have destroyed any British ships sent in to attack the enemy's ships aground ! and that the issue of the court-martial mainly rested on establishing the formidable character of the fortifications, a second despatch was called for. When, in my evidence, I was explaining to the court the little danger to be apprehended from these fortifications—one of the principal points before the court, Admiral Young stopped me with the query, " Will you consider, my Lord Cochrane, before you go on, HOW FAR THIS IS RELEVANT ? "

On my insisting upon further explanation, the judge-advocate attempted to stop me by demanding—" CAN THIS RELATE TO THE QUESTION ASKED ? " The president—seeing that I would not be stopped—remarked—" *Lord Cochrane states this as his reason for not taking a particular line of conduct.*" I stated it for no purpose of the kind, but to show that opposition from such fortifications was hardly worth taking into consideration, and thus continued :—

" I have felt that if I had answered ' *Yes* ' or ' *No* ' to all the questions which had been put to me, I ought to be hung, and that if a court-martial were held upon me and only the answers ' *Yes* ' or ' *No* ' appeared to those questions, I *should* be hung for them."

JUDGE-ADVOCATE.—" *I believe nobody has desired your Lordship to answer merely ' Yes ' or ' No ' !* "

A still more striking instance of the animus of the court was the following attempted stoppage of Captain Beresford's evidence.

CAPT. BERESFORD.—" The only thing I know with respect to the *Calcutta* being fired, was by a conversation between Lord Cochrane and myself in the presence of Capt. Bligh, Capt. Maitland, and others."

PRESIDENT.—" *Is this strictly evidence, Mr Judge-Advocate ?* "

JUDGE-ADVOCATE.—" *Yes !* I should think it is ; BECAUSE I CONCEIVE IT IS TO AFFECT THE EVIDENCE OF LORD COCHRANE " ! ! !

At the present day such proceedings in any tribunal would be thought impossible. There, however, they are on record— showing that the openly avowed object of the court-martial was the suppression and invalidation of my evidence by any means that could be brought to bear, rather than an inquiry into the conduct of the commander-in-chief on the merits of the case.

One point more must be noticed, relative to the manner in

which the court was conducted. Having reason to believe, as has been shown, that the inquiry was being directed against myself, I was naturally anxious to be present at the reading of the commander-in-chief's defence, in order to judge how far I might thereby stand affected. With this view I presented myself at the court on the fifth day of the inquiry, when it was known that the defence would be made.

To my surprise the court saw fit to refuse the privilege.

Lord Gambier stated at the outset of his defence, that he had been compelled to demand a court-martial in consequence of "the insinuations thrown out against him by Lord Cochrane, which not only compromised his own honour, but that of brave officers and men serving under his command."

I never threw out against his lordship a single insinuation, nor does one exist, either on the records of the court or elsewhere. I merely told Lord Mulgrave, as previously narrated, that I did not consider Lord Gambier's services worthy of a vote of thanks from parliament, and that on this ground, as bound by public duty to my constituents, I should resist it. As will presently be seen, this was also the opinion of many eminent men in parliament, and on the same ground too—that of public duty. If I committed any offence in this, it was that of refusing to have my name coupled with that of Lord Gambier in the vote of thanks, and resisting an offer of an independent squadron and a regiment, not to persist in my determination of opposing it.

That my objection to the vote of thanks to Lord Gambier included any of the officers serving under him was a gratuitous assumption to secure sympathy for himself. Not a single word did I utter against any officer; though, on the ninth and last day of the court-martial, it was with the greatest difficulty, and *after a positive refusal*, that I succeeded in getting a denial of Lord Gambier's unfounded assertion attached to the Minutes.

So clumsily was this accusation made against me, that Lord Gambier, despite the unwarrantable assumption just quoted, subsequently admitted my objection to the vote of thanks to have *been solely aimed at himself*, and not, as he had just said, at the officers and men of the fleet. Here are his lordship's words :—

" Lord Cochrane *warned* the noble lord at the head of the Admiralty that if his measure (the vote of thanks) were attempted he should, if standing alone, oppose it ; thus, without specifically objecting to thanks being given for the service performed, directing his hostility *personally at me.*" (*Minutes*, p. 107.)

That is—I should not have objected to a vote of thanks to the officers and men of the fleet, but only to himself *personally.* Yet in the same breath he accused me of traducing the officers and men of the fleet ; with the intention, no doubt, of sheltering himself under the pretence of my having traduced them also. Could anything be more puerile ? I gave no other " *warning* " to Lord Mulgrave than that which Lord Gambier correctly stated, and that I certainly did give, but without a word which could give rise to the slighest imputation on the officers and men of the fleet.

The fact is, that I never accused Lord Gambier at all, *not even to Lord Mulgrave*, to whom I only expressed an intention of opposing a parliamentary vote of thanks. It was the Board of Admiralty who accused him.

I now quit this miserable subject for ever. The real fact is, that from over-persuasion of those who were jealous of a junior officer originating and being appointed to carry out plans deemed impossible by others, Lord Gambier declined to second my efforts. This decision of his lordship was no doubt arrived at, when a council of officers were summoned on board the flag-ship, on the morning of the 12th, at which time the enemy's fleet was lying helplessly ashore.

That, after such council, his lordship never intended to make *any attack at all* on the French ships, is proved *beyond question*, by the subjoined testimony of Captain Broughton.

"A ship or two might have been placed, in my opinion against the batteries on the southern part of Ile d'Aix, so as to take off their fire AND SILENCE THEM. I mentioned to Sir H. Neale, when the signal was made for all captains in the morning, and I thought *they were attackable*—speaking of the confused state in which the French ships appeared to be at the time."

"*I heard my Lord Gambier the same morning say* (at this council) it *had been his intention to have gone against the batteries I now speak of, but as the enemy were on shore he did not think it necessary to run any unnecessary risk of the fleet when the object of their destruction seemed to be already obtained.*" (*Minutes*, pp. 221, 222.)

That is, he admits my exertions to have destroyed the French fleet (which was not destroyed—all except three ships having escaped), and plainly tells Captain Broughton that *he will do nothing more*! This should for ever decide the point.

If, however, proof be still wanted of the utter worthlessness of any opposition in the power of the enemy to offer, whether by fortifications or ships, it is to be found in the following statement at the close of Lord Gambier's defence :—

"I conclude by observing that the service actually performed has been of great importance, as well in its immediate effects as in its ultimate consequences ; for the Brest fleet is so reduced as to be no longer effective. It was upon this fleet the enemy relied for the succour and protection of their West India colonies, and *the destruction of their ships was effected in their own harbour, in sight of thousands of the French. I congratulate myself and my country that this important service has been effected, under Providence, with the loss only of ten men killed, thirty-five wounded, and one missing.* NOT EVEN ONE OF THE SMALLEST OF OUR VESSELS EMPLOYED HAS BEEN DISABLED FROM PROCEEDING ON ANY SERVICE THAT MIGHT HAVE BECOME NECESSARY."

By this voluntary admission of Lord Gambier I am willing to

R

be judged—feeling certain that posterity will be as fully convinced of the inability of the enemy to inflict material damage
on our ships, as was Lord Gambier himself, according to his
own testimony, as quoted in the above passage. As Lord
Gambier truly says, no damage worth mentioning *was* done to
any of our ships, to which I shall add, that at no period after
the enemy's ships were driven ashore were they in a condition
to inflict damage. This his lordship not only admits, but *proves*,
in the concluding paragraph of his defence, and yet the whole
point of the trial is made to rest on the surmise that had Lord
Gambier done *anything* against the enemy's ships aground,
the destruction of the British force must have been the consequence.
That is, *by doing nothing the enemy's ships were destroyed ; though
by doing anything our own would have been in danger* ! ! !

CHAPTER XXV

THE VOTE OF THANKS

FROM this time forward I never trod the deck of a British ship
of war at sea, as her commander, till thirty-nine years afterwards I was appointed by her present most gracious Majesty to
command the West India squadron ; the greater portion of the
interval being marked by persecution of which the court-martial
on Lord Gambier was only the starting-point.

The commencement of the parliamentary session in 1810, was
remarkable for its votes of thanks, and the refusal of all information which might justify them. This led Lord Milton
to declare in the House of Commons, that " votes of thanks,
from their frequency, had lost their value, and ceased to be an
honour. They had got so much into the habit of voting thanks
that it was almost an insult not to vote them."

On the 25th of January, 1810, Lord Grenville adverted in the
House of Lords to notice of motion for a vote of thanks to Lord
Gambier, for *his* services in destroying the enemy's ships in

Basque Roads ; and observed that as the last intimation on the journals respecting Lord Gambier was his arrest, it would be necessary that the *minutes* of the court-martial should be laid before the House, in order to enable it to judge of the necessity for a vote of thanks. To this Lord Mulgrave strongly objected, on the ground that it " would appear as if it was wished to retry the case." Laying the sentence of acquittal only before the House, said his lordship, would be "sufficient to render their proceedings regular, and would answer all the purposes of the noble lord." With this the House was obliged to be content, though how that sentence had been obtained the reader is now made aware.

On the 29th of January, in pursuance of notice previously given, I made a motion for the production of the *minutes of the court-martial* in the House of Commons ; as being, from the extraordinary discrepancy between the nature of the evidence and the sentence, absolutely necessary, in order to enable members fairly and impartially to decide whether the thanks in contemplation of ministers *were due* to Lord Gambier for the part he took in what had been by them denominated a victory in Basque Roads.

In support of this production of the minutes, I adverted to a previously expressed opinion of the Chancellor of the Exchequer (Mr Perceval), that Lord Gambier had been honourably acquitted, but that an officer's having done no wrong *did not entitle him to the thanks of the House*; which, if bestowed on trifling, or, indeed, on any but brilliant achievements, would dwindle into contempt, even with those on whom they should be conferred. Votes of thanks were already lightly esteemed in the navy, and I pledged myself—if the House would insist on the production of the minutes—to prove that " Lord Gambier's defence was contradicted by itself—by his lordship's official letters— and by his own witnesses ; many of whom, as to essential facts, were at variance with themselves and with each other." Lastly, I undertook to prove to the House, that the chart of the 12th of April was "in a most material point false—and in every respect a fabrication."

Having been put on my defence by direct accusation on the part of a ministerial supporter that I had not done my duty, I implored the House to give me an opportunity, not only of defending myself, but of laying bare matters of more importance to the country than either my judgment or character. I again pledged myself to prove all I had asserted, and to stake everything that was valuable to man on the issue, at the same time telling the House that, if the minutes were granted, I would expose such matters as might make the country tremble for its safety—and entreating it well to consider that there was another tribunal to which it was answerable, that of posterity, which would try all our actions and judge impartially.

At the conclusion of the preliminary debate, the Chancellor of the Exchequer rose to move a vote of thanks to Lord Gambier for *his eminent services in destroying the French fleet* in the Basque Roads ! My name, as having effected anything, was *purposely and very ingeniously left out* ! but warm thanks were accorded to those who directed the fire-ships,—not against the enemy, but against the banks of the Boyart and Palles shoals !

The passage in the vote of thanks is curious : " for their gallant and highly meritorious conduct on this glorious occasion, *particularly marked by the brilliant and unexampled success of the difficult and perilous mode of attack by fire-ships, conducted under the immediate superintendence of Captain Lord Cochrane* ! " Yet Lord Gambier stated in his defence, " The success of the first part of the enterprise arose from the terror excited by the *appearance* of the fire-ships ! *as they failed in the principal effect they were intended to produce.*" If the House had been in the possession of the minutes of the court-martial, would they have voted thanks to officers of whom the commander-in-chief says that they " *failed in their object* " ? Not a word of thanks to me for having conducted it, but to the commander-in-chief, then twelve miles off, his only merit consisting in coming three miles nearer, anchoring out of gunshot—and to men whom a ministerial supporter had praised by saying they had been promoted for " *disobeying my signals* " ! And this though the First Lord of the Admiralty had offered me his own regiment—a squadron of frigates, with *carte blanche* to do what I pleased with them—and a vote of thanks, conjointly with Lord Gambier, if I would not offer any opposition !

The value of such a vote under such circumstances had been rightly estimated, even by those who acquiesced in it. The value of the service rendered was paltry, in comparison with what it ought to have been ; and the vote, either to myself or my superiors, would have been worthy of it. I had from the first refused to have my name coupled with such pretence, as a fraud on national honours.

Yet, leaving me altogether out of the vote of thanks, so long as thanks were voted, and giving them to the commander-in-chief and the officers under " my immediate direction," was a specimen of party spite so transparent that it could deceive nobody. The Chancellor of the Exchequer, either ashamed of his subject, or forgetting the purpose in hand, most unaccountably gave me in his harangue *the credit of the whole affair* ! He could only have done this from two motives. Either he was too much a gentleman to permit his personal honour to be trampled under foot by his colleagues, or he could not have read the vote of thanks till he came to it at the conclusion of his speech. There is, however, a third hypothesis. The subjoined eulogy might have been pronounced to blind the House.

" The attack having thus recommenced on the night of the 13th, successively was followed up on the next day by the noble lord (Cochrane) with peculiar gallantry. The consequence was that no less than three sail of the line and a fifty-gun ship were completely destroyed. The House would not, therefore, he trusted, be disposed to refuse its thanks *for eminent services when performed under such great peril and risk*, whilst the enemy were possessed of the protection of their own batteries, and other advantages which they could bring into play for the security of their own vessels. *It was an enterprise of great and peculiar hazard and difficulty.* The result had been highly injurious to

the enemy, and had the effect of not only disabling but of removing the enemy's whole squadron from the possibility of being
for a considerable time available for the purposes of the naval
campaign. *Was not this an object of great magnitude?* "

From this speech it is clear that the Chancellor of the Exchequer considered that the whole success was attributable to
my exertions, and it is no less apparent that he contemplated
my being included in the vote of thanks.

Then why leave me out of the vote of thanks, and give thanks
to those who had nothing to do with this "*work of great
magnitude*"?

Lord Mulgrave made no such blunder in the House of Lords
nor even mentioned my name *except in terms of reprobation*—
possibly because I refused his lordship's temptation of a squadron
and a regiment to hold my peace! Yet it may be that the
Chancellor of the Exchequer made no mistake. His eulogy
might have been merely intended to appeal to the popular ear,
whilst contemptuously excluding me from the vote. Be this as
it may, the trick succeeded, and my voice was drowned amidst
the clamour of faction, as were the voices of those who supported me in the House.

Still I was not disposed to allow the vote to pass without
further protest. I again warned the House that "even their
verdict was not conclusive upon character, but that there was
another tribunal to which even that House was amenable, and
that the public would one day exercise a judgment, even though
the House might shrink from a just decision. I inquired what
portion of Lord Gambier's exploit merited thanks, or what had
been the nature of his exploit? He lay at a distance—never
brought his fleet to the place of action, or even within danger,
and yet for such supineness he was to receive the highest honours
of his country! The ground taken by ministers was frivolous
—that where the subordinates admittedly deserved the praise,
the superiors must receive it. The public *would one day read
the minutes, though the House would not. The public would*

judge from the facts, though the House would not. The public would not submit to have its eyes bound because the House chose to keep theirs shut. Let a single reason be adduced for this vote of thanks, and I was ready to vote for it—but the *reasons* which had been obtruded on the House were unworthy the name of *arguments.*"

A few remarks on what passed in the House of Lords, where similar thanks were voted, are necessary.

Lord Mulgrave said that it was with great surprise that he first heard that a noble lord serving under the noble admiral, and a member of another House, had intimated his intention to oppose the vote of the House of Commons, on the ground that his commander had not done his duty to *the utmost.* Lord Mulgrave, of course, alluded to my conversation with him nine months before, though I never said anything of the kind to his lordship. What I said was, "that the commander-in-chief had not done anything deserving the thanks of Parliament." Had the *minutes* been allowed to be produced in either House, this would have been proved beyond question, in spite of the *sentence of acquittal,* which was alone laid on the table.

Lord Mulgrave was no less unjust in attempting to convince the peers that I had done nothing but carry out *Lord Gambier's plan of fire-ships* ; referring them to Lord Gambier's letter of March 19th, 1809, in which, instead of recommending an attack by fire-ships, Lord Gambier had denounced such an attempt as " *hazardous, if not desperate,*" as would have appeared had the minutes of the court-martial been laid before them.

Mine, as I have previously explained, was not an attack by fire-ships alone, for such an attack could only have ended in the boarding of the fire-ships by the enemy's row-boats, and the murdering of the crews. It was an attack by means of explosion vessels, which should impress the enemy with the idea that every fire-ship was similarly charged, so as to have the effect of deterring them from boarding, and thus the fire-ships, had they been properly directed, must have done their work in spite of the enemy's row-boats.

Yet Lord Mulgrave followed Lord Gambier in this "*suppressio veri*." On the very day Lord Gambier had *not* recommended the use of fire-ships—though Lord Mulgrave's speech would lead the House, in the absence of the minutes of the court-martial, to infer that he *had* recommended their use—the commander-in-chief had stated that an attack with fire-ships would be "*hazardous, if not desperate*." A curious way, truly, of recommending the use of fire-ships ; though, had he recommended them, they would have been of no use without the explosion vessels, the terror created by which formed the very essence of my plan, and was the sole cause even of the trifling success gained. Again, said Lord Mulgrave :—

"Lord Cochrane arrived at Plymouth. He had on a former occasion been employed in blockading Rochefort, and was acquainted with the coasts. He was, therefore, consulted, and *spoke with greater confidence of the success of the attempt than those who wrote from that quarter*. It was not, however, merely the zeal and *desire of execution* he showed, but also the talent he displayed in meeting the objections *started by naval men*, which induced the Admiralty to employ his Lordship."

This representation was thoroughly incorrect. So far from there being any " desire of execution " on my part, I tried every means in my power to avoid being intrusted with the execution of my own—not Lord Gambier's—plans as Lord Mulgrave insinuated. He, however, unconsciously admitted that other naval men "started " such objections, that they could not be got to undertake an attack with fire-ships, and therefore the duty was *thrust* on me, with the addition of the explosion vessels I had suggested, thus convincing the Admiralty Board that an attack, on my plan, was both easy of execution and certain in its results. Lord Mulgrave's expression of " those who wrote from that quarter," viz. Lord Gambier, showed that the commander-in-chief had *no confidence* in fire-ships. Neither had I, unless accompanied by my plan of explosion vessels.

Still persisting that this was an attack by fire-ships merely, Lord Mulgrave told the House that it was nothing new, which was the case, if the explosion vessels were left out, but that—

"In the course of the last century there were two services performed by fire-ships ; the first in 1702 at Vigo, and the second off Minorca in 1792. But *what was the present service* ? Recollect, a fleet protected by *shoals and currents*, in sight of their own coast, and in presence of their countrymen. *Nothing in the annals of our Navy was more brilliant* !"

Who, then, performed that "*brilliant*" service, than which nothing could be more satisfactory ? Lord Mulgrave told the House that Lord Gambier did, *whilst lying with his fleet nine miles off*, and reluctantly sending two line-of-battle ships and some frigates to my "assistance," when almost too late to rescue me from the dilemma into which, in sheer despair of anything being done, I had voluntarily rushed, with the determination that if my frigate was sacrificed, while he was calmly looking on, he should take the consequences, and what they would have been I need not say. It was this act of mine, and this only, which caused the paltry service to be effected of destroying two line-of-battle ships and a store-ship, instead of the whole enemy's fleet !

Lord Mulgrave's statements were severely rebuked by Lord Holland :—

"Lord Holland represented in strong terms the light in which ministers placed themselves before parliament and the country by coming forward, so hastily in the first instance to procure thanks, and then suddenly sending Lord Gambier to a court-martial *with the thanks on their lips*. He thought that in a case of parliamentary thanks the case should be *clear and strong* to receive such a reward. What said Lord Cochrane in his reply to the Admiralty ? * '*Look at and sift the log-books* ! and not

* See p. 248.

ask me for accusations.' He (Lord Holland) condemned the precipitancy of ministers, who by their measures had endeavoured to *stultify the House as they had already stultified their own administration.*

"After sending Lord Gambier through the ordeal of a court-martial, Lord Mulgrave now came down, pronounced his praises, and called upon the House to vote him their thanks ! It was not in this manner that the French government conducted itself towards their admirals and generals. They instituted a very severe inquiry as to this affair at Basque Roads, and many of their commanders were most severely punished. They did not give thanks to General Monnet for his defence of Flushing, but, on the contrary, censured his conduct most severely.

"If the barren thanks of both Houses of Parliament were *often to be voted in this way, they would soon cease to be of any value.* The noble Lord (Mulgrave) had said a great deal about the battle of Talavera, and the resistance made to the vote of thanks in that instance. Now it did not appear to him (Lord Holland) that the battle of Talavera could have anything to do with the action of Basque Roads or with the conduct of Lord Gambier. But if resistance to the vote of thanks to Lord Wellington were adduced as a proof of party motives, it might well be considered a proof of party spirit on the other side to bring forward motions of thanks for services of such a description as were those of Lord Gambier."

However dexterous might be the ministerial legerdemain which could convert into victory the admitted intention of the commander-in-chief *not to fight,* Lord Melville alone exposed the real secret of the matter :—

"Lord Melville conceived the Admiralty to have acted extremely wrong in giving to Lord Cochrane a command so contrary to the usual rules of the service, and which must have been so galling and disgusting to the feelings of other officers in

Lord Gambier's fleet. He respected as much as any man could the zeal, intrepidity, and enterprise of Lord Cochrane, but it was wrong to presume that these qualities were wanting in officers of that fleet of superior standing to his Lordship. Such a selection naturally put Lord Cochrane upon attempting enterprises whereby great glory might be obtained."

Here lies the gist of the whole matter. Had I devised the plan of attack, and had the Board of Admiralty acceded to my earnest wish, and left it to my seniors to execute, or had I persisted in my determination to refuse a command which the Admiralty literally forced upon me, all would have been well. Even had Lord Mulgrave fulfilled his promise of satisfying the *amour propre* of the fleet—which he neither did nor intended to do—all might have been well. As it was, I was exposed to the full amount of hostility which formed my reason for declining the command in the first instance.

It was felt—as Admiral Austen plainly says—by the officers of the fleet in Basque Roads that a decisive victory would elevate me in national estimation over my seniors, as it unquestionably would have done. Lord Gambier was an easy man, and the " shoal and current " bugbear was successfully used to bring the fleet to an anchor in place of going on to the attack, he knowing no better, and having taken no trouble to ascertain the fact; in short confining himself to mere blockade. This was the fault of the commander-in-chief, but it did not justify him in bringing forward charts made up for the purpose of proving imaginary dangers from ruined fortifications and shoals where none existed. Nor did it justify the evidence of influenced witnesses to *prove* danger—in defiance of his lordship's own admission that *no ship suffered injury*! It did not justify his lordship in assuming many things in his defence, which were not in evidence at all, and many more things that were totally at variance with the evidence contained in the minutes. To have declined pushing an advantage to victory, in deference to the jealousy of senior officers, was one thing; to trump up a story of *an old store-ship breaking up a boom of more than a mile in lineal extent, and moored with a hundred anchors, was another*.

It will now be seen why the Government of that day refused the production of "*minutes* of the court-martial, almost every page of which would have rendered the defence of the commander-in-chief—or rather that of his solicitor, Mr Lavie, for I will do Lord Gambier the justice of believing that he did not write the defence read to the court by the judge-advocate —untenable for a moment. That the ministry of that corrupt day should have resorted to such a subterfuge can, however, scarcely add to the contempt with which history already regards them."

I told the House of Commons that "*posterity would judge their acts.*" Here, then, is matter for that judgment. That it was not made public at the time arose from two causes. First, that in those days the bulk of the press was influenced by the ministry ; and a jackal howl, from one end of the kingdom to the other, would have been, and was, the reward of my pains. Secondly, that until his Grace the Duke of Somerset gave me the chart and other official materials requisite to lay the matter before posterity, it was not in my power to do so ; except, as on my previous attempts at justification, by assertions, which would have had no more effect on the public mind than now would those of the factions which persecuted me. As I belonged to no party in the House, I found no friends but the few who, like myself, stood alone in their independence of party. Those were themselves disorganised, and deceived by the well-timed eulogy of the Chancellor of the Exchequer, into the belief that the vote of thanks included me also. The numbers of the independent party were, however, as nothing compared to the organised masses in power, or eager to place themselves in power. The debate was felt to have most seriously damaged the party to whom I was politically opposed, and that party ever afterwards made me a mark for their revenge. In this brief sentence may my whole subsequent history be comprised.

CHAPTER XXVI

REFUSAL OF MY PLANS FOR ATTACKING THE FRENCH FLEET
IN THE SCHELDT

JUST at the period of the court-martial on Lord Gambier, great
national expectations were excited by the combined military
and naval expedition to Walcheren, under the Earl of Chatham
and Sir Richard Strachan. The object of this armament, the
most formidable England had ever sent forth, was the capture
or destruction of the French fleet in the Scheldt, and of the
arsenals and dockyards of Flushing, Terneuse, and Antwerp, at
the latter of which ports Buonaparte was carrying on naval
works with great vigour.

The force employed for this purpose comprised 40,000 troops,
35 sail-of-the-line, 2 fifty gun-ships, 3 forty-four gun-ships, 18
frigates, and nearly 200 smaller vessels, besides dockyard craft;
the first portion of the expedition quitting the Downs on the
28th of July, 1809, and anchoring the same evening near the
coast of Walcheren.

It will not be surprising that I viewed the departure of this
force with regret; as had one half of the troops been placed,
as suggested in my letter to Lord Mulgrave, on the islands of
the French coast, and had half the frigates alone been employed,
as had been the *Imperieuse* and other vessels in the Mediterranean,
not a man could have been detached from Western France to the
Spanish peninsula, from which the remaining portion of the
British army might have driven the French troops already
there.

Full of these views, and knowing that short work might be
made of the Walcheren expedition, so as to liberate both the
naval and military force for service elsewhere, I laid before the
Admiralty a plan for destroying the French fleet and the Flemish
dockyards, somewhat analogous to that which would have proved

completely effectual in Basque Roads, had it been followed up by the commander-in-chief. My new plan had, moreover, received an important addition from the experience there gained, and was now as formidable against fortifications as against fleets.

The first measure of indignation against me for my late services to my country was the summary rejection of my plan, and not only this, but a refusal by Admiralty letter to proceed to the Scheldt to join my frigate, which had been sent there under the temporary command of the Hon. Captain Duncan, a most excellent and gallant officer.

Of the disastrous failure of the Walcheren expedition—the destruction of a large portion of the army by disease—and the retreat of the remainder, I shall not speak ; these matters being already well known to the student of English history. I will, however, assert—and the assertion will be borne out by the plan of the attack submitted by me to the Admiralty—that had my recommendation been adopted, even though not carried out under my own supervision, nothing could have saved the French fleet in the Scheldt from a similar fate to that which had befallen their armament in Aix Roads. Even—as with the disaster in Aix Roads fresh in remembrance, is probable—had the French fleet in the Scheldt taken refuge above Antwerp, it could only have placed itself in a *cul-de-sac* ; whilst there was ample military and naval force to operate against the dockyards and fortifications during the period that my appliances for the destruction of the enemy's fleet were in progress ; for I in no way wished to interfere with the operations of the general or admiral commanding, but rather to conduct my own operations independently of extraordinary aid from either.

The cost of this plan to the nation would have been ten rotten old hulks, some fifty thousand barrels of powder, and a proportionate quantity of shells. The cost of the expedition, which failed—in addition to the thousands of lives sacrificed—was millions ; and the millions which followed by the prolongation of the war, by the refusal of the Admiralty to put in operation any naval expedition calculated to effect a beneficial object—who

shall count ?   So much for war when conducted by cabinets !
But I was now a marked man, and the Government evidently
considered it preferable that the largest force which England had
ever despatched from her shores should incur the chance of
failure in its object, than that the simple and easily applied
plans of a junior post-captain should again jeopardise the reputation of his commander-in-chief.

It was very curious that whilst this animosity was being
directed against me in my professional capacity, I had shortly
before received from his Majesty George the Third, the highest
decoration of the order of the Bath for my professional services.

So little secret did the Government make of their determination not to employ me again, that the public press regarded this
determination as a settled matter.   It was nothing that I had
been instrumental in destroying the fleet so much dreaded by
our West India merchants and the nation generally, or that I
had offered to serve the French fleet in the Scheldt in the same
way.   I was now an obnoxious man, and the national expenditure
of millions for defeat, was by the ministry of that day deemed
preferable to cheap victory if achieved by a junior officer, to
whom the Chancellor of the Exchequer—whilst denying him
thanks for the service—had attributed the destruction of a
fleet quite as formidable as the one in the Scheldt.

It may be scarcely credible to the present age that the
Government should have openly announced such a determination.
On the principle adopted throughout this work, of adducing
nothing without proof, it will be necessary to place the preceding facts beyond dispute.   From one of the most talented
periodicals of the time I extract the following passage : " The
worst injury which the radical reformers have done the country,
has been *by depriving it of Lord Cochrane's services, and withdrawing him from that career* which he had so gloriously begun."
The pretence was, that I had *withdrawn myself* ! at the time I
was entreating the Admiralty to permit me to return to my
frigate !   This matter will shortly be made very clear.

One grave cause of offence to the ministry, in addition to my determination to oppose the vote of thanks to Lord Gambier, had been the part I took at the famous meeting held at the Crown and Anchor in the Strand. For a junior naval officer in that day to associate with such persons as Sir Francis Burdett and Major Cartwright was bad enough, but that he should *act* with them was a thing unheard of in the naval service.

At this meeting many irritating things were said, though not by me. The late trial of the Duke of York was freely handled, and Colonel Wardle, the principal promoter of it, held up to public admiration. The "borough-mongering faction," as it was forcibly termed by Sir Francis Burdett, was painted as involving the country in perpetual misfortune, and consigning to hopeless imprisonment all who ventured to expose their practices ; whilst it was said, even his Majesty could not carry on his fair share of government, being compelled to choose his ministers from a faction which not only oppressed the people, but controlled the King himself.

The resolutions moved by good old Major Cartwright at this celebrated meeting were at that time regarded as treason, though at the present day sound doctrine, viz. that "so long as the people were not fairly represented corruption must increase —our debts and taxes accumulate—our resources be dissipated —the native energy of the people be depressed, and the country be deprived of its best defences. The remedy was only to be found in the principles handed down to us by the wisdom and virtue of our forefathers, in a full and fair representation of the people in parliament."

This was perfectly true ; and singularly enough, after the lapse of fifty-one years, the very same question forms the principal feature of the present session of parliament, the debates on the subject in our day differing very little from their predecessors of half-a-century ago, if we may credit the following picture from the *Times* leader of April 23rd, 1860. "Call Reform what you will, it is almost anything you please, except legislation. *The belligerent parties will fight and cheat one another, and both together will cheat the people !*"

SIR FRANCIS BURDETT, BART.
[Born 1770.   Died 1844]

If after a battle of fifty years the people have not achieved the victory which early Reformers began, I have some right to call on the public to estimate the amount of obloquy which befell myself for my voluntary enrolment amongst the combatants on their side ; and in the belief that the public of the present day will do my memory that justice which through life has been denied me, I shall not shrink from laying these matters before them. If such a picture of our present legislators be truly drawn, what must have been that of the faction against which I had to contend ?

The speech made by me at the Crown and Anchor was very moderate, and indeed was spoken of by the ministerial organs as expressing less of the spirit of faction than any which had been delivered on that day. The worst part of it, so far as I can recollect, was that generally recorded, that " I hoped the time would come when ministers would not be employed all day in thinking what they were to cavil about all night, and all night in useless debate—whereby the real business of the country was neglected ; so much so indeed, that when the newspapers had reached me abroad, I felt ashamed at the manner in which the government of my country was conducted."

I had even gone further in moderation, though the ministry did not know it, viz. by observing to Sir Francis Burdett that I thought he was going *too far*. His reply was characteristic. " My dear Lord Cochrane, you don't know ministers. If you wish to get anything from them, you must go for a great deal more than you want. Even then you will get little enough." " Oh ! " replied I, " if those are your tactics, go on, I'll follow."

The real grievance was, however, my support of the motions in parliament which arose from the meetings at the Crown and Anchor. Mr Madocks distinctly charged the ministry with trafficking in seats, offering to prove to the House that Lord Castlereagh had, through the agency of the Honourable Mr Wellesley, been instrumental in purchasing for Mr Quintin Dick the borough of Cashel ; and that when in the matter of the

s

Duke of York Mr Dick had determined to vote according to his conscience, Lord Castlereagh intimated to that gentleman the necessity of voting with the Government, or resigning his seat, which was accordingly done. The ministry declined to accept the challenge.

The subsequent motion of Mr Curwen went further. But I must not forget that I am writing my autobiography, and not political history; I never made pretensions to parliamentary eloquence, and shall not inflict on the reader my humble efforts, excepting only those connected with the naval service.

On the 19th of February I moved for certain papers relative to the conduct of the Admiralty Court, and as my speech on that occasion was sufficiently comprehensive, I will adduce it with some slight explanations indicative of the practices which at that time were in full operation :—

" If these papers are granted it will be in my power to expose a system of abuses in the Admiralty Court unparalleled in this country, even exceeding those prevalent in Spain under the infamous administration of Godoy.

" The whole navy of England was, by the existing system, compelled to employ one individual to carry on its business before the Admiralty Court ; a person perhaps in whose competence or honesty they might have no confidence. But admitting his ability and integrity to be unquestionable, still the thing was preposterous. Would any man like to employ an attorney who at the same time did business for the other side ? Was such a regulation consistent with equity or common-sense ?

" Even the personal liberty of naval officers was answerable for some seizures, the produce of which notwithstanding went to the Crown, and the most abominable compromises sometimes took place. Whether the profits of these compromises found their way into the pockets of any particular individual I was not absolutely sure, but had evidence to presume that this was the fact. What indeed could be the design of confining the captors to one proctor, except that secrecy as to these questionable transactions may be preserved ? "

One case was my own. In a previous portion of this work is narrated the capture of the *King George* privateer, or pirate, for which seizure by any vessel of war a reward of 500*l.* had been issued. The *King George* in part actually belonged to parties connected with the Maltese Admiralty Court. As her condemnation was unavoidable, she was condemned as a *droit* to the Crown ; and costs to the extent of 600*l.* were decreed against myself, officers, and crew, for having taken her ! A subject which will hereafter have to be further alluded to.

The effect of this system was to indispose officers to look after prizes, and thus many an enemy's vessel was suffered to escape. One of my reasons for harassing the French on the coasts of Languedoc and Catalonia was, that it appeared more advantageous to effect something of service to the country, than to take prizes for no better end than to enrich the officers of the Maltese Admiralty Court, and at the same time to be ourselves condemned in costs for our trouble.

Some curious stories might be told of the effect of the system. It was my own practice, when any money was captured in a prize, to divide it into two portions, first, the Admiral's share, and next our own. We then buried the money in a sand-bank, in order that it might not be in our possession ; and, as opportunity occurred, it was afterwards taken up, the Admiral's share being transmitted to him, our share was then distributed at the capstan, in the usual proportions. As I never made any secret of my own transactions, the Maltese officials regarded me with perfect hatred ; they, no doubt, honestly believing that by appropriating our own captures to our own use, we were cheating them out of what they had more right to than ourselves ! By their practices they appeared to entertain one idea only, viz. that officers were appointed to ships of war for the sole purpose of enriching them !

In a case previously narrated, where I had, in Caldagues

Bay, taken thirteen vessels laden with corn for the French army in Barcelona, after having sunk two small ships of war protecting them—we sold the corn vessels and their cargo to the Spaniards for a trifle, dividing the dollars amongst us, after sending Lord Collingwood his share. We afterwards took the vessels of war, after raising them, to Gibraltar, where I purchased one as a yacht. Had I sent those corn vessels to Malta, and had them condemned there—in place of obtaining anything for the capture, a heavy bill of costs for the condemnation of such small vessels would have greatly exceeded the sum realised by their sale.

On the 9th of March, when these papers were laid before the House, I moved for others in order to elucidate them. This gave rise to another debate, in which some curious facts were brought to light by Colonel Wardle :—

" In the Navy Pay-office it was usual to promote junior clerks over the heads of men who were many years their seniors in the service. One junior clerk, eleven years in the office, was promoted to a place of 300*l.* a year, over the heads of senior clerks from twenty-seven to thirty years in the service. In another case a gentleman was obliged to retire against his will on 170*l.* per annum, and a *boy of fourteen* was appointed to his situation *with a raised salary,* and over the heads of many senior clerks. The Secretary of the Sick and Hurt Office was pensioned off at his full salary of 500*l.*, and an assistant appointed in his stead *with a salary of* 1000*l.* ! ! "

On the 12th of March, my respected colleague, Sir Francis Burdett, than whom a purer patriot never breathed, moved that Mr Gale Jones should be discharged from Newgate, to which prison he had been committed by order of the House, for placarding a handbill, the contents of which were construed into a violation of the privileges of the House. Sir Francis—conceiving that the people had privileges as well as those claiming to be their representatives, or rather that the popular voice constituted the power of their representatives—demanded the release of Mr Jones, on the ground that the House possessed no privilege to commit a man for asserting his right to discuss its measures, and that neither legally nor constitutionally could such privilege exist.

The debate which ensued, not coming within the scope of this work, may be omitted. Suffice it to say that Sir Francis published in *Cobbett's Weekly Register* a revised account of his speech, in which he declared that the House of Commons sought to set aside Magna Charta and the laws of England by an order founded on their own irresponsible power.

Accompanying this revised speech was a letter addressed by Sir Francis to his constituents of Westminster ; and these coupled together the House chose to construe into a breach of their privileges also. The result, as every one knows, was a motion for the committal of Sir Francis Burdett to the Tower.

My worthy colleague, however, refused to surrender. As there was no knowing to what lengths the despotism of the House might extend, a rumour of breaking into the honourable Baronet's house being prevalent, a number of his friends, myself amongst them, assembled at his residence in Piccadilly to see fair play ; but one morning, during our absence, an officer, armed with the Speaker's warrant, forcibly entered, and Sir Francis was carried off to the place of his imprisonment.

It is quite unnecessary to detail these circumstances, as they are well known to every reader of English history. On the day after my excellent colleague's capture the electors of Westminster held a meeting in Palace Yard, and adopted a petition which fell to my lot to present to the House.

The petition went even further than had Sir Francis, by denouncing the House as " prosecutor and juror, judge and executioner," and denying its right to exercise these combined offices. It taunted the House with evading the offer of a member to prove at the bar that two of the ministers had been distinctly charged with the sale of a seat on their benches, and that such practices were " as notorious as the sun at noonday." They therefore prayed not only for the release of their member, but for a reform of the House itself, "as the only means of preserving the country from despotism."

To have committed the whole of the electors of Westminster for adopting such a petition would have been inconvenient. To have committed me for presenting it would have been scarcely less dangerous, as depriving Westminster of both its representatives. The predominant feeling in the House appeared to be that of astonishment that a naval officer should dare to meddle with such matters. One member opposed its reception at all, another begged me to withdraw it, which I refused to do ; and, therefore, the House adopted the only possible alternative of " ordering it to lie on the table." The feeling towards myself may be conceived.

On the 11th of May Mr Croker proposed a vote for the ordinaries of the navy, when I embraced the opportunity of making what was at the time termed " one of the most remarkable speeches ever delivered in that House." The speech indeed was remarkable—not for its eloquence, for it had none, but for some very awkward statistics which *my enforced leisure* had enabled me to collect and arrange. And let me here remark, that when my parliamentary speeches are adduced, the object is to give a faithful picture of the condition as well of the House as of the navy at that period, not as specimens of an eloquence to which I had no pretension. My parliamentary efforts, such as they are, are on record, and the reproduction of a portion may save both myself and the reader the trouble of further dilating thereon.

One besetting sin of the administration was the bestowal of pensions, which was carried on to a wonderful extent. Wives, daughters, distant relatives, etc., of all sorts of people who had votes or influence claimed a pension as a matter of right. Another besetting sin of the Government was doling out pittances scarcely sufficient for the support of life to those who had fought and bled for their country.

Bearing this in mind, the reader will readily comprehend

the following " remarkable " address—as it has been termed by historical writers—to the House of Commons :—

" An admiral, worn out in the service, is superannuated at 410*l.* a year, a captain at 210*l.*, a *clerk of the ticket office retires on* 700*l. a year* ! The widow of Admiral Sir Andrew Mitchell has *one third* of the allowance given to the widow of a commissioner of the navy !

" I will give the House another instance. Four daughters of the gallant Captain Courtenay have 12*l.* 10*s.* each, the daughter of Admiral Sir Andrew Mitchell has 25*l.*, two daughters of Admiral Epworth have 25*l.* each, the daughter of Admiral Keppel 24*l.*, the daughter of Captain Mann, who was killed in action, 25*l.*, four children of Admiral Moriarty 25*l.* each. That is—thirteen daughters of admirals and captains, several of whose fathers fell in the service of their country, receive from the gratitude of the nation a sum *less than Dame Mary Saxton, the widow of a commissioner.*

" The pension list is not formed on any comparative rank or merit, length of service, or other rational principle, but appears to me to be dependent on parliamentary influence alone. Lieutenant Ellison, who lost his arm, is allowed 91*l.* 5*s.*, Captain Johnstone, who lost his arm, has only 45*l.* 12*s*. 6*d.*, Lieutenant Arden, who lost his arm, has 91*l.* 5*s.*, Lieutenant Campbell, who lost his leg, 40*l.*, and poor Lieutenant Chambers, who lost both his legs, has only 80*l.*, *whilst Sir A. S. Hammond retires on* 1500*l. per annum.* The brave Sir Samuel Hood, who lost his arm, has only 500*l.*, *whilst the late Secretary of the Admiralty retires, in full health, on a pension of* 1500*l. per annum* !

" To speak less in detail, 32 flag officers, 22 captains, 50 lieutenants, 180 masters, 36 surgeons, 23 pursers, 91 boatswains, 97 gunners, 202 carpenters, and 41 cooks, in all 774 persons, cost the country 4028*l. less than the nett proceeds of the sinecures of Lords Arden* (20,358*l.*), *Camden* (20,536*l.*), *and Buckingham* (20,693*l.*).

" All the superannuated admirals, captains, and lieutenants

put together, have but 1012*l*. more than Earl Camden's sinecure alone ! All that is paid to the wounded officers of the whole British navy, and to the wives and children of those dead or killed in action, do not amount by 214*l*. to as much as Lord Arden's sinecure alone, viz. 20,358*l*. What is paid to the mutilated officers themselves is *but half as much !*

" Is this justice ? Is this the treatment which the officers of the navy deserve at the hands of those who call themselves His Majesty's Government ? Does the country know of this injustice ? Will this too be defended ? If I express myself with warmth I trust in the indulgence of the House. I cannot suppress my feelings. Should 31 commissioners, commissioners' wives, and clerks have 3899*l*. more amongst them *than all the wounded officers of the navy of England* ?

" I find upon examination that the Wellesleys receive from the public 34,729*l*., *a sum equal to* 426 *pairs of lieutenants' legs, calculated at the rate of allowance of Lieutenant Chambers' legs. Calculating for the pension of Captain Johnstone's arm, viz.* 45*l*., *Lord Arden's sinecure is equal to the value of* 1022 *captains' arms* : *The Marquis of Buckingham's sinecure alone will maintain the whole ordinary establishment of the victualling department at Chatham, Dover, Gibraltar, Sheerness, Downs, Heligoland, Cork, Malta, Mediterranean, Cape of Good Hope, Rio de Janeiro, and leave* 5460*l*. *in the Treasury. Two of these comfortable sinecures would victual the officers and men serving in all the ships in ordinary in Great Britain, viz.* 117 *sail of the line,* 105 *frigates,* 27 *sloops, and* 50 *hulks. Three of them would maintain the dockyard establishments at Portsmouth and Plymouth.* The addition of a few more would amount to as much as the whole ordinary establishments of the royal dockyards at Chatham, Woolwich, Deptford, and Sheerness ; whilst the sinecures and offices executed wholly by deputy would more than maintain the ordinary establishment of all the royal dockyards in the kingdom !

" Even Mr Ponsonby, who lately made so pathetic an appeal to the good sense of the people of England against those whom he was pleased to term demagogues, actually receives, for having been *thirteen months in office,* a sum equal to nine admirals *who have spent their lives in the service of their country* ; three times as much as all the pensions given to all the daughters and children of all the admirals, captains, lieutenants, and other officers who have died in indigent circumstances, or who have been killed in the service ! "

This portion of the speech, true in every figure, was not incorrectly termed " remarkable " ; and it made an enemy of every sinecurist named, as I had afterwards but too good reason to know. Nevertheless, the administration had made a mistake. I was not permitted to be employed *afloat,* and was determined to effect all the good I could for the naval service by advocating its interests *ashore.*

But the worst was yet to come. My very excellent grand-mother, of whom I have spoken in the first portion of this work in terms feebly expressive of her worth, had a pension of 100*l.* for the services of her gallant husband, Captain Gilchrist ; and *though she had been dead eight years,* some patriotic individual had been *drawing her pension, as though she were still living* ! Given, a hundred dead widows, with a pension of 100*l.* each, and some one was at the national expense the richer by 10,000*l.* per annum !

On this point, I thus proceeded, no doubt to the intense disgust of the party enjoying the defunct pensions :—

" From the minute expenses noticed in the naval estimate, viz. for oiling clocks, killing rats, and keeping cats, I suppose that great care has been taken to have everything correct. It was, therefore, with great surprise that I found the name of my worthy and respected grandmother, the widow of the late Captain Gilchrist of the navy, continuing on the list as receiving 100*l.* per annum, *though she ceased to exist eight years ago* ! "

Notwithstanding the unanswerable argument of my grand-mother's pension, and equally unanswerable comparison of sinecures and naval rewards—the Secretary of the Admiralty, Mr Wellesley Pole, considered that he satisfactorily replied to both, by pronouncing my statements "inaccurate, and my complaints inconsistent! As to the pensions to the children of admirals, Lord Cochrane must know very well that *the widow or children of an admiral were not entitled, strictly speaking, to any pension* "!

To comprehend the preceding statements, it may be necessary to observe that we had at that time more than 1000 ships of war of all classes afloat, and that from the general bad character of their sailing and equipment, the enemy, who had little more than a tenth of the number, fairly laughed at us. Under any circumstances, the waste of money was deplorable, but under the corrupt system by which worthless ships were then introduced into the navy, to which subject allusion has been formerly made, it was utter paralysation of every natural effort.

The amount of obloquy these efforts to raise the condition of the naval service brought on me, amongst persons who held that afloat or ashore the duty of a naval officer was implicit obedience to the ministry of the day, will be readily understood. Reply to my statements being impossible, the ministerial organs made me the subject of numerous bad squibs, one of which is subjoined :—

> " You fight so well and speak so ill,
>   Your case is somewhat odd,
> Fighting abroad you're quite *at home*,
>   Speaking at home—*abroad* ;
>
> Therefore your friends, than hear yourself,
>   Would rather of you hear ;
> And that your name in the *Gazette*,
>   Than *Journals* should appear."

The wit is somewhat obtuse, but the feeling here expressed was no doubt sincere. The ministers indeed began to suspect that they had committed an error in preventing me from joining my ship, and shortly afterwards attempted to repair it by ordering me immediately to sea! With what effect will appear in the next chapter.

CHAPTER XXVII

MY PLANS FOR ATTACKING THE FRENCH COAST REFUSED, AND
MYSELF SUPERSEDED

IT has already been stated that the *Imperieuse* frigate under
my command had been placed by the Admiralty under the
orders of the Honourable Captain Duncan, son of the distinguished admiral of that name, as acting-captain; but that
permission to resume her command in the Scheldt had been refused
on my application to rejoin her; no doubt with the intention of
preventing me from effecting anything more which might become
obnoxious to another admiral.

Now that my presence in the House of Commons had become
inconvenient, the Admiralty affected to consider that *I was
unjustifiably absenting myself from my ship*! and an intimation
was given that I must join her *within a week*!

So far from my absence being voluntary, *it had been forced*
upon me from the necessity of attending the court-martial and
an acting-captain was to be put in my place. When I found
that this step was determined on, I asked that Captain Duncan
might be appointed, knowing that he would carry out my views
in the management of a crew to which I was attached, as from
long and ardous service they were attached to me. But notwithstanding this temporary appointment, I was anxiously urging
on the Board of Admiralty the necessity of further operations
in which it was my earnest wish to bear a part.

The correspondence which took place with the Admiralty
will not only show this, but the record may prove useful in case
of future wars.

On the 7th of June, 1810, I transmitted the subjoined letter
to the Hon. Charles Yorke, who had succeeded Lord Mulgrave
as First Lord of the Admiralty :—

" London,
" 7th June, 1810.

" Sir,—When I had the honour to present myself to you
the other day, I used the freedom to submit to your judgment
the mode by which the commerce of the enemy might, in my
humble opinion, be greatly injured, if not completely ruined,
and that such mode, whilst assisting the present, would be providing for the future, exigencies of the State. The subject has
pressed itself so forcibly on my attention, that I am induced to
address you by letter, which is perhaps the best means to avoid
engaging too much of your time.

" Passing over the points I then noticed as a stimulus to the
navy, which, unfortunately for this country, though for the
benefit of our inveterate foe, is checked and restrained in its
operations, I shall beg permission to call your attention to other
parts of the subject I had then the honour to introduce.

" I am the more impelled to the intrusion by the intelligence
recently received of the islands of Los Medas on the coast of
Catalonia having been taken by the French, who were doubtlessly
influenced by the motive *that ought to actuate us to possess ourselves of the islands on the coast of France*, or such of them as tend
to aid her best interests.

" In the present state of our navy, the French rest in the
fullest confidence of assured security, and are, therefore, entirely
at our mercy, as regards the objects in my contemplation.

" In the present state of French security, L'Ile Groa at the
mouth of the Loire, and L'Ile Dieu on the coast of Brittany,
may be easily seized by 800 men, in defiance of any opposition ;
and by a *coup de main* a fourth part of that number would be
sufficient. These islands would afford safe anchorage to our
cruisers, with the wind on shore, and when, in the winter season,
it is dangerous to approach them.

" The islands at the entrance of the port of Marseilles could
be taken by 100 men, and their importance is demonstrable by
their situation. United with the possession of one of the Hières,

they would enable us to cut off the communication between that part of France which consumes the commodities of Italy, and thus the trade of Leghorn and Genoa—once of importance to us—would be lost to our enemy, who now exclusively enjoys it.

" The port of Bayonne, whence the French supply their dockyards at Rochefort and Brest with timber, may be rendered useless by sinking a few old vessels laden with stones. In like manner the anchorage of Ile d'Aix might be destroyed—the passages in the entrance of the Garonne rendered impracticable—and that of Mamusson filled up.

" Proceeding on a more extensive scale, Belle Isle offers itself to particular notice, and would be a most valuable acquisition, as it gives shelter at all times to shipping. At Cette—commanding the entrance of the canal through which the whole produce of Italy and the shores of the Mediterranean are transported to the north of the French empire—the locks might be seized on with facility, and held or blown up, in defiance of the whole power of Buonaparte now in France. The island of Elba might be reduced with as little difficulty, and as it contains two excellent harbours, and protects the anchorage in the Piombia passage, it is well calculated to interrupt all intercourse between the Roman, Italian, and Tuscan States. Were it in our hands at this moment, it would be an invaluable depot for our manufactures, which, on cutting off the trade with France, would be in the greatest demand throughout the whole of Italy. It was given up at the termination of the last war in ignorance—as may be presumed—of the great advantage which it affords in this respect.

" I need not suggest to you, Sir, that if the measures on which I have thus slightly touched were carried into effect, it would—even should the enemy be disposed to disturb us—require a large portion of the force *intended for the subjugation of Spain*, to be diverted from its purpose. If these measures were to be followed up by a flying naval expedition of trifling extent, and with comparatively only a handful of troops, the enemy might be held in check, or at any rate their plans elsewhere would be frustrated in part, and the remainder must become insignificant from perplexity and embarrassment.

" I submit to you, Sir, that were it not for our naval superiority, and a few thousand troops were at Buonaparte's disposal, our coasts would not be safe—the vessels in our ports would be swept away—and very possibly the ports themselves laid in ashes. As we have at least physical powers, and more honourable incitements than Buonaparte to aid our energies and direct our objects, we ought bravely to pursue all that he would dare to attempt.

" If, Sir, these points should appear to interest you, and you should think it necessary to require of me further detail or information, I shall be happy to wait on you for that purpose at any time you may be pleased to name. I had intended to bring this subject before the House, but a variety of obvious reasons showed me the propriety of addressing you in the first instance.

" I have the honour, etc.   COCHRANE.

" The Right Hon. CHARLES YORKE."

In reply to this letter, I was told by Mr Yorke that the acting-captain had been appointed to the *Imperieuse* for " *my accommodation* " ! ! instead of Captain Duncan having been appointed from the necessity before mentioned ! Mr Yorke concluded his letter with a peremptory order for me to proceed to sea within a week :—

" ADMIRALTY,
" *June* 8, 1810.

" MY LORD,—I had the honour this morning of receiving your Lordship's letter of yesterday, communicating your Lordship's opinions on various points of service connected with operations on the French coast in the Bay as well as in the Mediterranean, which appear to be nearly of the same effect with those which I had the honour of hearing from your Lordship personally some days ago.

" I beg to return you my thanks for this communication of your sentiments, and have now to inform you that as your Lordship's ship, the *Imperieuse*, is now nearly ready for sea, and destined for the Mediterranean, and as *the period of the session of Parliament during which your Lordship has been accommodated with an acting-captain to command the frigate in your absence* (!) *has now nearly reached its close*, I presume that it is your intention to join her without loss of time, and to proceed in her to join Sir Charles Cotton, who will no doubt employ your Lordship in the annoyance of the enemy and in the protection of our Allies in the manner best suited to the exigencies of the service.

"I request that your Lordship will have the goodness to inform me as early as you can *on what day next week it is your intention to join your ship*, as His Majesty's service will not admit of her sailing being much longer postponed.

"I have the honour, etc.   C. YORKE.

"Capt. LORD COCHRANE."

The assertion that an acting-captain had been appointed to the *Imperieuse* for my accommodation as a member of Parliament was monstrous, for after the court-martial was ended I begged to be allowed to join her ; first, soon after the Walcheren expedition sailed, and again when it failed to satisfy the national expectations ; even then offering to destroy the enemy's fleet as had been done in Aix Roads. I afterwards asked permission to view the siege of Flushing as a spectator only, and *was refused*, the refusal being fortunately still in my possession :—

"ADMIRALTY,
"*Oct.* 11, 1809.

"MY DEAR LORD,—I have mentioned your request to the Naval Lords at the Board, and find it cannot be complied with.

"I am, my dear Lord, your very faithful servant,

"MULGRAVE.

"The LORD COCHRANE."

Notwithstanding Mr Yorke's version of the reason of my

absence from the *Imperieuse*, I determined to make one more effort for permission to carry out my plans for harassing the enemy's coast, and thereby preventing them from forwarding troops to Spain. My object was to get two or three frigates and a few troops under my command. Had I been able to accomplish this, what had been effected with the *Imperieuse* alone on the coast of Catalonia will be my excuse for saying, that such a force would have been the most valuable aid to the British army in the Peninsula.

Preferring, therefore, the service which I was desirous to render to my country to my own wounded feelings, I addressed another letter to Mr Yorke :—

" LONDON,
" *June* 11, 1810.

" SIR,—In acknowledging the receipt of your letter of the 8th I confess much embarrassment. The measures submitted to your judgment were, in my humble opinion, of great national importance. They had in view to weaken the hands of our enemy and strengthen our own. I therefore indulged in the hope that they would have received your countenance and support.

" It must have been apparent to you, Sir, that I did not offer them on light grounds, nor without calculated certainty of success in the event of their prosecution. I flattered myself with the hope of being employed in the execution of a service on which my previous observations would have enabled me to act with confidence.

" But although, Sir, you are pleased to thank me for my communication, you pass over in silence the objects it embraced ; and do away with even the expressions of courtesy bestowed on it by asking ' on what day *in this week* it was my intention to join my ship, as His Majesty's service would not admit of her sailing being much longer postponed ' ; thus leaving me to conclude that in taking the liberty of approaching you I had trespassed too far, and that to prevent my importunities in future you had deemed it advisable to order me to join my ship, and further, to join Sir Charles Cotton, who, you signify, 'would no doubt employ me in the annoyance of the enemy, and in the protection of our Allies, in the manner best suited to the exigencies of the service.'

" I have throughout life been accustomed to do my duty to the utmost of my power, and my anxiety to render the performance of it acceptable to my country, whilst it stimulated me to inform myself on the best means for that purpose, may have led me to intrude on those with whom alone rests the power of encouraging my expectations. Yet I might have imagined that my motives would sufficiently plead my excuse. On the present occasion I had an additional inducement in addressing myself in the first instance to you, Sir, instead of the House of Commons. I felt that I was paying the respect due to the First Lord of the Admiralty.

" It appears, however, that I have inadvertently offended, and am sorry for it, as the public interest may be injured by the step I have taken. I should have been gratified had you done me the honour to call for details of the sketch which I laid before you, when I should have been happy to supply a properly digested plan by which I propose to secure the objects here shadowed forth.

" Had this plan been brought under your consideration, I may venture to say that you would have directed it to be carried into execution ; and I should have envied any person whom you might have honoured with the charge of it ; however much I might have regretted the refusal to permit me to share in it, I should nevertheless have cheerfully rendered every information required of me, or that I might have conceived necessary.

" I have now no alternative than to submit to the wisdom of the House the propositions you have thought proper to reject, or rather suffer them to die away without further notice. I do not pride myself on the accuracy of my judgment, but may be allowed to understand those matters that come under my own immediate observation better than those who have had no experience in such kind of warfare.

T

"The capture of Los Medas by the French has confirmed me in the opinions I gave to Lord Mulgrave on my last *reconnaissance* of Ile d'Aix, and which I had the honour to state to you in my last. I again submit that a similar course pursued by His Majesty's Government towards France would distract the purposes of Buonaparte, and injure him infinitely more than any other step likely to be taken. The capture of even one of the islands enumerated in my former letter would be felt by him much as we should feel if a French force were to capture the Isle of Wight.

"In another part of your letter you say that I have been ' *accommodated with an acting-captain to command the frigate during my absence.*' I have to assure you that it was an accommodation I never solicited, and one which, far from conveying a favour, was extremely painful to my feelings, as it prevented my going on a service which I was extremely desirous of witnessing. I even made an application to Lord Mulgrave for permission to be a spectator only of the scene of Flushing, so as to avail myself of the opportunity to acquire information about the Scheldt and its environs, but was refused, although others not connected with the service obtained leave to proceed there.

"In conclusion, I beg permission to say that I have yet some objects of moment to bring forward in Parliament, and that as there is no enterprise given to the *Imperieuse*, I have no wish that she should be detained for me one moment.

"I have the honour, etc.   COCHRANE.

"The Right Hon. CHAS. YORKE.

"*P.S.*—Your letter, Sir, is marked ' private,' which I consider as applying solely to the destination of the *Imperieuse*, and, of course, shall be silent on that subject."

The reply of the First Lord was that it was "*neither his duty nor his inclination to enter into controversy with me* "! A proof how the interests of a nation may suffer from the political pique of a single man in power. Not an individual of the ministry considered me incapable of carrying into execution, even with an insignificant force, the plans foreshadowed ; yet they were treated with contemptuous silence, and a command to proceed immediately on a subordinate service.

" ADMIRALTY,
" <i>June</i> 12, 1810.

" MY LORD,—I have had the honour this morning of receiving your Lordship's letter of yesterday. *As I do not conceive it either my public duty so it is by no means my private inclination to be drawn into any official controversy with your Lordship, either in your capacity of captain of a frigate in His Majesty's service or of a member of Parliament.*

" For this reason I must beg to decline replying to several parts of your Lordship's letter, in which you appear to have much misconceived my meaning, as expressed in my former letter, or to observe upon the turn and direction which your Lordship is pleased to endeavour to give to our correspondence.

" I have thought it proper to lay the two letters which I have received from your Lordship, being on points of service, before the Board of Admiralty for their consideration ; and have only now to request to be distinctly informed whether or not it is your Lordship's intention to join your ship, the *Imperieuse,* now under orders for foreign service, and nearly ready for sea, as soon as Parliament shall be prorogued.

" I shall be much pleased to receive an answer in the affirmative, because I should then entertain hopes that your activity and gallantry might be made available for the public service. I shall be much concerned to receive an answer in the negative, because in that case I shall feel it to be my duty to consider it as your Lordship's wish to be superseded in the command of the *Imperieuse.*

" I am, my Lord, your most obedient servant,   C. YORKE.

" Capt. LORD COCHRANE."

A more unjust order from a lay lord of the Admiralty than this, to join the *Imperieuse* and proceed on foreign service, was never issued from the Admiralty.

Nevertheless, this ill-treatment determined me not to shrink from my duty, though I was resolved that Mr Yorke should neither get an affirmative nor a negative from me as to joining the frigate. If the command of the *Imperieuse*, under the orders of Sir Charles Cotton, were forced upon me I would take it, but of this the Admiralty should be the judges—not I. Had Lord Collingwood lived to reach England the Admiralty would not have ventured to thrust such a command upon me after my services of the previous three years and my plans for future operations, which, as I have once or twice said, would have saved millions spent on prolonged strife in the Peninsula.

In the vain hope that the national welfare would, on calm deliberation, rise superior to petty official spite, I again addressed Mr Yorke as follows :—

" PORTMAN SQUARE,
"*June* 14, 1810.

" SIR,—When I had the honour to present to you in writing those ideas that I had previously communicated verbally, it was far from my views and contrary to my intention to draw you into any unofficial correspondence. My solicitude to see the interests of my country promoted and the power of the enemy reduced were my only objects. I presumed that amidst the pressure of business any hints thrown out in desultory conversation might escape your memory, but that committed to paper they would meet your consideration. This was my chief reason for addressing you by letter.

" As a member of Parliament I never harboured a wish to intrude myself on your notice. I know that as a captain of a frigate I do not possess any consequence, and am conscious that I never assumed any. But, Sir, I submit that if information promising essential benefit to the State is procured, the source from which it flows, however insignificant, is not of the least moment.

"With an impression which I must lament, Sir, that you decline entering on those parts of my letter which alone prevailed with me to trouble you, I regret having done so. I am not in the habit of entreaty, but when the public service is to be advanced entreaty becomes a duty. I trust, therefore, that you will pardon me if I repeat the hope that you will be pleased to regard the subject in a more favourable light, and examine the grounds and principles on which my opinions are founded. I feel convinced that any other officer possessed of the knowledge necessary to form his judgment will tell you that the measures I have proposed may *to a certainty and with great ease be carried into execution* ; and that the enemy would, in consequence, be entirely crippled in his best resources.

"Had I been fortunate enough to receive the least encouragement from you I should have brought forward other objects than those noticed. Amongst these is one that has reference to the coast of Catalonia, where the maritime towns are occupied by troops of the enemy just sufficient to keep the peasantry in awe and exact from them provisions. These, by possessing the open batteries, the French convey coastways in fishing boats and small craft to their armies, which, from the scarcity of cattle, fodder, and the state of the roads, they could not obtain by any other means.

"The few troops stationed along the coast for these purposes might be seized and brought off with a trifling force employed in the way I have indicated. As a proof of this, the aide-de-camp of General Lechu and a whole company were brought off by the marines and crew of the *Imperieuse* alone, to whom they surrendered, well knowing that had they left the battery they would have been put to death in detail by the oppressed and irritated Spaniards.

"I am thankful, Sir, for your kindness in laying my letters before the Lords Commissioners. The flattering terms in which you speak of my humble abilities also demand my acknowledg-

ment; and, whilst again tendering them to the service of my
country, I beg permission to say that it is the first wish of my
heart and the highest aim of my ambition to be actively employed
in my profession, and that from former associations I prefer
the *Imperieuse* to every other frigate in the Navy. But as she
is to proceed immediately on foreign service, I fear it is impossible
for me to be in readiness to join her within the time specified.
    " I have the honour, etc.   COCHRANE.

" The Right Hon. CHAS. YORKE."

To this letter no reply was vouchsafed, and the Honourable
Captain Duncan was confirmed in the command of the *Imperieuse*,
which in the *following month* sailed to join Sir Charles Cotton
off Toulon.
    Parliament being prorogued within a few days after the date
of the last letter, I had no opportunity of bringing the subject
before the House.

CHAPTER XXVIII

VISIT TO THE ADMIRALTY COURT AT MALTA

AT the commencement of 1811, finding that, in place of anything being awarded to the *Imperieuse* for numerous prizes
taken in the Mediterranean, the Maltese Admiralty Court had
actually brought me in debt for vicious condemnation, I determined to go to Malta, and insist on the fees and charges
thereon being taxed according to the scale upon which the
authority of the court in such matters was based.
    It is not my intention to enter generally into the nature of
the demands made by the Maltese court, but rather to point
out the manner in which, after realisation of the prize funds,
costs were inflicted on the officers and crews of ships of war, till
little or nothing was left for distribution amongst the captors.

This will give a good idea of the practices which prevailed; preventing officers from harassing the coasting trade of the enemy, as the expenses of condemning small craft were ruinous, being for the most part the same as those charged by the court for the condemnation of large vessels.

One of the customs of the court was as follows : to charge as fees *one fourth* more than the fees of the High Court of Admiralty in England ; this one fourth was practically found to amount in some cases to *one half*, whilst any scale of charges by which the conduct of the court was guided remained inaccessible to the captors of prizes.

The principal officer of the court in this department was a Mr Jackson, who held the office of marshal. This officer, however, though resident in Malta, performed his duty of marshal by deputy, for the purpose of enabling him to exercise the still more profitable office of proctor, the duties of which he performed in person. The consequence was, that every prize placed in his hands as proctor had to pass through his hands as marshal ! whilst as proctor it was further in his power to consult himself as marshal as often as he pleased, and to any extent he pleased. The amount of self-consultation may be imagined. Right profitably did Mr Proctor Jackson perform the duty of attending and consulting himself as Mr Marshal Jackson !

Subjoined is an extract from the charges of Proctor Jackson for attending himself as Marshal Jackson :—

	Cr.	rls.	sc.
Attending (as proctor) in the registry and bespeaking a monition	2	0	0
Paid (himself as marshal) for said monition under seal, and extracting	9	0	0
Copy of said monition for service	2	0	0
Attending the Marshal! (himself) *and feeing and instructing him to execute the same !*	2	0	0
Paid the Marshal (himself) *for service of said monition !* (on himself)	2	0	0
Certificate of service ! (on himself)	1	0	0
Drawing and engrossing affidavit of service ! (on himself)	2	0	0
Oath thereto, and attendance ! (on himself)	2	2	3

By what ingenious process Marshal Jackson managed to

administer the oath to himself as Proctor Jackson I know not, but the above charges are actual copies from a bill in my possession, the said bill containing *many hundred* similar items besides. Some idea of its extent may be formed from the statement that, previously to a debate on the subject, I pasted together an exact copy of the different sheets of which the bill of charges was composed, formed them into a huge roll, and, amidst the astonishment and laughter of the House of Commons, one day unrolled it along the floor of the House, when it reached from the Speaker's table to the bar ! !

In addition to this multitude of fees and charges, the marshal also claimed, and received as his own especial perquisite, *one half per cent.* on the inspection of prizes, *one per cent.* for their appraisement, and *two and a half per cent.* on the sale. This, with *one fourth* added as aforesaid, made just *five per cent.* on all captures for the marshal's perquisite alone, irrespective of his other fees ; which, being subjected to no check, were extended according to conscience. So that, for every amount of prizes to the extent of 100,000*l.* the marshal's share, as a matter of course, would be 5000*l.*, wholly irrespective of other fees of court calculated on a similar scale. When numerous other officials had to be paid in like manner, also without check on their demands, it scarcely needs to be said that such prizes as were usually to be picked up by ships of war on the Mediterranean coast entailed positive loss on their captors ; the result, as has been said, being that officers avoided taking such prizes, and thus the enemy carried on his coasting operations with impunity. In other words, the most important object of war— that of starving out the enemy's coast garrisons—was suspended by the speculations of a colonial Admiralty Court !

Foiled in procuring redress in the House of Commons, where my statements were pooh-poohed by the representatives of the High Court of Admiralty as rash and without proof, I determined on procuring, by any means whatever, such proof as should not easily be set aside.

Embarking, therefore, in my yacht *Julie*, one of the small

French ships of war captured at Caldagues and afterwards purchased by me, as before narrated, I set sail for the Mediterranean.

On arriving at Gibraltar I considered it prudent to quit my yacht, fearing that so small a vessel might fall a prey to the French cruisers, and embarked on board a brig-of-war bound to Malta.

My first demand upon the Admiralty Court on arriving at that place was, that the prize accounts of the *Imperieuse* and *Speedy* should be taxed according to the authorised table of fees. This revision was refused.

Entering the court one day when the judge was not sitting, I again demanded the table of fees from Dr Moncrieff, then judge-advocate, who denied that he knew anything about them. As by Act of Parliament they ought to have been hung up in the court, I made careful search for them, but without success. Entering the judge's robing-room unopposed, I there renewed the search, but with no better result, and was about to return tableless; when, having been directed to a private closet, I examined that also, and there, wafered up behind the door of the judge's retiring-chamber, was the Admiralty Court table of fees ! which I carefully took down, and re-entered the court in the act of folding up the paper, previously to putting it in my pocket.

Dr Moncrieff instantly saw what I had got, and rose from his seat with the intention of preventing my egress. Reminding him that I had no cause of quarrel with or complaint towards him, I told him that guarding the judge's water-closet formed no part of his duties as judge-advocate ; and that it was rather his place to go and tell the judge that I had taken possession of a public document which ought to have been suspended in court, but the possession of which had been denied. He seemed of the same opinion, and suffered me to depart with my prize ; this in half-an-hour afterwards being placed in the possession of a brother-officer who was going over to Sicily, and promised to take charge of it till my arrival at Girgenti.

This " Rape of the Table," as it was termed in a poem afterwards written on the occasion by my secretary and friend, Mr Wm. Jackson, caused great merriment ; but the judge, Dr Sewell, was furious, not perhaps so much at the invasion of his private closet, as at losing a document which, when laid before the House of Commons in connexion with the fees actually charged, would infallibly betray the practices of the Maltese court. A peremptory demand was accordingly made of me for the restoration of the table, this being met by my declaration that it was not in my possession. The judge, believing this to be untrue, though in fact the tables were in Sicily, finally ordered me to be arrested for an insult to the court !

The duty of arresting me devolved on my friend in duplicate, Mr Marshal Mr Proctor Jackson. I reminded him that the court was not sitting when the alleged offence was committed, and therefore it could be no insult. I further cautioned him that his holding the office of proctor rendered that of marshal illegal, and that if he dared to lay a finger on me, I would treat him as one without authority of any kind, so that he must take the consequences, which might be more serious to himself personally than he imagined.

The proctor-marshal, well knowing the illegality of his double office, which was not known—much less officially confirmed in England—prudently declined the risk, on which the judge ordered the deputy marshal, a man named Chapman, to arrest me. Upon this I informed Chapman that his appointment was illegal also, first as holding the office of deputy marshal to an illegally constituted person, and secondly, from his also exercising the duplicate office of deputy auctioneer—the auctioneer being a sinecurist resident in London ! ! So that if, as deputy marshal combined with deputy auctioneer, he ventured to arrest me, he too must put up with the consequences.

This went on for many days, to the great amusement of the fleet in harbour, no one being willing to incur the risk of arresting me, though I walked about Malta as usual, Chapman following me like a shadow. At length the judge insisted on the deputy marshal-auctioneer arresting me at all risks, on pain of being himself committed to prison for neglect of carrying out the orders of the court. Finding himself in this dilemma, Chapman resigned his office.

On this a man named Stevens, unconnected with any other official position, was appointed in a proper manner; and all the legal formalities being carefully entered into, I no longer resisted, as that would have been resistance to law.

The manner in which the arrest was made showed a spirit of petty malevolence quite in keeping with the dispositions of men who were making enormous fortunes by plundering the officers and crews of his Majesty's ships of war. I was on a visit to Percy Fraser, the naval commissioner, when the newly appointed deputy marshal who had watched me in was announced, and on entering told me he was come to arrest me. On demanding his credentials, I found them to be signed by Mr Proctor Jackson, and as I wanted this proof of his acting as marshal illegally, admitted myself satisfied with them.

The deputy marshal then requested me to accompany him to an inn, where I might remain on parole. I told him that I would do nothing of the kind, but that if he took me anywhere it must be to the town gaol, to which place he then requested to me accompany him. My reply was :—"No. I will be no party to an illegal imprisonment of myself. If you want me to go to gaol, you must carry me by force, for assuredly I will not walk."

As the room was full of naval officers, all more or less victims of the iniquitous system pursued by the Maltese court, the scene caused some merriment. Finding me inflexible, the Vice-admiralty official sent—first for a carriage, and then for a picket of Maltese soldiers, who carried me out of the room on the chair in which I had been sitting. I was then carefully deposited in the carriage, and driven to the town gaol.

The apartments assigned for my use were the best the place afforded, and were situated on the top story of the prison, the only material unpleasantness about them being that the windows were strongly barred.   The gaoler, a simple worthy man, civilly inquired what I would please to order for dinner.   My reply was : —" Nothing !—that, as he was no doubt aware, I had been placed there on an illegal warrant, and would not pay for so much as a crust ; so that if I was starved to death, the Admiralty Court would have to answer for it."

At this declaration the man stood aghast, and shortly after quitted the room.   In about an hour he returned with an order from Mr Marshal Jackson to a neighbouring hotel-keeper, to supply me with whatever I chose to order.

Thus armed with *carte blanche* as to the *cuisine*, I ordered dinner for six ; under strict injunctions that whatever was prized in Malta, as well in edibles as in wines, should be put upon the table.   An intimation to the gaoler that he would be the richer by the scraps, and to the hotel master to keep his counsel for the sake of the profits, had the desired effect ; and that evening a better-entertained party (naval officers) never dined within the walls of Malta gaol.

This went on day after day, at what cost to the Admiralty Court I never learned nor inquired ; but, from the character of our entertainment, the bill when presented must have been almost as extensive as their own fees.   All my friends in the squadron present at Malta were invited by turns, and assuredly had no ward-room fare.   They appeared to enjoy themselves the more heartily, as avenging their own wrongs at the expense of their plunderers.

At length the Admiralty authorities thought it high time to decide what was to be done with me.   It was now the beginning of March, and I had been incarcerated from the middle of February without accusation or trial.   It was evident that if I were imprisoned much longer, I might complain of being kept out of my place in Parliament, and what the electors of Westminster might say to this, or what the House of Commons itself might say, were questions seriously to be pondered by men whose titles to office were unconfirmed.   They had at length discovered that I had committed no offence beyond the fact of having been seen to fold up and put in my pocket a piece of dirty paper, but what that paper might be, or where it was, there was no evidence whatever.

At length they hit upon a notable expedient for getting rid of me, viz. to get his excellency the Governor to ask me to give up the table of fees. This I declined, telling his excellency that as I had been incarcerated illegally I would not quit the prison without trial.

It was accordingly determined that I should be put on my trial, the puzzle being as to what offence I should be accused of. The plan, as I afterwards found, was to interrogate me, and thus to entrap me into becoming my own accuser.

On the 2nd of March I was taken to the Court-house, accompanied by the naval commissioner Mr Fraser, Captain Rowley the naval officer in command, and nearly all the commanding officers in port.

Two clerks, one a German and the other a Maltese, were said to have deposed to " seeing a person, whom they believed to be Lord Cochrane, with a folded paper." On the strength of this evidence, the following charge was made out :—" That I had entered *The Registry* of the Admiralty Court, and had there taken down the table of charges ; that I had held up the same, so as to cause it to be seen by the King's advocate, Dr Moncrieff, and had then put it in my pocket, and walked away."

To this I replied that " there must be an error, for as the Act of Parliament ordered that the table of charges should be displayed in open court, it could not possibly have been the paper which I saw in the judge's water-closet. That the paper showed by me to Dr Moncrieff was folded up, so that he was necessarily ignorant of its purport or contents. Finally, I denied having taken down the table of charges, as established by Act of Parliament, from the court-room." After this reply I demanded to be confronted with my accuser, for the purpose of cross-examining him.

This the judge would not allow, but said he should consider

my denial in the light of a plea of "not guilty." He then put to me a series of interrogatories, for the purpose of getting me to criminate myself ; but to these I refused to reply in any way, merely repeating my assurance that his Honour must have made a mistake, it being highly improbable that the lost table of fees should have been hung anywhere but in open court, as the Act of Geo. II. prescibed, viz. : *in an open, visible, and accessible place,* which his Honour's retiring-closet was not. Dr Sewell then admitted that the charges entered on the table of fees *had not been ratified by the King in Council*! and that he had therefore not caused them to be suspended in open court, according to the Act. On which declaration I protested against the whole proceedings as illegal.

Finding that nothing could be done, the judge then *asked me to go at large on bail*! This I flatly refused, alleging myself to be determined to remain where I was, be the consequence what it might, till the case should be decided on its merits. At this unexpected declaration the court appeared to be taken aback, but as I refused to be bailed, the judge had no alternative but to remand me back to prison.

On arriving there, my friends were of opinion that the affair had been carried far enough, and that I should apologise for taking the table of charges, and send for it to Girgenti. To this counsel I refused to listen, as I wanted the tables for exhibition in the House of Commons, and would in no way compromise the matter.

On this the senior naval officer, Captain Rowley, said to me : —"Lord Cochrane, you must not remain here ; the seamen are getting savage, and if you are not out soon they will pull the gaol down, which will get the naval force into a scrape. Have you any objection to making your escape ? " " Not the least," replied I, " and it may be done ; but I will neither be bailed, nor will I be set at liberty without a proper trial."

In short, it was then arranged that my servant Richard Carter, should bring me some files and a rope ; that I should cut through the iron bars of the window ; and that when everything was in readiness, on the first favourable night, a boat should be manned at the sally-port, and that I should be taken across to Sicily, to pick up the table of fees at Girgenti.

Some three or four nights were occupied in cutting through the bars, the marks being concealed in the day-time by filling up the holes with a composition. When all was in readiness, my friends and I held our last *symposium* at the expense of the Admiralty Court. The gaoler was purposely made very tipsy, to which he was nothing loth ; and about midnight, having first lowered my bedding into the streets, to be carried off by some seaman under the direction of my servant, I passed a double rope round an iron bar, let myself down from the three-story window, pulled the rope after me, so that nothing might remain to excite suspicion, and bade adieu to the merriest prison in which a seaman was ever incarcerated.

On arriving at the harbour I found the *Eagle's* gig in readiness, and several brother-officers assembled to take leave of me. The night was dark, with the sea smooth as glass, it being a dead calm. When pulling along the island we came up with the English packet, which had sailed from Malta on the previous day, she having been since becalmed. As she was bound to Girgenti, to pick up passengers and letters from Naples, nothing could be more opportune ; so, dismissing the gig, I went on board, and was on my way to England, doubtless, before I was missed from my late involuntary domicile at Malta. I had thus a manifest advantage in those days of slow transit, viz. that of arriving in England a month before news of my escape from Malta could be sent home by the authorities of the Admiralty Court.

As I afterwards learned, nothing could exceed the chagrin of the Admiralty officials at having lost, not only their table of charges, but their prisoner also. No one had the slightest suspicion that I had gone to sea, and that in a man-of-war's boat. Yet nothing could better show the iniquitous character of the Maltese Admiralty Court than the fact that my escape was planned in conjunction with several naval officers present in harbour, who lent me a boat and crew for the purpose ; the whole matter being previously known to half the naval officers present with the squadron, and, after my escape, to not a few of the seamen, all of whom must have been highly amused at the diligent search made for me the next day throughout Valetta, but still more at the *reward offered for those who aided me in escaping.* Yet not a word transpired as to the direction I had taken, or the time occupied in searching for me on the island might have been turned to better account by an endeavour to intercept me at Gibraltar, where I remained long enough to dispose of my yacht, and amuse the garrison with a narrative of my adventures since I left the Rock two months before !

CHAPTER XXIX

NAVAL LEGISLATION HALF-A-CENTURY AGO

On my return from the Mediterranean, having no prospect of employment, I devoted myself assiduously in parliament to the course I had marked out for myself, viz. the amelioration of the condition of the naval service ; whether by originating such measures of my own accord, or assisting others who had the same object in view.

At this period it was the custom to compel naval officers on foreign stations, in whatever part of the world located, to draw bills for their pay. The consequence was that the bills had to be sold at a discount sometimes amounting to 35 and 40 per cent., the whole of the loss falling on the officers negotiating the bills.

A motion to place officers of the navy upon the same footing as officers of the army was made by Captain Bennet, and strenuously opposed by the First Lord of the Admiralty, Mr Yorke, as an innovation on *old rules and customs,* which, when once sanctioned, no one could tell where it might stop.

Upon this I inquired " what greater difficulty there could be in paying officers of the navy abroad than in paying officers of

ADMIRAL THE HON. SIR ALEX. COCHRANE, G.C.B.

[Born 1758. Died 1832]

the army ?   There were consuls at all the foreign stations, who could certify what the rate of exchange really was.   Under the present system, to my own knowledge, officers on the Gibraltar station were 25 per cent., or a fourth of their scanty pay, out of pocket, and it was with great difficulty that they could provide themselves with proper necessaries."

The effect of these remarks was, that Sir C. Pole moved as an amendment that a Committee should be appointed to inquire into the state of the navy generally, and this was seconded by Admiral Harvey.

On the 6th of June I entered on the subject of the Maltese Court of Admiralty.   As the debate in the House is sufficiently explicit, previous comment is unnecessary.

" Vice-Admiralty Court of Malta

" Lord Cochrane rose to make the motion of which he had given notice.   The noble lord began by stating that he had before had occasion to trouble the House on this subject, but he then failed in his attempt to obtain justice, on the ground that there was not sufficient evidence of the facts stated to warrant the House in entertaining his motion.   He had since, however, personally been at Malta, and had procured such a chain of evidence, that if the House should now be pleased to entertain his motion, he had no doubt but he should be able to lay before them such a connected string of evidence of flagrant abuses in the Vice-Admiralty Court at that island, as would astonish all who heard it.

" He would undertake to prove that, if the Court of Admiralty at home would do their duty, one third of the naval force now employed in the Mediterranean would be sufficient for all purposes for which it was employed there, and that a saving might be made in the naval service alone of at least five millions sterling a year.   If the Committee for which he moved last year had been granted, the evidence to prove this might now have been before the House."

U

There was no question at the time, and many naval officers are yet living to confirm the assertion, that the rapacity of the Admiralty Courts and their extravagant charges for adjudication and condemning prizes did prevent the interception and capture of the majority of the numerous small vessels employed in the coasting trade of the enemy, this forming to him the most vital consideration, as the means of provisioning his armies. At the commencement of the war, the capture of large vessels coming from distant parts with valuable cargoes gave so much prize-money as to render both officers and crews careless about a little exertion more or less, but when the enemy's foreign trade was destroyed nothing remained to be looked after but small craft, and as the Admiralty Court charges had increased in an inverse ration to the worthlessness of small craft, few would run the risk of looking after them, with the certainty of small gain, and the more than probability of being brought in debt for their pains. The consequence was, that little or no destruction was offered to the enemy's coasting trade, which, important as it was to him for subsistence, ought to have been far more so to us, as its destruction would have deprived him of the means of subsistence.

Between the years 1803 and 1807, the naval establishment was increased from 200 to 600 vessels of war, notwithstanding which the coasting commerce of the enemy still went on, and it should have been obvious that when the navy was increased to upwards of 100 ships, *nothing more was done.* The amusement of cutting out coasting vessels when under the protection of batteries ceased to operate as an incentive. The logs of frigates showed that their commanders avoided the risk of keeping their ships in contiguity with the shore *at night,* and secured a good night's rest for their men by running into the offing. Hence the enemy's coasting convoys proceeded by night, and in the day ran into some port or other place of protection. The result in the frigates' daily journal,—" Employed *as usual,*" was no less true than comprehensive.

For telling such truths as these, an outcry was raised against me for depreciating the character of officers ! The case was my own. I took prizes in the Mediterranean and elsewhere by dozens, for which neither my officers nor crews got anything, the proceeds being swallowed up by the Admiralty Courts. I then turned to harassing the coast armies and forts of the enemy, without hope of reward, deeming this kind of employment the most honourable to myself, and the most advantageous to my country. So far from my pointing out the effect on the mind of officers in general being a reflection on their honour, it was only creditable to their common-sense. They could not reasonably be expected to sacrifice their rest and that of their crews, or to run their ships into danger and themselves into debt, for the exclusive emolument of the Courts of Admiralty ! I have no hesitation in asserting that had the ministry diminished the navy one half, and given the whole cost of the other half to the Admiralty Court officials in lieu of their charges, the remaining ships would of themselves have turned the course of the war, and their commanders would have reaped fortunes.

These remarks will enable the naval reader to comprehend what follows. They are not intended so much for a history of past maladministration as a beacon for the future.

" The noble lord then read a letter from a captain of a vessel at the Cape of Good Hope, complaining ' that the officers of ships of war were so pillaged by those of the Vice-Admiralty Courts, that he wished to know how they could be relieved ; whether they could be allowed the liberty to send their prizes home, and how far the jurisdiction of the Vice-Admiralty Court extended ; for that the charges of court were so exorbitant, it required the whole amount of the value of a good prize to satisfy them. In the case of one vessel that was sold for 11,000 rupees, the charges amounted to more than 10,000. This was the case at Penang, Malacca, and other places, as well as at the Cape.' He would not, however, wish to dwell on this, but put it to the feelings of the House, whether naval officers had any stimulus to do even their duty,

308 THE AUTOBIOGRAPHY OF A SEAMAN

when the prizes they took would not pay the fees of the Vice-Admiralty Courts merely for condemning them ? It had been stated the other day at some meeting or dinner by a very grave personage, the Lord Chancellor, that the ships of France were only to be found in our ports. If that statement were believed by ministers, he should be glad to know why we at this moment kept up 140 sail of the line, and frigates and sloops of war in proportion to that number."

What follows is very curious, as establishing the magnitude of the charges for adjudication in the Vice-Admiralty Courts. The bill for the condemnation of the *King George* privateer, the first vessel taken by the *Imperieuse*, had brought me 600 crowns in debt, and was of such magnitude that I had an exact copy made of it, and pasted continuously together. The result will be gathered from what follows.

" His Lordship then produced the copy of a Proctor's Bill in the island of Malta, which he said measured six fathoms and a quarter, and contained many curious charges. [*The unrolling this copy caused a general laugh, as it appeared long enough to reach from one end of the house to the other.*] This Proctor, the noble lord said, acted in the double capacity of Proctor and Marshal ; and in the former capacity feed himself for consulting and instructing himself as counsel, jury, and judge, which he himself represented in the character of Marshal ; so that all those fees were for himself in the one character, and paid to the same himself in the other. He then read several of the fees, which ran thus :—for attending the Marshal (himself) 2 crowns, 2 scudi, and 2 reals ; and so on, in several other capacities in which he attended, consulted, and instructed himself, were charged several fees to the same amount. An hon. member, not then in the house, had last year opposed the motion he had brought forward, for a Committee to inquire into this subject ; but, on seeing these articles of this his own Proctor's bill, his Lordship flattered himself that the hon. member would now join in the support of the present motion. The noble lord said he had produced the copy of the bill to show the length of it. He then showed the original ; and to show the equity and moderation of the Vice-Admiralty Court, he read one article where, on the taxation of a bill, the Court, for deducting fifty crowns, charged thirty-five crowns for the trouble in doing it. A vessel was valued at 8608 crowns, the Marshal received one per cent. for delivering her, and in the end the net proceeds amounted to no more than 1900 crowns out of 8608—all the rest had been embezzled and swallowed up in the Prize Court. He was sorry, he said, to trespass on the time of the House, on a day when another matter of importance was to come before them. He pledged himself, however, that no subject could be introduced more highly deserving their serious attention and consideration."

Notwithstanding the admission of the First Lord of the Admiralty that the papers were necessary, and that they were produced, it is scarcely credible that the Government subsequently refused to act in the matter, thus turning a deaf ear to proofs that the enactments of the Legislature were defeated by the rapacity of distant Admiralty Courts, which continued to impound without scruple the rewards which the Legislature had decreed for effective exertion.

The naval reader who may wish to know more respecting the extortionate fees of these courts may refer generally to Capt. Brenton's " Life of Lord St Vincent." I will extract one passage. He says (vol. ii. p. 166) :—" Lord Cochrane made a statement of some facts to this effect in the House of Commons, but he might have gone much further. The proctor's bill for a prize taken by the *Spartan*, when my brother commanded her, was 1025*l*., which, when refused payment and taxed, *was reduced to* 285*l*. ! "

Capt. Brenton thought " I might have gone much further." So I might, but with as little effect.

CHAPTER XXX

OPENING OF PARLIAMENT, 1812

THE opening of the session of 1812 was in many ways remarkable. The speech of the Prince Regent, read by the Lords Commissioners, made everything *couleur de rose*, both as regarded our foreign wars and domestic policy. Notwithstanding that we were on the brink of war with America, both Houses were assured that the affair of the *Chesapeake* had been " finally adjusted, though other discussions were not yet brought to a close." The finances were represented as being in a flourishing condition, and his Royal Highness had no doubt of the liberal disposition of Parliament " to sustain the country in the great contest in which it was engaged."

The hollowness of these representations was met by Lord Grenville, who contrasted it with the " critical circumstances of the times, and the present alarming state of the country. The framers of the speech, said his lordship, were the very men who by their obstinate blindness had brought the country to the brink of ruin, but who, in the midst of the distresses they had themselves occasioned, still held forth the same flattering and fallacious language. He would protest against a continuance of those measures which had brought such calamities upon the country. People might choose to close their eyes, but the force of truth must dispel the wilful blindness."

Lord Grey similarly denounced the policy which was " the source of present and impending calamities. Yet these very complications were brought forward in assertion that the system of the government had contributed to the security, prosperity, and honour of the country " ! etc. etc.

In the House of Commons an unusual circumstance occurred. After the speech had been read by the Speaker, Lord Jocelyn was rising to move the usual complimentary address, but Sir

Francis Burdett, having risen at the same time, first caught the eye of the Speaker, who decided that Sir Francis was in possession of the House.

One of the honourable baronet's cutting speeches followed, in which he denounced the ministers as an " oligarchy of rotten-boroughmongers "—who alike imposed upon the people and the Prince Regent. " A system of taxation had been created which ruined many and oppressed all. This fiscal tyranny being carried to its height, the lower orders had been reduced to a state of pauperism—whilst the desperate resistance which such pauperism was calculated to produce was kept down by the terrors of a military force. Depots, barracks, and fortifications had been established in all quarters, and foreign mercenaries, who had been unable to defend their own country, had been brought over to protect the native land of courage and patriotism, or rather to protect its rulers against an indignant and oppressed people, and to support the scandalous invasions of the liberty of the press, and the severe punishments with which those who ventured to express popular opinions were visited by the courts of justice."

This interruption by Sir Francis took the House by surprise, but still greater was its astonishment when the honourable baronet proposed, in place of the ordinary address to the Prince Regent, a memorial of remonstrance, laying before his Royal Highness all the instances of misgovernment and oppression— of infringement of the public liberty, and accumulation of abuses, which had been characteristic of the system pursued by Government for many years past.

As a matter of course, the address proposed by Sir Francis was read by the Speaker, amidst the ill-concealed dismay of those most affected by it. I then rose to second the address, denouncing the impolicy of the war, and more still the way in which it was conducted, so far as the policy of ministers was concerned.

The address proposed by Sir Francis and seconded by myself was, of course, unsuccessful. The mover of the address originally

intended was Lord Jocelyn, who, when I had concluded, made
not a word of allusion to any part of the speeches of Sir Francis
or myself, beyond stating that " *he wholly disapproved of all we
had said.*" Such was legislation in those days, that the arguments of those who did not belong to the ruling faction were
not listened to, much less answered. Lord Jocelyn's address,
which was only an echo of the Lords Commissioners' speech,
had, however, to be proposed as *an amendment* to that of Sir
Francis, and was carried without a division.

The feeling towards myself for having—as was said—" thought
fit to countenance Sir Francis "—needs not be animadverted on.
Yet I had given some good advice as to the way in which our
naval power was frittered away to no purpose. English historians, by their silence on this point, appear to have little
conception as to the extent of the evil.

As in seconding the address of Sir Francis Burdett, I had
mentioned Sicily, I will give a remarkable example of the
way in which war was carried on in that quarter *against the
French*! The reader may deduce from that why I was not
permitted to put my plans of harassing the French coast into
execution.

The following letter is from Captain Robert Hall, commanding what was singularly enough called the " *army
flotilla* " at Messina. The document is a curious one, and
may do something towards enlightening future English historians :—

"MESSINA,
"*Jan.* 14, 1812.

"MY DEAR LORD,—It is so long since I heard of you, and
being disappointed at not seeing you in this country, as the
papers gave us reason to believe, that I must take the liberty of
asking you how you are. We were led to expect you in the
Mediterranean with a flying squadron, but I am sorry to see
there is *now* no probability of it.

" I am serving here in an *amphibious* kind of way—having

the rank of brigadier to command an ' *army flotilla* ' ! but why it should be an ' army ' one I cannot find out, though I have well considered the matter *for the last eighteen months.*

" There is *an immense naval establishment here of a hundred and forty vessels of different descriptions quite independent of the Admiral* ! These are maintained by the British Government, at an expense of at least 140,000*l.* per annum. I have, in fact, lessened its expense by 60,000*l.* a year, merely by reducing the pay of the seamen to the standard of our own, though they have been paid at double the rate of English sailors, whilst the *padrones* of gun-boats, taken from the streets, *are paid more than our lieutenants.*

" It is a singular thing that this establishment cannot be thrown into its proper channel—the navy. The island of Zante has another flotilla of 60,000 dollars a month to protect it, and the commandant of the barren rock of Lissa—not content with his gun-boats—sent in, the other day, a serious memorial, stating the necessity of defending his island, by placing gun-boats *all round it,* wherever there were no guns on shore ! If this flotilla mania should reach our West India Islands, what will be the consequence ? At least, I should think, as army matters are conducted, an expense equal to one half that of the whole navy ! It is the duty of officers to serve where they are ordered, but this mixture of services is, I believe, altogether new, and may, if followed up, be fatal to the independent spirit of the navy. If that spirit perishes all ardour is gone, and we shall be like some foreign countries where the services are mixed—neither the one thing nor the other.

" My Lord, I believe you know me. You may therefore guess my feelings, after *eighteen years' service,* to be ordered to serve under a person *who is a perfect stranger to the service to which I belong.* What do you think of an order to make a passage to Zante in the dead of winter by *sailing close to the land in the Gulf of Tarento* ? It is too ridiculous—and really deserves the consideration of the Admiralty.

" If we can combine our naval and military tactics, it will be a greater effort of human ingenuity than has hitherto been devised. We may then dispense with the rapidity of our manœuvres and '*march in ordinary time.*' Figure to yourself *eighteen subalterns of different regiments commanding divisions of the flotilla*! When I took it out to sea, they were all sea-sick, and —— about the decks! Each of these subalterns received *seventeen and sixpence a day for this extraordinary and fatiguing service*;—nearly three times as much as a lieutenant in the navy!

"Endeavour, my Lord, to reconcile the meaning of such an establishment, glancing your eye at the same moment on the manner of conducting the flotilla establishment at Cadiz. We have at this moment *more troops on the Faroe line than the French have in both Calabrias*—independent of those which, under our nautico-military chief, sacrificed our friends in Catalonia.

"Yet there is a sad outcry here. We tell the Sicilians that they mean to murder us all, and there is no doubt their will is good enough. Numerous are the remonstrances against sending a single soldier out of the island. The firm and manly mind of Lord William Bentinck was proof to this outcry, and it is to be regretted that circumstances did not admit of this zealous and active officer accompanying the expedition himself. Nothing can equal my respect for Lord William Bentinck as a soldier and a gentleman, but I must say with old Neptune, when jealous of the interference of some '*long-shore*' *Deity*—

'Non illi imperium pelagi sævumque tridentem
Sed mihi—sorte datum est.'

What end, what purpose, can it answer, to put a naval establishment under the command of a person who acknowledges that he does not know how to use it? As it was formed under the auspices of my Lord Mulgrave, this arrangement may probably have been made with a view of simplifying naval matters. For example, my Lord, the long sentence of '*back the main topsail,*' might be more readily expressed by the short word '*halt*!'

'Filling and making sail,' according to the strength of the wind, might be called '*marching in quick or ordinary time*!' Instead of boatswain's mates to '*march off*' the different '*detachments*' of the watch, it would, according to our present system, be more regular to '*march them off with corporals*'! though in squally weather this might be inconvenient. In short, there might be many improvements. The *army officer* appointed to command one of our vessels mislaid what he called the '*route given him by the Quarter-master-General*'! '*lost his way*,' as he expressed it, and got ashore in the Gulf of Squillace. On his exchange he reported to me that 'the night was *so dark, he could not see the rock on which the vessel ran*'! and that when fast, 'a *board broke in her bottom*, so that the water ran in so fast he could not *scoop it out* again!' Thus it is that Mr Bull is humbugged. For my part, I have remonstrated repeatedly on the folly of this establishment, and it only remains with me to serve where I am ordered.

" Of the politics of this country the public journals will have informed your Lordship. We are certainly doing nothing in the way of amelioration, and all parties seem discontented. The newfangled constitution strikes too much home to be popular amongst those who profited by the old system. Our views are certainly for the prosperity of Sicily, yet no Sicilian thinks so. They dislike us, and I believe they know not why. Some of the knowing ones appear apprehensive of our assuming the government altogether ; and urge their fears of our treating them as we do the Irish Catholics ! The French partisans, of course, make the most of this state of things.

" It is to be hoped that Buonaparte's failure in Russia will blast his other prospects, or Sicily will be his in a short time, if we do not oblige the Government to adopt some energetic measures. If they would only put the troops we have here on shore in Calabria, there would be no necessity for gun-boats. They would excite an immediate insurrection, and would throw plenty of grain, of which we are in want, into Sicily. But if the Sicilian troops should intend running away on the approach of a

French regiment—as they did formerly—we had better remain and *colonise* at Messina.

"Your Lordship's faithful servant,   ROBERT HALL.

"The LORD COCHRANE."

The above will show the useless manner in which our best naval force and officers were employed—no less than the testimony to their own uselessness. Yet with upwards of a thousand ships in commission, we had no naval enemy to oppose, and persisted in employing our seamen anywhere but on the enemy's coast! For simply urging the common-sense employment of our numerous navy, and a proper investigation into the minor details which crippled its action, I was regarded as a common disturber of the ministerial peace.

CHAPTER XXXI

MY MARRIAGE

THE event recorded in this chapter is the most important and the happiest of my life, in its results,—the "silver lining" to the "cloud," viz. my marriage with the Countess of Dundonald. It has been said by a Scottish writer that "the Cochranes have long been noted for an original and dashing turn of mind, which was sometimes called genius—sometimes eccentricity." How far this may be true of my ancestors, I shall not stay to inquire. Laying no claim to the genius, I however dispute the eccentricity in my own case, notwithstanding that appearances, so far as relates to my past life, may be somewhat against me. Without a particle of romance in my composition, my life has been one of the most romantic on record, and the circumstances of my marriage are not the least so.

Early in the year 1812, it was my good fortune to make the acquaintance of the orphan daughter of a family of honourable standing in the Midland Counties, Miss Katharine Corbett Barnes. In consequence of the loss of her parents, the lady had been placed during her minority under the guardianship of her first cousin, Mr John Simpson of Portland Place and also of Fairlorn House in the county of Kent, of which county he was then High Sheriff. The story is the old one. Shortly after my introduction to this lady I made proposals of marriage, and was accepted.

But here an unexpected difficulty arose. I was at that time residing with my uncle, the Hon. Basil Cochrane, who had realised a large fortune in the East Indies. My attachment—though not my engagement—to my *fiancée* had by some means reached him, and he at once attempted to divert my purpose by proposing to me a marriage with the only daughter of an Admiralty Court official who had realised a very large fortune by the practices which have already been made familiar to the reader.

I cannot describe the repugnance which I felt even to the proposition, and pointed out to my uncle the impossibility of marrying the daughter of one of those persons whom I had so severely denounced ; adding that not only would such a step be a deviation from those principles which ought to guide a well-regulated mind in the selection of a wife, but must be destructive of my public character, which would be so clearly sacrificed for money, that it would render me contemptible to my constituents, and would prevent my again meriting public confidence. His reply was brief and caustic. " Please yourself : nevertheless, my fortune and the money of the wife I have chosen for you, would go far towards reinstating future Earls of Dundonald in their ancient position as regards wealth."

This conversation was communicated to the lady to whom I was affianced, on whom I urged a consent to a secret marriage, —a proposition in which she refused to acquiesce. My uncle, however, continuing firm in his resolves, I at length prevailed upon her to overcome her repugnance, and we were, on the 8th of August, 1812, married at Annan in Scotland.

On my return my uncle again renewed the subject, and one morning, during our walk, he informed me that he had made his will, leaving me one half his fortune. He, however, declared, that compliance with his wish as to my marriage with the heiress of the Admiralty Court official was essential to its eventual confirmation. On arguing this, on the same grounds as before, he observed that some other person of wealth must be sought for, as his object was to retrieve the family fortune. Meanwhile he required my assurance that I would not marry without his sanction. Compliance with this was declined for the best of all reasons, that I was already married.

The fact of our marriage was not long concealed, and I did not inherit a shilling of my uncle's wealth, for which loss, however, I had a rich equivalent in the acquisition of a wife whom no amount of wealth could have purchased. A yet more singular sequel has to be told. On the discovery of the marriage, my uncle, though then an old man, also married, and was easily made to believe that non-payment of a large sum due to him from Government, on account of some contracts undertaken before he quitted India, had been delayed on account of my parliamentary opposition to the ministry. This may or may not have been the case, but it induced my uncle to request that our future association might be less frequent. An intimation followed by the still more questionable course of his requesting an interview with Lord Liverpool, for the purpose of informing his lordship of the step he had taken with regard to myself, and assuring him that he had never countenanced my conduct in parliament. Singularly enough, my uncle's demands upon the Government were soon afterwards settled.

It was my wish here to have spoken of my wife's devotedness to me amidst the many trying circumstances in which I have been placed. They do not, however, come within the scope of this volume, as regards their chronological order; I therefore postpone their narration.

CHAPTER XXXII

THE STOCK EXCHANGE TRIAL

I NOW approach a period of my life in which occurred circumstances beyond all others painful to the feelings of an honourable man. Neglect I was accustomed to. Despite my efforts to rise superior to the jealousies of others, it has followed me through life. Exclusion from professional activity at a period when opportunity for distinction lay before me, was hard to bear; but I had the consolation of exerting myself ashore for the benefit of the noble service, in the active duties of which I was not permitted to participate. But when an alleged offence was laid to my charge in 1814, in which, on the honour of a man now on the brink of the grave, I had not the slightest participation, and from which I never benefited, nor thought to benefit one farthing, and when this allegation was, by political rancour and legal chicanery, consummated in an unmerited conviction and an outrageous sentence, my heart for the first time sank within me, as conscious of a blow, the effect of which it has required all my energies to sustain. It has been said that truth comes sooner or later. But it seldom comes before the mind, passing from agony to contempt, has grown callous to man's judgment. To this principle, I am thankful to say, I have never subscribed, but have to this hour remained firm in the hope and confidence that by the mercy of God I shall not die till full and ample justice of my fellow-men has been freely rendered me.

It may be thought that after the restoration to rank and honours by my late and present Sovereigns—after promotion to the command of a fleet when I had no enemy to confront—and after enjoyment of the sympathy and friendship of those whom the nation delights to honour,—I might safely pass over that day of deep humiliation. Not so. It is true that I have received those marks of my Sovereign's favour, and it is true that from that day to the present I have enjoyed the uninterrupted friendship of those who were then convinced, and are still convinced, of my innocence ; but *that unjust public sentence has never been publicly reversed, nor the equally unjust fine inflicted on me remitted* ; so that if I would, it is not in my power to remain silent and be just to my posterity. The Government of my country has, though often invoked, refused to re-investigate my case, as impossible in form, and from fear of creating a precedent. Nevertheless, I will, repugnant as is the subject, re-state the facts, and, posterity being my judge, have no fear as to the verdict. The coronet of my ancestors, and the honour of my family, which will, in the course of nature, ere long be committed to the keeping of a devoted and sensitively honourable son, demand no less at my hands.

It must not, however, be imagined that the recital of leading facts is for the first time adopted in pursuance of the dictates of family duty and affection. Neither would it have been possible to write my autobiography without entering on this most important and painful portion of my life, because such an omission would be fatal to my reputation, as it might be construed into an admission of my culpability.

At a period before the experience of the present generation, the circumstances about to be recorded were over and over again submitted to public judgment, but at a time when the rod of justice was suspended *in terrorem* over the public press, which did not venture openly to espouse my cause on its own merits. Yet even then my efforts were not in vain. The press, instead of being, as in those days it was, the organ of ill-concealed public dissatisfaction, has now become the exponent of the public voice ; which, through its medium, is heard and felt throughout the length and breadth of the land. Though approaching the subject with distaste, I do so with confidence that my unvarnished tale will not be told in vain.

For the more ready appreciation of the reader in the present day, as regards facts, the details of which the lapse of half-a-century has nearly obliterated, I may be permitted to introduce the subject by extracts from the works of two of the most learned and distinguished lawyers and statesmen of the age in which we live—two noblemen, of whose learning, of whose judgment and integrity it is unnecessary for me to say one word, because they are much above my praise, and therefore can receive no addition from it—viz. Lord Brougham, formerly our Lord High Chancellor, and Lord Campbell, the present Lord High Chancellor of England. I will take those of Lord Campbell first, because they embrace points into which Lord Brougham does not enter, and also because Lord Campbell, in addition to the dignity which he now adorns, for many years occupied the same high position as did Lord Ellenborough, when he presided at the trial to which the reader's attention is now directed.

Lord Campbell, at p. 218, vol. iii. in his valuable work entitled "The Lives of the Chief-Justices of England," says :—

"I have now only to mention some criminal cases which arose before Lord Ellenborough in later years. Of these, the most remarkable was Lord Cochrane's, as this drew upon the Chief-Justice a considerable degree of public obloquy, and, *causing very uneasy reflections in his own mind, was supposed to have hastened his end.*

"Lord Cochrane (since Earl of Dundonald) was one of the most gallant officers in the English navy, and had gained the most brilliant reputation in a succession of naval engagements against the French. Unfortunately for him, he likewise wished to distinguish himself in politics, and taking the Radical line, he was returned to Parliament for the city of Westminster. He was a determined opponent of Lord Liverpool's Administration; and at popular meetings was in the habit of delivering harangues of rather a seditious aspect, which induced Lord Ellenborough to believe that he seriously meant to abet rebellion, and that he was a dangerous character. But the gallant officer was really a loyal subject, as well as enthusiastically zealous for the glory of his country. He had an uncle, named Cochrane, a merchant,*

* This is an error. My uncle, an East India merchant, was the Hon.

x

and a very unprincipled man, who, towards the end of the war, in concert with De Berenger, a foreigner, wickedly devised a scheme by which they were to make an immense fortune by a speculation on the Stock Exchange.

" For this purpose they were to cause a sudden rise in the funds, by spreading false intelligence that a preliminary treaty of peace had actually been signed between England and France. Everything succeeded to their wishes ; the intelligence was believed, the funds rose, and they sold on time bargains many hundred thousand pounds of 3 per cents. before the truth was discovered.

" It so happened that Lord Cochrane was then in London, was living in his uncle's house,* and was much in his company, but there is now good reason to believe that he was not at all implicated in the nefarious scheme.   However, when the fraud was detected,—partly from a belief in his complicity, and partly *from political spite*,—he was included in the indictment preferred for the conspiracy to defraud the Stock Exchange.

" The trial coming on before Lord Ellenborough, the noble and learned Judge, being himself persuaded of the guilt of all the defendants, used his best endeavours that they should all be convicted.   He refused to adjourn the trial at the close of the prosecutor's case, about nine in the evening, when the trial had lasted twelve hours, and the jury, as well as the defendants' counsel, were all completely exhausted and all prayed for an adjournment.   The following day, in summing up, prompted, no doubt, by the conclusion of his own mind, he laid *special emphasis on every circumstance which might raise a suspicion against Lord Cochrane*, and ELABORATELY EXPLAINED AWAY WHATEVER AT FIRST SIGHT MIGHT SEEM FAVOURABLE to the gallant officer.   In consequence the jury found a verdict of GUILTY against *all* the defendants.

" Next term, Lord Cochrane presented himself in Court to

Basil Cochrane, a highly honourable man, not the one alluded to by Lord Campbell.
* It was my uncle Basil with whom I for a time resided.

move for a new trial, but the other defendants convicted along with him did not attend. He said truly that he had no power or influence to obtain their attendance, and urged that his application was founded on circumstances peculiar to his own case. But Lord Ellenborough would not hear him, because the other defendants were not present. Such a rule had before been laid down,* *but it is palpably contrary to the first principles of justice, and ought immediately to have been reversed.*

"Lord Cochrane was thus deprived of all opportunity of showing that the verdict against him was wrong, and in addition to fine and imprisonment, he was sentenced to stand in the pillory.† Although as yet he was generally believed to be guilty, the award of this degrading and infamous punishment upon a young nobleman, a member of the House of Commons, and a distinguished naval officer, raised universal sympathy in his favour. The judge was proportionably blamed, not only by the vulgar, but by men of education on both sides in politics, and he found upon entering society and appearing in the House of Lords *that he was looked upon coldly.*

"*Having now some misgivings himself as to the propriety of his conduct in this affair, he became very wretched.* Nor was the agitation allowed to drop during the remainder of Lord Ellenborough's life, for Lord Cochrane, being expelled the House of Commons, *was immediately re-elected for Westminster.* Having escaped from the prison in which he was confined under his sentence, he appeared in the House of Commons. In obedience to the public voice, the part of his sentence by which he was to stand in the pillory was remitted by the Crown, and a bill was introduced into Parliament altogether to abolish the pillory as a punishment, *on account of the manner in which the power of inflicting it had been recently abused.* It was said that these matters

---

* On one special occasion only.

† This vindictive sentence the Government did not dare carry out. My high-minded colleague, Sir Francis Burdett, told the Government that if the sentence was carried into effect, he would stand in the pillory beside me, when they must look to the consequences. What these might have been, in the then excited state of the public mind, as regarded my treatment, the reader may guess.

preyed deeply on Lord Ellenborough's mind and affected his health. Thenceforth he certainly seemed to have lost the gaiety of heart for which he had been formerly remarkable." (Lord Campbell's "Lives of the Chief-Justices," vol. iii. pp. 218, 219, 220.)

Such are the recorded opinions of one of the most learned and acute men of the age—one who now does honour to the judgment-seat of the highest tribunal of our country ; and who, at the time those opinions were given to the world, held the scarcely less dignified position of Chief-Justice of England, sitting in the very court in which that cruel sentence—the unmerited cause of so much misery to me—was pronounced. From such an authority—as much judicial as historic—may the reader form his own conclusions.

It is with no less satisfaction that I add the opinions of another learned and highly-gifted peer of the realm, who has also adorned the dignified office of Lord High Chancellor of England, viz. my friend Lord Brougham, to whose name, as the untiring advocate of everything nationally progressive and socially expansive, no testimony of mine could add weight.

In the year 1844, when I submitted to her Majesty's Government how incomplete I considered the restoration of my honours, I wrote to Lord Brougham, ever my constant and steadfast friend, to ask his opinion of the step I was taking. The subjoined was Lord Brougham's reply :—

"Grafton Street,
"*March* 29, 1844.

"My dear Lord D.—I think, upon the whole, the time is favourable.

"I have well considered the matter as of importance, and have read the papers through. I don't think the best way of bringing the subject before the Duke is to send that correspondence, but rather to make a statement, and I authorise you distinctly to add to it these two important facts.

"First, that William IV. only objected to the Bath being restored *at the same time* with your rank, and not absolutely at all times.

"Secondly, that your counsel were clearly of opinion that the verdict as *concerned you was erroneous*, and I always concluded that you had sacrificed yourself out of delicacy to your uncle, the person really guilty.

"The restoring you to rank without your honours is too absurd and unfair. It means ' we will take all we can get from you in service, and give you nothing.'

"Yours ever truly,   H. BROUGHAM."

No one knew better than his late Majesty, King William the Fourth, the injustice under which I had laboured, and the causes of the political spite which had been directed against me. Before his Majesty came to the throne he warmly interested himself in my behalf, and intimated to Sir Francis Burdett, that if I were to memorialise the Government, he would use his influence to procure my restoration. This was accordingly done, but in vain, his Royal Highness's influence *then* proving insufficient for the purpose, but not so after his Majesty's accession to the throne,

The following extract of a letter from Sir Francis Burdett, coming shortly before my restoration to rank, will show the continued interest taken by his late Majesty and those near him to remove unmerited obloquy from a brother sailor, notwithstanding the failure of his Majesty's previous effort when Duke of Clarence. The same intimation to Sir Francis Burdett being made, a similar memorial was laid before his Majesty in Council ; this time with effect.

"MY DEAR LORD DUNDONALD,—I went to the Levee on Wednesday to give your memorial to Greville, the Clerk of the Council, to present—but the King returned to Windsor immediately after the Levee and no council was held. Had it been, I can entertain no doubt that your memorial would have been presented and granted.

"I went to see Greville about it the next day—he was so kind and so desirous of doing everything in his power to expedite it, even proposing to take it out of its usual turn, that I cannot but feel quite satisfied and assured that there will be not a moment's unnecessary delay. A little patience and all will be right. I should like to see you for a day or two, and perhaps may.

"Yours sincerely,   F. BURDETT."

My restoration not long afterwards followed, and no one knew better than his Majesty the justice of reversing the unjust sentence which had so long and so undeservedly excluded me from a service which from my youth upwards had been my pride.

I shall ever consider this interference on my behalf as a testimonial from his late Majesty not only to my innocence, but also to my unjustifiable persecution, for had he not believed me innocent, his Majesty would have been the last person to interfere so pertinaciously. Still less when, on coming to the throne, his former influence had become authority.

I was not restored to my honours till the reign of her present Most Gracious Majesty, and on this restoration being made, I again requested of her Majesty's ministers a reinvestigation into the causes which led to my unjust conviction, alleging that my restoration to rank and honour might be construed into an act of mercy, were not my innocence of the Stock Exchange hoax fully established. In this sense I addressed the late Duke of Wellington and Sir Robert Peel. The following was his Grace's reply.

"WALMER CASTLE,
"Sept. 12, 1844.

"MY LORD,—I have just received the package from your Lordship, containing your Lordship's letter to myself of the 10th inst. and other papers, which I will peruse with attention according to the desire and for the purpose expressed in your Lordship's letter.

"I have the honour to be, etc.   WELLINGTON.
"Admiral the EARL OF DUNDONALD, etc."

The reply of Sir Robert Peel was more explicit, and gave as a reason why my request could not be complied with, that just, or unjust, it was not, from lapse of time, in the power of the Government to attempt to reverse a decision in a court of law.

                                        "WHITEHALL,
                                        "Nov. 7, 1844.

"MY LORD,—Her Majesty's servants have had under their consideration the letter I received from your Lordship, bearing date the 10th of September, 1844, together with the documents by which that letter was accompanied.

"On reference to the proceedings which were adopted in the year 1832,* it appears that previously to the restoration of your Lordship to your rank in the navy a free pardon under the great seal was granted to your Lordship, and, adverting to that circumstance, and to the fact that thirty years have elapsed since the charges to which the free pardon had reference were the subject of investigation before the proper judicial tribunal of the country, her Majesty's servants cannot consistently with their sense of public duty advise the Queen to reopen an inquiry into those charges.

"I beg leave to refer your Lordship to the letter which the Earl of Haddington, the First Lord of the Admiralty, addressed to your Lordship in the year 1842—as I am not enabled to make any communication to your Lordship on the part of her Majesty's Government differing in purport from that letter.

"I have the honour, etc.   ROBERT PEEL.
"Admiral the EARL OF DUNDONALD, etc."

Here was the whole secret why I had never been able to obtain an investigation of my case, and why the Admiralty,

* My restoration to rank.

which deprived me of rank and honour, declined to investigate it, notwithstanding that an appeal from the verdict had been refused by the Court of King's Bench, though I had then in court such additional evidence as must have set aside the verdict, which evidence will shortly be laid before the reader, who will now be in a condition to understand the following explanation of Lord Brougham, given, under the article " Ellenborough," in his " Historic Sketches of British Statesmen in the time of George the Third."

" On the bench, it is not to be denied that Lord Ellenborough occasionally suffered the strength of his political feelings to break forth and to influence the tone and temper of his observations. That he ever, upon any one occasion, knowingly deviated one hair's breadth in the discharge of his office is wholly untrue. The case which gave rise to the greatest comment, and even led to a senseless show of impeachment was Lord Cochrane's. * * * I must, however, be here distinctly understood *to deny the accuracy of the opinion which Lord Ellenborough appears to have formed in this case, and deeply to lament the verdict of guilty which the jury returned, after three hours' consultation and hesitation.*

" If Lord Cochrane was at all aware of his uncle Mr Cochrane Johnstone's proceedings, it was the whole extent of his privity to the fact. Having been one of the counsel engaged in the cause I can speak with some confidence respecting it, and I take upon me to assert that Lord Cochrane's conviction was mainly owing to the extreme repugnance which he felt to giving up his uncle, or taking those precautions for his own safety which would have operated against that near relation. Even when he, the real criminal, had confessed his guilt, by taking to flight, and the other defendants were brought up for judgment, we, the counsel, could not persuade Lord Cochrane to shake himself loose from the contamination by abandoning him.

" Our only complaint against Lord Ellenborough was his Lordship's refusal to adjourn after the prosecutor's case closed, and his requiring us to enter upon our defence at so late an hour—

past nine o'clock—that the adjournment took place at midnight,
and before we called our witnesses. Of course, I speak of the
trial at Guildhall only. Lord Ellenborough was equally to blame
with his brethren in the Court of King's Bench for that most
cruel and unjustifiable sentence, which at once secured Lord
Cochrane's re-election for Westminister when the House of
Commons expelled him upon his conviction.

" In 1833, the Government of which I was a member restored
his great warrior to his rank of Admiral in our navy. The
country, therefore, in the event of hostilities, would now have
he inestimable benefit of his services, whom none perhaps ever
qualled in heroic courage, and whose fertility of resources,
ilitary as well as naval, place him high amongst the very first
t commanders. That his honours of knighthood, so gloriously
on, should still be withholden is a stain, *not upon him*, but upon
he councils of his country ; and after his restoration to the
rvice, it is as inconsistent and incomprehensible as cruel and
unjust." (Lord Brougham's " Historic Sketches.")

A brief outline of the circumstances which led to the trial
will enable the reader to comprehend the grounds upon which
the opinions just quoted were based.

At the commencement of 1814 I was appointed by my uncle,
Sir Alexander Cochrane, then commanding the British fleet on
the North American station, as his flag-captain ; and in the
month of February was busily engaged in getting the *Tonnant*
line-of-battle ship, then fitting at Chatham as my uncle's flag-
ship, ready for sea. The presence of Sir Alexander being im-
peratively required upon the station, he had previously quitted
England in a frigate ; and it had been understood between my
uncle and myself that, on joining him with the *Tonnant*, the
most efficient measures should be adopted to compensate for
our late defeats with the better manned and equipped vessels of
the United States.

Previous to my uncle's departure at the latter end of 1813,
he had, in pursuance of this object, repeatedly though unsuc-

cessfully applied to the Admiralty for permission to engage an officer in the Duke of Cumberland's regiment of Sharpshooters, as having a reputation not only for skill in teaching rifle practice, but also for his pyrotechnic acquirements, as an engineer officer ; this proficiency having become known to Sir Alexander through his brother, who strongly urged the employment of the person alluded to, a Captain De Berenger, with whom Mr Cochrane Johnstone had been for some time acquainted. It was thus that I was subsequently brought in contact with a man who eventually proved my ruin, by involving me in an appearance of complicity in an attempt to raise the public funds by the dissemination of groundless news to the prejudice of the Stock Exchange speculators, one of those common deceptions which, I am told, were then, as now, practised by parties connected with the transactions of the Stock Exchange.

In the month of January Mr Cochrane Johnstone invited De Berenger to a dinner, at which I was present. Towards the close of the evening this person asked me to step aside with him for the purpose of conversation. His object was to request me to take him on board the *Tonnant* in any capacity, for having failed to obtain the consent of the Admiralty he would be happy to trust to Sir Alexander's generosity to employ him in any situation for which he was qualified. With this view he begged me to peruse his testimonials as adjutant of the Duke of Cumberland's rifle regiment, as well as other documents of a similar character.

Finding the testimonials satisfactory, I expressed my regret at not being able to take him in the *Tonnant* without an appointment, or at least an order, from the Board of Admiralty ; adding, that no person could possibly have less influence with their lordships than myself, and that therefore it was useless for me to apply to them on his behalf, especially as they had refused the application of Sir Alexander Cochrane. Knowing, however, that it was the wish of Sir Alexander that De Berenger should go if possible, I recommended him to exert himself to secure the influence of those under whom he appeared to have served so satisfactorily ; adding that, if he succeeded, I should have great pleasure in taking him in the *Tonnant*.

With these prefatory remarks the reader will readily comprehend what follows :—

About midnight on the 20th of February, according to the current report of the transactions hereafter to be named, a person calling himself Colonel de Bourg, aide-de-camp to Lord Cathcart, presented himself at the Ship Hotel at Dover, representing that he was the bearer of intelligence from Paris, to the effect that Buonaparte had been killed by the Cossacks— that the allied armies were in full march for Paris—and that immediate peace was certain. After this announcement he forwarded similar intelligence by letter to the Port-Admiral at Deal, with a view—as was supposed—of its being forwarded to London by telegraph ; thus making the Port-Admiral the medium of communication with the Government.

This person, as was afterwards known to the Stock Exchange only *through my instrumentality*, was the before-named De Berenger. The intelligence was false, having been concocted for the purpose of causing a rise in the public funds.

On the 7th of March, the Committee of the Stock Exchange published an advertisement offering a reward of two hundred and fifty guineas for the discovery of the person who had perpetrated the hoax ; a report being at the same time current that the pretended De Bourg had, on the morning of the 21st February, been *traced to my house in Green Street*.

At this time I had joined the *Tonnant* at Chatham, and was preparing to sail for the North American station, but on learning the injurious report above mentioned, and being aware from the ordinary channels of public intelligence of the nature of the transaction—being moreover indignant that the perpetrator of the deception should have dared to visit me, I determined to denounce him, in order that if he were really the guilty person, his name should be made public at the earliest possible moment, so that no time might be lost in bringing the matter home to him.

In pursuance of this determination I obtained leave of absence from the ship. On my return to town, I found that although the authorities were ignorant of the name of the person who came to my house on the 21st of February, public rumour did not hesitate to impute to me complicity in his transactions, simply from the fact of the suspected person, whoever he might be, having been there.

To rebut these insinuations was of the first importance. Accordingly I immediately consulted my legal advisers.

The result was that an affidavit was prepared and submitted to an eminent barrister, Mr Gurney, to whom I disclosed every particular relative to the visit of De Berenger, as well as to my own previous, though very unimportant transactions in the public funds. I was advised by him and my own solicitors to confine myself simply to supplying the authorities with the name of De Berenger as the person seen in uniform at my house on the 21st ultimo.

With this suggestion, wisely or unwisely—but certainly in all honesty, I refused to comply, expressing my determination to account *for all my acts* on the 21st of February, even to the entire occupation of my whole time on that day. Finding me firm on this point, the affidavit was settled by Mr Gurney, the barrister, and sworn to, the name of De Berenger for the first time thus becoming known to those who were in quest of him.

A circumstance may here be mentioned which has an important bearing on the subject. My letter to the Admiralty, giving my reasons for asking leave of absence for the purpose of rebutting the insinuations against my character, contained most material matter for my exculpation. It was written to Mr Secretary Croker, but when I afterwards moved for and obtained from the House of Commons an order for the production of my correspondence with the Admiralty, *this letter was not to be found, though all others asked for were* ! ! Had the letter been produced, it must have had great weight with the House, the adverse decision of which I mainly ascribe to its nonproduction. Unfortunately, in the haste of the application, no copy was taken.

I have been particular in recording dates, because it has been insinuated to my injury that I *had been tardy* in giving the information in my power. It is hence my desire to put on record that *the moment* the necessity for vindicating myself arose not an hour was lost by me in giving the Stock Exchange a clue to the offender, if such De Berenger should turn out to have been.

I will here notice another circumstance, viz. that the very Mr Gurney who had advised me in the matter of my affidavit, and to whom I had unreservedly communicated every circumstance connected with my private affairs, as well as those connected with the visit of De Berenger, was afterwards chosen by Mr Lavie, the *solicitor to the committee, as the leading counsel for the Stock Exchange at the subsequent trial against me*! I simply relate the fact, without comment.

It is not necessary here to weary the reader by the insertion of a lengthy affidavit, which accounted for every act of mine on the day of the alleged hoax. The main facts, as relating to the visit of De Berenger, are these. That early on the morning in question I had gone to a lamp manufactory in the city, for the purpose of superintending the progress of some lamps patented by me, and ordered for the use of the convoy of which I was about to take charge on their voyage to North America. Whilst thus engaged, my servant came to me with a note, which had been given to him by a military officer, who was waiting at my house to see me. Not being able to make out the name, from the scrawling style in which the note was written, and supposing it to have come from a messenger from my brother, who was then dangerously ill with the army of the Peninsula, and of whose death we were in daily expectation of hearing, I threw down the note, and replied, that I would come as soon as possible ; and, having completed my arrangements at the lamp manufactory, arrived at home about two hours afterwards, when, to my surprise, I found De Berenger in place of the expected messenger from my brother.

The comprehensiveness of the voluntary disclosure contained in the affidavit has been termed indiscreet, and may have been so, as entering on much that might be deemed unnecessary. But I had nothing to conceal, believing it could in no way affect me—nor would it have done so but for the trickery subsequently resorted to. There was nothing extraordinary in the document. A poor but talented man—a prisoner within the rules of the King's Bench—came to me in the hope that I would extricate him from his difficulties by taking him to America in the *Tonnant*. After my renewed refusal, on professional grounds, De Berenger represented that he could not return to the Rules in his uniform without exciting suspicion of his absence. The room happened at the time to be strewed with clothes, in process of examination, for the purpose of being sent on board the *Tonnant*, those rejected being thrown aside ; and at his urgent request I lent, or rather gave, him a civilian's hat and coat to enable him to return to his lodgings in ordinary costume. This simple act constituted my offence, and was construed by the court into complicity in his fraudulent conduct ! though under ordinary circumstances, and I was aware of no other, it was simply an act of compassionate good nature.

A very remarkable circumstance connected with this affidavit, and afterwards proved on the trial, was this—that on De Berenger's arrival in town from Dover, he neither went to the Stock Exchange, nor to his employers, whoever they might be, nor did he take any steps on his arrival in town to *spread the false intelligence which he had originated.* He was proved on the trial to have dismissed his post-chaise at Lambeth—to have taken a hackney coach—and to have proceeded straight to my house. The inference is plain, that the man was frightened at the nature of the mission he had undertaken, and declined to go through with it, preferring to try once more whether he could not prevail on me to take him on board the *Tonnant*, where he might remain till the ship sailed for North America.

Had I been his confederate, it is not within the bounds of credibility that he would have come in the first instance to my house, and waited two hours for my return home, in place of carrying out the plot he had undertaken, or that I should have been occupied in perfecting my lamp invention for the use of the convoy of which I was in a few days to take charge, instead of being on *the only spot* where any advantage to be derived from the Stock Exchange hoax could be realised, had I been a participator ini t. Such advantage must have been immediate, before the truth came out, and to have reaped it, had I been guilty, it was necessary that I should not lose a moment. It is still more improbable, that being aware of the hoax, I should not have speculated largely for the special risk of that day.

Neither, had I been his confederate, is it more probable that I should have declined to take him on board the *Tonnant*, when, by so doing, I could have effectually concealed him under another name, together with every trace of the plot, and could have either taken him with me, or have shipped him in safety to the Continent.

I will here repeat what has been previously stated, that before my affidavit the committee of the Stock Exchange was ignorant even of the name of *any* person, that my affidavit alone disclosed the necessary information. In other words, *I voluntarily gave the only information upon which the subsequent trial was based, and this disclosure was so complete as to leave the Stock Exchange nothing to do but to prosecute De Berenger.*

Let me ask the common-sense question, whether this was the act of a guilty person, who by concealing his knowledge could have effectually prevented all further investigation ? Or, to put the question in another form—would it not have been the act of an insane person, if guilty, to have denounced another to his own conviction, when by holding his peace both would have been safe from detection ? To have done such an uncalled-for act, would have been little in accordance with the *acumen* for which the public had for many years given me credit. In one respect, my affidavit might have been an error, but it was not the *error of a guilty man* ; viz. in not deferring to the opinion of my legal advisers, who wished me to confine myself to the single fact that the pretended De Bourg had been traced to my house, and that I suspected De Berenger to be the person.

My fault was, that being conscious—till too late—that nothing in the whole affair could in any way concern me—I was careless about my defence—had nothing to do with the brief beyond a few rough notes—and never even read it after it was finally prepared for counsel. This was not the act of a guilty man. Yet, had I been guilty, I should have had every chance in my favour of acquittal; first, by concealing the fact that De Berenger was the stranger who came to my house on the 21st of February, in military uniform—and, without this voluntary information on my part, the case must have disappeared; secondly, had I really been guilty, my chance of acquittal would have been greater than if innocent—because the knowledge of facts which I must have possessed if guilty, and *could not have possessed* if innocent, would have enabled me to make an effectual defence in place of the aimless defence which was made.

If proof of my non-participation in the hoax were required, it existed, so far as the statement of such a person was credible, in the handwriting of De Berenger himself, immediately after my affidavit disclosing his name in furtherance of the purposes of justice; a proceeding on my part which might naturally be supposed to embitter him against me. So far from this being the case, an innate sense of justice on the part of De Berenger led him to admit even the truth of the declaration contained in the affidavit as regarded himself.

" 13, GREEN STREET,
" *April* 27, 1814.

" SIR,—Having, I trust, given ample time and opportunity to those who have endeavoured to asperse my character to learn from your own mouth the circumstances which induced you to call upon me on the 21st of February last, I feel it now due to

THE EARL OF DUNDONALD, ADMIRAL OF THE RED
REAR-ADMIRAL OF THE FLEET
[Born 1775.   Died 1860]

myself no longer to delay this my earnest request, that you will afford me that explanation.

"I am, Sir, your obedient Servant,

(Signed)   "COCHRANE,"

"BARON DE BERENGER."

[De Berenger to Lord Cochrane :—

"KING STREET, WESTMINSTER,
"April 27, 1814.

"MY LORD,—I have the honour of acknowledging the receipt of your Lordship's favour, which has this moment been delivered.

"Rest assured, my Lord, that nothing could exceed the pain I felt when I perceived how cruelly, how unfair, my unfortunate visit of the 21st of February was interpreted (*which, with its object, is so correctly detailed in your affidavit*); but my agony is augmented, when I reflect that acts of generosity and goodness towards an unfortunate man have been, and continue to be, the accidental cause of much mortification to you : a fear of increasing the imaginary grounds of accusation caused me to refrain from addressing you.

"I have the honour, etc.

"CHAS. RANDOM DE BERENGER."

The tone of this letter, which, without answering in express terms my query as to the object of his visit on the 21st of February, declares the truth of my affidavit as to the same, and also to what occurred during the short time he remained there.

This indisposed me for further communication with the writer, who, finding such to be the case, commenced a series of vituperative epistles, the object of which was evidently the extortion of money. The whole of these letters were transmitted by me to the public press, without reply or comment, and were so published at the time.

Y

A no less important admission emanated from De Berenger. The press had by some means or other got hold of the fact that this man, whom I had denounced to the Stock Exchange, was *in communication with certain members of the Government for the purpose of implicating me* ! The communication does not appear to have resulted in anything further than was known from my affidavit, and I have reason to know that from fear of the man's character, the Government abstained from committing themselves with him.

" KING'S BENCH,
" *July* 19, 1814.

" Whereas several newspapers have asserted that I have written to Lord Sidmouth, whilst others state that I have addressed the committee of the Stock Exchange, etc., disclosing particulars to prove Lord Cochrane's guilt, I feel justified thus solemnly, publicly and positively to declare, That *since my confinement here,* I have neither written, or otherwise applied, directly or indirectly, to any of the offices of Government for the purpose of disclosure. That I have not written to any one on the subject of the 21st of February last, *since the 11th instant* (July), excepting one private letter to Lord Cochrane. That the assertions in the newspapers are totally false, etc. etc.

" CHARLES RANDOM DE BERENGER."

The plain inference is, that De Berenger did so *before the trial,* and whilst he was writing to me that the contents of my affidavit, as regarded himself, contained the exact truth. That he had such communication with both Government and Stock Exchange, before the trial, is beyond doubt, and part of the reasons which warrant my assertion, that a higher authority than the Stock Exchange was at the bottom of my prosecution. Deeply degraded as was the man, he affords the strongest *presumptive* evidence of my non-participation in the hoax.

I do not blame the judge for not taking these matters into

account, for, confident in my entire innocence, I could not set their importance or bearing, and did not even communicate them to my solicitor till too late.

Bitter after-knowledge has however convinced me of the error of carelessness—even from a consciousness of innocence —when once entangled in the meshes of law—a word by no means synonymous with justice.

Of the subject of the prosecution itself, I will here say one word. It was that of one set of stock-jobbers and their confederates trying—by means of false intelligence—to raise the price of " *time bargains* " at the expense of another set of stock-jobbers, the losers being naturally indignant at the successful hoax. The wrong was not then, and still is not, on the statute-book. Such a case had never been tried before, nor has it since—and was termed a " conspiracy " ; or rather, by charging the several defendants—of most of whom I had never before heard—in one indictment, it was brought under the designation of a " conspiracy." The " conspiracy "—such as it was—was nevertheless one, which, as competent persons inform me, has been the practice in all countries ever since stock-jobbing began, and is in the present day constantly practised, but I have never heard mention of the energy of the Stock Exchange even to detect the practice.

I do not make these remarks to palliate deception, even at the expense of Stock Exchange speculators. My object is, that the present generation, knowing that in my early life I was imprisoned and fined 1000*l.* for an alleged offence against the Stock Exchange fraternity, may understand the exact character of the accusation. It is clear that the influence and vindictiveness with which this most unjustifiable prosecution was carried out as against me, arose from motives far deeper than the vindication of stock-jobbing purity, viz. from a desire in more influential quarters to silence, if possible, an obnoxious political adversary ; the visit of De Berenger to my house, as disclosed by myself, and his acquaintance with my uncle as before stated, affording a basis for the accomplishment of this object.

Happily, Providence has implanted in the breast of man an amount of moral and physical energy proportioned to the wrongs and inflictions he may be called upon to bear, and, even in my eighty-fifth year, I am still left sound in mind, and with a heart unbroken, to tell my own story.

CHAPTER XXXIII

LORD ELLENBOROUGH'S CHARGE

HAD I been aware of a very curious coincidence connected with the trial which followed, my confidence, arising from consciousness of innocence, would have vanished in an instant; so that instead of indifference about the result, I should have seen the necessity of meeting every accusation with the most deliberate caution, supporting the same by every attainable evidence, in place of no evidence at all.

The fact alluded to is this—that the same Mr Lavie who had displayed so much tact on Lord Gambier's court-martial *was selected as solicitor to the prosecution in the present case,* to the exclusion of the appointed solicitor to the Committee of the Stock Exchange! The fact was significant, as affording additional suspicion that an influence other and higher than that of the Committee was at work.

As in various publications connected with Lord Gambier's trial I had spoken very freely of Mr Lavie as regarded the fabricated charts, there could be no doubt of his not unreasonable personable animosity towards myself. But when, *after the trial,* I became for the first time aware that he had been employed to conduct it, the enigma was solved as to how I, from having voluntarily given the only information upon which the case could have originated at all, came to be mixed up in one common accusation with a number of persons, of most of whose very names I had never before heard.

More than this, it then became but too apparent that from

the selection of Mr Lavie as prosecuting attorney, I was not so much the subject of a Stock Exchange prosecution as of the political vindictiveness of which I have spoken, and which had gone out of the usual course to secure his services. That there was collusion between a high official at the Admiralty and the Committee of the Stock Exchange on this point, I do not hesitate for one moment to assert ; nor do I think, from previous revelations in this work, that many of my readers will be inclined to differ with me.

The principal circumstance which was held to have implicated me in the hoax practised on the Stock Exchange was this :—That (as gathered from my own voluntary information) De Berenger came to my house on the 21st February ; but that instead of being dressed in a green uniform, as set forth in my affidavit, he was in scarlet uniform, that being the alleged costume in which he had disseminated the false intelligence at Dover. If this point could be proved, it was inferred that I must have had a motive in wrongly describing the uniform in my affidavit, and that motive could be none other than my own knowledge of the hoax which had been perpetrated.

The main question relied on by the prosecution related to the colour of De Berenger's coat, whether *scarlet* or *green* : the point held by the court being, that if *scarlet*, I must have made a false declaration in my affidavit as to its colour, and therefore must have at least known how De Berenger had been engaged. A *non sequitur* truly, but nevertheless the one relied on for my conviction as one of the conspirators.

The evidence was this—that when De Berenger arrived from Dover at the Marsh Gate, Lambeth, he exchanged the post-chaise in which he had been travelling for a hackney coach, in which he drove to my house,—which was true enough. The waterman on the stand was called as the first link in the chain ; but as he said "he did not see that he could recollect De Berenger, having only seen him for half-a-minute," this evidence is not worth commenting on, unless to remark that, failing to recognise De Berenger in court, the extraordinary course was taken of pointing him out, and then asking the witness if " he *thought* he *was like* the man who got into the coach ? " The reply was, " he *thought* he was, but he only saw him for half-a-minute."

The next witness brought forward was a man named Crane— the hackney coachman who drove De Berenger. In his examination, Crane did not say a word about the colour of De Berenger's coat, but in his cross-examination swore that he had on a " red coat underneath his greatcoat." At the same time he stated that De Berenger had with him " *a portmanteau big enough to wrap a coat in.*" Other witnesses proved that he had drawn down the sun-blinds in the vehicle, so that he had abundant opportunity to exchange his red coat in which he appeared at Dover, for the green sharpshooter's uniform, and this no doubt he had done. The person of whom the red uniform had been purchased also deposed, that he had carried it away from his shop in a portmanteau, so that there was no doubt of the capacity of the latter to contain the coat. In short, he left London in the uniform of the rifles, and put on the scarlet uniform at Dover, to assume the pretended rank of a staff officer. On his return to London he in like manner, no doubt, changed his uniform by the way.

The case against me then stood thus. *One* witness (the waterman), but no more, swore to the under coat of a person whom he had seen step from one vehicle into another ; and *one* witness, but no more (the hackney coachman), swore to the person whom he brought to my house, as having on a red coat beneath his military coat, but would not swear positively to the wearer. It was, however, to support this extraordinary evidence that my voluntary declaration in my affidavit, of lending De Berenger an old hat and coat, because he alleged that he could not return to his lodgings in the King's Bench in uniform, without exciting suspicion of his absence from the Rules, and thus endangering his securities—was charged against me as involving confederacy.

On the evidence here adduced—and there was not a tittle beyond it, on the subject of the coat—the point was held by Lord Ellenborough to be established that De Berenger stripped off the red coat in my house ! and as it was afterwards found in the river, his lordship charged the jury in a way which bore the construction of my having been also a participator in *that act*, though there was not a particle of evidence on the trial which could give even a shadow of such a conclusion, nor was there even a pretence on the part of the prosecution that such was the case. His lordship's address to the jury on this head is amongst the most remarkable that ever fell from the lips of an English judge.

" Now, gentlemen, he (*De Berenger*) is brought to the house of Lord Cochrane ; *further evidence afterwards arises upon the subject of his being there.* We will at present follow the dress to its conclusion. George Odell, a fisherman, says, ' In the month of March, just above Old Swan Stairs, off against the Iron Wharfs, when I was dredging for coals, I picked up a bundle which was tied with either a piece of chimney line or window line in the cover of a chair bottom ; there were two slips of a coat, embroidery, a star and a piece of silver with two figures upon it ; it had been sunk with three pieces of lead and some bits of coal ; I gave that which I found to Mr Wade, the Secretary of the Stock Exchange ; it was picked up on the Wednesday, and carried there on the Saturday. I picked this up on the 24th of March.' *You have before had the animal hunted home, and now you have his skin*, found, and produced as it was taken out of the river, cut to pieces ; the sinking it could have been with no other view than that of suppressing *this piece of evidence*, and preventing the discovery which it might otherwise occasion ; this makes it the more material to attend *to the stripping off the clothes which took place in Lord Cochrane's house*."

That this unwarrantable assumption, based on no evidence whatever, of De Berenger's stripping off his clothes at my house, could have anything to do with a coat found in the river, was positively absurd, and was not supported by a particle of evidence. Besides which, I had some reputation for shrewdness, and should not have been likely to tie up the coat " in an old chair cover, with three pieces of lead and some lumps of coal ! " when the winter's fire in my grate would in five minutes have destroyed the coat and its evidence together, had it been " stripped off " in my house, or had I been a party to its destruction. The position in which the coat was found, showed where it came from, viz. from the Southwark side of the river, where De Berenger's lodgings were.

It has been stated, that, conscious of my innocence, I took no personal steps for my defence, beyond forwarding a general statement of a few lines to my solicitors, that I never even read the completed brief which they drew up for the guidance of my counsel, nor was I present in court to suggest questions in cross-examination. After my conviction, however, it became necessary to seek additional evidence to support an appeal from the conviction, or an application for a new trial as against myself.

Lord Ellenborough refused the application, *because all the persons tried were not present to concur in it*, though the law gave me no power to compel their attendance. The evidence on which it was grounded, however, is none the less conclusive because Lord Ellenborough and his colleagues declined to receive it, or even *to hear it* ! ! but in place of so doing, at once delivered their outrageous sentence against me.

This appeal was grounded on the evidence of several respectable tradesmen, residing in the neighbourhood of Crane, the hackney coachman ; they voluntarily and unsolicited by me, but as an act of public justice, going before the Lord Mayor, and making the affidavits from which the subjoined extracts are taken. Not one of these tradesmen was even known to me or my solicitors :—

JAMES MILLER, butcher, of Marsh Gate, Lambeth, made affidavit that he saw De Berenger " get out the chaise into a hackney coach—that he was *dressed in green,* with a grey great-coat, and that *there was no red on any part of his dress.*"

JOSEPH RAIMENT, fishmonger, Westminister Bridge Road, made affidavit that he saw De Berenger "get out of the chaise into the hackney coach—that his greatcoat was partly open, and that *the under dress was dark green, like that of the sharpshooters.*"

CHARLES KING, stable-keeper, Westminister Bridge Road, made affidavit that he met William Crane accidentally, and asked him what he had been doing with Sayer ? * He answered, that " he had been to see De Berenger, in order to identify him, but *he could not swear to him, as many faces were alike.*" But he said, using a protestation in the most horrible language, too gross to repeat—" he would have a hackney coach *out of them,*" meaning, as deponent believed, the prosecutors. During this conversation, a person passed dressed in a grey greatcoat, which Crane said was just like De Berenger's, and that he (Crane) did not see De Berenger's under dress, *as his coat was closely buttoned up.*

" Deponent further saith, that after the trial he saw Crane's father, who told him that ' he was *going after the money* ' (meaning the reward), adding that ' *his son was considered a first-rate witness* ! ' On this deponent asked Crane the elder ' how he could consider his son in that light, as he knew very well that had he (deponent) been examined, he must have *beat him out of Court.*' To this Crane's father replied, ' that if he had appeared, there was the place where the clothes were bought, and the post-boy.' On deponent being severe in his remarks, the father said, ' I don't know what they did with the boy, *they had him two days locked up in the police officer's house, that he might not be tampered with.*' † Deponent asked him if there had been any advances by the opposite party. He said, ' None.'

" Deponent further saith, that he has seen William Crane since the trial, and on deponent accusing him of going too far

* A messenger of the Court.
† The post-boy admitted on the trial that he had several previous examinations, and that he *received 52l. for his evidence* !

with his evidence, he said, '*he would swear black was white, or anything else if he was paid for it*!'

"Deponent further saith, that before the trial, the said William Crane's coach and horses *were of a most miserable description, but that since the trial he has purchased a hackney coach and horses of the best description*!

"Deponent further saith, that the said William Crane's general character *is most infamous*, and his mode of expressing himself *so obscene and blasphemous* as to preclude deponent from stating the exact words made use of by the said William Crane. This deponent further saith, that Mr Keir, and the groom of Colonel Taylor, were present when Crane said that '*he would swear black was white, or anything else, if he was well paid for it.*'

"Deponent further saith, that *since* the trial the said William Crane has been enabled *to purchase a very good hackney coach, with horses and harness*, though *previous* to the trial his coach and horses were of the most miserable description. Deponent lastly saith, that the said William Crane *is a man of the most infamous character, and this deponent positively declares that he would not believe him on his oath*."

JAMES YEOWELL, of Silver Street, Falcon Square, ticket porter, made affidavit " that *a few days after the 21st of February*, William Crane told him that the person whom he took from a post-chaise and four at the Marsh Gate, was NO OTHER THAN LORD COCHRANE HIMSELF ! that he knew Lord Cochrane as well as he knew him (deponent). That he *had driven Lord Cochrane from the Opera House, and other places of amusement twenty times*, and described Lord Cochrane as a tall man, with a long face and red whiskers.

"Deponent further saith, that after the trial he (deponent) accused the said William Crane *of perjury*, in having sworn to De Berenger as the man taken up by him at the Marsh Gate, whereas he had *previously declared* before the Stock Exchange Committee that LORD COCHRANE WAS THE PERSON ! Whereupon Crane refused to converse with him further on the subject.

"This deponent further saith, that having on the same day

again met William Crane, he inquired if he had received the reward offered by the Stock Exchange Committee, when he, the said William Crane, admitted that *he had received a part, and expected more.*"

JAMES LOVEMORE, of Clement's Lane, made affidavit " that he heard the said James Yeowell interrogate William Crane as to the person of Lord Cochrane, and that Crane said that he knew Lord Cochrane as well as he did him (Yeowell), and that he had driven Lord Cochrane from the Opera House and other places of amusement, *twenty times*; and Crane further declared that *it was Lord Cochrane* whom he drove from the post-chaise and four at the Marsh Gate, Lambeth, and described his Lordship as a tall man with a long face and red whiskers."

Such was a portion only of the facts which I was prepared with in my appeal to Lord Ellenborough and his colleagues. But, as before said, the same judge refused to listen to the appeal, not on the ground of my having no evidence to rebut the perjury of Crane, but because *all the persons convicted were not present in court to join in the appeal.* It was the rule of court, which I had no power to alter, though, as has been seen in a recent chapter, Lord Campbell, in his " Lives of the Chief-Justices," states, that such a case had *only been ruled once, and that in this case it ought to have been overruled.*

In the two affidavits last adduced there is abundant proof that if the resource of the *red coat* had not been adopted, Crane was prepared to swear that *it was I whom he had driven from the Marsh Gate to my own house*! the conclusion being that I was the pretended De Berenger. Crane evidently knew my personal appearance, as did most persons in London, and said, further, that he knew me from having driven me *twenty times to the Opera*; the fact being that I was never at the Opera but twice in my life, and once in the vestibule, when I was refused admittance from not being in full evening dress, the deficiency consisting in wearing white pantaloons on a very hot day.

It should be remembered, that Crane stated this before the

Committee of the Stock Exchange *soon after the* 21*st of February,*
i.e., *before* I had given the clue to De Berenger in my affidavit
as the person who visited my house on the morning of that
day. *After* I had thus disclosed the name of De Berenger, the
project of proving by the perjury of Crane that *I was the pretended De Bourg,* was given up by the prosecution,—from the
dissimilarity of his personal appearance to mine ; and then—
but not till then—was the equally atrocious perjury of the *red
coat* resorted to.

A few more particulars relative to this *convict,* Crane—for
such was his subsequent fate,—are necessary to enable the
reader to judge of my prosecution and those who selected this
man as their chief witness.

Not long after the trial, the solicitor of Mr Cochrane Johnstone
wrote me to the following effect relative to a discovery made when
too late as to Crane's character :—

" This fellow has lately been prosecuted by Mr Dawson before
the Commissioners of the Hackney Coach Office, for brutality
and general misconduct. This offence was so flagrant that the
severest punishment was inflicted, and at present he is under a long
suspension. He is a worthless rascal, and if Mr D. can do your
lordship any service, you have only to command it."

Enclosed in the above communication was the following
extract from the *Times* newspaper of May 25th, 1814 :—

" On Friday last, William Crane, driver of the hackney coach
No. 782, was summoned before the Commissioners on a charge
of cruelty to his horses, and for abuse to a gentleman who noticed
his conduct. The circumstances detailed were so shocking as
to induce the Commissioners to observe that they never *heard a
more atrocious case.* They would have inflicted a pecuniary
penalty, but as it must necessarily be paid by his father, they
ordered him instead to be suspended from driving any coach for
three months."

The trial, which resulted in my conviction, *on this very man's evidence*, took place on the 8th of June, 1814, *only a fortnight after his conviction of the atrocity just quoted*! so that at the moment of giving his evidence this man was himself under punishment for an offence pronounced by the commissioners to be "*so shocking that they never heard of a more atrocious case*" ! ! ! Had this information been available at the trial, the jury would have paid but small attention to Crane's evidence.

Crane was convicted of stealing twenty sovereigns and other property under circumstances no less atrocious. He was sentenced to transportation for seven years, but at the expiration of three years *received a free pardon from the Government on his own petition*.

These facts will be sufficient to convince the reader of my innocence as regarded the evidence of Crane, the hackney coachman. Yet his evidence was laid before the jury as of the highest reliable kind, whilst the very facts relative to his character, even to his being under conviction whilst giving his evidence, Lord Ellenborough and his colleagues refused to hear, because all the parties convicted were not present in court. It is scarcely possible to imagine greater injustice and folly, even in that day.

It is impossible in an autobiography like the present to go into the entire case *seriatim*, as it would be easy to bring forward other proofs as clear as those now adduced. The evidence of Crane was, however, the important point. Whether was it the more probable, that a man in my position, with nothing to gain by it, should, in order to commit a fraud, conspire with several other persons of whose names he had never before heard, and then swear that I did not commit it—or, that such a man as Crane, at the moment of giving his evidence, himself under conviction and sentence for a heinous offence, should swear falsely to the colour of a coat for a pecuniary reward ? I, to whom the public voice, and the rewards of my Sovereign, had elevated to an honourable rank in my profession, or a hackney coachman, under conviction at the moment of giving his evidence, and known in his own line of life to have been the most depraved of one of the most depraved classes of society ?

My conviction was followed by expulsion from the House of Commons, and was voted by a majority of 140 to 44.

CHAPTER XXXIV

REMARKS ON LORD ELLENBOROUGH'S DIRECTIONS

A CIRCUMSTANCE strongly inferential occurred which went far to prove that De Berenger *had changed* his dress before coming to my house. On the first part of the journey he was proved to have worn a sword, unquestionably as essential to his assumed character. But before he came to my house, he had disengaged himself from the sword, for Crane swore that on entering, he " took out of the chaise a portmanteau and a *sword*, and went in." So that, according to the evidence of Crane himself, the chief witness for the prosecution, *he had made one material alteration in his appearance.* Why should De Berenger have worn his sword up to the last stage from Dover, during which he " pulled down the sun-blinds," and then have taken it off, but for the plain reason that he could not change his scarlet coat for his green uniform without first taking off his sword, which he had not replaced, but laid it on the chaise-seat during the operation. Not a word of this was allowed to go to the jury, though if—as Lord Ellenborough argued—he had been regardless of exhibiting himself to me in the false character of a military officer, he *would hardly have taken off his sword* ! These facts were not only proofs that a partial change of dress had been made, but that an entire change had been effected, to which the removal of the sword was absolutely necessary. Had my servants been called upon the trial, their testimony must have been decisive.

It has been stated, that at the instance of Mr Cochrane

Johnstone, Sir Alexander Cochrane applied to the Admiralty for permission to engage De Berenger, and the records of the Admiralty would then, as no doubt they will now, prove the fact. There was not a word passed on the subject at the trial, nor any witness brought from the Admiralty to decide the point. Yet Lord Ellenborough put it to the jury as beyond doubt, *that it was I or Mr Cochrane Johnstone, who was also a defendant in the same prosecution, who applied to Sir Alexander for his engagement*!—thus making this unfounded but important fact part of his direction to the jury.   Here are the judge's words :—

" There is no doubt that Sir Alexander Cochrane had, on some application from Mr Cochrane Johnstone, *or Lord Cochrane,* applied for him."

It is difficult to account for the judge's motive in making such a statement, wholly unsupported by evidence. Neither was there even an attempt to show that I had ever interfered or even interested myself in any application on De Berenger's behalf. The fact of Sir Alexander Cochrane having made the application was most important for my defence, because it added greatly to the probability of my statement in my affidavit, and accounted for the conduct of De Berenger in presuming to call on me to request a passage to America. This Lord Ellenborough completely neutralised by telling the jury that *it was I* who applied to Sir Alexander for his employment ; the impression made on the minds of the jury being, that notwithstanding I disclaimed all knowledge of the man, I had been on terms of intimacy with him before the application was made !

The judge then declared as follows :—" But it does not rest there ; for he himself lends to this person the immediate means of concealment,—he lets him have a hat *instead of his laced cap* ; *and what had such a cap to do with a sharpshooter's uniform ?* "

I had never said a word about a " laced cap," nor had I ever seen De Berenger's cap, for, as one of my servants testified, it

lay in the hall. After this direction to the jury and my consequent conviction, I made it my business to ascertain what kind
of cap was worn by the adjutant of Lord Yarmouth's rifle-*corps*,
and, to my great surprise and indignation, discovered that the
regimental head-dress of De Berenger was a black cap *with a
spacious gold band upon it, a long gold tassel pendant, and a death's
head and marrow bones in bronze*!—so that sharpshooters *had*
something to do with laced caps.

Still more extraordinary was the judge's observation to the
jury :—" The uniform of the rifle-corps is of a bottle-green
colour, made to resemble the colour of trees, that those who wear
it may hide themselves in woods, and escape discovery there."
This was in direct opposition to the evidence, for Lord Yarmouth
had actually testified in court that the uniform of the corps was
" waistcoat-green, with *a crimson cape*! "

I have merely taken these instances at random, and without
comment further than necessary to enable the reader to comprehend them. As my judge is no longer here to reply to me, I
abstain from comment, however much it might tend, now that
the party spirit which ruined me has died out, to establish my
innocence.

One most material point connected with the trial cannot be
overlooked ; one, in fact, which not only concerned the liberties
of obnoxious persons like myself, but also the liberties of every
man in the country. At the period of my trial, Lord Ellenborough
was not only Chief Justice of the King's Bench, BUT AT THE SAME
TIME A CABINET MINISTER ! ! ! This terrible combination of
incompatible offices was for the first time under constitutional
government effected in the person of Lord Ellenborough, and,
to the credit of subsequent administrations, for the last time
also. No other Chief Justice ever came hot-foot from a Cabinet
Council to decide the fate of an accused person, politically
obnoxious to the Cabinet ; the trial going on from day to day,
so as to become open no less to Cabinet than to forensic discussion.

The chance I had may be readily estimated, *with a Cabinet
minister for my judge*, and the Cabinet of which he was a member

composed of ministers to whom I had become deeply obnoxious by determined opposition to their measures ; having, in fact, given them more trouble than any other of my party, because my knowledge of naval abuses and profligate expenditure enabled me to expose both. It might, with one of my most bitter opponents for a judge, have been a still greater marvel had I been acquitted, than that I was convicted without and in opposition to evidence. Had Lord Ellenborough possessed a true sense of delicacy, he would never have presided at that trial. Still less would he have refused me a new trial when more perfectly prepared ; a proceeding no doubt adopted as the best means of silencing further discussion, which had begun to harass him personally, and to cause uneasiness to the ministry. The shortest course, if not the justest, was to screen himself and them by *immediately* crushing his adversary. But the injury went further than my conviction in the Court of King's Bench. After my subsequent expulsion from the House, which, as Lord Brougham rightly says, " *secured my re-election for Westminster,*" on its adverse note *hung the fate of the ministry.* Had that vote been in my favour, the Chief Justice could not have held his seat in the Cabinet, and his evacuation could scarcely have been otherwise than followed by that of the whole ministry. Of this, however, there was little danger, the great bond of adhesion to the ministry being the pensions and sinecures so freely distributed amongst an unreformed House of Commons.

The question, however, became thus one of ministerial existence. Had the House, as it ought to have done, irrespective of me or my case, repudiated the anomaly of a Chief Justice holding a seat in the Cabinet, the retirement of Lord Ellenborough must have been indispensable and *immediate.* He could not have maintained his political office for an hour. In place of an individual member being heard in his own defence, the question really was the right of a Chief Justice to hold a seat in the Cabinet, or in legal phrase, the issue was, Lord Cochrane *versus* Lord Ellenborough, the Admiralty, and the Cabinet. In the un-

z

reformed House of Commons Lord Cochrane, as a matter of course, went to the wall, no one expecting otherwise.

Of the guilt or innocence of the other parties convicted I know nothing ; but this I will say, that, if guilty, there was nothing in their guilt half so bad as the deliberate malice which on two occasions had conspired to ruin me. My appointment as flag-captain to my uncle was gall and wormwood to those who, for opposing a vote of thanks to Lord Gambier, had condemned me to five years' deprivation of employment, at a time when my services would have been honourable to myself and beneficial to my country. I had gained employment in a way beyond their control, and my unjust conviction of having participated in a trumpery hoax, which common-sense might have convinced them was beneath my notice, was converted into the means of preventing the future exercise of my abilities as a naval officer.

At my re-election for Westminister—the consequence, as Lord Brougham has well said, of the outrageous treatment to which I had been subjected—an incident occurred with which my wrongs became indirectly mixed up. Whilst the electors of Westminster were securing the triumphant return of one who was in durance, under an infamous sentence, the daughter of the Prince Regent was flying from court tyranny.

On the day preceding my re-election, the greatly beloved Princess Charlotte, then under age, escaped from her father's protection and, having called a hackney coach from the stand, at Charing Cross, fled to her mother's residence in Connaught Place. The public mind was at the time in a state of great excitement on account of the vindictive sentence passed upon me, and the electors of Westminster having determined to sustain me, every precaution was taken by their leaders to keep alive the public sentiment.

In the midst of this excitement the flight of the princess became known, together with the fact that she had been treated by her father with an amount of unbecoming violence and coercion, and through some of his acquiescent ministers outraged by an injudicious pressure, the object of which was to force upon her a marriage to which she had not only a personal objection, but towards which she had publicly expressed a decided and insuperable aversion.

Notwithstanding this, the Regent, regardless of his daughter's feelings, insisted on proceeding without loss of time with the preparations for her marriage ; and it was on repeating his fixed determination as regarded her fate, that she took the step of placing herself under her mother's protection, the terror inspired by the interview with her father being such that, without bonnet or shawl, she ran down the back staircase of Warwick House, and escaped by the servants' *entrée*.

Not many hours elapsed before the fact of her flight and its cause became publicly known. This act of political tyranny towards a princess, who, though so young, had, by her powers of mind and engaging manners from her childhood, secured the universal affection of the people, created an amount of sympathy which, coupled with the excitement and irritation at my outrageous treatment, almost amounted to public frenzy.

The Government became alarmed. Crowds beset the house of her late Majesty Queen Caroline, where their favourite was safely sheltered. The carriages of the royal family and of the ministers, including those of the Lord Chancellor, Lord Ellenborough, and the Law Officers of the Crown, were all in attendance, their occupants having been sent to use their influence with her Royal Highness to induce her to return, but in vain. She even refused to see any of the royal family except the Duke of Sussex, for whom she had sent, as well as for Mr Brougham, the latter to advise her in the difficult position in which she had been compelled to place herself. The advice was to return ; but she declared in strong terms that she could not overcome her repugnance to the violent treatment she had received, or to the attempt to force her into a marriage which she held in aversion.

The day following this scene was the day of my re-election for Westminster. The same overtures were repeated to the princess, but without making the slightest impression on her wounded feelings. At length the Duke of Sussex took his niece to the window of the drawing-room and drew her attention to the angry multitude assembled before the house, explaining to her that such was the public sympathy in her favour, and such the interest the people took in her happiness, that they would form a shield for her protection against which her oppressors would scarcely venture to array themselves.

Still the princess remained inexorable, till the danger of continued public excitement was pointed out to her. She was told by the Duke of Sussex, that the irritation was twofold, for *that very day was appointed for the re-election of Lord Cochrane for Westminster, after the unjust sentence which had been passed upon him, and which also formed another great cause of public excitement, whilst the two causes combined* might lead to a popular outbreak which it was to be feared would end in bloodshed, and perhaps in the destruction of Carlton House itself. It was further urged, that in case of mischief, no small portion might be laid by ministers to the account of her Royal Highness.

These considerations sensibly affected the princess, who was moved to tears, and exclaimed : " POOR LORD COCHRANE ! I HEARD THAT HE HAD BEEN VERY ILL USED BY THEM (meaning her father's ministers) ; SHOULD IT EVER BE IN MY POWER, I WILL UNDO THE WRONG."

With a magnanimity which her persecutors could neither feel nor comprehend, the princess then declared her perfect readiness to render herself a self-sacrifice, in order to prevent the dreadful result which she felt might be possible ; and shortly afterwards returned to Warwick House, accompanied by her uncle the Duke of York. Her courage and firmness relieved her from further importunity from her father and his ministers on the subject of the hateful marriage, which was broken off, and this noble-minded woman afterwards contracted with the King of the Belgians a marriage of affection, approved by the whole country.

Such instances of tyrannical oppression as these will be read with amazement by the present generation, though there are those yet living who can corroborate their recital. When even a princess of the blood royal, the idol of the whole nation, was not exempt from persecution, what hope had I of escaping ministerial vengeance, backed by a House of Commons, the majority of which consisted of sinecurists and placemen, whose fortunes *in esse* and *in posse* depended on their subservience to the place-givers ?

It is true, I had with me the sympathy of the public, and this alone sustained me under such an accumulation of injury. Men do not become popular for nothing ; but I have no hesitation in saying, to the honour of my constituents, that the injustice done to me by an adverse ministry gave me far greater popularity than anything I had accomplished in my professional capacity. For five years my adversaries had taken care that no fresh achievements in war should be added to my professional reputation ; and it was only when by my uncle's favour, I had once more an opportunity of distinguishing myself in spite of the Admiralty, that the concentrated malice of the faction I had offended by my pertinacious opposition in Parliament burst on my head in the shape of a prosecution, in which my judge was a member of the very Cabinet to which I was politically and personally obnoxious.

In a general point of view, there can be no two opinions on the impropriety of a Cabinet minister occupying the bench of the highest law court of the realm. In all state prosecutions—and mine *was* one—it would fall to his lot to decide in the Cabinet as to their commencement, though in my case this was apparently avoided, by the law officers of the crown keeping aloof from the proceedings ; care, however, being taken to employ as my prosecutor an attorney of tried shrewdness, having a personal dislike to myself. A judge thus politically connected had to leave the Cabinet in order to carry out its decisions, himself presiding at all trials which might result, adjudging and sentencing the unlucky offenders. Happily, no such combination of political and judicial offices has occurred since Lord Ellenborough's time, nor can it occur, unless some retrograde spirit of despotism shall again—to use the significant language of the *Quarterly Review*—" *tinge the ermine of justice with the colour of party.*"

The reader, who is now well acquainted with my services, can pursue the subject for himself. With the exception of the Red Ribbon of the Bath, which as the gift of my Sovereign I highly prize, my reward has been a life of unmerited suffering. Even the stipulations of the South American Governments, to whom I gave freedom, are violated to this day, from a conviction that no sympathy will be accorded by the Government of my own country.

These are the requitals for my " *hitherto unrewarded services.*"

Amongst the curiosities shown to visitors of the Bank of England, there was, and no doubt is still, a thousand pound bank-note, No. 8202, dated 26th June, 1815, on the back of which are endorsed the following words :—

" MY HEALTH HAVING SUFFERED BY LONG AND CLOSE CONFINEMENT, AND MY OPPRESSORS BEING RESOLVED TO DEPRIVE ME OF PROPERTY OR LIFE, I SUBMIT TO ROBBERY TO PROTECT MYSELF FROM MURDER, IN THE HOPE THAT I SHALL LIVE TO BRING THE DELINQUENTS TO JUSTICE.

(Signed)   " COCHRANE.

" KING'S BENCH PRISON,
   " *July 3rd,* 1815."

There is the reward bestowed on me by a ministerial faction, memorable only for its political corruption. With that protest I close the book.